NAZI
GOLD

NAZI GOLD

THE FULL STORY OF THE FIFTY-YEAR
SWISS-NAZI CONSPIRACY TO STEAL
BILLIONS FROM EUROPE'S JEWS AND
HOLOCAUST SURVIVORS

TOM BOWER

HarperCollins*Publishers*

HarperCollins books may be purchased for educational, business, or sales promotional use. For information please write: Special Markets Department, HarperCollins Publishers, Inc., 10 East 53rd Street, New York, NY 10022.

FIRST EDITION

Designed by Joseph Rutt

ISBN 0-06-017535-4

97 98 99 00 01 ❖/RRD 10 9 8 7 6 5 4 3 2

To Veronica

CONTENTS

ACKNOWLEDGMENTS

The impetus for this book was a telephone call in May 1996 from two friends, Mike Kinsella and Bob Royer. Kinsella, the chief of staff of Senator Alfonse D'Amato, and Royer, a Washington, D.C., lawyer, were searching in the National Archives for information about Swiss banks to use in the early stages of the senator's campaign. Their support and generosity thereafter were unlimited. Martin Mendelsohn arranged through the Simon Wiesenthal Center for funding for my initial visit and research. Gregg Rickman, Senator D'Amato's legislative director, has undoubtedly served as the tower of strength for the senator's campaign and was an enormous and indispensable help to me.

Robert Fink, my indefatigable and resourceful associate in New York, was, as always, invaluable, not least in several archives in New York, Washington, D.C., and elsewhere, and for tracking down important eyewitnesses.

In Switzerland, Mario Koenig spent ten weeks in the national archives and not only produced astonishing new material but provided incisive interpretation. I am very grateful to him and to others who unfortunately must remain nameless. Thanks to the original journalism of Irene Loebell of Swiss Television, I was better able to understand this story and Switzerland.

In Paris, Jane Lizop overcame the chaos of the French national archives—which are magnificently designed but are managed in such a way as to prevent proper research—and produced some absolute gems.

Among the many others who gave me valuable help are Moses Abramovitz, Edwin Adams, Morton Bach, Rolf Bloch, Herbert Cummings, Martin Doude van Trostwick, Eli Ginzberg, Max Isenbergh, Paul Jolles, Nat King, Ida Klaus, Paul Rechsteiner, Seymour Rubin, Hans Schaffner, Elan Steinberg and Israel Singer of the World Jewish Congress, Jacob Tanner, Gian Trepp and Herbert Winter. I received considerable but unattributable help from many Swiss bankers and government officials.

Peter James performed his unique magic in editing the manuscript; David Hooper of Biddle & Co. declared the book to be legally watertight; Anne-Marie Ehrlich found the photographs; and Diana Mackay, who sold the foreign rights, and Michael Shaw of Curtis Brown were, as always, great friends and supporters. To all, I am very grateful.

Most of all, I am grateful to my family, who never complain, always laugh and never cease to offer encouragement.

PREFACE

The contrast is stark and pertinent. The date was November 1940. Thousands of young Allied soldiers and airmen had just been buried in German-occupied France; Britain's cities were burning, thanks to the Luftwaffe's blitz; and sailors of the Royal Navy were drowning in freezing water as casualties of the Battle of the Atlantic. From occupied Europe and Germany, correspondents employed by the *New York Times*, still unencumbered eyewitnesses, dispatched reports about oppression, arrests, executions and tyranny, characterized as "Our Darkest Hour."

In that same month, two hundred of Switzerland's financial and political leaders—the pillars of that nation—petitioned their government to show greater sympathy toward the Nazis. The plutocrats were pushing at an open door. While Europe shuddered before the apocalypse, Switzerland was aligning itself with evil.

Both in the midst of the war and in the aftermath, as the horrors were gradually revealed, the Swiss never questioned the morality of that choice. Their justification was their country's isolation and traditional neutrality.

Switzerland's ethics did not go unnoticed or uncriticized in London, Washington, D.C., or Paris, but compared with the other revelations after the Nazis' defeat, this small country's misconduct was relegated as of minor importance.

Yet in 1997, fifty-five years after a group of Nazis finalized their plan at Wannsee, in a pleasant lakeside villa outside Berlin, to destroy the entire Jewish nation, Switzerland has finally been brought before the bar of history and asked to account for its Faustian pact. Switzerland is asked not only to explain its conduct toward the Jews and its relationship with those who plotted their destruction, but to justify something far worse.

Why, it is asked, did a group of self-professedly respectable Swiss citizens willfully profit from the crime that threatened the foundations of western civilization?

Crime often produces a windfall for the perpetrators, but greed, intrigue, and deception have not until now been associated with the affluent, faceless men who own and manage Switzerland's discreet financial institutions. "Switzerland," wrote F. Scott Fitzgerald, "is a country where very few things begin, but many things end." The hopes of many refugees ended in Switzerland, and they were murdered soon afterward. But their money remained secure, too secure, in Switzerland's banks.

The fate of those Jews—some perhaps featuring as the naked innocents in the smudged photographs and jerky newsreels filmed by their enthusiatic murderers—has been chronicled as a result of an astonishing legacy. Carefully, even lovingly, the Nazis recorded the minute details of their crimes in correspondence, memoranda, and the minutes of their conferences. The surviving archives indisputably proved individuals' guilt.

Similarly, the Swiss collaborators and profiteers also recorded their thoughts and decisions on paper. Although the most pertinent of those files still remain hidden from public inspection in the banks—and might well be shredded—sufficient government records had been innocently deposited in Bern's national archives to substantiate a compelling case against previous generations.

Until recently, the incidents and conversations described in this book would have been dismissed as irrelevant or inconceivable. In my book *The Paperclip Conspiracy*, published in 1987, one chapter was devoted to Switzerland's conduct during and after World War II. However, compared with the revelation that the Allies had protected and employed incriminated German scientists, Switzerland's protection of the Nazis' loot and their expropriation of Jewish deposits aroused no interest. One decade later, it is Switzerland's misfortune that its image as a land of awesome Alpine scenery, clockwork efficiency, and immaculate cleanliness is tarnished by those same sordid but irrefutable revelations.

As the story unfolds, it becomes painfully clear that facts about Switzerland ten years ago were only hints of a far graver iniquity than could be imagined. After studying archives in Paris, London, New

York, Washington and especially Bern and speaking with those who shaped events after 1945, I found a new truth gradually emerging. This is not just a story about a handful of pitiless bankers hoarding the wealth of a ravaged continent while spurning the pleas of defenseless survivors of the Holocaust; it is a sensational accusation that a country whose citizens, over the past half century, boasted to their neighbors about their enviable wealth, was quite knowingly profiting from blood money.

LIST OF ABBREVIATIONS

AJC	American Jewish Committee
AJDC	American Joint Distribution Committee
CIA	Central Intelligence Agency
DIV	Deutsche Interresenvertretung (German Interests Section), Swiss Political Department
DM	Deutschmark
FBI	Federal Bureau of Investigation
FEA	Foreign Economic Administration, U.S. Treasury
FF	French franc
FFC	Foreign Funds Control, U.S. Treasury
HMG	Her Majesty's Government
IARA	Inter-Allied Reparations Agency
IRO	International Refugee Organization
MI6	British Secret Intelligence Service
OSS	Office of Strategic Services (U.S.)
POW	Prisoner of war
RM	Reichsmark
SBA	Swiss Banking Association
SBC	Swiss Bank Corporation
SD	Sicherheitsdienst (SS Security Police, Nazi Germany)
SF	Swiss franc
SIG	Swiss Federation of Jewish Communities
SS	Schutzstaffel (elite stormtroopers, Nazi Germany)
UBS	Union Bank of Switzerland
WJC	World Jewish Congress

I

CONFRONTATION AND TEARS

Hatred shone in their faces. Distrust echoed in their voices. The chill inside the conference room struck deeper than the winter air in the ancient square outside.

Tragedy had compelled the nine men to sit around the long wooden table, but their common sentiment was anger. None had suffered, but all were suspicious. Humanity was confronting greed and, after seven years of strife, the innocent had finally won one victory: the agreement to gather on the afternoon of November 17, 1952, in the parliament building.

All nine men were Swiss, but the majority regarded two of their number as foreigners, not properly acceptable as ancient Helvetii. These two were both Jews, representatives of an intimidated minority who could not boast of courage or prowess. The majority were lawyers and bankers, protectors of their nation's wealth, proudly successful in excluding their country from the moral conflicts that for centuries had plagued their neighbors. At the head of the table sat Markus Feldmann, the new minister of justice and the police, renowned as an ambitious workaholic but carelessly short-sighted about the conflict he was seeking to broker.

"We're here," announced Feldmann, "to discuss the fate of money deposited by foreigners in Switzerland who were killed because of Nazi violence and wartime events." The sanitization of the vocabulary used to refer to the Holocaust had been perfected in Switzerland ever since Adolf Hitler became chancellor in neighboring Germany. For the twelve years of the Third Reich, none of the non-Jews in that room had protested about the criminality occurring beyond their frontiers and, in the aftermath, none been troubled to consider the truth. Comfortable survival and self-enrichment remained their entrenched gospel, and any challenge to that credo prompted instant suppression. Such a challenge had now arisen. "Parliament has decided," continued Feldman, "that we need a decree or regulations to deal with the money in question."

The "money in question" was the unaccounted-for millions of Swiss francs—some insiders would eventually confess to "hundreds of millions"—which had been deposited in the Swiss safe haven by Europe's Jews as much as thirty years earlier. Those Jews had been murdered, their records had disappeared and their secrets were known only to their trustees, represented by the Swiss around Feldmann's conference table—secrets that they were unwilling to divulge.

Naturally, the minister looked to Emil Alexander, the reticent but experienced director of the ministry's Justice Division, to provide an unobjectionable summary of the reasons for their meeting: "At first, when the question of the so-called heirless assets became a reality," began Alexander, "we tried to deal with it practically. People applied at banks claiming that their missing relations had left behind a fortune deposited in a Swiss bank, and the Bankers Association made inquiries among its members." To Alexander's right sat Max Oetterli, the Swiss Bankers Association's pugnacious forty-six-year-old secretary. Oetterli had fought hard to prevent this meeting and had no intention of leaving without expressing his hostility. "The results," summarized Alexander, referring to Oetterli's work, "were usually very thin, which is not very surprising, because the people who came to the banks based their applications on a hunch." Oetterli agreed with that and with what followed.

"Those inquiring at the banks," continued Alexander, "were usually unable to prove that the person was dead or even missing. A further complication is that making inquiries in some countries, especially Eastern Europe, is dangerous. Another great difficulty is that some deposits were registered under false names which the inheritors don't know. And some people did not deposit their money in banks but entrusted it to private people like lawyers, notaries and business associates. Those identities are of course unknown to the people hunting for their inheritance. Finally, after all this time, there is a chance that money could be lost because of the statute of limitations."

Around the table, even men who were foes agreed with the lawyer's summary. Alexander had arrived at the purpose of their meeting. Protests during recent months had persuaded the government to consider a law compelling Switzerland's banks, insurance companies and others to declare any assets in their custody owned by murdered Jews. "The banks," confirmed Alexander, "insist that they do not want to enrich themselves with this money; that they would not apply any time limit to reclaiming the deposits and that we can discuss later what to do with any unclaimed money." Oetterli again nodded, but his face hardened as Feldmann signaled to George Brunschvig, the president of the Swiss Federation of Jewish Communities (SIG). Brunschvig's lobbying for a new law had incensed the bankers.

"Experience shows," began Brunschvig, bruised by his past encounters with Oetterli, "that those bankers involved seldom give satisfactory information. The only guaranteed way of discovering these deposits, we believe, is by introducing a new law." Brunschvig glanced for support at his colleague Paul Guggenheim, a respected professor and lawyer.

"We've really got two problems," said Guggenheim. "First, how to find the heirless assets; and then to decide who will receive the money." Glancing at Oetterli, the professor continued, "I don't like the bankers' proposals because they don't guarantee that all the financial institutions will be honest. That's why a law is vital." The Jewish lawyer, outraged by the perfidies practiced by Oetterli and his ilk since 1945, dropped any pretense of courtesy. "I'm not very impressed by the bankers' plea that a law would damage their absolute requirement of secrecy. On the contrary, it seems to me that they are more damaged if they keep on with their denials of having any money." At the last moment, Guggenheim tempered his bluntness with an olive branch: "With goodwill, we can surely find a solution to this problem."

Goodwill was far from Oetterli's thoughts as Alfred Wegelin, the managing director of the Schweizer Volksbank, launched the counterattack: "We strongly disagree about this problem. We're wide apart." Sympathy and understanding about recent history were not emotions extended to the two Jews. "We bankers want to find a solution to the deposits of those who are dead. That's why we support the efforts to help the inheritors. But they must abide by the law. Today a deposit could be described as an heirless asset and sometime in the future the owner will turn up—especially if they live in Eastern Europe." For the banker, the only solution was to do nothing: "The money is very safe in the banks. It's always available for the inheritors."

Albert Matter, the director of the Basler Kantonalbank, sitting beside Wegelin, would over the next years prove to be as insensitive as Oetterli, yet on this occasion he began with an apparent reassurance. "Banks certainly do not want to enrich themselves with the so-called heirless assets. There's no danger that claimants will lose their money because they don't appear for a long time. We're always ready to help people who come to us looking for money, so long as it's within a certain framework." Sneers came as easily to Matter as palliatives: "But don't forget. It's not only people who have deposited money with us who have disappeared. People who owe us money have also gone." Matter's bank had evidently endured some uncomfortable moments. "We've had to put that fact down to experience," he concluded. Some in Europe had experienced the Holocaust while Matter and his colleagues had experienced bad loans. Some Jews,

Matter's colleagues griped, had even allowed themselves to be murdered in order to escape repayment of their loans.

The gulf appeared unbridgeable. For the minister, directing a small army of secret-police officers spying on their fellow countrymen, the thought of prying into banking secrets was nearly intolerable. In the tradition of Swiss ministers, Feldmann's role was not to govern but to serve the different interests of the community. Switzerland's bankers, he accepted, did not require the government's protection, only the assurance of noninterference. Together, the bankers were stronger than the state, and they applied pressure when their interests required it. "Clearly," said the minister passively, "the Jewish group want a law and the bankers don't. The representative of the Bankers Association should tell us how he imagines future cooperation."

Oetterli took the stage, narrowing his eyes and hunching his shoulders. His mood was far from benign. "All our experience convinces us that the problem is vastly exaggerated." He emphasized each word, at once aggressive and derisive. "Many claimants seem to have convinced themselves that—because a missing relation once passed through Switzerland—he must have deposited a fortune here." Mocking the Jews came naturally to Oetterli, especially in the battle to protect his members. "The proposed law will be a serious breach of banking secrecy and will damage Swiss banking. If there are any heirless assets, the safest place for them is in the bank. Their future, if they are really shown to be heirless, can be discussed later." Oetterli had often mentioned talking about the heirless assets "in twenty or thirty years' time," ignoring the urgent needs of the survivors.

"Have all your inquiries worked smoothly up to now?" asked Feldmann.

"Our members have tirelessly sought to help inquirers," replied Oetterli. "We do everything we can. Unfortunately, the documents provided are often inadequate."

The implication that Oetterli and his members were assisting claimants infuriated Guggenheim. Inquiries to the Bankers

Association about accounts—which were considered only if accompanied by a hefty fee—had aroused what the headquarters in Basel had called "a number of legal and practical problems." To Guggenheim, they were "the completely impossible requirements" of proving the death of a depositor, the proof of heirship and the precise identification of the bank account.

"Proof of death in a gas chamber is extremely difficult," Guggenheim had long complained. "All we know is that the deceased was last seen entering a concentration camp and is not known to have ever emerged." Moreover, the requirement that the accounts be identified was impossible. The Jews had chosen to deposit their money in Switzerland because it guaranteed anonymity. They were not always likely to reveal their ruse to their families.

"The Bankers Association isn't proposing anything new," snapped Guggenheim. "We're not going to get any further because hardly any of the banks are prepared to give information voluntarily." But Oetterli was manifestly unimpressed. Charge and countercharge had become routine, even though the representatives of the Jews were mild men who feared exciting enmity. Oetterli was beyond persuasion, but Feldmann's sympathy was vital, and Guggenheim addressed his comments to the politician.

"Six million people have disappeared and that exceptional fact requires special remedy. Because of those terrible events not only whole families but whole communities have disappeared. In many cases there aren't going to be any inquiries at the banks. Only if a law orders a census of deposits can we find the lost deposits. Other countries have adopted similar measures for this special problem. And the same should happen here—even if it's not easy. There are definitely deposits at the banks whose owners have not contacted their bank since 1942. A law ordering that those deposits be declared cannot undermine banking secrecy."

"It's absolutely clear that we have to consider a major moral problem," agreed Feldmann, only to be interrupted by the clamor of bankers insisting on their reverence for the sanctity of the law. "A new law is inevitable," insisted the politician. "No one can deny that this issue is political, psychological and moral. The cause was something monstrous. The bankers don't want a law. I propose to order the drafting of a law, and we can discuss it later."

Most mortals, faced with such determination, might have held back to await the minister's proposals. Oetterli was different. Loathing his adversaries and outraged that a politician should dare to contemplate interfering with the sovereignty of Switzerland's banks, he threatened to withdraw all cooperation: "Any law would be monstrous and will cause a great row." Oetterli's choice of the word *monstrous*, the very word Feldmann had used to refer to the Holocaust, was deliberate and provocative. Switzerland's bankers, accustomed to having their warnings respected, understood how to exploit the weaknesses of the nation's stagnant and secret political system. For Oetterli, the bankers were the keepers of the flame and the protectors of the nation's future. Certainly they were unaccustomed to contradiction from Jews. But Brunschvig felt that he had been unusually provoked. "What amazes me is Herr Oetterli's threats to withdraw his cooperation if there's a law. We can't overcome that. Yet your investigations have revealed practically nothing." Everyone understood Brunschvig's unspoken accusation. Hiding behind the secrecy laws, the bankers were conspiring to delay, or to deny that the assets existed, or to demand that they should not be returned to their owners. Frustrating all inquirers, the bankers' tactics persuaded even the most determined claimant to abandon the quest. It amounted to a fraud on the victims and the survivors. "Only a law," concluded Brunschvig, "can solve the problem."

"I'm very skeptical about the Bankers Association's position," agreed Guggenheim. "They seem to have little understanding about the heirless assets."

Now the tension in the room burst out into open warfare. "I am absolutely amazed," shouted Oetterli, "that you're actually considering confiscating money entrusted to us."

"There's no question of expropriation if there's an owner," snapped Guggenheim, irritated by Oetterli's familiar distortion.

"We're talking about using property which is no longer owned by anyone for social purposes."

There was nothing more to say. The disagreement was fundamental. Two entrenched interests were unwilling to yield. "My timetable," announced Feldmann, "is to hold a conference in February to discuss the draft law."

It was 4:30 in the afternoon. Bern, Switzerland's federal capital, was dark. Gravely, Markus Feldmann said good-bye to his visitors. As the eight walked out of the parliament building into a dimly lit square, the floodlights illuminating the solidly built structures nearby confirmed the realities of power in Switzerland. On the left was the Berner Kantonalbank, the headquarters of a regional center of finance. On the right was the headquarters of Switzerland's National Bank. For twelve years, the representatives of Nazi Germany's central bank had walked through its stone doorway to be welcomed by their Swiss friends. Even after Hitler's defeat, the bank's directors—ignoring the Allies' outrage—had continued to look after the interests of Germany. Their motives were not humane. Self-interest was the supreme guide for all of Switzerland's banks, which was the precise reason why, soon after Markus Feldmann bid farewell, he bowed to Oetterli's demands and abandoned the notion of serving morality. Any thought of a new law was jettisoned.

NEW YORK—OCTOBER 16, 1996

The aged, tearful faces revealed a lifetime's suffering. Under jarring neon lights in an eighth-floor conference room within sight of the Statue of Liberty, the witnesses could hardly disguise their unique odyssey. Surrounded by murmuring journalists, lawyers and officials, the five women and one man, cast as victims and survivors, were united by a recurring nightmare and a searing loss. They had been nurtured amid wealth and love in Jewish communities scattered across Europe, but their childhood security had been shattered and their loving parents murdered by unforgiving persecution. By twist of fate and good fortune, unlike six million others, they had survived

Auschwitz and other infamous slaughterhouses to enjoy the affluence of New York. Even that salvation, over the years, had not dented the sorrow or the anger aroused by their bitter inheritance. Too late to exact retribution against the murderers of their parents, they had eagerly accepted an invitation to travel on that bright October morning in 1996 to a drab federal courthouse to testify on behalf of an unusual indictment.

Over the decades, respected judges within that concrete building had heard innumerable accounts of New York's sordid crimes and bewildering inhumanity, but no witness had been summoned to relate a similar chronicle of profiting from mass murder—an unprecedented theft committed by the apparently respectable citizens of the world's most peaceful nation. Renowned as diligent bookkeepers, those burghers had insulted, ignored and ultimately forgotten the six witnesses and many more who had pleaded for understanding. Now the witnesses gloried in an unexpected opportunity to revive some unfinished business and compel the bookkeepers to submit a final account.

Compared with the countless horrors committed during the Holocaust, the witnesses' complaint had in the past understandably been judged of lesser importance. After the initial flurry in the months after the war, when some of the murderers were caught and executed, deliberate blindness and a biological amnesty had saved the majority of murderers from the hunt and retribution. Only the sudden discovery, over the following decades, of Adolf Eichmann, Klaus Barbie and Dr. Josef Mengele had reminded the world of the crime and the failure of justice. Even so, many of those murderers caught in recent years had been spared thanks to the myth that the survivors, old and obsessed, had become unreliable eyewitnesses to the worst crime in European history. Nevertheless, as the manhunt faded, one final reckoning was revived: to settle the account with the Holocaust's profiteers.

The witnesses were indelibly scarred by Nazi persecution and their grievance was against a breed of men, brazenly immune to their suffering, who pontificated about their service to mankind yet had stolen their family's money. Some names had become notorious for earning fortunes from the suffering of the Jews. Recrimination had been directed at the roll call of Germany's biggest corporations and banks, which had employed slave labor and banked profits earned in the concentration camps. But few had thought to regard the silent, starch-shirted bankers and lawyers in beautiful, clean, neutral Switzerland as unconscionable profiteers.

Charges of hypocrisy were too mild for those witnesses waiting to tell the world about their fractured lives. The calculated theft was merely the final degradation that they had suffered. For fifty years the injustice had been neglected and condoned as one of history's footnotes. Now, at the end of their lives, they finally commandeered the spotlight.

Their attention was focused on the slight, dark-suited, dapper man who, just after 10:30 A.M., entered the room surrounded by young aides. The witnesses' presence in the court building was at his invitation, and their evident gratitude was uninfluenced by the controversy surrounding their hero. In his native New York, which he represented, Senator Alfonse D'Amato is revered and reviled. Accused of many sins, he positions himself as a home-loving Italian-American maverick traduced by smug Ivy Leaguers. The senior Republican senator, first elected in 1980, was an unlikely champion of Jewish causes, but his critics had been silenced by the effectiveness of his latest campaign. Seated behind a small table, D'Amato, in his jagged Brooklyn accent, opened the hearings of the Senate banking committee: "We're very concerned that Swiss citizens and corporations blatantly benefited from the Holocaust while the interests of the survivors were totally ignored." His voice rising slightly, the senator issued his challenge: "We want to know where all the hundreds of millions of dollars of assets that the Nazis deposited in the banks went." And then the threat: "It's time for justice. Time to get the truth. We want to know where it is. Who has it?"

The witnesses beamed. The politician was addressing their concern. Along one side of the room, Swiss journalists were scribbling intently. Their readers, especially the bankers and politicians in

Zurich and Basel and Bern, would the following day study their reports with concern and even fear.

To shame those Swiss stalwarts, D'Amato summoned his first witness, Elie Wiesel, the Auschwitz survivor and a spokesman for the Holocaust's victims. A winner of the Nobel Peace Prize, Wiesel dignified the political theater set so near to Wall Street. Surviving hell has its downside, and his breaking voice recalled the horrific and irremovable scars of an experience he shared with the witnesses. Wiesel is tormented by the Germans' destruction of his close family in Hungary and by the loss of his beloved father, whom he barely knew before he died in Buchenwald. Ever since emerging from a life lived among the dead, he has been dedicated to explaining the mad savagery—the "balance sheet" of life—he and his fellow victims endured. "They didn't simply want to kill Jews, as horrible as this may sound," he told D'Amato. "They wanted Jewish money." Then he made a memorable accusation: "Is there no limit to pain? Is there no limit to outrage?" His words cautioned those critics and lobbyists seated behind him—hired to deride the hearing as cheap politicking.

The senator smiled. The survivor had justified the campaign and provided the explanation for the embarrassment it was causing. After a judicious cough, the politician disclosed an offer. In 1995, the Bankers Association had suggested to the World Jewish Congress, "Drop all your claims," and in return the Jews would receive $36 million. That had been rejected. "We want an accounting," demanded D'Amato, justifying the WJC's refusal. Rebuffed, the Swiss had proposed a commission to report in five years. "It's the old game," ribbed the politician. "Delay, delay, time, time. We're not satisfied with that."

He had reached the heart of his indictment, what he dubbed "one of the most incredible things." The witnesses had all lost fathers who, attracted by the guarantee of anonymity and protection from prying governments, had deposited money in Swiss banks. But the same system had denied their children that inheritance at their most vulnerable moments. The banks, spat D'Amato, demanded "a death certificate." As he leaned toward the microphone, his anger sounded only too genuine. "I mean, can you believe this?" He looked along the line of witnesses: "Somebody is a victim in a concentration camp and an heir comes forward and the banks say, 'Well, give us the death certificate to prove that your loved one, one of your parents, was killed.'" Eyes darting, D'Amato leaned farther forward: "I mean, preposterous! Turning you down on the basis that you could not provide a death certificate!"

The indictment was a dreadful one. Evil bureaucrats had murdered their parents and malicious bureaucrats had denied them their inheritance. Bursting with indignation, Estelle Sapir, called as the first witness, depicted the frustration.

Sapir, small, withered and speaking broken English, had last seen her father through barbed wire in a French prison camp. "Try to survive," he urged her. Their prewar lifestyle of governesses and maids, all the tokens of great wealth, had been long forgotten in their daily struggle. The only legacy was a bank account in Switzerland. In 1947, Sapir arrived at Crédit Suisse in Basel, Switzerland's second-largest city, clutching a document miraculously preserved during the war in their family home in Poland. Dated 1938, the flimsy deposit slip of the Crédit Suisse bank found among her father's papers showed that he had deposited money at the Basel branch. "I saw a young man come out from behind," spluttered Sapir, "and the first thing he asked me, 'Show me the death certificate for your father.' And I answer him, 'How can I have a death certificate? I have to go find Himmler, Hitler, Eichmann and Mengele.' And I start to cry. I run out from the bank, into the street. The same day, I went back to the bank, but could not compose myself. Never went back to Switzerland. Never went back to Switzerland. Never." Without proof of death, exclaimed Sapir, reliving the humiliation, the banker refused to look at the proffered deposit slip. Ever since, scarred by inhumanity, the "child of privilege" had been struggling to survive in New York's downtrodden districts.

"This is just unconscionable!" exclaimed D'Amato. "How many others fall into this shameful category?" Sapir had not finished. Oblivious to D'Amato's words, she was still recalling her treatment by the bankers: "The Swiss were so arrogant to me. They have been so arrogant. They knew, I'm just coming from the war, from the Holocaust. They were absolutely not human to me."

And there was a sting to her tale, one that gave credibility to her testimony. Money deposited by her father in British and French banks had been paid within days of her application in the postwar years. Without a death certificate and ignorant of any details, the British and French banks had traced her father's account and handed over thousands of dollars to Sapir and her mother. Banking secrecy had not denied Sapir her inheritance. "It's funny," she would reflect later. "My father was able to protect his money from the Nazis, but not from the Swiss."

Eleven TV news cameras had recorded Sapir's anguish, good reason for D'Amato to be pleased. His final witness was Lewis Salton, born in Cracow, Poland, eighty-five years earlier. Salton's father, a lawyer, collected and traded valuable stamps. Among his principal contacts was Luder Edelmann, a dealer in Switzerland. Purchases and sales of stamps with Edelmann were transacted by Salton through a Swiss bank account. In September 1942, Salton's father was murdered by a Nazi firing squad, and his mother was gassed. Miraculously, in one of those feats that reveal the ingenuity of the survivors, Salton escaped death and, after traveling for one and a half years across Siberia to Korea and across the Pacific to Panama, arrived in New York.

When travel to Europe was permitted, Salton journeyed to Switzerland to track down his father's account. As was the case with so many other claimants bereft of documents and precise knowledge, Salton's inquiries proved abortive. Unlike the banks in Britain, France and New York, the Swiss uttered their refusals without any sense of regret. Fifty years later, Salton, the wealthy inventor of hot plates for the catering industry, was candid to D'Amato about his "sad story": "Frankly, I don't need the Swiss money, but I would love to get it for sentimental reasons."

D'Amato nodded. In language not normally associated with banking, the senator vented his spleen. "Trust was totally broken and smashed. And used in the most vile of ways where you do not have a number. A fraud was committed on all of the people, and it continues today." The investigation, the senator declared, would benefit from "my dogged determination," not only to embarrass the Swiss but also to uncover a "conspiracy of silence which unfortunately this country [the United States] and its officials aided back in 1946 when we signed the Washington Accord."

WASHINGTON — OCTOBER 16, 1996

Two hundred and thirty miles south, on the same day, the staff of the Swiss embassy hosted a party in Washington for a departing colleague. Surrounded by immaculate lawns, the sprawling embassy compound exuded wealth, security and certainty—the very qualities of Switzerland itself. The hosts, modestly dressed, quietly spoken and impeccably polite, were aggrieved by that morning's events in New York. Over a warm buffet, they voiced their suspicions about D'Amato and his motives. In their lifetime, their nation has been associated only with spectacular Alpine landscapes, international charities, enviable prosperity, quirky traditions and a respected banking and business community. An occasional news flash had mentioned Switzerland, but the sustained attention now engineered by D'Amato and the World Jewish Congress had been unsettling for those unassertive, gray-suited bureaucrats. They characterized D'Amato as hysterical, abrasive, dishonest and uncomprehending of Switzerland—in short, as a duplicitous ogre. The contempt was mutual. Despite repeated requests, the senator had refused to meet the Swiss ambassador. This unusual insult reinforced the diplomats' disdain.

Among those career diplomats was Christoph Bubb, the embassy's young legal counselor. Worship of laws, regard for the inviolability of formal agreements, have always been paraded as the cornerstones, even the gospel, of Switzerland's existence. "Legality is a small country's only defense" is its ritual chant. Sipping fizzy water, Bubb admitted that Switzerland's wartime conduct could be criticized. The nation's treatment of Jewish refugees was regrettable, but its vaunted neutrality between the Allies and the Nazis had been sadly misunderstood. Talk of skeletons and dirty laundry was probably accurate, but the idea that Swiss bankers had profited from the war, or had collaborated with the Nazis, or had kept looted gold, or had actually stolen money belonging to the Jews was inconceivable. Inconceivable. Nurtured on facts sanitized by his compromised predecessors, the diplomat spoke of "honesty in the genes" and dismissed accusations of his nation's collaboration with the Nazis. "Inconceivable."

Over the years, Bubb's predecessors had rebuffed claims for the Jewish assets by reference to laws, contracts, formal undertakings and international agreements sanctified after negotiation by a solemn signature. In his world, emotions and references to morality only clouded the issue. Responding to the allegations that Switzerland had knowingly accepted looted gold from the Nazis, he expressed an infallible conviction that his countrymen never broke laws. "Perhaps the gold was booty," he suggested. "Swiss bankers would then be entitled to accept that gold." Similarly, Bubb smiled at the suggestion that Swiss bankers would have deliberately kept the deposits of murdered Jews. "Our bankers," he said with a smirk, "obey the law."

LONDON — 1996

Charles Sonabend possessed proof of the Swiss bankers' deceit. Born in Brussels, Belgium, in 1931, Sonabend, with his family, had become the victim of both the Nazis and the Swiss. In July 1996, the businessman, living in comfort in London, had revisited Switzerland to read Swiss police reports dated 1942 and 1963, detailing his family's arrest and deportation and a subsequent investigation into the fate of their two suitcases, one entrusted to police custody and another to a family friend in August 1942. Inside one suitcase, according to the 1963 police report, was at least $1,400 in banknotes. According to Charles Sonabend, there was much more. But one sentence in the police report aroused his excitement: "The remaining $200 was deposited in Herr Sonabend's bank account at the Berner Kantonalbank."

For the past fifty years, Charles Sonabend had been searching for his father's Swiss bank account. In 1942, he had later been told by his father's Swiss business associate, the account contained "at least SF200,000"—over $1.7 million in current values. But every bank to which Sonabend and his sister applied after 1946 denied all knowledge of a family account. Without any details, Sonabend had been helpless. That impotence disappeared after the discovery of the 1963 police report. Quite irrefutably, in 1942 there had been a Sonabend bank account.

Apprehensively, on an overcast July morning in 1996, Sonabend visited the headquarters of the Berner Kantonalbank overlooking the parliament building, where forty-four years earlier Max Oetterli had aggressively denied that Swiss bankers were withholding money deposited by Jews. Greeted in the small reception area by Peter Lienhard, a stout, bearded bank employee, Sonabend was ushered into a first-floor windowless room. The message he received was brief and unapologetic: "There is no trace of any bank account." If an account had remained dormant for ten years, the bank would have automatically initiated a process to destroy the records. No paper trail remained proving that an account ever existed.

"Nothing more can be done," Lienhard told the visitor.

"It could have been stolen," said Sonabend.

"That's possible," replied the banker. "We have terrible difficulties tracing old records." Collective amnesia infected all the bankers.

"This is immoral and wrong," insisted Sonabend.

Bid swiftly farewell, Sonabend stood forlornly on the street outside the bank. As with thousands of other claimants, a sense of futility began to sap his energy. Peter Lienhard had been so "correct"—so similar to the attitude of the Swiss police and SS officers who had determined the family's fate fifty-four years earlier.

2

THE SEEDS OF
CRIME

During the night of August 12, 1942, Charles Sonabend, then age eleven, had anxiously followed his father, Simon; his thirty-eight-year-old mother, Lili; and his sister, Sabine, fifteen, up an Alpine mountain path in eastern France toward the Swiss border. Led by a French guide, they stumbled, frightened, over unseen rocks, alarmed by unfamiliar sounds, racked by the terror of discovery. At daybreak, the fugitives' fear dissolved. Looking down into a rich green valley, their guide triumphantly announced: "You're in Switzerland."

"We're free," sighed Charles Sonabend. "Saved." Neutral Switzerland, the home of the Red Cross, would provide sanctuary from their persecutors. The sunlight glancing off the tall Alpine trees and the effect of the fresh mountain air encouraged the family to cast off the hatred and dread instinctive to refugees. Fear of Gestapo officers, of inhumanity and of imminent deportation to a death camp was extinguished by this tranquil vista. It was a return to normality. Their trembling, so long a permanent affliction, ceased.

The Sonabends' journey from Brussels had started two weeks earlier when Simon, a forty-three-year-old importer of Swiss watches, received a summons from the SS ordering that the family report for "resettlement in the East." Sonabend was not fooled, and he understood the fate that awaited his family. Ever since the

German invasion of Poland in September 1939, he had received letters from his brothers in Warsaw describing the Nazi treatment of Jews and the mass shootings and even mentioning rumors about gas chambers.

Simon Sonabend, with his family, had tried to escape the Nazis in May 1940. Fleeing toward Dunkirk after the German blitzkrieg invasion of France, Belgium and Holland, the Sonabends had been marooned twelve miles from the coast in an abandoned British army base and missed the last boat across the channel. Anxiously, they returned to occupied Brussels. Over the following two years, Simon continued to import Swiss watches, secretly arranging for at least SF200,000 to be deposited by the manufacturers in a secret bank account in Switzerland.

For years, Jews, like people of every nationality, had used Swiss banks to deposit money to escape paying local taxes and as insurance should they need to flee their own countries. Some opened accounts in their own names, others anonymously. Some simply pushed banknotes, gold coins and jewelry into safe-deposit boxes, reassuringly protected by thick stone walls. Others bought property or insurance policies. For those fearful that banks, despite their formalities, might nevertheless reveal their secrets to the police or to their own governments, the alternative was to entrust their savings to Switzerland's lawyers, notaries, trustees, and insurance companies, or to their business associates to be registered in other names. That protection became critical in the months after Hitler became chancellor in January 1933. Swiss bankers began receiving requests from German-Jewish clients that their deposits should be either transferred to Germany or handed over to a representative who would personally call at the banks. German Jews, the Swiss realized, had become the victims of Gestapo blackmail. Many of those requests were refused until the bankers were satisfied that the Jews genuinely wanted their money handed over to their jailers. To reinforce their clients' protection, the bankers had successfully lobbied for a federal law, passed in 1934, punishing those responsible for unauthorized revelations of banking secrets. Although there was no evidence that the 1934 law was conceived to benefit the Jews—the bill was introduced only eighteen days after Hitler became chancellor—the law had, by 1942, convinced most Gestapo officers that importuning Jewish depositors was an unprofitable activity. Countless Jews had already been gassed or shot without revealing the secrets of their finances, while others, on the eve of their death or separation from their children, had passed on the secret: "There's money for you in Switzerland." Occasionally—in the desolate prison, in the crammed railway wagon or surrounded by the dying in concentration camps—these people whispered the secret numbers. But, in the turmoil of suffering, the heirs barely noted what seemed an irrelevance. For those still free but persecuted, the existence of a secret fund in Switzerland was akin to divine reassurance.

In July 1942, to avoid "resettlement in the East," Simon Sonabend found a Frenchman who agreed to smuggle his family into Switzerland. The cost, for providing false French passports and guiding the family from Brussels across France and through the mountains into Switzerland, was SF125,000 (about $800,000 in today's values)—a fortune, but affordable for Sonabend.

In the days before their departure, Simon deposited diamonds and gold bars with four friends, secretly recording the details inside a chest of drawers. Other gold bars were hidden in a chimney. More gold bars, diamonds stuffed into lipstick canisters and currency then worth about $20,000 were concealed in the two bags that the Sonabends carried to Besançon, near the Swiss border.

Two days earlier, a telegram had arrived at the Foreign Office in London from its embassy in Bern. In stark terms, a British diplomat quoted a "reliable" intelligence source—Gerhard Riegner, the secretary of the World Jewish Congress—reporting Hitler's secret orders to exterminate four million Jews "at one blow." That report only confirmed all the eyewitness reports received by officials in the Foreign Office, the State Department and Switzerland's Political Department about the deportation of French, Dutch and Belgian Jews eastward and their mass execution. Descriptions of those murders had been broadcast on BBC radio from London and were heard in Switzerland, where local newspapers reported a speech by

Winston Churchill denouncing the Nazi murder of one million Jews. Swiss citizens were even themselves eyewitnesses of the mass murder. Across occupied Europe, Swiss diplomats, doctors and travelers, protected as neutrals, observed and reported to Switzerland the horrors inflicted upon the innocent. Some eyewitnesses, such as Dr. Rudolf Bucher, a Zurich physician, gave dozens of speeches in Switzerland during that summer of 1942 about their experiences—of seeing deportations and mass shootings, of hearing rumors of the gas chambers. Considering that information, the Sonabends had good reason to believe that they were safe. But they had been unaware of Dr. Heinrich Rothmund, the director of the police section of the Ministry of Justice and the Police.

Tall, broad-shouldered, athletic and a respectable Christian, Rothmund nursed a hatred of Jews noteworthy in Switzerland only because of the power he wielded. Indoctrinated for centuries by its dogmatic priests, Switzerland's God-fearing community was steeped in a primitive hatred of the Jews as the killers of Jesus Christ. Long after Jews had been granted civil rights in neighboring countries, Switzerland continued to discriminate and persecute Jews until, the last country in Europe to do so, it granted them political rights in 1886. Ever since, Switzerland's small Jewish community had meekly acquiesced in their countrymen's anti-Semitism. Trepidation rather than pride had spread among the small community on February 4, 1936, when David Frankfurter, a twenty-five-year-old Jewish medical student and the son of a rabbi in a small Yugoslav community, assassinated Wilhelm Gustloff, Hitler's personal representative in Switzerland. Frankfurter had immediately surrendered to the police, explaining the murder as a gesture to draw attention to the plight of the Jews in Germany. His eighteen-year prison sentence was a warning to all Swiss Jews to remain inconspicuous and unprotesting. Accordingly, none had dared to protest when, to conform with Nazi Germany's laws, Jewish bankers, members of long-established Swiss families, had been requested by their countrymen to resign their directorships and memberships in the council of the Zurich stock exchange.

Dr. Heinrich Rothmund's unpredictable moods swung between meekness and hysteria, reflecting a driven, authoritarian, conceited official who alternately displayed despotism and charm, gentle wit and harsh cynicism. By 1942, acting at the behest of Switzerland's establishment and the majority of the people, its authoritarian police apparatus was dedicated to keeping the country "pure" and to saving it from being "overrun with Jews." Rothmund was tied to that ideology, and the reports from Germany and Eastern Europe could not sway his feelings toward those whom he considered a sinister threat.

Switzerland's attitude toward Jews applying for asylum was sealed by a new law passed on April 7, 1933. Those fleeing from the Nazis as religious rather than "political fugitives" were denied the status that automatically granted asylum under the Swiss constitution. By 1942, just 9,150 foreign Jews were legally resident in Switzerland, only 980 more than in 1931. The fortunate few were the rich who had cooperated in allowing the Swiss to profit from their misery. Unscrupulous Swiss businessmen like Richard Holtklott had been tipped off by Swiss diplomats about Jewish property and factories in Germany and occupied Europe that could be purchased cheaply. Among the victims of that trade was Frederick Weissmann, the owner of Emil Jacoby, a shoe factory in Berlin. After running the business for thirty years, Weissmann was compelled by Germany's Aryanization laws to sell the factory. The purchaser, for one mark, was Bally Shoes, the Swiss giant, which had acquired for similar amounts a succession of other Jewish assets in Germany. Weissmann's only comfort was that Bally arranged an entry visa to Switzerland, which saved his life. The less prosperous Jews were the subject of Rothmund's influence, first manifested on March 26, 1938, just two weeks after Hitler triumphantly arrived in Vienna and annexed his homeland to the Reich.

Desperate Austrian Jews were entering Switzerland in growing numbers, and Rothmund proposed to the Federal Council—the government, or Bundesrat, consisting of seven ministers—that the refugees should be denied visas and expelled. "We must protect ourselves with all our strength," he told the nation's rulers, "and, when necessary, without mercy, against the immigration of foreign Jews, most especially those from the east." As the Jews' predicament worsened and distraught Jews were forcibly repelled at the Swiss border, Rothmund was dispatched on July 6, 1938, as the Swiss delegate to a conference to discuss the plight of Jewish refugees. At President Roosevelt's initiative, thirty-two nations had agreed to meet in Switzerland, but when the Swiss government refused to host the meeting they convened instead at nearby Évian, on the French shore of Lake Geneva.

Few knew more than Rothmund and the Swiss government about the persecution of Jews in Germany and Austria. During an enjoyable tour around Oranienburg, the concentration camp near Berlin, Rothmund had lectured his hosts over lunch in the camp about Switzerland's successful control of the Jewish threat and had later congratulated himself on the respect shown to him. His report on his return praised the German method of teaching citizenship. By then, the fate of the Jews—harassed, stigmatized, robbed, jailed and murdered by their kinsmen—was openly boasted about by Germany's leaders in their much applauded public speeches. Over 250,000 Jews had fled Germany and Austria—52,000 to Britain, 30,000 to France, 33,000 to Palestine, 100,000 to the United States and 3,000 to Sweden. Switzerland had allowed 14,000 to enter but had compelled more than half to leave. As the persecution worsened, Switzerland's restrictions increased. For Rothmund and his sponsors, the Jews were unwanted mouths, millstones, even vermin among the horde of foreigners seeking protection under Switzerland's Red Cross. The conference at Évian aggravated the Jews' tribulations. Instead of helping the Jews, the delegates, most notably the Australian, voiced fears of a stampede and of importing "a Jewish problem."

Heartened by international solidarity, Rothmund returned home to consider the crisis. Enforcing Switzerland's exclusion of Jews had become difficult, not least because identifying the Jews among the Germans arriving at Switzerland's borders was not always easy. Aryan Germans were upset by the questions and—more irritating—the

Swiss were embarrassed when Jews were inadvertently admitted. A cumbersome way of identifying the Jews would be to require visas for all Germans traveling to Switzerland. To avoid that unfortunate measure, on August 13, 1938, Swiss diplomats approached the government in Berlin with an unusual request. By then, desperate Jews were crossing the Swiss border illegally. Exhausted, hungry and often destitute, they were usually arrested and driven back toward their tormentors. From Bern, Rothmund pushed hard for special discrimination. Dr. Hans Frölicher, the pro-Nazi Swiss ambassador, asked the Nazi government whether Germany would be prepared to mark the passports of Jews with a distinctive sign. Previous requests had been unavailing because the German policy had been to encourage Jewish emigration, but eventually, on September 7, after persistent Swiss pressure, the Germans yielded. All Jewish passports were to be prominently stamped with the letter *J*.

Rothmund remained dissatisfied. Although Switzerland was at this time housing no more than 12,000 political and religious refugees, the police chief traveled to Berlin to demand further concessions. After successive bouts of negotiation, the Nazis finally agreed that German border guards would prevent Jews from crossing the frontier. The Swiss demand for cruelty had been accepted.

Over the following weeks, the pressure to escape into Switzerland intensified. Kristallnacht, a two-day orgy of mayhem and murder directed against Germany's Jews on November 9–10, 1938, was launched by Hitler in a speech promising "the annihilation of the Jewish race in Europe." More German Jews unsuccessfully attempted to cross the Swiss border. The following year, on the outbreak of war, France's Jews also sought sanctuary in Switzerland, risking their lives as they passed through thick forests and across ravines and mountain ranges. The French were followed by Belgian and Dutch Jews. Nearly all of those who overcame the obstacles and crossed the frontier were forcibly ejected. To all appeals for humanity Rothmund stayed impervious, despite knowing the fate of those returned to German-occupied Europe. Even the knowledge that warehouses across Switzerland were full of unclaimed luggage dispatched by hopeful Jews who had failed to complete their journey did not dent the police chief's resolution. Voicing the sentiment of his masters, he told inquirers that tiny Switzerland should not underestimate the threat posed to law and order or "overstrain" its limited food supplies.

The irony was lost on most people. Until 1942, the Swiss government would compel the 5,000 members of Switzerland's Jewish working community to finance entirely the care of the Jewish refugees. Wealthier refugees were forced to pay additional taxes to support poorer refugees, and no refugee was allowed to work, pending compulsory internment. American Jews had contributed toward the cost until a director of the National Bank threatened to cease converting "Jewish dollars." Rothmund and Eduard von Steiger, the new minister of justice and the police and a Nazi sympathizer, had cowed Switzerland's Jewish community into petrified subservience. Long before the Sonabends crossed the frontier, Switzerland had without a qualm adopted Germany's racial policies. Uncertainty permeated the lives of those Swiss Jews to whom the Sonabends innocently appealed for help.

After a short train journey from the border, on August 13 Simon Sonabend had led his family to friends in Biel, the center of Switzerland's watch manufacturers. Welcomed with evident trepidation by Swiss Jews, the two children were transferred to another house while their hosts explained their predicament to Simon Sonabend. Swiss law required foreigners staying the night to be registered at the local police. A handful of Swiss, realizing the consequences, had illegally hidden their uninvited guests, but Sonabend's hosts, fearful of breaking the law, insisted on notifying the police about the refugees. Sonabend's tearful entreaties were resisted. Even Jews born in Switzerland were being threatened by the government with denaturalization. Rothmund's edict had ruptured the bond among Jews and their friends.

On the morning of Saturday, August 15, 1942, two policemen arrived at the house where the children were staying. Gruffly, they were ordered to pack. "We can't travel," replied the bewildered boy.

"It's the Sabbath." Jeering, the policemen bundled Charles, his sister, and later their distraught, frail mother into a car. Their immediate destination was the Convent des Ursulines, a picturesque sixteenth-century mansion bordered by narrow cobbled streets and overlooked by the Jura Mountains in Porrentruy. Nearby was France. The nuns had agreed to imprison the Belgians until their deportation. The convent, packed with Jews and other refugees, had become a staging post for Auschwitz, a symbol of Switzerland's pact with the Nazis.

Simon Sonabend had been incarcerated in the town's jail. Italic script in the prison's heavy black ledger recorded the fate of prisoner number 1,151. Unlike other illegal French immigrants, who were fined ten francs, Sonabend was described as a "Jew to be deported." Just before his departure, he revealed that he had entrusted one suitcase filled with currency, jewels and gold to a Swiss associate (another suitcase was held by the police). Meticulously, the police recorded the prisoner's statement and asked Simon for his signature. Unlike Switzerland's bank records, the police and prison records would survive the next fifty years in unblemished condition.

That same day in Bern, Rothmund had issued a new instruction concerning the treatment of Jewish refugees. Four weeks earlier, he had discussed with von Steiger their common fear that Switzerland would be overwhelmed by Jews. The frontier, Rothmund had reiterated, was difficult to guard, especially against those prepared to suffer any injury to save their lives. The solution, he recommended, was to issue an uncompromising order that every Jew crossing illegally into Switzerland was to be forcibly returned to occupied Europe. Von Steiger, enjoying a holiday in the mountains and feeling no sympathy toward the "arrogant and disgruntled people . . . with dollars and jewels," approved the law on August 13, 1942. Among the first victims of Rothmund's new decree were the Sonabends.

In the late afternoon on the following day, two French policemen called for Lili Sonabend and her two children. Escorted from the mansion along the cobbled path to a waiting car, the woman suddenly panicked and cried for mercy. In the words of the subsequent police report, "Madame Sonabend pretended they would be shot if deported." Lili collapsed screaming onto the pavement, attracting over fifty outraged townsfolk who protested against the family's deportation. The nuns, by contrast, remained immobile. For their own safety, the police allowed the Sonabends to return inside the building.

The following night, August 17, the Sonabends, terrified but resigned to their fate, were driven to the French border. The routine, by then familiar, would be repeated by thousands of other Jews. In darkness on strange roads, children would cry for their mothers; old women would be forced to walk, begging the police to shoot them rather than that they should take another step; fathers would plead and scream for their families to be saved; and wives would sob as their husbands were dragged through the dirt. All uttered the same entreaties: that the police should know that they were leading them to inevitable death, that they should know that the Gestapo, whom they had mercifully evaded just days before, awaited their return. Nearly all were met with the same icy indifference. At best, the police remained silent, convinced that they had to obey orders or lose their jobs—like Paul Grüninger, a police chief in St. Gall who had been dismissed in 1940 for allowing 3,000 Jews to cross the border. At worst, the officers spat out, "You're Jews and you're getting what you deserve."

Controlling his emotions, Simon Sonabend also uttered a plea. His family, he begged, should be deported to Free France in the Vichy zone, where there would be a chance of survival. Nonchalantly, the Swiss police rejected his request. "The Jews," decided the police, "are to be handed over to the Germans." Charles Sonabend recalled, "The Swiss were cynical and treated us as criminals." That cynicism, ordained by Rothmund's office and by his political master, manifested itself in the police requirement that Simon Sonabend pay SF6.80 for the taxi that took his family and their police escort to the border.

Clutching their luggage and denied any map to establish their whereabouts, the Sonabends walked hesitantly into the darkness. "My parents were too traumatized to carry on fighting," Charles realized in later years. "My father didn't think of waiting and then going back into Switzerland. Blindly we walked toward the SS." Once inside France, forlornly hiding under bushes, their hope that they would not be found by German patrols proved futile as sniffer dogs approached. Handing over their only suitcase, they were escorted to the local frontier post. "The SS," Charles Sonabend later reflected, "questioned us more politely than the Swiss police."

By then, the Swiss policemen had returned to their base. In their report, they recorded that the routine deportation had passed uneventfully. Attached to their report was the receipt issued by the taxi driver. The file was placed in an archive and the family was forgotten.

The following day, in Belfort prison, Charles met his father for the last time. Together they prayed. Just before the eleven-year-old bid farewell, he was told of the valuables hidden in Belgium and of the bank accounts in Switzerland and New York. The cell door closed. While the two children were taken to a local orphanage, the parents traveled to Paris and then on cattle trucks toward Poland. Charles and his sister soon arrived in Paris themselves. But the recent mass roundup of Jews had exhausted the local police. As a temporary measure, the two orphans were given shelter with Jewish families.

In Switzerland, the police handed Sonabend's suitcase to a friend. Prying it open, he found more valuables. Having taken what he deemed was owed to him, the friend (according to the police report) deposited the remaining $200 in Sonabend's account at a local branch of the Kantonalbank. At that moment, two weeks after their deportation, the Sonabends arrived at Auschwitz. They died shortly afterward.

The Sonabends' murder coincided with an outpouring of grief, anger and shame in Switzerland. Churchmen who had witnessed the suffering of the refugees protested to von Steiger that Switzerland's reputation for asylum had been contaminated by allowing just 9,600 refugees to remain in the country. The ban, complained the protesters, was harming rather than protecting the nation. In reply, the minister spoke of his fears that the refugees might import health risks and of his passionate desire to obey the law. Switzerland, he

exclaimed, was "an overcrowded little lifeboat." Addressing the
Federal Council on September 22, von Steiger praised his own policies, predicting that history would one day record, "We have fulfilled
the duty of humanity with independence and honor as in the past, and
with reason guiding our emotions." As a gesture, the minister
announced a slight relaxation of his policy. Exceptions would be tolerated to the expulsions, but there was no question of Switzerland's
making a sacrifice on behalf of the persecuted.

In Washington and London, there was no reaction to von
Steiger's announcements. Neither Allied government offered assistance to the Jews. While Foreign Office officials had categorized as a
"wild story" Riegner's information about German policy "to elimi-
nate 'useless mouths,'" senior officials in the State Department, still
denying the existence of the Holocaust, withheld the telegram from
World Jewish Congress officials in Washington as "unsubstantiated"
and continued to block attempts to allow entry into the United States
by those Jewish refugees still able to escape from Europe. A revolt
against that prejudice was germinating among the new recruits in the
U.S. Department of the Treasury, which was located in an imposing
building opposite the White House. Within the department, a band
of American crusaders were scrutinizing the role of Switzerland and
the other neutrals toward the Nazis, a scrutiny that would eventually
engender the campaign to restore the Jewish assets to their owners.

3

THE CRUSADE

Sam Klaus, a passionate gumshoe, an outstanding lawyer and a fervent Nazi hunter, shone among the American crusaders. An intelligent man, dynamic and resourceful, Klaus boiled with anger as he learned of Germany's treatment of the Jews, and he was determined to do all he could to prevent, for all time, any renewal of Germany's threat to world peace. He was no less driven by an invincible urge to find the Nazis' loot. To Klaus, Switzerland epitomized the enemy. For their part, the Swiss regarded Klaus—principled, powerful and Jewish—as their preeminent foe.

Klaus was born in Brooklyn in 1904. His father, a successful and cultivated tailor working on lower Madison Avenue, died shortly afterward of cancer. Klaus's mother remarried a grocer, and the family moved into a poor neighborhood, "redolent," according to Klaus's sister, "of Dickensian habits." A victim of diabetes and of misery at home, Klaus could in later years recall from his childhood only one benediction: his stepfather's insistence on a Hebraic education and a commitment to Jewish causes, especially the development of Palestine. Hard work eased his exit from that ghetto. Graduating at the top of his class from Columbia Law School and rising to become one of New York's best lawyers, Klaus enjoyed a well-established reputation by the outbreak of war. Automatically disqualified from military service in 1942 for health reasons, he joined others with a similar background in the Treasury who, in later years, affectionately recalled "Sammy" Klaus as a small, dark, intense bachelor with a passion for collecting rugs, always straining after perfection, who marched in the vanguard of an unusual crusade.

The mastermind of the crusade was Henry Morgenthau, the secretary of the Treasury since 1934, an affable, ardent New Dealer, a friend and neighbor of the president, who was driven by a credo that Europe's peace could be secured only by permanently destroying Germany's industrial might, reducing the warmongering nation to manufacturers of cuckoo clocks. Armed with ideas, guile and tenacity, Morgenthau's crusaders were a group of outstanding economists and lawyers, graduates of Harvard and Columbia, many of whom had risen from poor Jewish communities through their ambition, intelligence and industry. United by their desire to cripple Nazi Germany and by their concern for Europe's abandoned and destitute Jews, they were influenced by a variety of sources, prominent among them Israel Sieff, a British Zionist, who hosted weekly dinners in Washington to discuss the fate of Europe's Jews.

The most senior of Morgenthau's crusaders was Harry Dexter White, a New Dealer empowered as an assistant Treasury secretary to direct American policy across Europe. Inside the White House, Morgenthau's standard-bearer was Isador Lubin, a member of the president's "brain trust." Officially ranking as a government statistician, Lubin was one of those confidants of President Roosevelt who, like Colonel Bernard Bernstein (a Treasury representative assigned to General Eisenhower's headquarters to plan the occupation of Germany), had become uneasy about the collaboration by Europe's neutral countries with Nazi Germany.

Klaus was assigned within the Treasury to the Foreign Economic Administration (FEA) division, tracking and controlling Germany's foreign trade. Just as in the bygone era when the imperial navies and armies of warring nations laid siege to castles and blockaded ports, the Treasury in Washington, which relied heavily on the Ministry of Economic Warfare in London, had plotted an economic offensive against Germany and occupied Europe to prevent crucial supplies from reaching the Nazis. During that first year, 1942, immersed in constant discussion with other innovative lawyers and economists,

Klaus toyed with the problem of how eventually to seize the increasing flow of Nazi loot deposited in the neutral countries.

Since 1940, a trickle of intelligence reports from London had suggested that German bankers, industrialists, politicians and Nazi functionaries were accumulating technology and money, particularly in Switzerland, estimated to be worth $1 billion (over $10 billion in today's values). Reading those reports, Morgenthau's men suspected that after Germany's defeat the remnants of the Nazi leadership would use the secret funds deposited in the neutral countries as the seed money to establish the Fourth Reich. To forestall that resurgence of Nazism, Sam Klaus's own plan, set out on May 11, 1944, less than a month before the Normandy landings, was to launch a worldwide hunt to uncover and prevent the sale and disappearance of German property and loot after the war. Code-naming it the Safehaven program, Klaus recommended that Allied governments persuade the neutrals to seize all the German property deposited in their countries.

In July 1944, Sam Klaus was jubilant, convinced that he had won a major battle. Forty-four nations had met at Bretton Woods, a resort in New Hampshire, under the banner of the United Nations' Monetary and Financial Conference, to plan the world's postwar economy. On Klaus's initiative, the FEA representative persuaded the conference to adopt Safehaven as Allied policy. To the crusaders, Resolution VI, which demanded that the neutrals prevent the Nazis from hiding funds and loot in their countries, was a weapon that would shackle the enemy and their collaborators.

The preamble of the resolution stated: "Anticipating defeat, enemy leaders and their nationals are transferring assets to and through neutral countries in order to conceal them and to perpetuate their influence and power. . . ." The resolution called upon the neutrals to "take immediate measures to prevent any disposition or transfer . . . of looted gold, currency, art objects, securities and financial or business enterprises [and] to take immediate measures to prevent the concealment by fraudulent means or otherwise" of stolen assets or assets belonging to enemy leaders and their associates. The loot, the resolution demanded, should be returned by the neutrals to the Allies.

Back in Washington, on August 5, FEA representatives met officials from the State Department and Treasury to agree on their strategy to prevent the neutrals from frustrating the resolution. Using the threat of economic sanctions to compel the neutrals' compliance was, Klaus argued, vital. But by the end of the meeting the lawyer recognized that his passion for an aggressive policy was not shared by the State Department. Tellingly, the diplomats were even unwilling to relinquish to the FEA their control of communications to the neutral governments. Safehaven's success depended, Klaus knew, upon the attitude of the neutrals' governments, and if the U.S. Treasury Department was denied direct access to Swiss government officials, the program would be handicapped. "Where voluntary cooperation proves insufficient," urged Klaus, "we must be prepared to use direct pressure upon the neutral governments." The diplomats disagreed. Continuing a blockade after the war, asserted the State Department officials, "would not be warranted." The department's cooperation would be restricted to approving a request to American diplomats in the neutral countries to "investigate and report any evidence that enemy capital has been or is being invested in those countries."

Aggrieved by that disunity, Klaus flew to Europe on August 23 accompanied by Herbert Cummings, an equally zealous anti-Nazi employed in the State Department. Soon after their arrival in London, the secrecy of the mission evaporated. Seeking out journalists, Klaus spoke aggressively about Safehaven's threat to the German conspiracy. The imminent arrival of American troops on the Swiss border—they had fought their way across southern France—galvanized the crusader into predicting dire consequences if Switzerland and the other neutrals did not cease their close collaboration with Germany. Flying from London to the neutral capitals—Stockholm, Madrid, Lisbon, Ankara—the two officials called at American embassies to brief and exhort their colleagues to investigate German activities, to identify the deposits of looted assets and to find out how the Germans had camouflaged or cloaked their property within local corporations. Their reception seemed friendly and the assurances of cooperation unconditional, yet by the time the two officials arrived by airplane in Switzerland, their confidence had dimmed.

Like all new visitors to Switzerland, Klaus was beguiled by the country's civility and its sheer beauty: the snowcapped mountains, the rich green meadows and Bern's stone buildings erected along cobbled roads centuries earlier—roads down which Napoleon Bonaparte had ridden his horse to visit his banker and possibly a mistress. To discount that facade required exceptional knowledge and experience that even the Allied diplomats, stationed in Bern, hardly possessed. Few outsiders had penetrated the minds of the rulers of the four-million-strong bourgeois-peasant community who had lived since 1848 in a confederation of three cultures and three languages— German, French and Italian.

Klaus was soon versed in the mythology and the boasts, which declared Switzerland to be Europe's oldest democracy, long ruled by elected representatives rather than royalty. Switzerland, he was told by his hosts, could trace its roots back to 1291 and had survived as a nation since 1848 only because pervading tensions from neighboring countries could be defused by the nation's resolute neutrality, which had been recognized by the Declaration of Paris in 1815 and reaffirmed by the Treaty of Versailles in 1919. Neutrality, the chorus endlessly repeated, was essential to Switzerland's survival, because involvement in a European war would inevitably fracture the country's delicate balance and precipitate its disintegration.

Although Switzerland's leaders would in later years simultaneously lament and flaunt their country's isolation during that era, Sir Clifford Norton, the unassuming British ambassador, had perceptively compared the Swiss to passengers sitting in the air-conditioned salon of a liner steaming through a hurricane in the tropics. The Swiss, he wrote to the Foreign Office, could see momentous events through the portholes but resisted going on deck to experience or understand the conditions. This self-induced blindness had become instinctive to a people denied any recent participation in the dramatic political and social changes beyond their borders. In fact, over recent years, the condition had been exacerbated. As Switzerland became increasingly dependent on foreign trade, Swiss assertions of independence resounded ever more shrilly. The Swiss, as John Ruskin, the art critic, had remarked sixty years earlier, were not heroes but stubborn, proud, avaricious folk lacking any subtlety, enthusiasm or wit, yet boasting a unique brand of common sense and obstinate rectitude.

Inevitably during that brief visit, there were limitations to Klaus's understanding. He did not realize that Switzerland was not so much a country ruled by a central government as a collection of local communes separated by different cultures and united only by a legalistic confederation, by conservatism and by ambivalent history. The government, or Bundesrat, consisted of seven ministers, appointed for life or until they cared to retire, who annually rotated the nation's presidency. Klaus and the economic warriors were negotiating with the servants of self-appointed interest groups, supremely knowledgeable about financial matters and bred, as Switzerland's interests required, to present stubborn indifference toward the rest of the world. These policies had had stark and unpalatable consequences. Ever since Europe's Thirty Year War in 1618–48, while its neighbors had suffered, Switzerland had reaped healthy profits from neutrality.

By 1944, Klaus and many other Allied officials were pondering the question of profits earned by Switzerland from the massacre of millions on the other side of its frontiers. In Switzerland, unlike the rest of Europe, copious supplies of food, alcohol, chocolates and medicine were still available for a population that had experienced little change in its self-satisfied, enviable lifestyle. The country's economy, limited only by the severe rationing of fuel and coal, was undamaged. There was a large surplus of foreign exchange and, while the Swiss had been spared the torment of bombed homes, severed limbs and lost savings, their country's powerbrokers contentedly awaited the inevitable turn of history when new fortunes could be earned resupplying the war-ravaged continent.

Recent protests to Bern from London and Washington about Switzerland's close relations with the Germans and about the secretive assistance provided by Swiss banks to the Nazis had been rebuffed, albeit politely. Reports about discussions between Leland Harrison, the long-serving American ambassador, and Swiss officials revealed that Klaus was dealing with people who, while apparently sympathetic to Allied ambitions, politely acknowledging the virtues of Allied policies and offering their assistance, seemed immune to the reality that their profitable and eager dalliance with the Nazis would soon end.

The Allied armies had just liberated Paris (August 25, 1944), and were expected to cross the Rhine within weeks; meanwhile 300 divisions of the Red Army were remorselessly driving the Germans into retreat along the eastern front. As a neutral, Switzerland was theoretically uninterested in the fate of the Third Reich, but the destiny of Swiss investments in Germany, worth approximately $2 billion, and Swiss possessions in the United States, worth $1.9 billion and frozen by presidential order since June 14, 1941, would soon be determined by Allied diktat. The reality was the imminence of Allied control over Switzerland's very survival. All the country's imports from the port of Genoa—fuel, fodder and raw materials transiting across newly liberated France—would depend upon the Allies' goodwill, and recently that had been sorely strained. Like so many other Jews, Klaus had been emotionally affected by the new, vivid reports of the Holocaust and had been appalled by the unceasing reports that Switzerland was eagerly cooperating with the Nazis while turning a blind eye to the monstrosities. The enemy was just seventy miles away from the capital, Bern, and Klaus was not disposed to look favorably upon those willfully overlooking the mass murder of the Jews. The moment was approaching when Switzerland would have to account for its behavior since 1939, and the Allies possessed the power to insist on Switzerland's compliance with Safehaven.

Success for the crusaders—to discover the German loot and Jewish assets and to thwart those influential Swiss bankers and industrialists closely associated with the Germans who determined Switzerland's policy toward the Allies—required informants within the clan. By 1944, Switzerland's Trappist silence had proven hard but not impossible to violate.

Monitoring Switzerland's relationship with Germany was the responsibility of Allied diplomats and their intelligence services. At the outbreak of war, Frederick "Fanny" van den Heuvel, the head of MI6's station in Switzerland, had established a network of informants and sympathizers in government departments, banks and telegraph and telephone centers, and among those Swiss army, police, immigration, customs and intelligence officers who were defiantly hostile to the Germans. In unison, MI6 officers reported Switzerland's pride in achieving a brilliant balancing act that despite the country's collaboration with the Germans, appeared to guarantee its national independence. To deflect criticism of partiality, Switzerland's rulers created a myth to exalt the nation's bravery in protecting its neutrality. The hero of that myth was General Henri Guisan, a popular gentleman farmer elected as the army's commander-in-chief against a pro-German candidate. Under Guisan's plan of national defense, in the event of a German invasion there was to be nominal resistance along Switzerland's frontiers while the army retreated to the Alps, abandoning the bulk of the population and industry. Based in that natural fortress, the Swiss would repel the enemy. When the German invasion did not materialize, Switzerland's rulers referred repeatedly to a "miracle": the miracle of General Guisan, the brave commander whose bold strategy had outfaced the mighty Nazis and saved the nation.

British intercepts and decoding of secret German messages in the Ultra operation had soon exposed the myth. There was no evidence that Hitler had planned an invasion of Switzerland. On the contrary, the evidence revealed Germany's appreciation that most pro-Nazi Swiss opposed German occupation. Berlin acknowledged, according to the intercepts, the advantages of nurturing and exploiting Switzerland's German population to create a haven for German interests.

Under the direction of Amtgruppe D/13h, an SS department in Berlin responsible for Swiss affairs, Germany's infiltration and recruitment of sympathetic Swiss was masterminded through the embassy in Bern and through consulates in Switzerland's major

towns. Thousands of Swiss nationals had been recruited to dissemi-
nate Nazi propaganda in the theaters, cinemas and newspapers in
order to capture Switzerland's sympathy. The country's predominant
German-speaking community had welcomed a colony of about
72,000 German nationals, of whom 24,000 were considered by the
Allies to be suspect. Allied intelligence reports had noted blatant pro-
Nazi activities in Davos, the Alpine resort, where certain banks and
three Catholic sanatoria had been identified as centers of German
espionage and the repository of huge sums forwarded by German
diplomats and Nazi leaders. Even the Red Cross, a private organization based in Geneva, Allied intelligence had discovered later, was
used with the knowledge of the Swiss government as cover by
German intelligence officers to spy on Allied activities across Europe
and North Africa. A five-page report drawn up by the OSS (forerun-
ner of the CIA) and entitled "Enemy Agents and the Red Cross"
named twenty-eight suspected officials as "either German agents or
associates of German agents, who are using the Red Cross organization as a cover for securing and transmitting military information."

Unhindered by Swiss security police, the rival German intelligence agencies, the Sicherheitsdienst (SD) and the Abwehr, had
recruited Swiss volunteers for a special Waffen SS unit and an SS bat-
talion and had created a network of informers. Clandestinely, agents
directed from an intelligence center in Dijon, France, had targeted
Swiss and Allied personalities. After the war, Swiss counterintelligence
acknowledged that the Germans had successfully developed a "finely
developed net over the whole country"; this was confirmed by the
eventual arrest of 1,389 Swiss accused of treachery. That cozy relationship was rooted in the natural bonds developed over the centuries
between neighboring countries, but MI6 officers, joined in 1942 by
Allen Dulles, the chief of the OSS station, noted sinister aspects of that
union, which sparked the interest of officials in London and
Washington and inspired Sam Klaus to propose the Safehaven program to prevent Germany from profiting from the war.

The clues appeared in the intercepts. To finance intelligence
operations, the German Foreign Office and the SD were depositing

in Swiss banks funds extorted by the Gestapo from Jews or from sales of stolen diamonds and gold. Glad to receive a generous fee, the bankers asked no questions, and when the clients required help, the bankers provided advice. Among the clatter of telegraphic traffic from Berlin to Switzerland intercepted by the British was a telegram dispatched by the Reichsbank on February 21, 1941, to the German consulate in Zurich, Switzerland's banking capital. The diplomats were asked to discover from the Swiss Bankers Association whether the Reichsbank could depend upon the Lombard Bank "as thoroughly reliable and suitable for very confidential special transactions." Reichsbank officials wanted to use Lombard's well-established overseas relationships as a cover for imports to Europe and clearly relied upon the Bankers Association for honest advice. The reply on March 5 was negative: "Because of Jewish involvement and ties with England, Lombard Bank cannot be recommended." Those traces were symptoms of what Klaus and all other economic warriors in London and Washington regarded as a pernicious conspiracy.

Fearful of Allied interference or seizure of their foreign interests, German bankers and industrialists managing the giants—Siemens, AEG, Bosch, Mercedes, IG Farben and Telefunken—had seduced Switzerland's lawyers and financial institutions into organizing illegal transactions to camouflage German corporations as pristine, neutral entities. The Germans hoped that their legal ruse would protect their companies from appearing on an Allied blacklist or, in the event of a Nazi defeat, from being subjected to Allied seizure, while still enabling them to serve the German war economy.

The headquarters of that special effort, opened on September 8, 1939, was the Foreign Exchange Control division, the Devisenstellen, within the Ministry of the Economy in Berlin. Specialists sworn to unusual secrecy had created and supervised the camouflage or "cloaking" of German property abroad as independent non-German enterprises. Switzerland was the foreign center of that operation. Germany's leading corporations hired Swiss trustees to organize the legal framework that concealed a German company's ownership, while accumulating and hiding its funds during the war. To protect those transactions, the Swiss and German partners either concocted fake sales or simply exchanged oral understandings based upon trust. The only trace of those transactions spotted by MI6 officers was frequent journeys to Germany by Swiss lawyers visiting their clients.

Dr. Walter Keller-Staub at 5 Bahnhofstrasse in Zurich was typical of those Swiss lawyers noted by MI6 as chosen by the Nazis to protect their interests against the Allies. Among Keller-Staub's German clients owning interests in oil, shipping and manufacturing across the world were the Reichsbank and Alfred Krupp, Germany's giant armaments manufacturer. The Swiss lawyer was the front, approved by the Swiss government, designed to conceal German activities and collect royalties in Allied countries.

IG Farben, the world's biggest chemical manufacturer, used the services of Felix Iselin, an outspoken pro-Nazi lawyer based in Basel. Iselin's activities were personally controlled by Hermann Schmitz, the corporation's brilliant chairman in Berlin, who had sanctioned the production of poison gases to murder the Jews as a "patriotic duty," according to the corporation's directors. Anticipating the need for camouflage, Schmitz had created in 1929 IG Chemie, Farben's subsidiary in Switzerland, to be responsible for the empire's foreign interests, although he retained direct control in Berlin. In June 1940, rightly fearing that the company's colossal industrial power would prompt its seizure by the Allies, Schmitz appointed Iselin as IG Chemie's chairman to pretend that all of IG Farben's foreign subsidiaries were owned by a Swiss rather than a German company. Thereafter, Iselin was regularly monitored by MI6 as he scurried to Berlin to consult Schmitz, returning to Basel to transfer German funds to neutral countries or telephoning New York to issue orders as if he were in charge of a Swiss company. In London and Washington, the economic warriors such as Sam Klaus had collected files of data in the expectation that after Germany's defeat Switzerland would cooperate in seizing those assets.

Experience had, however, shown that Switzerland, reluctant to help the Allies, succumbed only to irresistible pressure. In 1939, London's declaration of worldwide economic warfare against

Germany had evoked no more than smiles in Bern. The announcement that those Swiss who assisted the Germans would be blacklisted
while those who suffered while helping the Allies would be rewarded
had hardly been noticed. Since Britain relied upon Switzerland to
protect British prisoners of war in Germany and to provide a base for
the British intelligence services in Switzerland, London deemed even
a protest to be incautious, despite the accumulating evidence of
Switzerland's steadfast tolerance of Nazi crime.

The attitude in Washington was markedly different. By early
1941, to protect their growing deposits from the Germans, Swiss
banks and some of their richest clients had prudently transferred millions of dollars, suitably cloaked within omnibus accounts, to their
branches in New York, accompanied by sealed envelopes containing
the depositors' instructions. Unexpectedly, at the behest of the U.S.
Chiefs of Staff, who were outraged by Switzerland's cooperation with
Germany, President Roosevelt froze the Swiss bank deposits on June
14 (along with those of Germans and other neutrals), forcibly exposing their activities and cautioning the Swiss government against completely ignoring Allied interests—even though, in the event, the
United States was not to enter the war for another six months. The
effect of the warning was short-lived.

On July 1, 1941, after Germany, as a show of force, had halted for
three weeks the transit of all Swiss imports through its territories and
stopped supplies of coal, iron and steel, Switzerland had consolidated
Berlin's goodwill in an unusual pact: the Swiss-German clearing
agreement. Since Germany had spent all its foreign exchange and
gold, the Swiss government agreed to provide massive loans to the
Nazis. Dressed up as credits to pay Swiss exporters pending payment
from Germany, the clearing account was meant to be balanced by the
year's end. Instead, the Swiss approved a mounting deficit: SF7 million every month. By December 31, 1942, Germany had borrowed
SF850 million to buy Swiss-manufactured weapons to fight the war.

With Switzerland established as a trusted contributor to
Germany's war economy and protected from Allied bombing, Swiss
precision engineers produced and exported to Germany ammuni-

tion, antiaircraft shells, guns, fuses, aircraft parts, radio equipment, machine tools, turbines, engines, locomotives, machinery and chemicals. As the war went on, Swiss contractors undertook research for new radio transmitters, antiaircraft instruments, machinery and improved metals, and supplied parts for the V-1 and V-2 rockets, jet sprays for diesel motors, clutch couplings for tanks and safety caps for artillery shells. On a more mundane level, Dr. Waldo Gerber, a well-known Swiss Nazi sympathizer and director of Mercedes, arranged for German cars to be repaired in Switzerland while Maschinenbau Hilti in Liechtenstein contracted to install new machinery in Germany. Symbolic of Switzerland's incorporation within the Nazi economy, German trains regularly traveled across Switzerland transporting war supplies to Italy, and German towns along the frontier drew electricity from Swiss power stations. By the end of 1941, Swiss exports of chemicals to Germany had increased by 250 percent, exports of vehicles by 450 percent, and exports of metals by 500 percent. In return, Switzerland imported gold, oil, iron and coal produced by slave labor.

Conveniently, those relationships and profits were protected by hypocrisy. For, while Switzerland's industrialists supplied weapons to the Nazis, the Swiss government had prosecuted an insignificant Swiss soldier for treason for selling his rifle to a German agent and, after his conviction, unhesitatingly approved his execution.

Protests by Allied ambassadors about the loans and the trade were countered by the Swiss with lectures about their principles, their convictions and the risks they took to preserve their sovereignty. Neutrality, Swiss officials told Sir Clifford Norton, meant only military neutrality. Economic neutrality was an unknown legal concept. Since only Germany could supply coal and iron, Germany was given freedom to choose what it required in return. Not only did Switzerland "feel aggrieved" by the Allies' "unreasonable" demands that it should limit its trade with Germany, Norton was told, but it demanded a similar right to trade with Japan, claiming that right as a neutral. In London, the demand was classified as a crude desire to earn extra profits out of the war. In Bern, the bankers complained that trading with both sides had become "unpleasant" and "a difficult task."

The focus of Sam Klaus's anger was the Bahnhofstrasse, a pleasant, narrow, tree-lined road leading from Zurich's main railway station into the city center. Above and between the expensive shops selling fashion and watches were the offices of over one hundred banks, lawyers and notaries who could guide the wary or uninitiated foreigner into the mysteries of numbered accounts and the discreet disappearance of their savings. Marked occasionally by small brass plates, these offices traded in an ostentatious tact.

At the outbreak of war, most of Switzerland's leading banks had existed for less than a century. The Crédit Suisse was founded in 1856 when Switzerland, still hampered by its ethnic disparity, had only just begun, unlike the rest of Europe, to industrialize and build railways. Benefiting from the absence of government influence or even interest in their affairs, the country's bankers, by seemingly divine edict, established their own rules, their own code of morality, and their freedom to conduct themselves exclusively in their own cause. Although this was still unknown to Klaus or even to the Swiss government, Switzerland's banks, in 1937, without need for legal authority, had unilaterally and without any announcement ceased paying interest on foreign deposits. Their subsequent explanation—that excessive "hot money" was pouring into their coffers—patently disguised their ruse to extract extra profits from captive clients. Profiting from incomparable secrecy, Switzerland's small breed of bankers had become greedier and more immoral than most, enjoying the special status bestowed upon those who simultaneously were senior officers in the country's citizen army and regularly undertook diplomatic missions abroad on behalf of the government. The proof of that prestigious status, certainly an incentive for foreign clients seeking special services and discretion, was the laws guaranteeing depositors anonymity and protection from inquisitive governments.

Cloaking of bank accounts in Switzerland had started in 1922 after a threatened tax on Swiss capital instigated a massive transfer of money to London. To protect their business from the government and attract the return of customers, Swiss banks offered to depositors confidential numbered accounts and the promise of concealment. Posing as the depositors' ally, Swiss bankers could legally protect accounts owned by foreign Jews from demands illegally made on their behalf in Switzerland by Gestapo agents; and subsequently the same bankers could cite that law to rebut condemnation of their collaboration with the Nazis and criticism of their conduct toward Jewish refugees who had fled the Gestapo. In reality, the banks had silently exploited the law for their own profit and in collaboration with the Nazis. In these matters, the Germans had discovered that Crédit Suisse's discretion was particularly reliable. Among the victims of that understanding was Laura Mayer, a Belgian living in Malmédy. Soon after the German occupation, Mayer was forced to sign transfers of her wealth held in Swiss banks. Her letters, clearly written under duress, were accepted from German officials by Crédit Suisse without inquiry. The bankers could not imagine that a reversal of German fortunes would expose their perfidy. After the war, Mayer would encounter a smoke screen of secrecy barring her inquiries in a manner that was still not understood by Klaus or the other Allied officials.

Unlike Mayer's, the deposits in Swiss banks by Germany's leaders were protected. Franz von Papen, the former chancellor, was reported to have placed SF500,000 in a bank in the Reifessenkasse, St. Gall; Joachim von Ribbentrop, the foreign minister, and Hjalmar Schacht, the former Reichsbank president, had used a female employee at the German embassy to deposit money in banks near Zurich; even Hitler was suspected of having used at least three different accounts, including that of Max Amman, his loyal publisher, for the royalties from *Mein Kampf*. No one, however, was as active as Hermann Göring, whose Swiss agents, especially Andreas Hofer, arranged for looted valuables, particularly paintings stolen from galleries and private collections across Europe, to be stored in Swiss bank vaults.

The more sophisticated Germans were laundering stolen money through Swiss banks by offering their loot at discount prices in exchange for secure deposits either in current accounts established under the names of Swiss nationals in Switzerland or in existing Swiss bank accounts in the United States. Swiss bankers had also become specialist dealers in stolen shares and securities. German couriers, using diplomatic protection, crossed regularly from France to deliver bags of stolen certificates to a network of untroubled custodians. One batch, spotted by British intelligence, had been stolen in the Paris office of the Westminster Bank and was delivered to the "notorious" Ted Hoch of the Swiss Bank Corporation (SBC). Hoch was managing a lucrative trade, obtaining from obliging lawyers, at $100 a shot, false affidavits attesting that the stolen foreign shares and securities belonged to Swiss nationals. Those stolen securities, resold on the Zurich and Geneva stock exchanges, were so cheap that British diplomats had protested to the Swiss government about the blatant dishonesty. A Swiss investigation in 1942 had confirmed SBC's falsifications, but in the face of political pressure, it was dropped "in the public interest." Papering over the embarrassment, Swiss officials reassured the British that "a better system of control could not have been devised."

Reviewing that history, Klaus concluded that Switzerland's laws encouraged both the trade and the crime. According to Swiss law, if possession remained unchallenged for five years, the thief was guaranteed ownership of his loot. Instinctively attracted to healthy profits, the Swiss contemplated no change of their laws, although their country, since the consolidation of the German occupation of Europe, had become a depository of loot.

Regularly, Allied intelligence sources revealed that Crédit Suisse, the Union Bank of Switzerland and the Basler Handelsbank were receiving currencies and gold worth millions of dollars from Germany either to be credited to secret accounts or to be transferred to other European neutral countries, to Shanghai or to South America. Bührle and other prominent banks, noted as "terminal stations," were being used by German industrialists to hoard foreign currency. The Reichsbank's ledgers recorded that at least RM15 billion ($6 billion) would be transferred into Switzerland, although the Swiss would claim it was just RM1 billion. In the opinion of Walter

Sholes, the American consul in Basel, Switzerland's bankers had transformed themselves into "pro-Fascist financial operators . . . who have not hesitated to work hand in glove with National Socialist and Fascist business interests." Walter Ostrow, the U.S. Treasury representative in Bern, reported that Switzerland, as Germany's international banker, was damaging the Allies by financing Germany's purchase of critical war supplies from neutral countries. Echoing Sholes and Ostrow, Klaus had drawn up a powerful indictment based upon intercepts and agents' reports revealing the close collaboration between the Swiss banks and the Germans, although the full manifestation of the bankers' prejudice was concealed even from the likes of Klaus by a carefully continued image of tactful modesty and discretion.

Exploding myths and laws was integral to Klaus's crusade. His ambition, to continue economic warfare into peacetime, threatened Switzerland's tranquillity, although most Swiss were unaware of that plan. Uninhibited by any political opposition, Switzerland's rulers had imposed total censorship and had carefully protected their people from foreign criticism and controversy. One among many unreported events was a petition signed in November 1940 by 200 Swiss leaders urging the government to observe stricter neutrality—which, considering the list of their complaints, implied a demand that Switzerland should display greater sympathy toward the Nazis. The signatories of the petition were representatives of Switzerland's biggest banks, including Peter Vieli, director general of Crédit Suisse and chairman of the Bankers Association's German Committee, and Paul Jaberg, director of the Union Bank of Switzerland, who also boasted a series of directorships among the nation's insurance and manufacturing companies. Both banks controlled vast Swiss investments in Germany and in return offered a haven in Switzerland for German savings and a cloak for their customers' nefarious activities.

Among those customers was Paul Schmidt-Branden, a former director of the Dresdner Bank in Berlin, resident during the war at the Park Hotel in Locarno, the beautiful lakeside resort in the canton of Tessin. Like other Germans enjoying the congenial atmosphere of the town, Schmidt-Branden discreetly brokered business for his Nazi clients—he helped Walter Funk, the Reichsbank president, transfer his private funds from the United States to the safety of Switzerland—but there were more sinister activities he undertook with Swiss bankers. In particular, he had recruited Swiss banking officials to reveal the accounts of Jews living in German-occupied countries.

Henry Löwinger, an Austrian Jew, was a victim of that arrangement. After his arrest in Vienna, he was visited by Gestapo officers with an offer based upon precise knowledge of his account at the Swiss Bank Corporation in Zurich. In return for his fortune, Löwinger was told, he would be allowed to cross into Switzerland. After agreeing, he and his wife, accompanied by Gestapo officers, drove to the Swiss border near Constance. Waiting on the border was his Swiss lawyer, who had arranged the SBC account. After signing the transfer of their fortune over to the Gestapo, the Löwingers walked into Switzerland, penniless but alive. "It was possible only because the Nazis had information from inside the Swiss banks," complained Löwinger, suspecting that an official in the bank had been recruited or even planted by the Gestapo. Unknown to Löwinger, SBC's relationship with the Nazis had been consolidated by its most senior managers and directors. Fifteen of the bank's twenty-four directors were identified by the U.S. Treasury as pro-Nazi, closely involved in financing and easing the foreign transactions of Germany's major industries. Investigators would conclude that the bank was "one of the principal accomplices of the Nazis." Passing information to the Gestapo about a Jew's secret account flowed naturally from that relationship.

Discreet conversations between British and American diplomats and Swiss officials in a bid to curtail Switzerland's illegal trade with Nazi Germany had produced no response, even after the German defeat at Stalingrad in December 1942. On January 5, 1943, both governments issued a public warning that Switzerland's ownership of looted property supplied by Germany would not be recognized. The Swiss government ignored the message.

On January 15, Switzerland's trade agreement with Germany expired. The news that Swiss negotiators were traveling to Berlin to negotiate a revised agreement and were offering more loans to allow Germany to buy munitions and war supplies irritated the governments in London and Washington. Swiss nonchalance, Sir Clifford Norton reported to the Foreign Office, was based not merely on Switzerland's need for German coal, ore and fuel but on the fact that ministers had been "over-persuaded [by] Swiss industrial interests ... that Switzerland is in honor and self-interest bound to carry out the letter of the 1941 Agreement which suits these interests perfectly." The Swiss, it appeared, were happy about their contribution to Germany's policies.

In London, Dingle Foot, a junior minister at the Ministry of Economic Warfare, was instructed to persuade the Swiss to dampen their loyalty toward the Nazis, at least by reducing the number of Swiss specialists servicing Germany's war machine. The threats available to Foot when he met Walther Thurnherr, the Swiss ambassador, on April 15, 1943, were unimpressive: a suspension of "navicerts," which allowed safe passage across the sea for Swiss merchandise, and restrictions on imports of fodder and military supplies for the defense of Switzerland. Foot's "severe warning" that Switzerland "had gone further than was necessary in meeting German demands" made such an imperceptible impression that Anthony Eden, the foreign secretary, personally intervened.

Allied armies in North Africa were on the eve of launching a massive attack against Rommel, and Eden was preparing for a critical visit to Washington. Yet the following day, April 16, Eden believed it worthwhile to meet Walther Thurnherr himself. Initially, the foreign secretary's manner was polite. "The measure of Germany's present difficulties," he told the ambassador, "is the measure of Swiss strength. The harder the Germans bluster, the greater Switzerland's strength." The ambassador nodded. Encouraged by the diplomat's apparent agreement, Eden added, "Switzerland should do all it can not to prolong the war." But it gradually dawned on Eden that the Swiss were treating his "serious concern" with incomprehension.

After Thurnherr had declared that he too was "preoccupied by the information reaching him," he launched into a self-eulogy about the problems Switzerland faced in fending off Germany's demands and still remaining neutral. Clearly, the diplomat did not understand the issue: Nazi Germany was an evil that needed to be destroyed. Allied servicemen were dying, yet Switzerland was not only supplying the Nazi war machine but was actually accepting Nazi loot, which had little bearing upon neutrality. To explain the moral issue, Eden realized, was pointless. Despite witnessing the dislocation, rationing and bomb damage inflicted on London, Thurnherr evidently felt no shame about Switzerland's relationship with Germany. Although, unlike his countrymen, he was not immune to the war, the diplomat knew that the Swiss, without television pictures and with no experience of warfare, could not imagine how their neighbors were suffering and scarcely cared. In truth, few Swiss, including Thurnherr, could envisage the defeat of Germany. Eden therefore bid the diplomat farewell with a threat: If the new Swiss-German agreement was damaging to British interests, "our action is likely to be unwelcome to you." The Foreign Office's only recourse was to seek Washington's support.

Five days later, on April 21, the American government issued its sternest protest. Announcing its "profound concern," the administration "expressed its most forceful objections" that the Swiss negotiations with Berlin would cause a "substantial rise" in Swiss exports to Germany, strengthening Germany's military potential and prolonging the war. To emphasize its anger, navicerts (as noted earlier, these guaranteed the free passage of Switzerland's imports across the seas) were suspended. That gesture was the Allies' only weapon.

Switzerland's reaction was immediately gauged by Sir Clifford Norton. Regularly, Norton met Marcel Pilet-Golaz, the arrogant foreign minister who hardly troubled to hide his sympathy for the Germans, a sentiment shared by the majority of the Federal Council. By 1943, even Norton, a timid character, had become exasperated by Pilet-Golaz's use of the words "loyalty" and "neutrality." Loyalty, to Pilet-Golaz, meant Switzerland's right to "make agreements with both sides and keep them loyally." Concerning neutrality, Pilet-Golaz compared his country's neutrality to that of the United States until the attack on Pearl Harbor—a deliberate distortion that ignored Washington's decisive support for Britain until the Japanese attack. To Norton's irritation, the minister further boasted that preserving Switzerland's neutrality was itself a victory and justified his country's profiting from the war. Yet Norton was also mollified by the politician. Pleading that he was truly pro-Ally but was hampered by the Federal Council, Pilet-Golaz had pledged that Switzerland would guarantee a "marked decrease" of exports to Germany during 1943. "I do not like the position in which Switzerland finds itself," Pilet-Golaz told Norton, apparently sympathizing with Britain's complaint, "but it is not our fault." An embargo, explained the minister, would reduce Switzerland's food imports, causing unemployment and unrest. Since he had made an identical pledge to reduce trade in 1942, which had later been dishonored, the Foreign Office and the State Department were resigned to the fact that the Swiss would always choose the Germans in preference to the Allies unless, as occurred on May 8, 1943, there was an opportunity to drive a wedge between Switzerland and Germany.

Walther Thurnherr, the Swiss ambassador, informed Eden that Switzerland's trade negotiations with Germany had broken down and asked whether the sanctions could therefore not be lifted. Since Switzerland was continuing to supply munitions while a new treaty was discussed, the Allies' response was tough. Supplies of food and fodder were banned for three months. Stung, Switzerland agreed to reduce war exports to Germany, especially ball-bearings, by 60 percent for the remainder of the year. Allied sanctions were relaxed, but the goodwill proved to have been wasted. In October, ignoring the Allies' concerns, the Swiss signed a new trade agreement in Berlin, granting the Nazis a further SF270 million loan to buy Swiss munitions. British ministers were furious. Switzerland's repeated promises to reduce exports to Germany, it was clear, would never be honored. "The more we damage Germany," Foot told Thurnherr, "the more the Germans need the Swiss." Thurnherr was unimpressed. "HMG

[His Majesty's Government]," continued Foot, "take an extremely serious view of this arrangement." After the war, he threatened, "Switzerland would not be allowed by the Allies to recover their huge loans to Germany." The ambassador naturally cabled a report of that conversation to Bern. It was read, filed, ignored and soon forgotten. Warnings uttered in London and Washington were the echoes of ghosts, not credible to the burghers of Zurich and Bern, who regarded the likes of Sam Klaus as the enemy.

Contemplating in Switzerland's summer sunshine the history of the Allies' relations with the neutral country over the previous four years, Klaus understood that one trade between Bern and Berlin— the smooth passage of gold ingots across the frontier—was a cornerstone of their intrigue. Standing in Bern's Bundesplatz, looking at the underwhelming portico of Switzerland's parliament, Klaus glanced to the left and found himself gazing at bland features of Switzerland's National Bank.

A nation's morality is occasionally betrayed by its architecture, but the edifices of Switzerland's democracy, he reflected, revealed little of the national character. Yet if a swastika had been chiseled into the stone under the National Bank's portico, it would have offered a fair hint of Switzerland's sentiment toward the Nazis.

4

LOOTED GOLD

Dr. Alfred Hirs, the small, taciturn deputy president of Switzerland's National Bank, was one of those Swiss who refused to meet Americans or Britons, especially types like Klaus. Utterly loyal to his country and his bank, the fifty-five-year-old Hirs by contrast always welcomed representatives of the Reichsbank, Germany's central bank in Berlin, who were financing the war against Bolshevism. In that cause, Hirs, like so many Swiss of German ancestry, had regarded as guilty the Jewish refugees who were illegally entering Switzerland to save their lives, while the Nazis he greeted as men of honor. That prejudice was more than useful to Walther Funk, Germany's minister of economics and president of the Reichsbank, and to his deputy, Emil Puhl.

The two Germans faced a unique challenge for central bankers. Germany's insatiable wartime demands had, by the outbreak of war, exhausted its official gold reserves, estimated at $120 million. The Reichsmark, the German currency, was rarely acceptable by the neutral countries as payment for the fuel required by Germany's ships, for the essential minerals needed by its armaments industries or for the specialized products used by its military. Instead, Portugal, Spain, Sweden, Turkey and especially Switzerland demanded either Swiss francs, their own currency, or gold. After selling all the Reichsbank's gold, Funk had identified only one other available source of foreign currency: the gold reserves of those European nations conquered and occupied by Germany.

In 1938, Germany had absorbed Austria's gold reserves. One year later, the Reichsbank seized Czechoslovakia's gold. After occupying Warsaw in 1939, the bank was disappointed to discover that adroit Polish officials had moved the reserves for safety to Romania, a temporary frustration resolved by negotiations with the government in Bucharest. In early 1940, Denmark's small gold hoard was transported to Berlin. Only after June 1940 did Funk's rich windfall materialize, as France, Belgium and Holland surrendered. Initially, Funk's emissaries were thwarted. Cautious officials at the French National Bank had shipped the treasure to the United States. The Belgians had also taken precautions. At the end of 1939, their National Bank had entrusted 1,751 gold ingots worth $223 million to France's National Bank for safekeeping. Soon after the German invasion in May 1940, the director of the Belgian National Bank had urged his French colleague to dispatch the ingots on a British cruiser to London. Instead, the French transported the gold to Dakar, in the West African colony of Senegal. Pending German negotiations with the French collaborationist government in Vichy to return the gold to Europe, Funk's sole source was Holland's gold reserves.

On the eve of Germany's invasion, 192,360 kilos of gold—35 percent of Holland's reserves—were stored in vaults in Amsterdam and Rotterdam. In the first hours after the Wehrmacht crossed the border on May 9, 1940, the gold in Amsterdam was safely shipped over to Britain. Another boat sailing from Rotterdam carrying 937 bars (11,012 kilos) struck a mine and lay marooned near the coastline. By 1942, 816 bars had been recovered by the Germans and, with 102,743 kilos discovered in the Rotterdam vaults, were transported to Berlin. In total, 146,016 kilos of Dutch gold worth $161 million would be meticulously recorded in the Reichsbank's ledgers as stored in their vaults. Emil Puhl was dispatched to Bern to offer the gold to the Swiss National Bank.

Ernst Weber, the National Bank's president, and Alfred Hirs were eager to oblige. Ever since the initial shock of France's collapse, which left Switzerland encircled by Axis and fascist territory, the National Bank had become the Reich's foremost supplier of foreign exchange for international trade, a profitable and politically acceptable task for a financial institution always eager to provide dividends for its private shareholders. For, in common with most of Switzerland's politicians, bankers and industrialists, Weber and Hirs were convinced of Germany's ultimate victory and were untroubled by the Allied perception that the bank was acting as a partner to the Nazis.

Neither Swiss banker doubted Puhl's credibility, since he, unlike most other senior directors of the Reichsbank, had unmistakably displayed his loyalty to the Nazi Party by refusing to resign in 1939. Nor did the two Swiss bankers question whether the Reichsbank owned or had proper legal authority over the gold that Puhl offered. Even during 1942, when the first Dutch ingots arrived in Bern, some still wrapped and stenciled in a way that revealed their origins, no questions were asked. Only after MI6 officers in Switzerland warned London about the gold deliveries did Weber and Hirs realize that there could be requests for explanations.

In answer to Foreign Office inquiries, the Swiss government stated that the Germans were buying escudos, the Portuguese currency. Asked why the Germans did not ship the gold direct to Portugal, the Swiss answered that their National Bank was merely acting as a channel because the Germans wanted to conceal their financial transactions. For the moment, despite the implausible reply, the Allies were helpless. Although Germany's use of looted gold was classified in Washington as "systematic plunder" and "unlawful," Switzerland's conspiracy with the criminals was barely addressed. The Allies' records reflected a similar weakness. The amount of gold found by the Germans in Holland, Allied officials had recorded, was "very little." That would prove a costly error.

In the prevailing atmosphere, the acceptance by Weber and Hirs of the looted gold was unexceptional. MI6 and OSS officers in Switzerland had observed a developing pattern reminiscent of the Middle Ages. An unceasing stream of Germans were arriving in Switzerland to sell looted art, jewelry, foreign currency, shares, securities and privately owned gold confiscated from Europe's innocents. Unlike the Jews, the Germans encountered no difficulties entering

Switzerland. In fact, they were welcomed despite the crudeness of their trade.

Identified Swiss traders accepted diamonds, seized by the SS from Jewish dealers in Antwerp and Amsterdam, which were regularly carried into Switzerland in German diplomatic pouches. Other Swiss traders dealt exclusively in stolen banknotes. The most sinister trade was the jewelry of Jews deposited for "safekeeping" as they entered the camps, and the gold extracted from the teeth of dead Jews hauled from the gas chambers. Some of that gold had been first delivered to the Reichsbank in Berlin for smelting into anonymous ingots, but bags of gold and jewels, stored initially in vaults in Berlin, were dribbling into Switzerland to be deposited with Swiss traders willing to ignore their provenance.

Sympathetic Swiss customs officials had confided to British intelligence officers that since the outbreak of war, crates containing masterpieces had crossed the borders on trucks and were even exchanged for cash at the Basel railway station, on Switzerland's frontier with Germany. Regularly, German officials and SS officers, traveling as diplomats, arrived at art dealers in Zurich and Basel offering paintings and artifacts plucked from private homes in occupied Europe and received a handsome price, albeit far below their true value. The more notable were the agents acting on behalf of Göring, Goebbels, Hitler, and von Ribbentrop, who had plundered famous works by Impressionists and old masters from galleries and private collections in France, Holland, Belgium and Italy, either for their homes in Germany or for deposit in Switzerland as security for the future. By 1944, the British government estimated that the Germans' loot was worth $144 million; the New York Metropolitan Museum of Art estimated that it was worth $2.5 billion.

Since the Swiss government had allowed the country to become an accomplice and beneficiary of the plunder of Europe, the attitude of Weber and Hirs toward the Reichsbank's offer of gold was unremarkable. Yet, as prudent men, the two bankers had taken precautions. The gold supplied by the Reichsbank, they assured themselves, was—despite the Allies' warnings—not looted.

After the summer of 1943, the Swiss National Bank began receiving new deliveries of gold from Germany. All the ingots were clearly marked as German and were stamped with dates before 1939. In reality, the ingots were the recast bars of the Belgian gold. In late 1942, that gold had arrived in Berlin from West Africa and, after resmelting in a foundry, had been stamped as German and offered to Sweden in payment for supplies of ore. The Swedish government, accepting the Allies' warning that there could be only one explanation for the leap in Germany's gold reserves since 1939, half-heartedly rejected Berlin's offer. Similarly, the Portuguese government refused payment in gold from Germany for wolfram, a mineral vital for the manufacture of metal. Finally, Funk and Puhl offered the same gold to Weber and Hirs. Unlike every other neutral, Switzerland, through its bankers, accepted unconditionally. To the Reichsbank officials' delight, Switzerland would, acting as a "screen" for other neutrals, convert the gold into foreign currency and dispatch at least seventy trucks to the central bank in Lisbon carrying the looted Belgian gold.

Weber had good grounds for being suspicious. Paul Rossy, a vice president of the Swiss National Bank, in a message reporting that the government in Lisbon had refused to accept gold shipped directly from Germany, had declared that the Portuguese would not object "if the gold went through our hands. We should think about that." Weber and Hirs acted on that option, despite a personal warning about the gold's provenance.

In March 1943, Yves de Boisanger, the president of the Banque de France, had protested to the Reichsbank about its intended misuse of Belgium's gold. De Boisanger was thanked by his Belgian colleagues. His protest was, nonetheless, ignored by the Germans. De Boisanger had visited Bern during the summer and took the opportunity to warn the Swiss bankers about the theft. Understanding the implications with unerring precision, Weber created an alibi for future use. In his diary, the bank's president wrote, "One cannot discover the origin of the imported gold. . . . We haven't got a clue."

Realizing that his oral warning had been ignored, de Boisanger wrote a formal letter to Weber in November 1943 stating that the

Swiss bank was accepting looted gold. Weber chose again to ignore the information, although it was repeated in a message from the Swiss bank's representative in Washington. Experience over the years had given Weber good reason to doubt the Allies' commitment to punish Switzerland for accepting looted gold.

In 1943, the State Department had been reluctant to support a Foreign Office campaign warning neutrals about accepting Axis gold. When, in June 1943, the State Department finally agreed to a joint protest, the Foreign Office noted that the Americans had acted "clearly without enthusiasm. . . . They did not wish to participate." Over the following months, Washington's attitude had changed as the neutrals' gold reserves increased to an astonishing degree. Spain's had risen since 1939 from $42 million to $104 million, Sweden's from $160 million to $456 million, Turkey's from $88 million to $221 million, and Switzerland's from $503 million to $1,040 million. Most of that trade in gold had flowed through Bern. The evidence of German criminality was overwhelming, and the attitude in Washington was modified accordingly.

On February 22, 1944, Morgenthau publicly warned Switzerland and the other neutrals against importing, storing or purchasing gold from Berlin. The United States, stated the declaration, "does not and will not recognize the transference of title of looted gold." In the future, any gold whose honest ownership was not clearly established, warned Morgenthau, would not be accepted in payment by Washington. Suspicious of the Americans' motives, the British government reluctantly issued its own declaration, announcing its refusal to recognize the "unlawful disposition of the looted gold."

Publicly, the government in Bern did not respond, but the silence did not reflect inactivity. Inside the bank, Weber and Hirs were creating a paper trail of legal advice justifying the acceptance of the gold and listing the precautions that had been imposed. Their strategy was not unusual in Switzerland. To avoid future recrimination, most Swiss officials in government, banking and industry regularly falsified the written minutes of their meetings. Dishonesty was a cultural code that individual Swiss had mastered to protect the nation's image and prosperity. The only precaution Weber and Hirs deliberately omitted, despite the Allies' warnings, was to properly question the bankers from Berlin about whether the gold ingots arriving in Bern were newly cast. Swiss sovereignty and neutrality, Hirs and Weber believed, did not require the National Bank to bow to the Allies' warnings. Isolated in Bern from the fevered atmosphere of the world beyond, the bankers were genuinely outraged when, on May 11, 1944, Washington repeated its request that the Swiss stop accepting gold from Germany. Defiance was the natural response from those immune to the Allies' crusade for honesty, especially since their recalcitrance was endorsed by their government.

In a widely heralded public speech in mid-May, Walter Stampfli, the Swiss president, boldly lectured the Allies. "Switzerland has never tried to infringe the rights of others," he said, "and we know how to defend our right to exist." To enhance his counterblast, the president insisted that Switzerland had "scrupulously observed" all its obligations as a neutral. Economic neutrality, he intoned, was "an unknown legal concept." The credibility of Stampfli's assertions was nevertheless thin. Swiss industries, he said, were forbidden to "supply arms and machinery which can be used in actual warfare" and he promised that Switzerland, while faithfully observing the universal principles of human rights, would refuse asylum to anyone whose actions were "incompatible with the fundamental traditions of law and humanity" or who had committed any war crimes. Considering that over 30,000 Jews had been dispatched across the frontier to the Gestapo, while Gestapo officers had entered Switzerland with impunity to deposit their loot, Stampfli's speech was hardly calculated to persuade those embarking on the most risky venture in military history.

Three weeks later the Allied armies landed in Normandy. On the eve of that invasion, the British government issued a specific warning to Switzerland not to provide "unchallengeable sanctuaries" for war criminals or for the proceeds of war crimes. Over the following days, as the Allies' success was gradually assured, intelligence reports from Switzerland exposed the extent to which that warning was being ignored and revealed the hollowness of Stampfli's assurances.

When the prospect of an Allied victory grew more likely by the day, OSS officers reported that the flow of loot from Germany into Zurich became a flood of "gigantic sums" as "alarm" gripped the Nazis. Truckloads of gold were spotted arriving from Berlin at the German embassy in Bern. In a series of snapshots of this frenetic activity, Allied intelligence officers in every neutral capital noted the same pattern: flights, accompanied by couriers, arrived from Berlin transporting gold bullion and other suspected loot, and were met by German diplomats. Indifferent to the change in the Allies' fortunes, Swiss bankers, satisfied that their government was continuing normal relations with Germany despite holding substantial stocks of coal that would have allowed a rupture of relations without serious financial consequences, accepted the loot. Morgenthau again asked the Swiss not to receive looted gold from Germany, but again Bern ignored the appeal. The reaction to all those reports in London and Washington had become markedly different.

In the Foreign Office, Dennis Allen was untroubled both by the Nazi leaders' storing "nest eggs" to be used after the Allied victory and by the neutral governments' ignoring Allied warnings. "I do not see," he commented lamely, "what more we could do to prevent it." Neutral countries, he added, displaying little imagination, "would not be in a position to stop such transfers." Any further initiative or action, his colleagues agreed, should be left to the Americans, "if they can think of any."

Klaus could think of many reprisals and left Bern preoccupied by a single thought: to make the Swiss in particular suffer for their profitable collaboration with the Nazis. "Tight and capable of looking after their own interests," Klaus remarked to Herbert Cummings. "And they still seem to be overlooking the killing of the Jews." In Washington, Klaus's report created a stampede of officials in different departments, agencies and divisions eager to join the crusade. Safehaven had become so popular that it risked suffocation in the bureaucratic struggle to win control.

5

"AN IMPENETRABLE RACKET"

Jack Troutbeck had only one word for the Safehaven crusaders: troublemakers. Along with his senior Foreign Office colleagues, Troutbeck despaired: "In their dealings with Switzerland, the Americans have lost all sense of reality." Ever since fifty British and other Allied airmen had been murdered by the Gestapo after escaping from a POW camp in Silesia in April 1944, the British government had feared that without Switzerland's "exemplary" care, the lives of more than 100,000 Allied POWs would be endangered. The State Department was easily persuaded of the danger. "The Gestapo might run amok," a State Department official agreed, "and commit wholesale murder of British and American prisoners." For Troutbeck that danger for all practical purposes overrode Whitehall's latent interest in compelling the Swiss to disgorge the Nazis' loot. The crusaders' indifference to Britain's opinion about Safehaven sealed his antagonism.

Piqued by the absence of any mention of cooperation with Britain in the State Department's messages to its embassies ordering "measures" to implement the Bretton Woods Resolution, Whitehall grew still more irritated with the crusaders as evidence of their aggression materialized. Threats, complained Troutbeck, were ineffective and counterproductive.

A conversation between E. H. Bliss, of the Ministry of Economic Warfare, and Lehman Aarons, a lawyer at the General Counsel's Office in the U.S. Treasury in London, confirmed the disagreement. "My ministry," said Bliss, noticeably unperturbed by Swiss activities, "is only beginning to think about the problem of German assets in neutral countries." Showing remarkable sympathy for Switzerland, he added, "For Switzerland, cloaking by the Germans is neither illegal nor wrong." The neutrals, he argued, in stark contradiction of American policy, were not legally obliged to surrender German assets to the Allies unless they were provably stolen. "We believe," he declared, "that the neutrals can use the German money to offset their own claims against Germany."

Aarons was stunned by Bliss's heresies. The flood of German assets pouring into Switzerland, he countered, was "flagrant." The Allies would make Switzerland "unneutral" after the war and "induce" their cooperation to hand over all of Germany's assets as reparations. Bliss stared, unconvinced. The issue was sterile and the crusaders were dangerous. Britain had only reluctantly committed itself to the Bretton Woods Resolution, and the Foreign Office's instructions to its embassies reflected a notable lack of urgency. Acknowledging that Britain's diplomats would be "very busy," London directed that information should be collected only if possible, "without too much trouble." And no more. Unlike the crusaders in Washington, Troutbeck, Bliss and the rest of their colleagues were untouched by the latest human tragedy unfolding in Europe, prompting more millions to pour into Switzerland—the profits of a strange trade in humans.

Throughout 1944, reports from Germany and Eastern Europe had chronicled the remorseless murder of the Jews. News agencies dispatched reports of ghettos being emptied and the inhabitants murdered. The fate of the Jews was confirmed by Swiss relief agencies in stark terms. "Deportation means the most brutal annihilation of the innocent," recorded the annual report of the Swiss Labor Relief

Agency for 1942–43. Swiss newspapers published eyewitness reports of degradation and distress as the Jews were herded to their death in fields, camps and rail wagons. In September 1943, a Swiss newspaper had repeated an estimate from New York that five million Jews had so far been murdered. In New York and London, the fate of Europe's Jews was widely discussed. Even the *Neue Züricher Zeitung* had bluntly concluded in December 1943, "The Jewish Question has become a Jewish slaughter." Reflecting the skepticism of the Swiss government's censorship department, which criticized the reports as "foreign atrocity propaganda of the worst kind," Eduard von Steiger, the minister of justice and the police, repeated to complainants that Switzerland could not afford to allow more than 600 refugees to enter the country every month.

Five months later, that obduracy had become untenable. Intelligence reports from the exiled governments and eyewitness accounts by escapees from Auschwitz and other camps were accepted even by former skeptics as irrefutable proof of mass murder. In May 1944, the reports from Hungary that Adolf Eichmann was organizing the deportation of over 700,000 Jews to Auschwitz were widely disseminated in New York, London and Geneva. In Budapest, Carl Lutz, the Swiss vice-consul, was appalled by the impending tragedy. Heroically, despite reprimanding letters from his distrustful superiors in Bern, Lutz issued 21,000 letters of protection for Jews, five times the number issued by Raoul Wallenberg, the Swede. Nevertheless, daily, after May 14, 1944, over 10,000 Jews were being shipped to Auschwitz. In just over three weeks, 355,000 would be murdered. Reports of the crime were published in Switzerland despite the censor's criticism that they bore "propaganda value." The Swiss did not react in the same ways. While more refugees were being given sanctuary, some cantons continued to refuse to provide any shelter. But, bowing to pressure from American Jews, von Steiger agreed that thousands of Jews would be given refuge. Overnight, Switzerland became one venue of the negotiations between representatives of the Jews and the senior SS officers in Hungary. The motive of the SS officers was money. Saving the lives of rich Jews, astute SS officers recognized, was a lucrative sideline and the natural safe haven for their ransom was Switzerland.

Negotiating under the supervision of Heinrich Himmler and Adolf Eichmann was SS Colonel Kurt Becher. Becher was an opportunist, born in Hamburg in 1909, whose career started in Dachau, progressed to the murder of Jews in Poland and Russia and climaxed in 1944 in Hungary. In Budapest, Eichmann was negotiating with Jewish representatives to exchange the lives of one million Jews for 10,000 trucks. The result of Eichmann's negotiations was a train carrying 1,686 Hungarian Jews that arrived in Switzerland from Hungary via Belsen on June 29, 1944. With Heinrich Rothmund's approval, the Jews were admitted to Switzerland, and others would follow later. Becher had negotiated the conclusion of that transaction—on the St. Margarathen bridge spanning the Swiss-German border—with Saly Mayer, the head of the Swiss Federation of Jewish Communities (SIG), and he discussed further deals in the Hotel Baur-au-Lac in Zurich with Roswell McClelland, an American diplomat representing the War Refugee Board. Ostensibly, the SS officer and the American were discussing humanitarian issues, but in reality Becher, the businessman, was seeking to profit from the Holocaust.

As a sideline, Becher was extorting money from Jewish families for his use after Germany's inevitable defeat. Later identified by American interrogators as "charged with providing safe haven for Nazi funds," Becher was collecting and hiding the valuables confiscated from Jews on the eve of their deportation to Auschwitz and offering the richest Jews their lives in exchange for their fortunes. Among the beneficiaries were the Weiss family, the owners of Hungary's biggest industrial complex, who were escorted to safety in Switzerland and Portugal by Becher's subordinates after transferring their entire wealth to the SS. The tariff fixed by Becher for other Jews to secure their safe passage to Switzerland was up to SF300,000, deposited under the supervision of a German officer in a Swiss account. Becher's charm secured from the Swiss consulate in Budapest the invaluable entry visas for the Jews, and Swiss banks unquestioningly arranged the transfers and accepted the deposits.

Among the Swiss "bankers" handling the ransoms in Switzerland was Baron Eduard von der Heydt. Living in Ascona, the former German banker of the kaiser was suspected of having obtained Swiss nationality in 1937 as a cover for protecting the assets of Nazi industrialists, politicians, diplomats and intelligence chiefs. In 1944, von der Heydt's employees disclosed that "large quantities of gold," smuggled into Switzerland under diplomatic protection, had been buried in the cellars of his grand house. Swiss police confided to OSS officers that their search of his hotel room in Zurich, on suspicion that he was a banker for German agents in North and South America, had unearthed lists of Germans suspected of bringing valuables to Switzerland.

Von der Heydt and Becher were protected, as Marcel Vaidie, the French finance attaché, in Bern commented, by the secrecy shielding all Swiss banking operations. "In the past," Vaidie reported to Paris, "Swiss banks have been involved in shady transactions." The Americans' demand for controls, he noted, had always been rejected and now the Swiss excuse was "inadequate manpower" for carrying out the controls. "The Swiss thesis," he added, "is supported by unconvincing arguments and their position appears to be weak."

The knowledge that Nazis were depositing their profits from the Holocaust in the same Swiss banks that since the outbreak of the war had been havens for the German loot pouring into Switzerland—more than ever since the German defeat at Stalingrad in January 1943—galvanized the crusaders into demanding that the Swiss bankers implement a code of behavior first proposed by British and American officials to representatives of the Swiss Bankers Association in Lisbon in July 1944.

"The Allied governments," noted the Foreign Office in the aftermath, "wish to make it clear to the S.B.A. and to the Swiss banks generally that they reserve complete freedom to impose all appropriate sanctions on any bank or financial institution engaging in transactions inimical to Allied interests." The association's leaders, anticipating an enjoyable annual conference in Zermatt, ignored the warning. Believing that under international law Switzerland was not bound to obey either of the combatants, the bankers told the Allied officials that they refused to withdraw any offers of loans to the Germans; that they anticipated long discussions with the Allies about their directives to Swiss banks; and that they demanded that the Allies recognize the ownership of any asset, meaning German loot, imported into Switzerland before June 1, 1944, regardless of how the owner had obtained the property. Neutrality, insisted the bankers, their self-satisfaction growing rather than diminishing, implied treating both the Allies and the Germans equally. Demanding a dilution of the resolution agreed at Bretton Woods, they offered one concession: the voluntary self-regulation of their own conduct. In sum, the Swiss had adopted a looters' charter amounting to a repudiation of Allied interference.

Unlike that of the British, the reaction among U.S. Treasury officials was outrage. Orvis Schmidt, the big, effusive director of Foreign Funds Control and an energetic crusader, raged among his colleagues that the Swiss banks' demand for "equal treatment" was a ruse to protect their profits and the German loot. The Swiss government was willfully obstructing the Allies by refusing to halt the flow of loot into the country or to control the country's banks despite the explosion of deposits by the murderers. With the fate of the war having swung so dramatically in the Allies' favor, Schmidt and the crusaders pushed at Morgenthau's open door, urging the adoption of a tougher stance. Switzerland's proposals for voluntary self-control were rejected as "so inadequate in almost all material respects as to offer no basis of agreement." The resolution at Bretton Woods demanded that Switzerland "take immediate measures," and the bankers' reaction, the crusaders calculated, would be the litmus test of Switzerland's commitment to Safehaven.

In early September, as American troops swept through southern France toward the Swiss border, the Bankers Association suddenly agreed to a seemingly tough code of behavior. Realizing that, with Switzerland's access to the sea under Allied control, it would be astute to acknowledge that new restrictions were "unavoidable," despite the limitations that would be imposed on their activities, the bankers decided to feign retreat in order to prevent the imposition of Allied sanctions against Swiss offenders. The Bankers Association's statement of intent seemed all-embracing.

"Collaboration in any form with the Germans," the association announced, "must be avoided in all circumstances." In the future, the bankers agreed, they would exercise "great care" and terminate "fictitious account balances," "anonymous accounts" and the "blurring of the real picture" of any transaction. To comply with those undertakings, the Swiss agreed to cease trading any foreign securities without affidavits, to refuse all deposits from Germany or occupied Europe, to stop leasing new safe deposits and to grant no new loans or credits or complete any currency transactions with Germans. Finally, the Bankers Association promised to investigate any "doubtful" cases of affidavits certifying the non-German ownership of securities and punish any member of the association for dishonesty. Endorsing that scheme, the Swiss government urged Washington to rely, like the British, on the Bankers Association certification.

To the British, the offer seemed satisfactory and a diplomatic success, but, to Whitehall's surprise, the U.S. Treasury balked. Not trusting the Bankers Association to prevent German cloaking, Schmidt demanded that the association's certificates and behavior be guaranteed by the Swiss government or by the National Bank. Alternatively, the Swiss government was to appoint the association as its official agent. The U.S. Treasury had identified the problem with great precision and expected the Swiss government to produce a solution. Instead, the reply from Bern was negative. Blaming the "political situation" and the independence of the cantons, the Swiss told the Treasury Department that the Bankers Association was not prepared to devolve its responsibility and authority on to the government. The ultimate authority in Switzerland clearly resided with the bankers.

Safehaven had reached a watershed, but the inevitability of military victory encouraged the crusaders to believe that Swiss resistance would be crushed. Their flag was raised on September 13 when Roosevelt and Churchill met in Quebec, Canada. High on the leaders' agenda was the Allies' treatment of occupied Germany. To

Churchill's surprise, Roosevelt introduced a plan that had been unveiled in Washington on September 2 by Morgenthau. The treasury secretary's policy was draconian. To prevent the repetition of history, Morgenthau proposed that the sinews of German militarism were to be destroyed: The country was to be deindustrialized, its factories demolished, its mines flooded and millions of its people sent to Russia as laborers. What remained would be a nation of peasants and cuckoo-clock manufacturers who could pose no threat to peace.

Stunned but anxious to avoid an argument after Morgenthau pointedly remarked on Britain's dependence on the United States for staving off bankruptcy, Churchill gave his agreement to the plan over dinner. Days later, as the implications for Europe were understood, both Roosevelt and Churchill retreated from the plan. For the moment, Morgenthau retained his influence, but the legacy was an irreconcilable split between State Department and Treasury officials, and greater distrust in London of the crusaders.

Those tensions coincided with the crusaders' obtaining increasing evidence of Switzerland's willful collaboration with the Nazis. Few were more pertinent than a report from a "reliable" French intelligence source, circulated in Washington in November 1944, about a secret meeting held on the eve of the liberation of Paris. On August 10, 1944, representatives of Germany's industrial giants, including Krupp, Messerschmitt and Rheinmetall, had met senior SS officers at the Hotel Rotes Haus in Strasbourg. Their purpose was to discuss the very plan that Sam Klaus had anticipated. Senior Nazi Party officials had admitted that the war was lost and urged that the new strategy was to survive and win the peace. Large sums of money should be sent abroad in secret in the care of sympathetic bankers and industrialists. Among the named Swiss banks were the Basler Handelsbank and Crédit Suisse. Eventually, according to the plan, that money would be used to finance the Nazi Party's attempt to build a new empire. Emphasizing the importance of cloaking the German deposits to make them seem "absolutely independent," the SS's expert insisted that success depended upon restricting knowledge of the plot to a few people. The rewards, the SS officer promised his audience, would follow once the party had rebuilt its strength.

State Department analysts did not doubt the credibility of the report. Captured German documents suggested that the Nazis' postwar plans were already in operation, and others were "ready to be launched on a widespread scale immediately upon termination of hostilities in Europe." The department's briefing continued, "It is clear that the Germans have done everything within their power to build up in the neutrals . . . an impressive financial stake which can be used to revive Germany's industrial and military potential after the war." By false invoicing, stockpiling goods in Switzerland, transferring funds under apparently innocent guises of "dummies" and "cloaks" and deferring payments on phony contracts, the Germans had secreted their loot.

To frustrate that plot and overcome Switzerland's continuing stubbornness, on December 6, 1944, shortly after the Red Army consolidated its advance toward Germany, the State Department circulated its first definition of Safehaven. The proposal, officials explained, was to register all known enemy assets outside Germany and survey enemy individuals and their activities around the world if they might be part of an attempt by Germany to preserve economic, political or military potential.

In early January 1945, as new intercepts revealed that Swiss banks, especially Crédit Suisse, were regularly transferring German loot and gold to Argentina, new drafts of the Safehaven program outlined the crusaders' intention to surround, intimidate and virtually invade neutral countries—especially Switzerland—to root out the Germans and their loot.

The State Department's more moderate list of demands, published on January 15, pinpointed Switzerland's obligations. The neutral was to prevent the export of any German property, to prevent the concealment of Nazi loot, to restore loot to its owners and to disclose all German assets to the Allies, whose authority over all German property was to be unchallenged.

In a long letter to American missions in neutral countries, each embassy was directed to appoint a Safehaven officer to coordinate and solicit help from local intelligence services and to utilize contacts with local banks, businesses and government. The Safehaven officer was provided with a list of the data required. Every property right and patent, every form of financial instrument and investment, and all forms of possessions stored in banks or in safe deposits or cloaked under false names were to be uncovered and recorded. In the hunt for information, every scrap of paper, every record book and every piece of correspondence was deemed to be valuable, including the check, stubs, deposit slips and receipts. Every suspect technician, financial expert and manager—any of whom could be disguised as a common laborer—was to be interrogated. To "secure the objectives," Switzerland was, on State Department instructions, to be squeezed by every means, including the threat of a maritime and land blockade, a freeze on all financial transactions and blacklisting from all international organizations. The American embassy in London was to be the coordination center, and Safehaven officials were to cooperate closely with the British.

To Troutbeck the instruction was a declaration of war against neutral countries—and utter madness. All his apprehension about the crusaders was confirmed. Similar fears among his colleagues were reinforced by an assessment of the crusaders' fervor from the British embassy in Washington. "Any resurgence of enemy activity" in the neutral countries, reported a diplomat, "is to be quelled in its inception." Impelled to bring "the utmost pressure" on the Swiss government if it failed to confiscate German property or to restore property to the legitimate owners, the crusaders were "prepared to use direct pressure upon the neutral governments . . . where voluntary cooperation proves insufficient." Britain, emphasized the diplomat, was expected to join the crusade. Troutbeck did not bother to record his personal feelings about that suggestion. Maintaining the facade of Allied unity was more important than argument. "We cannot disinterest ourselves in the problem," agreed a War Cabinet committee on February 27, 1945, because Washington was "deeply interested in this question." But even reading the State Department's directive produced exhaustion. The sheer quantity of work to collect the information required was daunting. The Germans were hardly likely to volunteer their secrets, and much of the relevant intelligence material was scattered around Washington and Whitehall. Compared with the Americans, the British wearily admitted, they simply lacked the dedicated staff even to start a hunt in London.

Confirming the pessimism, William Sullivan, the British commercial secretary in Bern, reported that, after months spent trying to penetrate and understand the secrets of the Swiss and Liechtenstein banks, he had to admit "the impenetrability of the racket." Nothing, not even a list of companies, was published. Finding the truth, he confessed, would be impossible.

The Swiss Bankers Association was not inclined to make the task any easier. "No Swiss banks," declared an official on the day that the State Department policy was published, "have ever carried out or collaborated in the transfer abroad of funds belonging to the leaders of the National Socialist party." That disclaimer was accompanied by a protest by the Bankers Association to the Allies and the suppression in Switzerland of news reports from Washington explaining why $1.9 billion of Swiss assets were frozen in the United States. Walter Sholes, the American consul in Basel, concluded, "it is quite evident that Swiss bankers have no intention of taking the Swiss public into their confidence in matters affecting Swiss banking practices. . . . The Swiss public continues to remain in the dark on the general subject."

The frustration among Treasury and State Department officials was turning to anger. In October 1944, Switzerland had imposed an embargo on exports of war material and frozen some bank accounts in German-occupied countries to prevent the compulsory transfer of possessions to the Nazis, but, protested U.S. Treasury officials, these were meaningless—even insulting—gestures, since the Wehrmacht had now abandoned those countries. In confirmation of Swiss nonchalance, the government in Bern had even rejected during January an Allied offer of raw materials from scarce stockpiles if Switzerland reduced trade with Germany. The offers were ignored. Switzerland still permitted Germany to transport military cargo along its rail network to Italy to be used against Allied soldiers, claiming it was bound by the St. Gotthard Convention. Similarly defiant, it granted Germany loans knowing that there was no chance of repayment, while the German companies supplying coal and steel were allowed to amass Swiss francs in Swiss bank accounts for use after the war. Switzerland's bankers were confident that the Allies would never discover the secrets because most important German deposits had been registered under Swiss names. The duplicity was not overlooked by Morgenthau and his disciples. Even as they observed Bern's pretense of complying with Washington's requirements, they read a new batch of intelligence reports from Europe contradicting Swiss assurances. Their antagonism was inflamed.

The reports from Switzerland described convoys of trucks traveling from Munich and Nuremberg carrying "large sums" of money and securities to Swiss banks and the German sanatoria in Davos. Other reports mentioned widespread looting by the SS and their transfer of stolen property to Switzerland. There were reports that Göring and Himmler were negotiating with Jean-Marie Musy, a pro-Nazi Swiss politician, to transfer prominent French politicians, including Marshal Pétain, Pierre Laval, Edouard Daladier and Léon Blum, and the king of Belgium to Switzerland if the Nazi leaders were also allowed refuge in the country where their own loot was deposited. Reports from Sweden and Switzerland mentioned a flood of German patent applications, and from Madrid there was a report that fourteen crates of stolen furs, sent from Paris, had arrived via Switzerland. In Washington, the Safehaven officers were convinced that the continent was awash with gangsters, but there was a dearth of real information. Groping in the darkness, the investigators knew that one group in Europe could by themselves stymie Nazi criminality, and they were outraged by their mixture of venality and sanctimoniousness.

Switzerland's refusal to cooperate in the final defeat of the Nazis infuriated Morgenthau. At the secretary's behest, Roosevelt dispatched Lauchlin Currie, the FEA's deputy administrator and a New Dealer, with Orvis Schmidt to Europe. Although uninvited by the Swiss, they were ordered to arrive in Bern and extract compliance with a list of demands. Both shared the Treasury's uncompromising attitude, although by now Harry Dexter White's proposals for reprisals against Switzerland had become draconian.

In his bid to destroy German power, White was unapologetically prepared also to cripple Switzerland if the government in Bern refused to obey U.S. demands. Without threats, White believed, it was "futile" to expect the Swiss to reveal and control German assets. Sanctions were the only language the Swiss would understand. To intimidate them, White proposed cutting their coal supplies and even pushing the country toward bankruptcy by permanently freezing their $1.9 billion assets in the United States. His ideal solution, he told Morgenthau, would be to advance loans to friendly American investors to buy control of Switzerland's leading banks. Morgenthau did not demur, even at that outlandish notion. White's aggression mirrored the common sentiment within the building.

One obstacle, Morgenthau knew, remained: those senior State Department officials opposed to Safehaven. Despite endorsement from many departments, including a letter from General Clayton Bissell, the chief of military intelligence in the Pentagon, urging that Safehaven was "of utmost importance," the State Department remained cool. Morgenthau suspected that London's influence should not be underestimated.

Filled with moral outrage and ready to punish the Swiss, Currie arrived in London on February 1, 1945, to receive an unpleasant surprise. The British were less than lukewarm about joining the mission. Wearied by the discomforts of wartime, lacking the passion of the crusaders and short of the kind of talented intellectuals recruited by Morgenthau's Treasury Department, officials in Whitehall remained incurably skeptical about Safehaven. "We won't be going to Switzerland," Bliss said with a smile. Swiss stubbornness, the Briton told Currie, guaranteed the mission's failure.

Unspoken was British concern about the crusaders' attitude toward Swiss banks. Reports from Switzerland about arguments between British and U.S. intelligence officers concerning the treatment of the Johann Wehrli Bank in Zurich revealed deep disagreements. The basic facts were not in dispute. Despite its steadily declining fortunes since 1914, when Wehrli himself, a member of one of Zurich's patrician families, had entertained Germany's kaiser, the bank had revived since Hitler's accession. Under the direction of Karl Kessler, a Swiss Nazi sympathizer who had met von Ribbentrop and other senior Nazi officials, the bank had counted among its clients the Reichsbank and several big German manufacturers and had served as a conduit for German money to Madrid and South America, while helping German officers obtain visas to enter Switzerland.

Unlike the activity of the major Swiss banks, Wehrli's activities had been easily monitored by both British and U.S. intelligence officers. Intercepts revealed Wehrli's regular telegraphic transfers of money and securities around the world, and an employee had been recruited as an informant. That unusual breach of a Swiss bank's security had exaggerated the importance of the bank's affairs but simultaneously exposed the disagreements among the Allies.

At the request of Walter Ostrow, the U.S. Treasury official in Bern, Wehrli had submitted himself for questioning in the American embassy. The Swiss had little alternative because his failure to oblige could have resulted in blacklisting and freezing of the bank's activities throughout the world. Ostrow had wanted information and Kessler's dismissal. Wehrli resisted, concealing the fact that his bank had provided SF42 million to German intelligence officers. Suspicious of the banker's collaboration, Ostrow recommended that the bank and Kessler be blacklisted. British intelligence officers in Bern were furious. Wehrli, in their opinion, was a "valuable intelligence source." Ostrow disagreed. Wehrli's information, the American reported, was worthless. Moreover, he consistently lied. Worst of all, Ostrow believed that Wehrli was being protected by Captain Max Binney, his son-in-law, who was the British vice-consul in Lugano. Claiming that Binney was a dangerous influence on the bank's behalf in London, Ostrow accused the British of protecting the Swiss relationship with the Nazis. Inevitably, his campaign interested the crusaders in Washington and confirmed British suspicions.

Britain's attitude toward Switzerland had shifted ever since Churchill had publicly thanked the Swiss for their assistance in December 1944. Specifically discounting the profits Switzerland was earning, the prime minister had acknowledged "the sole international force linking the hideously sundered nations and ourselves" and praised the neutral with "the greatest right to distinction" as "a democratic state, standing for freedom in self-defense among her mountains, and in thought, in spite of race, largely on our side."

This combination of appreciation for Switzerland and recrimination toward the crusaders confounded Currie. Yet, realizing that his appearance in Bern without the British would signal weakness, he hunted through the capital to find ways of dragging the British, unwillingly if necessary, on to his mission. Calling upon every local U.S. diplomat to support his cause, he pleaded the importance of Bretton Woods and then threatened dire repercussions if the British expected financial assistance from the U.S. Treasury to ward off bankruptcy. One week later, fearing embarrassment and worse, the British government bowed to the pressure. Dingle Foot, the parliamentary secretary at the Ministry of Economic Warfare, was assigned to accompany Currie.

On February 8, 1945, the two flew to Paris to recruit a French representative for the mission. To Currie's disappointment, French ministers were equally reluctant. Annoying the Swiss, he heard, would endanger France's supplies of food, wood, paper and chemicals from Switzerland. For other reasons, bewildering to Currie, France was also unwilling to allow supplies to Switzerland to transit across France. But eventually the same entreaties and threats cajoled the French into nominating Paul Charguéraud, a temperamental diplomat, as a member of the mission.

The trio arrived in Bern by train on February 11. Three thousand spectators, curious to see the first official Allied mission in Switzerland since the outbreak of war, had gathered at the station to cheer. Deliberately grim-faced, Currie climbed slowly into a car, determined that the Swiss should sense that he embodied a threat. But first there was an emollient.

As a courtesy, Currie delivered a letter from Roosevelt to Eduard von Steiger, Switzerland's president that year. Expressing understanding for Switzerland's isolation and its relationship with Germany during the war Roosevelt added, "I know in these circumstances that you will be eager to deprive the Nazis of any further assistance . . . [while] you will lend every assistance to our efforts in the postwar period to track down and seize the property of our foe."

Switzerland had good reason to fear a backlash from Washington. The war had reached a particularly bitter stage. Americans and Europeans were dying in sight of final victory in the cause of freedom while the Swiss, amid tranquillity, continued to trade with the killers. At Eisenhower's headquarters in Versailles, the military staff was furious that Switzerland, whose motives had been suspect since 1943, was resisting the Allies' requests to reduce its supplies to the Nazis and was thus prolonging the war. An urgent recommendation had been sent to Washington that Switzerland be frozen into submission by enforcing a complete blockade. The Swiss could only hope that France and Britain, whose unease with U.S. policy was no longer a secret, would temper the Americans' anger by explaining the realities of life for a small neutral nation and would mitigate the Americans' outrage about the protection of German plunder by Switzerland. To minimize the accusation further, the Swiss government leaked to journalists the news that all the gold shipped by the Germans to Switzerland had been spent.

The groundwork for the negotiations had been prepared by Walter Stucki, an ambitious troubleshooter who would dominate Switzerland's postwar relations with the Allies. Stucki was tall, serious, energetic and overbearing. He had been born in 1888. Although his father and grandfather had been teachers, the family's background as peasant farmers was never quite forgotten. Despite studying law in Bern, Paris and Munich and speaking good English and French, Stucki was rooted in the glory of insular Swiss neutrality. As an admirer of the eighteenth-century dictatorships, he had been elated by his appointment as ambassador to Vichy France in 1940. Marshal Pétain, France's military commander in chief in World War I and the leader of the collaborationist government, was Stucki's idol. Throughout the war, mindful that the French army had in 1940 abandoned its secret treaty obligation to defend Switzerland, Stucki had adopted a suspicious attitude toward France, but his admiration for Pétain had never wavered. In his address in Vichy's City Hall on the eve of France's liberation on August 29, 1944, Stucki had shouted that Pétain "is a noble figure . . . and I wish to put it on record that I shall always remain a great admirer of this great Frenchman who dedicated his life to France." Although that section of his speech was erased from the recording provided for a radio broadcast, once back in Switzerland Stucki regularly listened to the complete recording of what he deemed to be his finest hour. Regularly invited to regale his countrymen with tales of his service in Vichy, the government official never omitted to praise Pétain and to denigrate the French resistance and the *maquis* as "bandits." Invariably, Stucki's German-speaking audiences agreed.

Stucki's return to Switzerland had been marked by unusual political turmoil in the country. Marcel Pilet-Golaz, the pro-German foreign minister, had been replaced by Max Petitpierre, a polite forty-six-year-old private international lawyer, lacking political experience but with strong connections to industry and banking. The unsuccessful candidate for the post, baffled that his seemingly inevitable inheritance had not materialized, was Stucki. His consolation was an appointment as director of the Political Department, the Swiss Foreign Ministry. Effortlessly, he persuaded himself that, despite his subordinate position, the young, weak minister would unquestioningly and gratefully rely upon an experienced director. In any event, as Switzerland's most powerful civil servant, Stucki took it for granted that he deserved the appointment. In the opinion of a British diplomat, Stucki was "renowned as a man of ability and ambition, but possessed few if any endearing traits. He is much feared and respected, but little liked."

Among the many dissimilarities between Petitpierre and Stucki was their attitude toward Switzerland's bankers. Stucki, coming from a patriotic, parochial mountain background, harbored instinctive suspicions toward the nation's financiers. By contrast, Petitpierre regularly attended the Bankers Association's annual conferences, a display of respect toward that fraternity, among whose members was one of his brothers. The new minister was therefore inclined to ignore the Allies' denunciations of Swiss bankers and the allegations about Nazi loot.

Just two days before Currie arrived in Bern, Petitpierre received a long letter marked "urgent" from Dr. Boris Lifschitz, a respected sixty-six-year-old lawyer with a large practice in Bern. Indignant about Swiss dishonesty, Lifschitz told Petitpierre that Swiss and Liechtenstein bankers and corporations not only had accepted massive quantities of loot—"money, shares and patents"—and other deposits from the Germans on the understanding that they would be returned after the war, but had transferred other fortunes to the United States, Argentina, Brazil, Sweden and Portugal. "Understandably," Lifschitz wrote, "there is no reason for the banks to change their habits now." Anxious not to appear a traitor, he insisted that, while he intended no harm, he wanted the minister to be aware of the facts, not least that "Hitler probably did not invade Switzerland because Switzerland and Liechtenstein were considered by the Führer to be his two 'safes.'" Urging Petitpierre to acknowledge the truth, Lifschitz recommended that he use Currie's imminent arrival to "rescue Switzerland from an embarrassing position because we cannot avoid handing the hidden assets to the Allies." The minister was unimpressed. The bankers had long insisted that the Nazi money had already been transferred out of Switzerland. Perhaps it was well hidden. In any event, he ignored Lifschitz's advice.

Lauchlin Currie's opening speech to Stucki on February 13 mixed offers of friendship with hints of threats. "Every hour the war is prolonged," he told Stucki, "means more lives, and the lives of our young men are very precious to us." Switzerland, he continued, "furnished great assistance to our enemy [and] alone continues to trade regularly with Germany." Currie's implication was clear. Respecting the legality of Switzerland's neutrality was not a problem, but the Allies would not understand Switzerland's standing aloof during the final battle: "There can be no question of neutrality of spirit. It is inconceivable in our view ... to maintain an attitude of Olympian aloofness or indifference as to the outcome" of the war. The current issue, concluded Currie, was whether Switzerland would protect the Nazis' loot and thereby enable them "to preserve the power of the Nazi party and plan again for world domination."

Stucki found nothing to sympathize with in Currie's peroration. Neither his country's sovereignty nor its right to earn profits was negotiable. On the other hand, an accommodation to secure vital imports of food and raw materials was clearly desirable while Switzerland maneuvered itself away from its alliance with Germany into a new understanding with the Allies. So Stucki, with remarkable self-restraint, appeared to listen with forbearance as Currie concluded that Switzerland's unequivocal compliance with Resolution VI of Bretton Woods was a minimal requirement.

Stucki had delegated the negotiations to Professor William Rappard, a U.S.-educated economist who was a teacher at Geneva University and was soon to become known as Stucki's "ghost." Beguiled by Rappard's fluent English and American mannerisms, Currie grew more optimistic as he explained the Allies' demands. Switzerland, he insisted, should amend the banking secrecy laws, cease transit between Germany and Italy, stop most exports to Germany, freeze all German assets, deliver a complete census of German-owned property in Switzerland, allow Allied investigators to operate in Switzerland and hand over all the looted gold. The headline requirement, he concluded, was reparations: Germany's loot should be returned to its owners and Germany's assets should be transferred to the Allies to be used to rebuild Europe.

Rappard had no mandate or indeed any wish to agree to those demands. Switzerland, he believed, had no reason to apologize for its wartime activities, although the government, sensitive to political realities, understood the advantage of appearing to bend toward the Allies. On February 15, Switzerland's trade agreement with Germany lapsed. To secure Currie's goodwill, the government announced the following day a freeze on all German property situated or administered in Switzerland that belonged to any individual or company resident in Germany or German-occupied country.

Elated, Currie and his two colleagues quickly convinced themselves that the Swiss had bowed to the awesome power they represented and had ordered the banks to breach the secrecy laws to discover German assets. That was the first of their mistakes. The banks, anticipating the freeze and aware that it did not affect non-German assets, had already helped their important clients to avoid the Allies' threat by transferring German-owned assets into accounts under false names, usually English names, with addresses in China or South America. Naturally, the banks deducted a fee for their services, which the client gratefully paid.

Currie's second mistake was not to understand the timing of the announcement. In Stucki's calculations, the concession had been approved only after he had been "sure that the Germans could not harm us anymore and we could use their assets to pay off our loans." Stucki's timing was calculated to deceive. "We chose the moment carefully," he explained later, at the end of the negotiations. "If we had frozen the assets before the agreement, then the Allies would have given us nothing in return. If we had imposed the freeze at the end of the negotiations, it would have suggested that we were bowing to Allied demands." Stucki's coup disoriented but did not in the end fool the three Allied negotiators.

Within hours of the Swiss announcement, Dingle Foot, a lawyer, had spotted the loopholes. The law, providing numerous exceptions and only gradual enforcement, was glaringly deficient. "It's more a warning," Foot exclaimed, "to Germans to hide their wealth and escape future controls." Stucki was adamant. Switzerland, said the official, was bound by legal obligations and depended upon "vital imports." Trade with Germany could not be completely halted. Currie and Foot protested. Stucki's reply was abrupt: "Switzerland is neutral."

Over the following three weeks, the Allied negotiators were introduced to Swiss intransigence and feigned passion for abiding by the law. Switzerland's neutrality, repeated Stucki, prevented its compliance with the Bretton Woods Resolution. The Allies' demand for a census of Axis assets in Switzerland, he explained, breached a Swiss law of 1907 that protected its commercial relations with Germany. Allied investigators would not be allowed to operate in Switzerland. That was a breach of both Switzerland's neutrality and its sovereignty. The trio of negotiators were flummoxed. British warnings to the crusaders, bitterly resented, had proved justified. The Swiss were unmoved by reports of Allied soldiers dying for democracy. The virtues of sovereignty and the Swiss franc could not give way to sentiment.

Stucki now moved to establish the basis for negotiations. German assets in Switzerland, he declared, which the Americans estimated to be worth $600 million, were valued by the Swiss at only $250 million. Concerning the gold Switzerland had bought, Rappard insisted that the Allies were mistaken. In 1939, Germany possessed more gold than the ingots worth SF1,191 million, which had been delivered since March 4, 1940. "The dates on the ingots," said Rappard, "are prewar." Chargueraud, whose government had a keen interest in the fate of the Belgian gold, challenged the credibility of the dates. "It's not absolute proof," Rappard conceded, sensing—when Currie had mentioned the possibility of a blockade of food and fuel—that the negotiators' patience was evaporating. The threat of Allied sanctions, which could so easily cripple Switzerland, could no longer be ignored. Threats had been rewarded by an Allied breakthrough.

To Currie's relief, at the beginning of March, Stucki offered to sign an agreement. In Stucki's opinion, he was merely offering the cosmetics of compromise and concessions. In Currie's opinion, the Allied mission had succeeded.

Under the agreement, signed on March 8, Switzerland undertook that supplying electricity to Germany would cease and that Switzerland's trade and transport facilities for Germany would be limited to prescribed and minimal amounts. On the critical issue of loot, gold and German assets, Switzerland agreed to purchase no more gold from Germany except for diplomatic purposes; to prevent any more loot from entering the country; to search all German shipments for loot; to prevent Germans from selling their loot or assets; to return looted property and help claimants recover their possessions; and, while maintaining the freeze on all German-owned property, to complete a census of all German property in Switzerland and of German property owned by Swiss nationals. In return, Swiss imports of food, fodder and industrial materials would be allowed transit through France. Currie's success seemed sealed by an insertion, on Stucki's insistence, in the concluding statement: "The Swiss government wishes to point out that these restrictions impose heavy sacrifices on Swiss interests."

An addition to that agreement—an eight-page letter from Rappard to the Allies—was equally important, both for its admissions and for its deceptiveness. Concerning gold, Rappard assured the Allies that Switzerland's National Bank had controlled all imports of gold. That clearly was untrue. The future entry of foreigners into Switzerland, he promised, would be strictly controlled. That would also prove false. Finally, he promised the Allied negotiators that the Bankers Association's regulations, supervised by the National Bank, had prevented any Nazi loot from being deposited in the country. That too was unbelievable, but Rappard's assurances, concerning stolen assets and the heirless assets of the Jews in Switzerland, were accepted as true. Rappard promised that not only would the Swiss government prevent the country from being used for the "disposal, concealment or reception" of looted assets but, within the framework of Swiss law, "every effort will be given to [help] dispossessed owners to reclaim their assets found in Switzerland."

Currie's euphoric telegram to Washington, declaring that after "strong resistance and a stalemate yesterday, the Swiss delegation capitulated today," aroused jubilation in Washington. Orvis Schmidt's report to Morgenthau echoed that rejoicing. "The Swiss recognize for the first time in Swiss history that all banks, lawyers, holding companies, etc., will be forced to disclose to the Swiss government the names of the true owners of assets being held through Switzerland. This commitment was obtained with great difficulty and only because the American delegation was adamant." The Swiss government, Schmidt added, was committed "not to release German blocked assets" without consulting the Allies. Convinced by the report, Morgenthau congratulated Currie for having "thwarted the Nazis' plan for using Switzerland as a financial hideout." Only after captured German documents were analyzed two years later did the British realize that the Swiss, and especially Stucki, had practiced "virtual deceit."

In London, Rappard's promises were also taken at face value and aroused considerable fears. The crusaders' zeal for interfering in Swiss banks had originally alarmed Bliss, and the thought that they might have succeeded redoubled his concern. "This will have the effect," concluded a Downing Street official, "that banks will be compelled to reveal the ownership of numbered accounts in certain cases." Confirmation of British fears appeared in a *Financial Times* report from Bern. Swiss bankers, according to the newspaper, had posed an embarrassing question when discussing the amendment of Swiss banking secrecy laws to discover the heirless assets. Were British banks, a spokesman asked, also proposing to allow government access to accounts in British banks to discover any heirless assets? "We need to go slow on this," commented Eddie Playfair, a spirited senior Treasury official. "We don't want to be forced to reveal British banking secrets." As feared, the crusaders were causing damage. "We will be best served not to cooperate with that group," agreed Bliss. Close to panic, Foot had been instructed in an urgent telegram, "You are not (repeat not) doing anything which would lead to requests for disclosure of information by British banks."

The Swiss raised the stakes. If the law was changed, a British diplomat was told, an investigation of British accounts in Swiss banks might be automatically authorized. That suggestion was greeted in the British Treasury as "explosive stuff" requiring "great wariness." Any disclosure of British assets in Swiss banks was "red-hot" and required "very careful handling," squealed officials. The potential heresy was twofold: the thought of permitting anyone to pry into British accounts; and the notion that the Swiss considered treating German and Allied assets in Switzerland on an equal footing. Equal treatment, in the British view, was "rejected as irrelevant and insulting." Altogether, it was the predictable consequence of the troublemakers in Washington. Safehaven, it was agreed, required careful monitoring.

Just one week after the Currie agreement was signed, freezing all German accounts including the Reichsbank's, Emil Puhl, the Reichsbank's deputy, arrived in Zurich. Puhl's brief was to undo Currie's achievements and reverse what the German called Switzerland's "bootlicking of the British and Americans." Wary of Allied sabotage and conscious that his activities were observed by Allied intelligence agents, Puhl was under no illusion that Switzerland's National Bank would eventually be negotiating with new German bankers. American soldiers had already crossed the Rhine at Remagen near Bonn and were poised to sweep further into the Reich. On the eastern front, the Red Army was close to Berlin. Swiss citizens had scurried home from Germany describing in fearful tones the air raids and the destruction. Even Ernst Weber and Alfred Hirs, having dispatched an emissary to meet the new president of the Banque de France in liberated Paris, had every reason to discount the value of any negotiations with the Reich's apparatchik. But the fortunes of war had not altered the Swiss bankers' prejudices. Hirs castigated Pierre Mendès-France, the provisional French finance minister, as "the rich Jew."

As usual, Puhl planned to overnight at the Schweizerhof, opposite Bern's railway station, and at the Hotel Baur-au-Lac in Zurich, two of Switzerland's best hotels. His assistant was Friedrich Kadigien, a German living in Switzerland renowned as a financial adviser to Göring and the SS. Kadigien's lucrative sideline was converting stolen French francs into Swiss francs and, on behalf of the German government, disposing of the rough and industrial diamonds forcibly collected after 1940 from the 1,200 diamond factories and dealerships owned by Antwerp's Jews. By then Puhl was well acquainted with the crimes of the SS. Among his responsibilities in the Reichsbank was to supervise the receipt of gold dental fillings and wedding rings torn from the corpses of murdered Jews. The contents of these bags had been smelted into anonymous ingots and also sold to Switzerland.

Ostensibly, Puhl's "endless discussions" with Weber and Hirs were little different from their many previous encounters negotiating the monthly delivery of gold from the Reichsbank to purchase vital supplies for German industry. As always, the two Swiss officials displayed exemplary courtesy, reaffirming Puhl's conviction about the strength of German-Swiss relations. Nevertheless, the Swiss bankers were reluctant to satisfy his request that the Reichsbank's assets be unfrozen. After all, Puhl was asking them to renege on Switzerland's agreement with Currie, signed just seven days previously, to block all German assets. Constantly reminding Puhl of the changed circumstances was the unprecedented presence during their formal negotiations of two Swiss government officials, Dr. Robert Kohli of the Political Department and Dr. Jean Hotz of the Department of Commerce, who, with Heinrich Homberger, the president of the Vorort, the Swiss industrialists' powerful union, effectively determined Switzerland's foreign economic policy.

Nevertheless, Puhl pressed on. His offer was to pay for urgently needed munitions and repayment of German debts with six tons of gold waiting in storage just across the border in Constance. Weber and Hirs were noticeably sympathetic, but the government officials, aware of the Allies' threats, demanded payment in coal and iron. Their demand revealed that the Swiss were ignorant of the chaos enveloping Germany. The deadlock appeared unbreakable. Yet, quietly, Weber encouraged Puhl to continue negotiating.

Puhl understood Swiss bankers. Anxious for their debts to be repaid, Germany's friends would urge their government to be flexible and release the Reichsbank accounts. Instinctively, Puhl sought out those bankers, sympathetic to Germany, who had profited from their intimate association with the Third Reich—the presidents of Crédit Suisse, the Union Bank of Switzerland, the Swiss Bank Corporation and the Basler Handelsbank. All those banks had earned fortunes during the war and their presidents were interested in protecting not only their customers' credit in Germany, but also their future interests. The number of bank presidents prepared to visit Puhl in his hotel, "despite the enemy observing everything," surprised even the Germans.

Faced with the possibility of receiving no payments—an especially grim prospect for the Swiss creditors, who together were owed SF1 billion—the bankers became attracted by Puhl's offer of transferring looted gold and Swiss francs, bought with looted gold and deposited in the Swiss National Bank, to cover debts and expenses of SF25 million. After two weeks, under pressure by Swiss businessmen to obtain money, Kohli began speaking to Puhl about the importance of maintaining Switzerland's "good relations" with Germany despite the inevitability of defeat.

Completion of the transaction was assigned to Hirs. Mindful of the Allies' warnings about Switzerland's acceptance of looted gold, Hirs asked Puhl about the source of the six tons stored in Constance. The German admitted that the gold had formerly belonged to one of the occupied European countries. Unperturbed, Hirs did not inquire any further. Possession was all that mattered. Staunchly pro-German, Hirs and the Swiss politicians felt sympathy for the vanquished. Whatever criticisms were uttered by the Allies against the Nazis, the Bank and the Swiss politicians had been dealing with the "good Germans," whom it was hoped the Allies would respect and trust. For his part, Puhl was pleased to reveal, after signing the secret agreement on March 30, that Hirs "did not ask for any assurances concerning the source of this gold shipment."

Single-handedly, Puhl had unraveled the Allied blockade of German assets and the Reichsbank's accounts. Without self-recrimination, the Swiss had agreed to accept delivery of three tons of looted gold and SF10.1 million bought with other looted gold from the Germans—thereby breaching their agreement with Currie. Puhl allowed himself a moment of self-congratulation for his "considerable achievement" and blessed the strength of the German-Swiss relationship, predicting that it "will not stop now."

Concealment and deception were practiced arts among Swiss diplomats. Having taken the measure of Currie's gullibility, the Swiss diplomats in Washington concealed with an application of thick syrup the deception surrounding the Puhl agreement. Treasury officials were assured by Swiss diplomats that Currie had succeeded. "He gave nothing to the Swiss," stated Stucki, soft-soaping the Americans. The Treasury officials beamed. Stucki, described as "very influential in Switzerland," had even sent a "special" message to Washington. "He conveys to you," reported a Swiss diplomat to an American official, "his best regards and his expression of the highest esteem."

In the euphoria aroused by the Soviet army's bombardment, which was creeping ever closer to Hitler's chancellery, and by the rapid pace of the Anglo-American armies sweeping across the heart of Germany, few Allied officials probed or even noticed Switzerland's bad faith. In a continent ravaged by war, traumatized by occupation and in peril of starvation and disease, hunting for loot had a low priority.

Sam Klaus and other crusaders had envisaged an ambitious police operation—more akin to a huge dragnet—to hunt down the loot and the looters across Europe, yet sporadic intelligence intercepts were revealing Safehaven's failure. A "sudden increase in diplomatic mail" reported to be traveling from Spain to South America—from thirteen packages every month to seventy-eight in two weeks—and a convoy of 1,800 Spanish fishing boats traveling southward, carrying ice in their holds to conceal the loot, exposed the impossibility of control. In a note to the British cabinet, Sir Stewart Menzies, the chief of MI6, the intelligence service, warned that the Nazis' clandestine agencies had deposited "considerable funds in Switzerland" in banknotes and diamonds under the names of private individuals. Gestapo officers, he warned, having smuggled "large amounts of Dutch diamonds" into Switzerland, were shipping them on to South America.

Menzies's warning was endorsed by William Cavendish-Bentinck, the chairman of the Joint Intelligence Committee. Safehaven was fundamentally weak, warned Cavendish-Bentinck. Detailed lists had been prepared of German companies hiding property and cash in Switzerland, but there was no single group, he told the Foreign Office, gathering that intelligence and giving instructions to prevent neutral countries from receiving and hiding more German loot. An intelligence group for Safehaven, proposed by Lord Selborne, the minister of economic warfare, had not materialized. The indecision and fears would, Cavendish-Bentinck advised, bear inevitable consequences: "The Germans will have little difficulty hiding and disposing of bearer bonds, shares, gold and precious stones and in hiding the proceeds where we shall never find them."

In the countryside of southern Germany, declared by Hitler as the Final Redoubt where the Nazis would make their last stand, the SS and Reichsbank officials were finding houses, mines and barns and digging holes in fields across the Bavarian countryside to hide caches of currency, jewels and gold hurriedly transported from Berlin. Quietly, the more wily were entrusting the plunder to Nazi supporters to smuggle across the border into Switzerland.

Among that band of the sly was Kurt Becher. Systematically, the SS officer, having moved from Budapest to Vienna, was blackmailing the rich to deposit funds in his accounts in Switzerland. Among the vulnerable Hungarians was Thomas de Pechy, a thirty-eight-year-old industrialist. While Becher held Pechy's girlfriend as hostage, the industrialist was dispatched to Switzerland to sell copper and metal products and to deposit over SF1 million in Becher's account. Pechy arrived in Switzerland on March 6. Inside his car were suitcases filled with securities, jewels and other valuables "belonging" to the SS officer. Staying at the Hotel Baur-au-Lac in Zurich, Pechy telegraphed Becher to announce that his loot was safely deposited. On the payment of more money to a Swiss liaising with the Gestapo, Pechy obtained the release of his girlfriend. Swiss police retrieved the bribe but did not curtail Becher's activities. The German, immersed in a myriad of deals, had in the meantime sold more copper stored in Germany to Swiss industrialists while traveling with suitcases filled with jewelry, banknotes and gold that would be also deposited in Switzerland. Becher would use that fortune in the postwar years to build a multimillion-dollar wheat-trading empire based in Bremen and would prosper as one of West Germany's richest businessmen.

Soon after Germany's unconditional surrender on May 8, 1945, Becher was, like many Germans, temporarily arrested. Across Europe, the rejoicing was mixed with recrimination and revenge. In Switzerland, the politicians, industrialists and bankers, anxiously awaiting signals indicating their own fate, sought to repress their emotions. Fearing social unrest and recrimination, the country's rulers considered mobilizing the army to control protesters, maintaining censorship and continuing the restrictions placed on parliamentary sessions. Limiting democracy in peacetime appealed particularly to those who had sympathized with Germany.

Under Eduard von Steiger's control, Switzerland was to mark the end of the war in Europe with solemn church services and muted ringing of church bells. On his strict instructions, there were to be no expressions of joy that Nazi Germany had been defeated, no public meetings, and no thanks for the Allies' sacrifice. Addressing the nation on the radio, von Steiger gave thanks only that Switzerland had escaped the ravages of war and blessed the self-discipline of the Swiss people and the glory of the Swiss army. The handful of Swiss who had supported the Allies and sought to help the refugees were abandoned as outcasts. Paul Grüninger, the police chief of St. Gall who had offered protection to Jewish refugees, lived in poverty until he died; Carl Lutz, the consul in Budapest, was shunned for impugning Switzerland's neutrality by protecting Jews; and the Red Cross official whose intervention at the Mauthausen concentration camp in spring 1945 had prevented an SS massacre was condemned for disobeying orders and was forced to emigrate from his country. In May 1945, while awaiting the Allies' judgment, Switzerland's rulers sought survival by first suppressing their potential critics.

6

CRACKS

Aggressive, motivated and imbued with a deep sense of rectitude, James Mann, a Kentucky lawyer hired by the Treasury, arrived in Bern on May 15, 1945, as Harry Dexter White's latest emissary. After one year's service with the War Refugee Board in Washington, compiling information about Nazi concentration camps, Mann was raring to go and had predicted, "I'm going to bring the Swiss to their knees." Like all American visitors, he was attracted by the Alpine scenery and Switzerland's "appearance of quiet, peaceful life," but less predictable was his encounter with the leisurely atmosphere among the American diplomats in the legation. After two weeks in Bern, Mann was wild with anger. The relationships between the Swiss and the American diplomats, Mann observed, were "impediments to action." Safehaven was suffocating.

The butt of Mann's frustration was Daniel Reagan, the State Department's counselor for economic affairs nominated as Safehaven's "coordinator." Conscientious and cautious, Reagan shared his department's suspicion of Treasury types like Sam Klaus, whose personality and ambitions threatened to disrupt the smooth diplomacy cultivated with officials in the Political Department. Unwilling to release any control over Safehaven that might harm the United States' diplomatic relations, Reagan forbade the Treasury men from entering into unfettered conversations with Swiss officials, the U.S. military attaché, or Allen Dulles and his OSS officers.

The senior Treasury representative in Bern penalized by

Reagan's edict was Walter Ostrow, the crusader. Working from a private house rather than the main embassy building, Ostrow suspected that he was being deliberately denied information. Like the four State Department officials dedicated to Safehaven in the legation, Ostrow was frustrated by Reagan's reluctance to allow investigations, which obliged the Safehaven team to rely on local British intelligence officers as their best source of credible information. "Herman Kasper left here," wrote Mann about his predecessor, "with a feeling that his mission had been a failure and that the situation was hopeless."

Mann's complaints echoed Sam Klaus's damning comments in Washington three weeks earlier. In a blistering memorandum sent to Orvis Schmidt about Switzerland and the Currie agreement, Klaus listed Switzerland's "omissions," "disregard" and "complete disregard" in its reaction to protests: "Nothing was done." The Swiss were not seizing and handing over German and Jewish assets, protested Klaus, and even in Washington Safehaven was disintegrating. Only days after Germany's surrender, the U.S. Office of Censorship had refused, citing legal and ethical reasons, to continue monitoring the neutrals' mail and telegraphic communications. Safehaven's best source of information—the American intercepts—had disappeared. All that remained was a dwindling number of British intercepts and reports by army intelligence and OSS officers in Europe. Even those diminishing sources, Klaus complained, were compromised by the jealousy, misunderstanding and confusion sparked by the rivalry of agencies and personalities in Washington, fighting either to promote or to restrain the program. Without a unified voice, Safehaven was languishing. Schmidt, still basking in the accolades for negotiating the Currie agreement, was unconvinced. Sam Klaus, he jibed, was a "perfectionist."

OSS officers, investigating the Swiss-Nazi connection in Europe, also suspected that Safehaven was being sabotaged. The villain, they confided to Drew Pearson, the noted columnist, was Allen Dulles. The OSS's wartime chief in Bern, they believed, was compromised by his own use of Swiss banks for sensitive transactions, by the potential embarrassment if the Swiss were to release details of his private life in Switzerland, and most of all by the Dulles brothers' legal work in New York and Washington for Nazi corporations and banks. So many senior OSS officers, Pearson's informants explained, were either related to or employed by the scions of America's big corporations and major banks—the Mellons and the Morgans—that their instinct would be to forge alliances with incriminated Swiss-Germans rather than orchestrate their harassment.

Pearson's publication of that grievance at the end of May coincided with a "strictly confidential" letter sent by Walter Ostrow and James Mann to Harry White in Washington. The Treasury team in Bern, wrote Ostrow, were being "deliberately treated as outsiders and intruders" by Leland Harrison, the ambassador, and Daniel Reagan. Those two State Department officials, alleged Ostrow, "are systematically sabotaging our efforts to look after Treasury interests." Reagan in particular was accused of disregarding the Currie agreement and Safehaven policy, and reducing Mann's position to "a continuous perilous act of tightrope walking." Still denied access to information, Mann himself added that "nothing is ever done" on Safehaven and that the scale of uninvestigated loot was enormous.

Officially, the Swiss disputed that a hoard of German treasure was hidden in their country, but two sets of official statistics undermined their credibility. The declared deposits in Switzerland's banks had rocketed from SF332 million in 1941 to SF846 million in 1945, and Switzerland's gold reserves had doubled from $503 million to $1,040 million. Mann's suspicions were aroused by notable discrepancies. Whereas the Swiss valued German assets in Switzerland at $250 million, the American embassy's latest estimate of German investments in Switzerland, private deposits in banks and looted art stored in safe-deposit boxes was over $1 billion. British intelligence had positively identified fifty-three stolen paintings in Switzerland, but Swiss sources had suggested that "hundreds of paintings," stolen shares and manufactured materials, stocked in Swiss warehouses, were worth at least $500 million. The discovery of gold coins worth $1.5 million in the German embassy's safe, the remains of the treasury used for German espionage, supported Mann's perception of hidden loot and Swiss deceit. Asked by Safehaven officers to hand over the looted gold, Swiss officials prevaricated, murmuring their anxieties about establishing the true owners—in Germany.

Reports of discoveries in Germany of looted gold substantiated the long-feared specter of Nazi plunder. U.S. troops had found, packed with bullion, a twenty-four-carriage train dispatched by the Reichsbank, which had been halted near a mine in Merkers, itself packed with looted treasure. French troops seized a gold train that had been halted en route from Hungary. By early June, the U.S. military government had amassed more than 4,000 boxes and containers filled with over 15,000 gold and silver bars, jewelry and coins in fifteen locations originating from concentration camps, the Reichsbank or the SS. Rapidly their inventory grew to include 22,000 gold and silver bars, 3,326 bags of gold coins and 8 bags of gold wedding rings.

Reports about bags of wedding rings and scraps of gold, previously dental fillings, horrified the crusaders in Washington. Newsreel film shot by cameramen accompanying the army units liberating the concentration camps and eyewitness reports about those who had survived unlocked emotion, anger and desperation to help over 100,000 sick and homeless Jews, survivors of the camps, who were seeking shelter all across Western Europe. Reports also mentioned the anguish suffered by surviving Jews when they failed to repossess their own property in Germany, Austria and Eastern Europe. There were stories of Jews arriving in Switzerland to recover their savings and property only to be turned away by banks imposing strange stipulations; some people complained that the Swiss government, despite its undertaking to Currie, had not passed the legislation to help claimants retrieve looted possessions. Occasionally mentioned in those reports was another unprecedented imbroglio. Money and property deposited in Switzerland belonged to families obliterated by the Holocaust. Under the laws of all three Western Allies, that property was heirless and its fate was undetermined.

Heirless assets had been first discussed during 1944 among the lawyers in the war division of the Department of Justice in

Washington. Some would credit Herbert Wechsler, an imaginative lawyer, with the inspiration for raising the subject, while others would suggest that Jewish lawyers, talking over a cup of coffee, had been puzzling over the question of how to prevent the U.S. Custodian of Alien Property from seizing the American property of German Jews. By early 1945, all agreed that the money would be best used to help the victims of Nazism, although any plan depended upon British agreement.

Despite the crusaders' forthright determination to use the heirless assets to help the Jews, the British were ambivalent. Ever since the German Jews had been dispossessed by the Nazis' discriminatory legislation and had been officially stripped of their German nationality by a decree of November 21, 1941, Whitehall officials had resisted making any commitment to assist the survivors.

On April 21, 1944, not long before D-Day, William Frankel of the Board of Deputies of British Jews had called at the Foreign Office to discuss compensation and the restitution of property owned by German Jews in Germany. E. F. Henriques of the Trading with the Enemy Department was less than pleased. "This question may eventually give us more trouble than the whole of the rest of the problem of what to do with Germany," Henriques noted after Frankel's visit. "We shall be under very strong pressure (particularly in the United States) to allow Jews not only to stamp on the Germans' faces—after *we* have knocked them down—but to strip them naked as well."

Henriques's attitude was shared by his colleagues. For some months they had been drafting directives for the conduct of the Allied armies governing occupied Germany, including guidance about handling claims by Jews to repossess their homes. By May 1944, the officials' reluctance to help the Jews had been established. Henriques set the tone. It would not be "wise," he wrote, to force Germans to compensate the Jews. It was important, he continued, to avoid allowing the defeated Germans to think that "the United Nations are formally supporting the claims of the Jews against them or seeking to reestablish the position of the Jews in Germany, which no German is likely to want, however much after the war they may disapprove of Hitler."

The Germans, British officials decided, would not be compelled to pay compensation to the Jews or to restore property to the dispossessed—however desirable that might be on moral grounds—because it would be "dangerous to do so." Instead, the Allies would limit themselves to the abolition of the Nazi laws. To enforce that negative policy, Allied troops were to be ordered to resist pressure from the Jews, although they might encourage, only if the Germans voluntarily agreed, a percentage of compensation as the best the Jews "can expect to receive." Only if the actual expropriator still possessed the stolen property could the military government, at its discretion, insist on restitution. Henriques's prejudice appeared to be justified by references in Safehaven reports from Spain and Turkey—all totally unverified—mentioning that Jewish businessmen were cloaking property and money in neutral countries on behalf of German clients. The property rights of the Jews had attracted little sympathy in Whitehall. Even so, once the policy had been agreed on, opposition arose.

Exiled governments in London had told British officials that German looting of their national heritage had "aroused profound patriotic resentment" and plans had been prepared to recover the loot. Fearing "double odium" if the Allies failed to help the Europeans and also obstructed their efforts once the Allied armies occupied Germany, British officials admitted that they could no longer "appear indifferent." The Foreign Office altered its policy. The restoration of any looted property not belonging to Jews would be supported. "Restitution of identifiable property," commented the Foreign Office's Jack Coulson with obvious reluctance, "will have to be admitted." The problem, he said, would be to extract the property from the neutral countries. To help claimants, the neutrals would need to complete a census of German-owned property and that, he sighed, posed another problem. The Swiss might refuse to obey instructions sent by Allied officers in Germany or would find excuses, like suggesting that the property had been encumbered by a debt. "One thing must be accepted," Coulson stipulated. "It is only where the United Nations writ can run or is admitted that the property can be seized." Without the neutrals' cooperation, agreed Coulson's unenergetic colleagues, there was little hope of recovering any loot.

The more deeply the British officials pondered the problem, the more their pessimism grew. Restoring looted property, whether Jewish or non-Jewish, had become inextricably entangled with the approved policy of seizing German assets and loot in Switzerland and the other neutral countries for reparations; and the obstacles, political and legal, were enormous. Property could not be seized simply because it was owned by a German, because that German might have lived for years outside Germany, and the complexities of a foreign corporation could nullify the definition of pure German ownership. "Information is so diffuse," admitted Troutbeck, failing to reconcile the Allies' ignorance about German investments in the neutral countries with Washington's enthusiasm that all German property in Switzerland must be turned over to the Allies.

By March 1945, British pessimism had become defeatism. Simply declaring German or looted property in Switzerland as owned by Allies, declared Eddie Playfair, would not be recognized by the Swiss: "We shall doubtless have to make some bargain with the neutrals to allow them to satisfy some or all of their claims out of German assets before they are willing to surrender to us the balance." But he anticipated the worst: the Swiss would not recognize the Allies' orders confiscating German property, and the Germans would similarly disobey the Allies. In tune with his colleagues' ideas, Playfair introduced a fundamental caveat. German property seized in Switzerland, he declared, should not be used for general relief in Europe but belonged to the Allies as reparations for their losses. That, he knew, was totally contradicted by the United States' policy of helping the Jews.

On May 23, 1945, twenty-six American and British officials met at the Ministry of Economic Warfare in an elegant building in Berkeley Square in London's Mayfair to discuss Safehaven. Their politeness did not disguise their mutual suspicions. While the British and American officials shared a desire "to destroy German assets from motives of security" and a distrust of Switzerland's intention of grabbing German assets for its own purposes, the British were suspicious of the Americans' refusal substantially to reduce the blacklists. The Americans, assumed W. A. Brandt, a British economic warrior, wanted to use Safehaven "to make money [by] eliminating German influence." Brandt's suspicions had been aroused by Avery Peterson, a diplomat at the U.S. embassy, who had asked for British help in hunting down "obnoxious Germans." That hunt, Brandt suspected, was to suppress commercial competition, which was not in British interests. "In my opinion," agreed Michael Vyvyan, a Foreign Office official, "the political danger of overseas Germans is grossly exaggerated and it might even be in our interests to have some irritants of this kind in the Western Hemisphere affecting American relations with Europe." The suspicion was mutual. The Americans knew that the British harbored similar ambitions: "to get financial benefit" from German property. The mistrust, suggested Albert Robbins, a lawyer attached to the Ministry of Economic Warfare, was damaging: "If there's no cooperation in the field, I fear that the neutral governments may play us off against each other." The losers could only be the Jews, especially the refugees, denied a government and an army of occupation to champion their cause. The winners could only be the Swiss and the Germans, puffed up by their coup against Currie. The meeting ended with an exchange of platitudes about supporting Safehaven but no agreement about the consequences.

Touring Switzerland in June 1945, Orvis Schmidt had become incensed. Klaus's warnings, derided only four weeks earlier, had been only too justified. The Swiss were ignoring their undertakings to Currie. Morton Bach, a Safehaven officer in Bern, had moaned to Schmidt about how polite and unhelpful the Swiss bankers were proving. Eberhard Reinhardt of Crédit Suisse, unfailingly courteous when asked for assistance in the search for loot, always replied, "I can't quite recall"; while Edgar de Rahm, of the Banque de Paris in Geneva, consistently declared of his search for loot, "I'm afraid there's no progress." The best reply Bach could ever expect from any banker was "We'll look into it."

Safehaven, Schmidt realized, was less effective than Washington believed. Switzerland's measures, he reported to Morgenthau, were "so inadequate that German war criminals outside Germany or in Switzerland are free to utilize their funds held in Switzerland." German property, especially where it was slightly cloaked, was untouched by Swiss controls. "The Swiss make it easy for the Nazi industrialists and other war criminals to conceal their assets held not only in Switzerland but in Swiss names throughout the world." Unless the Treasury could "pierce this veil of secrecy," warned Schmidt, U.S. policy would be sabotaged. His solution was to threaten Switzerland with sanctions, ban supplies of coal and other essential commodities and impose a complete freeze on all Swiss bank accounts in the United States. Fired with indignation, the crusaders took their battle to Europe's first postwar summit of Allied leaders.

Despite his uninspiring official title, the United States Commissioner of Labor Statistics, Isador Lubin, wielded considerable influence in Washington. Based in the east wing of the White House, Lubin was a member of Roosevelt's brain trust and was recognized by all as a "civilized Jew from Harvard who knew how to hold his fork." Passionately active during the war as the president's link in the bid to rescue Hungarian Jews, Lubin in 1945 immersed himself with other crusaders in the efforts to save the Jewish survivors.

In a memorandum to the president, Lubin wrote that at least 100,000 persons "are particularly unfortunate victims," since either their possessions had been stolen or they had been forced to hand them over to their oppressors. Penniless, they were also stateless. Unprotected and unaided by any government, they were unable or unwilling to return to their homes. Securing money for relief would be difficult; but, Lubin speculated, one certain source was German assets in Switzerland. Their fate would be decided at the Allied summit conference to held in July at Potsdam, near Berlin. With Roosevelt's agreement, Lubin was appointed the American representative to negotiate on reparations. But the president's intervening death altered Lubin's status. As a reward for faithful services, Ed Pauley, a senior Democrat official, was appointed by Harry S. Truman as Lubin's superior. Since Pauley was more interested in photo opportunities to promote his political ambitions at home, however, Lubin retained his authority without the prestige.

Lubin's financial proposal seemed uncontroversial. Two percent of the reparations taken from the nonmonetary gold seized in Germany and the German assets seized in the neutral countries, he suggested, should be allocated to an international agency for the benefit of the 100,000 Jews. The only exception would be Jews living in Germany, who should be helped by the German government. But the crusade was not confined to securing mere money. It also concerned the fate of the Jews. "They stand," Lubin told Truman, "in immediate need of relief, of resettlement in a more promising environment and of aid in rehabilitation." His implication was unequivocal. The survivors should be allowed to rebuild their lives in Palestine, a British-mandated colony. Lubin understood the controversy his plan would generate.

Ever since Britain had been granted formal control over Palestine in 1919, as part of the settlement at the end of World War I, successive ministers were caught by a dilemma. Palestine was properly deemed by the British to be a vital military position for the defense of the Suez Canal, the shipping routes to the empire in India and Britain's considerable investments in the emerging Middle East oil fields. To have abandoned Palestine in 1919—in the midst of extraordinary turbulence—would have been military and political folly. Britain's dilemma arose out of the natural conflict between maintaining good relations with all the Arab rulers and a promise made to Chaim Weizmann in 1917 by Arthur Balfour, the foreign secretary, that "His Majesty's Government view with favor the establishment in Palestine of a national home for the Jewish people, and will use their best endeavors to facilitate the achievement of this object." The Balfour Declaration, however, contained a critical proviso: Nothing was to be done by the Jews "which may prejudice the civil and religious rights of the existing non-Jewish communities."

From 1917 onward, a trickle of European Jews, committed Zionists, had settled in Palestine, provoking concern among the

Arabs. Hitler's appointment as chancellor of Germany in 1933 prompted increasing numbers of Jews, denied sanctuary in other European countries, to settle in Palestine, and their arrival had aroused Arab protests. Britain's strategic interests were indisputable. After the outbreak of war, retaining the Arabs' loyalty against Nazi Germany was vital, and the arrival of any Jewish settlers was deemed to endanger the Allies' strategy against the Germans in the Middle East and North Africa.

That consideration, as Isador Lubin knew, had cost the lives of thousands of persecuted Jews. During his own wartime bid to save the Hungarian Jews, the British had prevented persecuted Jews from entering Palestine, even though their alternative destination was Auschwitz. The anger among the United States' Jews against Britain for that inhumanity was limited only by their ignorance of all the covert manipulations adopted by British diplomats to prevent the Jews from escaping from the Nazis and because State Department officials had similarly denied sanctuary to Jews. The past, Lubin believed, was best forgotten if he was to find allies for his new plan.

Traveling via Moscow, Lubin arrived in Berlin with Abraham Bergson and Moses Abramovitz, a thirty-three-year-old economist employed by the OSS as a senior analyst of German industry. Abramovitz had previously clashed with Morgenthau, arguing that Germany was incapable of affording gigantic reparations, but he shared the desire to "do justice" to the Jews. Morgenthau would resign during July, but the Americans were able to welcome the appointment of Sir David Waley, an industrious and widely respected fifty-eight-year-old Oxford-educated Treasury official who had won the Military Cross in World War I. Jewish and a Zionist, Waley supported the creation of a homeland for Jews in Palestine but tactfully concealed his sympathies.

Lubin's memorandum, "Reparations and Restitution for Stateless Persons," appalled most of Waley's colleagues. Only one aspect was attractive. Lubin proposed to limit the Allies' expenditures by financing the care of the survivors from German property in Switzerland. "By treating the problem of people who are robbed and made stateless by Hitler as a problem of reparations and restitution," explained Lubin, "we will shift the burden to Germany." Anything that saved money attracted British support, but Lubin's general sentiment was less palatable. A new International Board of Trustees, he suggested, should pursue the claims of murdered Jews and use the heirless assets to "secure equipment to help the stateless Jews settle in Palestine." That was unacceptable to the British. But, as an insignificant item in the vast agenda preoccupying the Allies at Potsdam, it was relegated for future discussion. Lubin's success, with Waley's help, was to include in the final agreement the stipulation that 2 percent of the reparations were to be used for refugee relief.

On July 31, 1945, the Four Powers—the United States, Britain, France and the Soviet Union—formally ordered the neutral countries to transfer all property owned by the Axis powers to the Allies. To the euphoric victors, momentarily forgetting the legal problems, it seemed that every German asset in Switzerland was there for the taking. If the Swiss objected, warned Lubin, the Allies would blockade their country. Sanctions would shatter Swiss stubbornness. Joining the enthusiasm, Foreign Office officials were unusually brazen: "Switzerland must recognize the complete authority of the three Western powers and deliver anything that the Allies took a fancy to." Switzerland, said another official, should be offered "the smallest cut for their claims that we can negotiate." The dissident who cautioned, "If we take a fancy to too much, the neutrals might kick," was momentarily ignored.

One week later, reality dawned. In scrawled memoranda, unemotional British lawyers cooled expectations. Simply waving resolutions would hardly persuade the Swiss to comply. They warned that, if Switzerland denied the validity of a foreign decree by asserting its sovereign rights, the Potsdam declaration would be worthless. The proposed solution was persuasion: "It will pay us to work by collaboration with the neutrals. If we try a bluff that does not work . . . there is not much that can be done." Recent history did not encourage the British. Nor were they gratified to find that Lubin and the crusaders were censuring them for pessimism.

In Bern, whose village atmosphere diffused any sense of reality, Leland Harrison was witnessing Swiss perfidy. Staff members from the British embassy, asserting their rights as representatives of the new government of Germany, had inhabited the vacant homes of Germany's expelled diplomats and were encountering fierce Swiss demands for their departure. Swiss officials spoke about keeping German property in trust "for the eventual legal government of Germany" and refused to allow the Allies access to the files taken from the abandoned German embassy. The Swiss proclaimed it their duty to protect the interests of all Germans, including Nazis, and had established a German Interests Section, the Deutsche Inter-resenvertretung or DIV, to protect German property against the Allies' claims. As if in the same breath, Robert Kohli, in the Political Department, told Harrison that Swiss investigators were plowing through police files, tax reports and other sources to seek German assets—he irritatingly refused to reveal any particulars—and also mentioned Switzerland's demand for the recovery of the SF1 billion wartime loan to Germany. Perplexed, Harrison reported to Washington that while he could not understand the "actual reasons for [Swiss] slowness" he still trusted that the Swiss had the "greatest interest to remove the sources of suspicion." Despite eight years' service in Bern, the American diplomat was an easy victim of Swiss deception.

Outwitting the Allies was an option Swiss ministers had instinctively embraced in the first days of peace. Apologies and resignations were not common in Switzerland's political tradition, and some prominent figures whose dalliance with the Nazis had been exposed easily shrugged off any embarrassment. Like Walter Stucki, the nation's leaders rallied to expressions of pride about Switzerland's wartime record. Surviving as a neutral, Stucki believed, had been a victory akin to the Allies' defeat of the Nazis. Like the Allies, Switzerland had been a victim of the Third Reich, but, thanks to guile and bravery, it had avoided occupation. Switzerland, Stucki proudly told the Allied ambassadors, had also suffered. No fewer than 376 Swiss nationals had been killed abroad, and 55 were still missing.

Two Swiss had been executed in Germany and ten in France. To emphasize the inviolability of Swiss neutrality, Max Petitpierre remarked in a distinctly inflammatory tone that France, the most vulnerable of the Allies, would be required to pay "two million francs" in compensation for that enormity. Later, the Swiss conjured up the statistic that sixty-three Swiss nationals had died in France, and the new government in Paris was presented with a bill for FF82 million. The Swiss who had died were black marketeers, common criminals or collaborators who had served the German cause. Masquerading as neutrals, those Swiss had sought to profit from France's discomfort, yet Philippe Pérrier, the senior diplomat assigned to deal with the claim, believed that France had no option but to make a counteroffer of FF55 million. "It is galling," he wrote, "to offer monetary compensation to the heirs of certain foreigners who had failed to observe total neutrality while in our country and who had freely and openly taken a position in favor of our enemies." But France, burdened by the legacy of Vichy, preferred to bow to Swiss demands rather than risk embarrassment.

Alberto Caflisch, the secretary of the Swiss Bankers Association, and his fellow members expected similar tactics—"the technicalities of business"—to sabotage the Allies. Born in 1898, the son of a long-established Swiss family, Caflisch had grown up in Naples, Italy (where his grandfather had established a business), before returning to Switzerland to tread a familiar path. After studying law at three Swiss universities, Caflisch was employed by a bank and then joined the association in 1946 as one of four secretaries. It was the association's practice to bully ministers until the government lent support to their opinion. Even before the war ended, Caflisch goaded Petitpierre to shrug off the affidavit scandal. Switzerland's "supreme interest," he preached to the politician, was not to erode worldwide respect by undermining the banks' credibility. The banks' new affidavit system, he had assured the minister, was "foolproof." Nevertheless, his campaign to protect the ownership of the stolen shares and securities accepted by its members had encountered a reluctance among politicians to alienate the Allies. Unused to unsympathetic reaction to the bankers' requirements, Caflisch repeatedly appealed to Petitpierre to appreciate that any breach of the secrecy laws and any disclosure of clients' names would "irreparably damage" the banks' reputation. Petitpierre listened. Allowing the Allies to infringe Switzerland's sovereignty and force unwelcome disclosures, he agreed, was unacceptable. But the agreement with Currie was a formal, legal document, and although it was being stealthily sabotaged, he said without regret, it could not be completely ignored. The minister's feeble response encouraged Caflisch to wage war. Escalating a disagreement into a crisis suited the association's tactics. In particular, it suited the bankers to launch a "battle of the names" against Max Schwab, the sixty-three-year-old director of the Swiss Compensation Office within the Political Department, who until recently had served as a commander of an artillery regiment.

Recruited in 1934 from the National Bank to control the flow of foreign currency passing through Switzerland, Schwab was a lawyer sharing with Stucki, an old school friend with whom he had played soccer, a distrust of bankers and servility toward the sanctity of the law. If incompatibilities between his principles arose, Schwab was usually inclined to interpret the law narrowly to the bankers' advantage. Humanity and flexibility were not qualities he displayed in the administration of his office, an approach that won him praise as "a man of integrity." Currie's belief that the Compensation Office could be trusted to implement the agreement was naive. During the war, the office's personnel had worked closely with Nazi financial agencies, including the Reichsbank, and their inclination to join the Allies in punishing the Germans was questionable. Yet the fate of the crusaders' plans to secure the German assets and help the Jews depended upon Schwab. Under the Currie agreement, Schwab was authorized to compile a census and supervise the freezing of all German property in Switzerland. Most important, he was also authorized to list the names of all German owners of bank accounts. That authority—to breach the bank secrecy laws—horrified Caflisch. The risk of leaks was appalling, and his members' businesses would be irreparably damaged. His only consolation was Petitpierre's sympathy when the bankers resisted Schwab's entreaties to abide by the Currie agreement.

Schwab approached his new task honestly, but within days he was stumbling. The obstacle, he confided to Stucki, was the decree ordering the freeze on German property. It was, he complained, "unsatisfactory." The banks, said Schwab, insisted on secrecy, and yet, without revealing names, it would be impossible to complete the freeze and the census. How could the Compensation Office determine the ownership of property, he asked, if the banks denied possessing that knowledge, refused to cooperate and relied upon the law protecting bank secrecy? "The banks say that it's not their duty," he told Stucki in frustration, "to query an owner's nationality." Safehaven's fate depended upon Max Schwab's securing a victory over Caflisch.

Schwab expected the department's support against the bankers when in mid-April he arrived in Robert Kohli's office with Caflisch for what had been billed by the Political Department as a meeting to settle the dispute. Instead, Kohli's response to Caflisch's aggressive defense of bank secrecy was "shaky." Stung by the banks' vehement opposition and by Caflisch's outlandish accusation that the Compensation Office was responsible for all the problems, Kohli became uncertain how Switzerland could ever feign compliance with the Currie agreement. By the end of the meeting, the intimidated official procrastinated: "We need to consider this further."

On April 28, 1945, Schwab approached Kohli privately. Relying upon the banks, said Schwab, was unsatisfactory. While most banks could be trusted, some of their employees, as shown by the false affidavits, were probably untrustworthy. "If we cannot obtain the names of the owners of assets," he proposed, "we will have to rely upon denunciations or information from other sources." Kohli did not react to Schwab's idea. Confronting or investigating the bankers was distinctly unappealing.

By July, on the eve of the Potsdam conference, Emil Puhl's confidence that the Swiss bankers would protect the Germans appeared justified. Alberto Caflisch, having recognized the seriousness of the American campaign to recover the German loot, shifted his position.

Adopting a pious approach, he told Petitpierre that Switzerland's banks, unlike the lawyers and fiduciaries, were wholly innocent. No Swiss bank, soothed Caflisch, would ever have assumed "the role of a fence by unlawfully acquiring property." Moreover, Petitpierre ought to be mindful of Switzerland's interests. Even if Swiss lawyers and fiduciaries were custodians of loot, "it is hardly the responsibility of our country to establish the nature of the illegality, causing a foreigner to lose his valuables. That's up to the foreign governments. Switzerland's responsibility is only to decide what is the definition of loot and how to protect the innocent purchaser of stolen goods." Finally, the minister should bear in mind Switzerland's interests. Infringing banking secrecy would jeopardize the nation's prosperity. To Caflisch's satisfaction, Petitpierre nodded. Three months after Currie's visit to Bern, the minister was bending. Switzerland's interests, he murmured, were similar to those of the bankers. The plans to seize German property seemed to be stillborn.

"I'm astonished," exploded Schwab. At the beginning of July, he appealed to Stucki. Both men's distrust of the banks and their shared dislike of Petitpierre propelled Stucki to challenge Caflisch. The Currie agreement and the decree declaring the freeze had been negotiated by him. The banks would not be allowed to tarnish his honor. Relying on the decree, he ordered the banks to disclose their clients' names to the Compensation Office. Caflisch seemed to have been defeated. The Compensation Office's thirty employees, Schwab told Allied diplomats soon after, were finally empowered to start to investigate German camouflage and "register and immobilize all German assets."

Unaware of that battle and the apparent victory, Leland Harrison sent a pessimistic report to Washington. To break the deadlock, Seymour Rubin, a crusader in the State Department, was dispatched to London.

Born in 1914 in Chicago to an estate agent, Rubin had graduated in law at Harvard and practiced for six years before his appointment as acting director of the State Department's Office of Economic Security responsible for Safehaven. Like Sam Klaus and the other crusading lawyers, Rubin, a liberal Jew, saw advantages in linking the Jewish claims against Switzerland to the Allies' demand for reparations from German property. Keeping the two issues interdependent strengthened the case for obtaining the heirless assets and allocating a proportion of the reparations to help the refugees.

In the days after Germany's surrender, Rubin had argued with local British diplomats against abandoning all sanctions against Switzerland. "We need them to extract the looted assets," he urged. "Morality demands it." By threatening to refuse deliveries of coal, oil and food, the British could always subjugate puny Switzerland. British pleas that trade with the neutrals was essential for their country's economic recovery had been discounted by Rubin as a "flagrant breach of faith." Britain, he alleged, was planning to undermine the Allies' unity for reasons of "commercial expediency" and was "sabotaging" Safehaven. Rubin's arguments prevailed. A "hard core" blacklist of Swiss nationals and corporations, conceded the British, could continue for one more year. Rubin's first breakfast at the Cumberland Hotel after his arrival in London from the Potsdam conference highlighted the cause of that dispute. Eagerly anticipating a traditional English breakfast, he had found himself gazing at artificial eggs and ersatz sausages. Pushing the plate aside and heading through the bomb-damaged capital to the U.S. officers' mess at the opulent Dorchester Hotel, the residence of the world's millionaires in peacetime, Rubin at least understood British concern that alienating the neutrals would jeopardize the reconstruction of the nation's economy.

But Rubin could not imagine the proportions of the crisis facing Britain. In the euphoria of victory, few understood that since 1940 the British economy had been technically bankrupt. Not only had all the nation's reserves been spent on the war, but its debts were vast. Compounding the crisis, Britain's remaining undamaged factories were slow to return to peacetime production and so failed to earn the profits from exports that were needed both to finance vital imports and to repay the loans. Magnifying that burden, Britain was maintaining a vast military and naval presence across the world, accepting

responsibility for policing the peace and pacifying the constant out-
breaks of turbulence that followed Germany's and Japan's defeat.
Anguished and exhausted civil servants in London, searching for
solutions to solve the perils of Britain's finances, could understand
the moral and political arguments for Safehaven but feared the financial consequences. To attack the neutrals at the expense of Britain's
economy seemed to be nothing but folly to them. That was an attitude that the crusaders could not begin to comprehend.

Rubin arrived at the Foreign Office on August 15 and was shown
into an unremarkable room with a worn conference table and shabby
chairs. A small man, Rubin did not possess an aura guaranteed to
excite curiosity or win attention. His strengths, as with so many crusaders, were his intellect, energy and commitment. Around the table
were fourteen British, French and American officials, dedicated like
Rubin, but to other causes. Rubin was the nervous salesman facing
unrevealing customers. "Thank you very much for coming to
London at such short notice," said Gerald Villiers, the British chairman. "Your contribution is sure to be very valuable." Rubin understood that the Foreign Office types—like some of his State
Department colleagues in Washington—were occasionally anti-
Semitic, definitely conservative and always searching for excuses not
to vilify the Swiss. Attacking Safehaven as complicated and responsible for confusing the Allies' political strategy, they echoed views similar to those Rubin had heard in Washington.

Conversations in Berlin had alerted Rubin to another obstacle.
British lawyers were convinced that the Swiss were not legally bound
to comply with the Allies' demands. His tactic would be to present a
new Safehaven: no longer just an operation to destroy German financial power but a crusade to confiscate money to help the Nazis' victims. His audience, Rubin hoped, would be refreshed by his original-
ity. Accepting the strength of the Swiss case, he explained to them
that Switzerland should be approached using morality as a argument:
"The Allies have suffered tremendous damage. Their armies and
civilian populations have suffered severe losses, their properties have
been destroyed by enemy bombing, their territories have been looted

in order to fight the war against fascism. During this time, the neutrals have to a great extent profited from trade with both the Allies and the Axis. In any case they have avoided similar sacrifices to the Allies. . . . To rebuild the family of nations, the neutrals should contribute to rehabilitation, and the German assets—which do not belong to the Swiss—can be used for Europe's reconstruction. And to avoid a drain on the neutrals' economies, the money raised by selling German assets would be spent in the neutral countries."

The predictable Swiss reply, continued Rubin, would surely be legalistic: that Switzerland's claims against Germany had precedence over the Allies' claims. Since everyone in the room agreed that Switzerland's wartime loans to the Nazis—over SF1 billion—should not be recognized, he proposed the rebuttal: "Switzerland gave the loans for their own benefit despite Allied warnings. The Swiss chose to accept German orders during the war despite the faint possibility of eventual full repayment. Those loans allowed the Germans to prolong the war against the Allies at the cost of Allied lives and property. There is every moral basis why the neutral claim should rank far below the Allied claims based on reparations." Rubin sat back. The atmosphere had warmed.

Understanding the incipient antagonism around the room toward the crusaders, Eddie Playfair, the Treasury's representative, smartly championed Rubin's plan. Acknowledging that British differences with the Americans were "so many and so acute," Playfair appreciated the absence of draconian threats: "We cannot simply deny every neutral claim and demand that they hand over all German property. We need to differentiate. We'll get nowhere if they refuse to cooperate." Pierre Francfort, the French representative, agreed: "We cannot be too tough." "Appealing to morality," chimed Villiers, "is better than brandishing a mailed fist in their faces." Playfair concluded the session. Playing the morality card against the hardheaded Swiss had appealed to the Treasury official: "The quiet confidence, a manly sob repressed at the thought of our suffering compared to theirs, an honorable suggestion of cooperation in carrying out a program to which no moral creature can object." The advantages of

Rubin's plan were manifest: "We need to show that we are being just rather than vindictive."

When the fourteen met again the following day, their earlier enthusiasm had become dimmed by forebodings of the legal obstacles that the Swiss would throw up against the Allies. No government, after all, could force another government to hand over property. Rubin sparked with the solution: the Allies, relying on the terms of Germany's surrender, had assumed the rights of the German government and could demand the return of German property. His audience again appreciated the proffered solution. Rubin departed encouraged by British suggestions that Switzerland seemed amenable to the Allies, but he nevertheless feared that Britain, financially desperate, intended to placate the Swiss. Naturally Stucki, aware of the U.S. agenda, spotted the advantage of prying the British away from the crusade.

Meeting Sir Clifford Norton, the British ambassador, in Bern on August 24, Stucki deftly applied balm to a sensitive diplomat. "This is the moment," soothed Stucki, "when Great Britain can expect favorable answers to her demands. Never have the Swiss people admired the British people more. Not only the military victories, but the general election showed the world what a living democracy really is. [Attlee's Labor Party had defeated Churchill in July.] It is a lesson to us all. I feel I am speaking for the whole of Europe when I say that the wind of freedom is blowing again and the whole of Europe realizes that it is to London, and London alone, that we should look for leadership." The duplicity of that assertion was exposed that very month, when an Allied intelligence officer acquired a secret assessment that had been written in May 1945 by Gerhard Kaehlitz, a Swiss government official, describing Switzerland's wartime economic relationship with Germany. Kaehlitz had emphasized the advantages the Swiss had gained from the increase of trade that they had enjoyed with the Nazis. But that truth was irrelevant to the British government. Ignoring the Americans' irritation, Whitehall eased the wartime freeze on Swiss assets in Britain and, encouraged by Swiss compliments, proposed to weaken the Allies' sanctions. The beneficiaries were Swiss bankers.

7

THE NAZIS'
FRIENDS

Dr. Alfred Schaefer, the managing director of the Union Bank of Switzerland, one of the nation's biggest, understood the importance of deception in the months after the war as he sought to conceal his bank's profitable relationship with Nazi Germany. The son of a building contractor, he had been just thirty years old when he was appointed to one of Switzerland's most influential banking posts. He had always realized that Stucki's agreement with Currie to weaken the banking secrecy laws threatened to expose embarrassing truths. The Union Bank, he believed, was safe so long as the government resisted the demands of Leland Harrison and the Treasury officials in Bern to implement Stucki's decision to erode banking secrecy. Yet pressure from the Americans, he feared, backed by the continuing freeze on Swiss property in the United States and the Allies' ability to control Switzerland's imports, might prove irresistible.

To combat aggressive Americans like the Kentucky lawyer James Mann, whose dislike of the Swiss was becoming uncontrollable, Schaefer's staff, like many other Swiss bankers, businessmen and lawyers, were clandestinely traveling to Germany, using entry permits secured by bribes, to "connive" with clients in the efficient concealment of their assets in Switzerland. Despite all the promises uttered to Currie by Stucki and Kohli, and despite Switzerland's new laws prohibiting undeclared trade with the Germans, British diplomats in Bern observed that the Swiss were seeking "permanently [to] escape the tentacles of the Allies." Not the least of the discoveries by the Safehaven investigators was that known German companies were unexpectedly listed as Swiss.

The evidence against Schaefer was emerging from a vulnerable point in the conspiracy: sensitive files in Germany to which the Allies enjoyed unrestricted access. American investigators in Bavaria were obtaining confessions from employees of the Munich Reinsurance Company, one of Europe's biggest insurers, disclosing how their company, using German residents in Switzerland and Swiss nationals who were Nazi sympathizers, had secretly moved funds into Switzerland with the Union Bank's help. Under the guise of insurance premiums and transfers of shares, UBS had become the company's "owner" to prevent confiscation by the Allies.

Unaware that the camouflage was disintegrating, on August 30, 1945, Schaefer launched a public offensive against the Allies. Attacking Switzerland's critics as demagogues, he sanctified banking secrecy as vital to "maintain public order" and akin to the hallowed secrecy protecting priests, doctors and lawyers. Emphatically he told his audience, "Swiss banks have never been a safe haven for Nazi funds." That sort of funds, the banker insisted, "should not be found in democratic Switzerland." Skeptics would later note Schaefer's phrase "should not" rather than "could not." The banker's finale was an unexpected invitation. U.S. banks, said Schaefer, should trust the Union Bank's expertise and its "invaluable services" when considering investments in Europe.

Schaefer's declamation did not impress William Sullivan, the British commercial attaché in Bern responsible for Safehaven. He understood in the course of that summer that Swiss law was protecting theft, and Stucki's promise to help Jews recover their possessions had proved to be a "meaningless gesture." Despite their promises, the diplomat realized, the Swiss were using the five-year statute of limitations to block any pre-1940 claims by Jews. "It transpires," he reported to London, "that the Swiss have no intention whatsoever of doing anything governmentally about it. The standpoint is that their existing civil law provided machinery for this purpose and that therefore it was up to each dispossessed owner to take individual action in the Swiss courts." Switzerland's "dilatory tactics," he was convinced, were calculated to test the strength of the Allies' determination and undermine their promises to Currie.

Successive reports of rejected claims convinced Sullivan that Swiss banks were protecting German property while blocking access to property belonging to Jews emerging from the camps. A case pursued by Erwin Haymann, a lawyer in Geneva, seemed typical. Retained by the widow of an Italian Jew murdered by the Germans, Haymann possessed good evidence that SF1 million had been deposited at Crédit Suisse in Geneva. Yet every attempt to secure the money was stalled by the bank.

Swiss insurance companies were also ignoring claims by Jews. German and British Jews possessing life insurance policies taken out with the Basler Lebens Versicherungs Gesellschaft (the Life Insurance Company of Basel) had discovered that the money owed under their policies had been paid out by the company to the Nazis. Without the Jews' agreement and without any legal obligation to do so, the insurance company had obeyed a 1938 Nazi law and transferred millions of francs to the German government. The Swiss had not even troubled to tell the policyholders. The complaints, arriving after the war, were rejected by the Swiss company as "irrelevant under Swiss law." Foreign Office officials privately condemned the Swiss as "unscrupulous" but refused to help the claimants.

The obstacles, Sullivan suspected, were maintained deliberately by the Swiss to prevent the restoration of looted assets. Major Swiss companies like Bally Shoes, which had bought Jewish-owned businesses in Germany at bargain rates, risked losing their prizes. A Jew like Frederick Weissmann, the owner of a shoe factory in Berlin before the war, might hope to retrieve his factory—bought for a peppercorn by Bally—but Swiss law would bar his claim.

In Washington, Sam Klaus, Sy Rubin and the other crusading lawyers concluded that the Swiss could be humbled only by passing a special law dealing with two complaints: Switzerland's treatment of the Jewish claims and its response to the Allies' demands for German property as reparations. Their legal remedy was inventive. The Allied Commission in Berlin, the lawyers argued, was the government of Germany under the terms of the unconditional surrender. As the government, it should issue a decree declaring that all German property in Switzerland belonged to the occupying armies and insist on its surrender. The instruction that the law be passed was cabled to Berlin in August. "I personally regard this law," General Eisenhower told Field Marshal Montgomery, "as a most important step in the policy to deal with Germany's problems as a whole. Early action is imperative." Any delay, declared Eisenhower, would allow the Germans time to conceal their assets.

Montgomery's advisers in London stared blankly. "There are just going to be long discussions about the law," sighed Gerry Villiers at the Foreign Office. "The Swiss will be forced to defend themselves and won't easily withdraw. It will get us nowhere." British forebodings that the Allies had no legal right to assume powers greater than those possessed by the defeated Nazi government were dismissed by Eisenhower. "I regret your attitude," he told Montgomery, brushing British opposition aside.

The pressure from Washington, supported by Paris, to threaten the Swiss was irresistible. "We'll do it unilaterally if you don't agree," scoffed a U.S. Treasury lawyer in London. "Our hands are forced," conceded Villiers, fearing that any law would simply encourage the Germans and the Swiss to hasten their concealment of the loot. Reports by Sullivan from Bern confirmed the problem. "On what Swiss law do they base their claim?" Stucki had demanded of the Briton.

"They're perfectly correct. . . . We haven't got a leg to stand on," moaned Henriques after reading Sullivan's report. The British official's anger was not directed at the Swiss. "The Americans," complained Villiers, "have a habit of assuming the propriety and legality of something they do, which if done by anyone else they would regard as highly illegal and unethical. . . . The difficulty is that the

Americans are itching for a fight with the neutrals on this issue." The Americans, he said, did not understand the consequences: "This will go far in wrecking any chance of success which the Rubin proposal may have."

Rubin had already received a blast of Swiss anger. Over dinner on September 13 with Ernst Schneeberger, a friendly Swiss diplomat in Washington, Rubin was lectured about Swiss neutrality. "It's no different," said Schneeberger, "from America's during the First and the early part of the Second World War."

"What about Switzerland's supplies of guns to the Nazis?" asked Rubin.

"Switzerland had proposed to ban all weapons supplies on September 1, 1939," replied Schneeberger, "but the British and French governments protested that they needed Swiss supplies. So Switzerland changed its policy. Afterward, as a neutral, Switzerland had supplied the other side."

Rubin was unimpressed. The Swiss always wriggled out of their embarrassment by rejoining with a counterembarrassment. Justifying equal treatment of the Nazis and the Allies revealed the questionable quality of Swiss morality. The Allies' sanctions were ludicrously described by the Swiss as a "heavy moral burden," while Stucki's moral victory over the bankers in July had proved to be pyrrhic.

In Bern, James Mann was dismayed. At a crisis meeting in the embassy, the Safehaven experts listed all Switzerland's broken pledges. The promised census and freeze on German property, said Mann, was "a joke." While Schwab's officials in the Compensation Office ignored all the evidence of Swiss nationals' collaboration and their profiting from deception, the Germans were blatantly concealing or selling their property. The Swiss were antagonistic and clearly approved of dishonesty. Compounding the insult, Swiss officials and ministers constantly uttered assurances to American diplomats that Switzerland had not become a safe haven for loot or war criminals and then accused the Allies of waging war against Switzerland. The facts, complained Mann, suggested the contrary: "Switzerland's policy is to stall as long as they possibly can." At the end of the meeting, it was agreed that a telegram would be sent to Washington urging a protest, with the threat of sanctions if the Swiss refused to comply.

Brigadier General B. R. Legge, the U.S. military attaché in Bern, was also furious. The Swiss, Legge reported, were "guilty of dilatoriness and evasion amounting to bad faith in carrying out the provisions of the Currie agreement regarding blocking of German assets." German property, supposedly "frozen," was being sold by Swiss middlemen for ridiculously small amounts, while the census of German assets was "inadequate." Even property that had clearly been looted was not being returned to its owners, complained Legge. Banks were refusing to open safe-deposit boxes known to contain the Nazis' loot, and while Swiss government officials advised claimants to assert their rights through the tortuous and expensive processes of the civil courts, the possessors were encouraged to sell the loot. The Swiss, he said, were "playing a delaying game," pleading an inability to modify the five-year limitation on claims just to protect the guilty, hoping that the Allies would tire of the effort. Washington's resolve, he protested, was weakening. Instead of threatening to impose an embargo on Switzerland, Washington had authorized increased Swiss imports of coal and food. Legge's protest was circulated in the State Department: "Swiss violations of both the letter and the spirit of the Currie agreement have been multiple and frequent." But the veracity of Legge's complaint about Switzerland's "bad faith" was questioned. Proof, commented John Birch, a State Department official determined to restrain the Treasury crusaders, was needed.

Birch was holding back a message drafted by Orvis Schmidt to the Bern legation. Critical of Swiss dishonesty, Schmidt suggested an "overall, final approach" to the Swiss with a list of demands and the threat of sanctions. Birch castigated Schmidt's accurate draft as exaggerated. There was, he advised Rubin, "little value in sending this to Bern." Sensitive to the change of mood in the department following the first serious disagreements with the Soviet Union concerning the government of Germany, Rubin agreed: "I feel strongly that this should not be sent."

Still waiting for a reply to his protest, Mann watched the change of attitude and policy within the embassy. Daniel Reagan, the economic counselor, had been replaced by Harry Conover, an outright opponent of Safehaven and a critic of the Currie mission. Mann's fierce rows with Conover had become a regular feature of embassy life. The "relaxation on our part," Mann wrote to Harry White, was causing Safehaven's "deterioration." Mann's new culprits were the British, alias the "weak sisters." Sir Clifford Norton and Gerald Selous, the new commercial secretary, he wrote, were deliberately "dragging their heels" on Safehaven and spreading rumors that encouraged the Swiss to believe that "the Allies do not mean business." With distaste, Mann observed Norton being "very clever," smilingly offering Switzerland an easy ride and soft-pedaling Britain's antagonism toward Petitpierre because "goodwill and trade" had come to matter more to the British than the wartime objectives. Bluntly, Britain's motives for adopting "undermining tactics," Mann believed, were associated with its negotiations to obtain a loan from Switzerland.

Mann's despairing assessment was justified. To avoid seeming antagonistic, Norton had objected to any threats of sanctions and himself informally approached Petitpierre on October 12, 1945. Speaking as "an old friend of Switzerland," Norton said that he was "disturbed" by the lack of Swiss cooperation and by the absence of Swiss "frankness" about German property. Understanding the background to Norton's self-restraint, Petitpierre appreciated the advantage of encouraging the split between the Allies. There had been "a good deal of delay," the foreign minister admitted, blaming "disagreements" among the Compensation Office, the bankers and the lawyers about releasing the names of depositors and clients. Norton was unperturbed. Petitpierre's sympathy for the bankers was barely disguised and that, Norton believed, was to Britain's advantage.

Petitpierre's relations with financiers were close (one of his brothers was a banker, the other a speculator). The revolving door between the Political Department and Switzerland's banks was well established. Petitpierre regarded Peter Vieli of Crédit Suisse, a former Political Department official, and the other former civil servants who had become employees of the Bankers Association as confidants and associates rather than adversaries. Instinctively, he relied upon bankers, more educated about the real world than government officials, for information, even about the attitudes of foreign governments. Bankers were trusted ambassadors. Particularly pertinent for Britain—and this explained Norton's sweet talk—was the recent report by Albert Nussbaumer, a Swiss banker who had negotiated on behalf of the Bankers Association in Washington in 1944. In August 1945, during a visit to London, Nussbaumer had called at the Treasury. In a conversation with Hugh Ellis-Rees, the banker was told about Britain's "friendly attitude" toward Switzerland. Nussbaumer's report, mentioning the bankrupt nation's hunger for credit, finally arrived on Ernst Weber's desk at the National Bank. Weber approved financial support for Britain, a gratifying decision that would not be forgotten in London. Securing that sympathy was Norton's motive in resisting James Mann and cosseting Petitpierre. However, even Petitpierre was unaware that the evidence substantiating Mann's outraged claims about Swiss crimes had actually been secured by his own Compensation Office, under its director Max Schwab.

Suspecting that Swiss bankers, lawyers and corporations were disobeying the law, Schwab, as a dutiful official, sought to discover the cause of the "disagreements" that Petitpierre had mentioned to Norton. In particular, Schwab wanted to know whether Mann's allegations about the bankers were true. Without telling Petitpierre, he placed telephone taps on a network of suspected Swiss bankers and lawyers. Within weeks, the transcripts confirmed that Swiss bankers and lawyers were helping Germans to hide their property. These isolated instances, Schwab assumed, reflected a widespread conspiracy. He knew that his evidence, in unpatriotic hands, would explode Petitpierre's facade of concerned assurances that the Compensation Office was trying "to fulfill its extensive and difficult task." Therefore, he decided, the discovery would not be revealed to outsiders—not even, for the moment, to Petitpierre.

Marooned and frustrated on the outside, Orvis Schmidt of the

U.S. Treasury's Foreign Funds Control, in the midst of a new visit to Switzerland, was incensed by his latest discoveries. There were, he had counted, 214 German-controlled companies in Switzerland. Probably there were many more, and none of them had been brought under the Allies' control. Switzerland's secrecy laws, he fumed, were concealing the truth—that the German giants were "honeycombing" the continent with their secret investments. Summoning journalists, he warned that, if Switzerland created difficulty, it was "imaginable" that the Allies would seize Swiss assets in Germany worth $4 billion. The crusaders had declared war.

"America's terrorizing the neutrals," commented Villiers, shaken by the prospect of strife. On October 30, 1945, Allied Law No. 5 was approved in Berlin, confiscating all German property in Switzerland. Only the property belonging to refugees, especially Jews, was exempted from seizure and sale. Overnight, dozens of Swiss lawyers, bankers and businessmen slipped across the border into Germany to consult clients about protecting their property. While Villiers fretted in London, James Mann, delighted by the crusade's new potency, traveled in early November to an American prison camp for senior Nazis in Germany to find embarrassing evidence that would disabuse the good burghers of Bern if they believed that the war had been fought to make "the world safe for Swiss embroideries." In a drafty wooden hut, Mann met Emil Puhl, the Reichsbank's deputy director. Surrounded by suspected war criminals with good reasons to hide their wartime activities, Puhl was by contrast unashamedly forthcoming. To Mann's delight, the banker boasted that during his negotiations in Bern earlier that year the Swiss had been eager to "maintain a friendly relationship" with the Reichsbank "in the future"—meaning after the war—and had knowingly accepted looted gold. That admission, Mann knew, was an invaluable prize to be treated with care as Swiss behavior became murkier.

On November 30, Mann, Selous and Marcel Vaidie, the French representative, met Schwab in Zurich to hear about the census of German assets. The divisions among the Allies were more evident than ever. While the French simply sought to extract the highest sum of money from Switzerland, Selous had recently complained to London that British ambivalence on Safehaven was producing the "worst of both worlds." Max Schwab was also in a predicament: there was government policy and there was the truth. A group of journalists had just been reassured by him that the Allies' doubts about Switzerland's goodwill were, "with a clear conscience, unjustified." The Compensation Office, he insisted, possessed "far-reaching powers" to ferret out concealed funds and plug any loopholes. Supported by new laws, homes would be searched and safe-deposit boxes, now blocked, would if necessary be forcibly opened. But in his conversation with the three Allies, Schwab admitted a different story. The hunt was failing, he confessed, because few were telling the truth and the banks were saying nothing at all.

Unsympathetic toward Schwab's dilemma, Mann angrily accused the Swiss of lying. The Compensation Office, he said, was allowing the Jews, the innocents, to suffer while protecting the looters. Schwab urged patience. A new law, he explained, to be published on December 10, would allow the legal owners of looted property the right to reclaim their assets even if the possessor had obtained them in good faith. Some of the problems encountered by the Jews, inextricably entwined with the Allies' demand for German assets in Switzerland, would be solved. The reality, Schwab knew, was different. Destitute German Jewish refugees were being used as a tool to defeat the Allies, and the government's intention was to inflame their plight. Among the victims would be Walter Garten.

Garten, a German Jew from Berlin, had arrived in Switzerland in 1945 from a concentration camp, intending to live in his house in Zurich and to use savings, deposited in a Swiss bank, to recover his health. To his surprise, Compensation Office officials told him that, in compliance with Allied requests and Allied Law No. 5, all German accounts and assets in Switzerland were frozen. Listed for seizure and confiscation by Schwab's office were Garten's home and bank deposit, immune over the previous twelve years from the Nazis. Schwab's edict, based, the Swiss official asserted, on an honest interpretation of the law, had struck the most vulnerable Germans—those

100,000 Jews who had survived the camps. Finding their homes destroyed or denied access to their property by the new residents, they were forced to live in Displaced Persons camps, anxious to build new lives in other countries. Sick survivors of Auschwitz, some even waiting in Switzerland for emigration to Palestine, were left penniless, unable to pay for their tickets to escape the Swiss. Schwab's other victims were among the 150,000 German Jews who had emigrated to Britain, the United States and Latin America, leaving property, insurance policies, shares and savings in Switzerland. Everything was being seized, and the legal excuse was an Allied law intended to confiscate German property and loot to fund the rebuilding of Europe and finance relief for sick refugees.

Allied Law No. 5 had targeted for confiscation the property of "Germans in Germany," meaning those Germans resident in Germany on February 16, 1945, the day the Swiss decree froze all Germany property. The American lawyers who drafted the law had neither intended nor anticipated that German Jews would be affected. Not only were all persecutees specifically excluded on moral grounds, but a Nazi law in 1941 had deprived all German Jews of their nationality—so in 1945 they were stateless. Schwab, encouraged by the Political Department and the banks, denied that interpretation. The Allies, he claimed, had revoked that Nazi law, so the stateless Jews were once more German. Hence a German Jew incarcerated in Dachau or Buchenwald was, under Schwab's definition, "resident in Germany" in February 1945. Naturally, American lawyers protested. The Allied law, they countered, had repealed the Nazi law but was not retrospective. Stateless Jews were not reinstated as Germans. Schwab was not persuaded. Declaring that mass denaturalization was contrary to Swiss law and therefore invalid, he had decided to ignore the 1941 decree as proof of statelessness and to create legal obstacles for the Jews. Each refugee was obliged to present the original Nazi decree depriving that named individual of his or her German nationality. Without that document, said Schwab, the property of the Jew would be frozen and eventually sold. Insensitively, all individual investigations were delegated to the Swiss police, the same

organization that had expelled over 30,000 Jews across the border
into the custody of the Gestapo.

"As a Jew, I suffered but survived the war," wrote Richard
Mathius from Berlin to President Truman, "but I am now destitute
except for my savings of SF10,000 in Switzerland. I cannot get at
them. It is causing me great suffering which I, as a victim of Hitler, do
not deserve. Can you help me?" As the pleas for help from anguished
Jews arrived in Washington, Rubin and the other crusaders were
dumbfounded. Having lost their relatives, Jews were now being
denied their property. German Jews were suffering the same discrimination as the worst German Nazi, except that Swiss sympathizers
were helping the Nazis to circumvent the rules. Tens of thousands of
homes, businesses, valuables and bank accounts, looted by Nazis,
were enjoyed by the criminals while their victims remained penniless
and destitute, often even unable to leave Germany. The pledges to
Currie had been ignored.

The Swiss, Rubin suspected, were callously intending to use the
property of German Jews as German assets, available for reparations
or, even worse, to repay Nazi Germany's debt to Switzerland. "It's
immoral," he cried, echoing the desperation of many. "German Jews
who became stateless do not want their German nationality
restored." Switzerland, he protested, should be compelled to cease
punishing the Jews. The implications for the heirless assets were terrible. Under Switzerland's new rules, the Jews' money, deposited in
Swiss banks, was to be used to pay off Germany's debts to
Switzerland. The murderers of the Jews would profit from their
crime. Alternatively, if the Swiss did not hand over the heirless assets
to Germany's creditors, the money would be taken by the Swiss
banks.

Rubin urgently addressed Schwab's deputy, Max Ott, a lawyer
specializing in foreign currency. "It was never intended," he insisted,
"that the persecuted should be affected by the Allied law." Individual
Jews, he pleaded, could not prove their statelessness, because the
Nazis had deprived most Jews of their nationality collectively rather
than by individual orders. Surely that fact, Petitpierre's officials were

challenged, was provable, just as it was possible to establish whether a German was a former member of the Nazi Party or the SS—the intended targets of the law. Ott was adamant. "It's impossible," he replied, "to distinguish between those Germans who had been persecuted and the others."

Ott did not reveal that some weeks earlier the Compensation Office had proposed to exclude the property of German Jews from confiscation. Its initiative had been decried by those Swiss interested in protecting the Germans. The pro-Nazi lobby calculated that discriminating against Jews—by refusing to distinguish between Jews and Nazis—would benefit the campaign against the Allie's confiscation of German assets and the protection of banking secrecy.

Championing that discrimination against the German Jews was the secretive office within the Political Department called the German Interests Section, or DIV. Based at 78 Willadingweg in Bern, the DIV had been established on May 9, 1945, to care for the interests of Germany against the Allies. Indicative of its intentions, its second director was Dr. Hans Frölicher, the former Swiss ambassador in Berlin, whose appointment was confirmed only after the original candidates, anti-Nazi Germans, had been rejected as untrustworthy. During his service in Berlin, Frölicher had regularly complained to Bern about any Swiss newspaper article he deemed to be unsympathetic toward the Nazis and on his return to Bern, mourning past glories, he made no attempt to disguise his regret about Hitler's downfall. Protecting German interests against the Allies was his final tribute to the old Reich.

Ostensibly, Frölicher's duty was to care for the property of German railways, German diplomatic buildings and other state-owned assets in Switzerland. But he extended his remit to include caring for the interests of the 20,000-member pro-Nazi *Deutsche Kolonie* living in Switzerland, the Nazi sanatoria in Davos, the German assets demanded by the Allies, and all the valuables and loot owned by Germans hidden across the country. Legally, the whole fortune had been frozen by the decree of February 16, 1945, and ought to have been transferred to the control of the Compensation

Office. But, to Frölicher's satisfaction, he regularly received from Stucki's office the minutes and reports of the joint commission appointed to implement the Currie agreement. Glancing through the records, he could spot those German interests requiring protection and argue that the property targeted by the Compensation Office was owned by Swiss nationals rather than German, or he could endorse a bank's refusal to release any assets. Unlike German Jews, who were denied any assistance in finding their property, Aryan Germans found that Frölicher assisted their cause, not least by urging Stucki and Schwab not to distinguish between Germans and German Jews. "That prevents any harsh treatment of the Germans," explained the official, pushing at an open door among his colleagues in the Political Department, who were nonchalantly shrugging off criticism that prominent Nazis resident in Switzerland were receiving better treatment than the Jews. With the department's blessing, Frölicher wanted money intended for Europe's reconstruction and for the Jewish refugees to help unrepentant Nazis enjoying Switzerland's security and comfort.

Switzerland's perpetuation of wartime discrimination particularly struck the Swiss Association of Jewish Refugees. Writing to Petitpierre, the association's president asked the minister to explain one incongruity. "During the war," he wrote, "the Swiss police had effortlessly identified every single Jew. Why is it now so difficult to do the same?" Moreover, before and during the war the Swiss had applied Nazi racial laws to decide whether an individual was a Jew. Why did Switzerland not now want similarly to accept the Nazis' Nationality Law of 1941? After all, the Swiss government had accepted and applied that very same law during the war. "Public authorities must remain consistent," mocked the association, "and cannot change their position!" The anonymous official in the Political Department who read the letter recorded his reaction. In the margin of the letter, alongside the association's plea that "surely the declaration by an individual that he is Jewish can suffice," he scoffed. "That would suit the Jews very well!"

Max Schwab was uneasy about the confusion. To seek a resolution he met Political Department officials on September 10. Personally, he explained, while he rejected the argument that German Jews had lost their nationality, he was prepared to allow limited exceptions to the freeze: namely, for the Jews but not for anti-Nazi Germans. Each application, however, would require investigation, and the decisions would not be publicized. Initially, that proposal was opposed by Robert Jezler, of the Police Department, who shared Heinrich Rothmund's anti-Semitism. Effectively, Schwab's initiative was vetoed. But, unexpectedly, one month later, Jezler changed his mind. The banks, which had sought to profit from the Jews, were one source of his disorienting somersault.

In 1942, the Volksbank, deluded by the myth that the Jews were rich and the bank's earnings would be enhanced by a windfall, had volunteered to accept deposits from all those Jewish refugees allowed to remain in the country. The bank had been surprised and disappointed. The Jews' deposits were small. In the summer of 1945, to recover its anticipated profits, the bank had imposed exorbitant fees for administering the deposits, by then inaccessible because of the freeze. The police had become irate and frustrated. Wanting to drive the Jews out of Switzerland as fast as possible, Jezler had become obstructed in the execution of his policy by the foreigners' excuse that it was impossible for them to travel unless they had access to their money. Reversing his argument, Jezler wrote to Schwab on October 12 that the Jews were not intended to be targets of the freeze and that the banks, rather than extorting money, should show "generosity" to anti-Nazis. The Compensation Office "should adopt a more open-minded and generous policy." The freeze was not intended to harm the Jews, and it would be "politically and morally justified" to release all of their assets just as the Jewish groups requested. "If we accept that solution, we avoid treating identically the tyrants and their victims," wrote the former persecutor of Jews, who nevertheless explained that the police would "not find it easy" to identify a Jew. Jezler's final argument hinted at the source of his reversal: "Financially it's not very important. Only a few of the refugees possess more than SF20,000." Banking secrecy existed within clearly defined limits.

To settle the confused dispute, Schwab asked two eminent professors to submit their interpretations of the law. To his discomfort, their opinion supported the Jews. Dr. Hans Reisser, a retired government lawyer, submitted that Switzerland had always accepted the validity of Nazi laws and that during the war the statelessness of the Jews had been recognized by Swiss law. Switzerland, he added, had even exempted the Jews expelled by the Nazis from the laws freezing their funds. Accordingly, the Jews were still stateless and no Jewish property, he advised, should be frozen. Clearly puzzled by the debate, Reisser added, "In June [1945] we agreed that it would be wrong for stateless Jews also to lose their assets. . . . It was also agreed that stateless people should be free to ask the DIV for new passports which would be stamped 'stateless.'" Uninfluenced by political pressure, Reisser resisted the abandonment of Switzerland's traditional posture of rigid adherence to the law.

Supporting his colleague, Dr. Adolf Schnitzer, the second lawyer consulted, recommended that Switzerland should rely on the refugees' declaration of Jewishness. Reading that advice, an anonymous official in the Political Department commented in pencil, "Never rely on them." The cheating Jews, he declared, should never be trusted.

Disquieted by the absence of legal endorsement, Schwab summoned a conference at the Hotel Bernerhof on December 17 to establish the government's policy. Initially tilting toward alternate sides of the fence, at the end of the day, supported by the pro-Germans in the Political Department, he chose to ignore the lawyers' advice. The freeze, it was decided, would apply to all Jews and anti-Nazis—although, depending on any proof provided, there could be exceptions. Effectively, the Holocaust was to be disregarded and Switzerland's wartime policy toward "stateless" Jews would be reversed. Jews and Nazis were to be treated identically.

8

THE PAWNS

Salvation for the Jews depended upon Moses Abramovitz, the thirty-three-year-old New York economist and crusader, still inspired by Roosevelt's legacy. In July 1945 at Potsdam, Abramovitz had argued that 2 percent of reparations, including the German assets in Switzerland, should be used to relieve the plight of Europe's refugees. Four months later, on November 9, he arrived in Paris for a conference of fourteen nations to establish, in accordance with Article 8 of the Potsdam Agreement, a Commission on Reparations. His ambition was to secure the allocation of money "for the rehabilitation and resettlement of non-repatriable victims of German action"—namely, the Jews.

The leader of the United States delegation, James Angell, a professor of economics at Columbia, was not much committed to the ideal of helping Jews. Fortunately, Angell relied upon his deputy, Abramovitz, for advice, to write his speeches and to negotiate the agreement with the other nations. Since all the other nations had suffered financial hardship from the war and were instinctively loath to approve any reduction of their share of reparations from Germany, their sympathy for refugees could not, Abramovitz knew, be assumed. "We're doing our best," he told the lobbyist of the Jewish Agency, perpetually prowling the corridors and berating the American delegates with the image of helpless Jews suffering in the camps, "but there are thirteen other countries here who don't want to see their share of the pot reduced."

The other delegates had arrived with varying antagonisms and prejudices. Abramovitz's tactic was to arouse their emotions by composing tear-inducing speeches for Angell about the death camps, the gas chambers and the discovery by the American army of hoards of wedding rings and gold fillings extracted from the corpses and abandoned by the SS in caches and Reichsbank vaults. "The emotion will change them," Abramovitz promised. Although the investigators estimated the value of that nonmonetary gold to be no more than $5 million, it was a symbol of inhumanity that would neutralize the most selfish demands. That gold if no other, it was agreed, belonged to the stateless Jews. To that money the Americans added the heirless assets.

Mention of the extermination camps always affected David Waley, the Treasury official, but Whitehall's instructions to the British representative were to oppose reparations for Jews and to condemn special pleading for the victims of Nazism. There were, Waley was briefed to argue, far fewer stateless refugees than suggested and, while stateless persons should be given special help, their numbers should be reduced, not least by sending German and Austrian Jews back home "if possible." Embarrassed by the prejudice shown by his London colleagues, Waley had been limited to uttering a private caution. The Americans, he warned, "obviously attach considerable importance" to the proposals submitted earlier by Sy Rubin and Chaim Weizmann, the president of the Jewish Agency, and the British should resist opposition unless there were "really strong reasons."

Rubin had returned to London in September to discuss the fate of the heirless assets. Still unaware that most of the heirless assets in Switzerland did not originate with German Jews and therefore did not fall under the Safehaven program, Rubin suggested to Jack Troutbeck that the Allies could assume that the heirless assets were "almost entirely" the property of German Jews, and should negotiate to obtain that money entirely for the benefit of the increased number of 250,000 destitute and stateless Jews languishing in the Displaced Persons camps.

Rubin's proposal, initially welcomed, was followed by a long and emotional letter to the Foreign Office from Chaim Weizmann. After reciting the unprecedented suffering of the Jews, the murder of six million, and the loss of assets worth "over £2 billion," Weizmann turned to the heirless assets in Switzerland. "It should need no argument," he suggested, "to prove that property rendered masterless by crime should not . . . fall to the governments which committed the crimes, or to any other governments, or to strangers having no title to it." He asserted that those properties "belong to the victim and that victim is the Jewish people as a whole." Up to that point, Troutbeck could accept Weizmann's argument. Although there was no reason in law to regard the surviving Jews as "heirs" of those who perished, Troutbeck could divine no reason to prevent the heirless assets from passing to the Jews. But Weizmann's conclusions were anathema. "The heirless assets," the Zionist insisted, "should be used to help Jews settle in Palestine." Similarly, any reparations from Germany, such as machinery, he proposed, should also be sent to Palestine.

The suffering of the Jews had not awakened much emotion in the Foreign Office during the war, and in the aftermath the sympathy had, if anything, declined. Unwilling to antagonize the Arabs, the Foreign Office opposed Jewish emigration to Palestine while lamenting Britain's slender prospects of extracting a share of the German assets in Switzerland to alleviate its financial predicament. "I feel little confidence that there will be anything for the U.K. by way of reparations from Switzerland," complained Playfair in the Treasury. "If the Swiss succeed in keeping all the German assets, we shall have to give up more than our fair share of what becomes available to other claimants." Yet he declared a "natural and personal sympathy" for Weizmann. While characterizing as "fictional" Weizmann's description of the Jews as "a nation," he nevertheless believed that the U.S. proposal to use the reparations for refugees was "realistic" and possessed "great attractions" for winning public support. "It corresponds," Playfair wrote, "to a strong sense of natural justice." Giving money to Jews in Palestine, he told Foreign Office officials, should be considered in a positive spirit in the interest of fairness.

Playfair's entreaties fell on deaf ears. Rubin's and Weizmann's "monstrous suggestions" were condemned as "special pleading," and as having "dangerous implications" for other claimants whose prospect of "having to compete with the Jews would be rather alarming." Weizmann's combination of heirless assets, reparations and Palestine drove Whitehall into opposing the allocation of any reparations, including the heirless assets, to the Jews. The mood in Whitehall became unremittingly hostile.

New submissions to the Foreign Office by Jewish refugee organizations and the Board of Deputies of British Jews about the rights and interests of the German Jews and the need for general assistance to Jews were perfunctorily acknowledged. Compensation to Jews for their losses out of reparations, minuted H. S. Gregory, "has no logical justification whatever the sentimental appeal may be. In fact it would mean that we should be paying for what the Nazis did." Jack Coulson argued that Britain should seize all German-owned property in Britain to pay off German debts, including property owned by German Jews. Disdaining any help for the German Jews, Gregory encouraged his colleagues "to keep out of this as long as you can." German Jews, he thought, should be pushed back into Germany. Troutbeck's replies to the Jewish organizations, acknowledged only after long delays, blamed "administrative conditions" for failing to implement their "difficult" requests.

To encourage the Jews to return to their homes and so limit their claim on reparations, the Foreign Office disputed the existence of "stateless Jews." Within the Foreign Office, officials had agreed in June 1945 that the Jews had never lost their nationality because the Nazi law of 1941 had been revoked—an opinion that was conveniently shared by Max Schwab and the Swiss government. Nothing was publicly said about that assumption, but after the submissions by Rubin and Weizmann had been categorized as "a mistake," the Foreign Office's policy became uncompromising: there were "extremely few truly stateless persons" in Europe. Accordingly, a request by the Jewish Agency to meet British officials was rejected and Weizmann's letter remained unanswered.

Outraged by the British suggestion of forcibly sending German Jews back to live among their persecutors, Abramovitz sought allies to defeat Whitehall's bigotry. His best ally, he discovered, was Waley. The Englishman understood that ultimately his Whitehall masters would be compelled to bow to American pressure and, after consulting Playfair, confided to Abramovitz that Whitehall's retreat depended upon Angell's persuading all the governments concerned of America's resolution to obtain money for the Jews.

Abramovitz's problem was Angell's inability to deliver a fluent speech that would persuade the doubters and the antagonists, especially the British. His solution was to seek Waley's help. While they were closeted together in a solitary office, the Englishman composed the speech that the American delegate would deliver to influence the Foreign Office in London. The result was an unapologetic plea by Angell for the survivors of the Holocaust: "It would be neither just nor humane to insist that Germans and Austrians who had to flee from their homes because of political or religious persecution should now return to live among the people who persecuted them so bitterly and who are responsible for the murder of so many of their relatives or political associates." Equally, it would be wrong, said Angell, to repatriate Jews from Eastern Europe forcibly: they would be threatened if they returned to their communist-dominated countries.

Angell proposed that $25 million should be allocated to the stateless refugees, to be financed by using all the nonmonetary gold found in Germany and 0.5 percent of the German assets secured in the neutral countries. The neutrals, especially Switzerland, were to be asked to hand over German assets and the "funds deposited . . . by victims of Nazi action who have since died and left no heirs." To assuage the British, although Jews would be entitled to 90 percent of the money, the directive to the international committee to be established to administer the fund would omit any mention of migration to Palestine. Twelve nations were persuaded by Angell. Only the British seemed to be opposed.

Faced with isolation, Waley was reluctantly instructed by London to support Angell's scheme and to renounce any suggestion of forcible repatriation of Jews. The agreement, pledging $25 million and the heirless assets to Jewish refugees, was signed on December 21. Privately, some British officials were furious. The Jews, remarked Gregory of the agreement, would not be satisfied with just $230 for each refugee, and the "blackmail from the Jewish community in the States will begin all over again." The agreement and the negotiations with Switzerland, he added, raised "concern" about those American officials "imbued with some spirit of the Crusaders, inclined to see sinister figures and machinations at every turn." With the approval of like-minded colleagues, he condemned the crusaders for sitting in judgment on the Swiss. Among the crusaders automatically included in Gregory's condemnation was Bernard Feig, the U.S. Treasury representative in London responsible for Safehaven.

Feig was sitting in judgment not only on Switzerland but also on Britain. Safehaven was in "crisis," he believed, and the prospects of success were "rapidly diminishing." The blame, he thought, lay with Switzerland's sabotage and dishonesty. The Swiss undoubtedly felt "smug" reading British press reports that there was no risk of sanctions. The sweetening atmosphere toward Switzerland was evidenced in the U.S. Treasury report of an elaborate luncheon hosted in Zurich in January 1946 by Peter Vieli, the director of Crédit Suisse, in honor of Lauchlin Currie. Vieli spoke eloquently about Switzerland's loyal contribution to Europe's peace and reconstruction, and yet in 1940 he had signed a petition urging the Swiss government to show greater sympathy toward the Nazis. Pertinently, Crédit Suisse, like Switzerland's other banks, still refused to seize German assets and loot. Even the British, Feig knew, had evidence of that rebuff.

Gerald Selous, the commercial counselor at the British embassy in Bern, had asked the Political Department about the results of the "opening of safe deposits" as promised by Stucki and ordered by a decree issued on November 30, 1945. Selous also asked for the results of the census of German assets: the bank accounts, shares, gold, jewelry, works of art, patents, businesses and property. Schwab's reply was familiar, although his tone had become markedly more unyielding. The census, he explained, was delayed because some German-owned companies valued their property at just SF1 and because lawyers and bankers refused to breach the secrecy laws. Even though Schwab parroted the line that the banks showed "no bad faith," he knew that they would readily abandon the secrecy laws if it was deemed politically expedient. For example, Bernhard Sarasin, the new president of the Bankers Association, would disclose to Petitpierre the accounts of the Parti du Travail, the left-wing radicals, because the indiscretion served the banks' political interests.

Those double standards, Feig observed, extended to the Switzerland's treatment of the stateless Jews. Claimants, seeking to retrieve their property under the new rules, were finding that Swiss officials ignored not only the official Nazi documents proving their statelessness, but even existing documents in Swiss police files. The exemptions from the new rules promised to persecuted Jews were proving to be a farce; meanwhile the non-Jewish Germans were protected. To combat the Swiss, Feig had sought allies in Whitehall, sounding out W. A. Brandt at the Ministry of Economic Warfare on the possibility of publicly raising the threat of sanctions. Brandt's rejection of this idea had been abrupt, and diplomats in the American embassy had resisted Feig's entreaties to exert pressure on the British. In desperation, he wrote to Washington suggesting that President Truman appeal to Clement Attlee, the British prime minister, to join in issuing a threat to impose sanctions on Switzerland. His recommendation was ignored. The omens for the impending showdown between the Allies and Switzerland were not encouraging for the crusaders.

9

WASHINGTON SHOWDOWN

In the early days of March 1946, Walter Stucki, director of Switzerland's Political Department, was more verbose, more agitated and more aggressive than usual. Snapping at his subordinates and lording it over his political master Max Petitpierre, Stucki was preparing for his appearance in the spotlight. In an unexpectedly cold, formal manner, the American government had invited Switzerland to send a delegation to Washington to negotiate a settlement of the outstanding differences: the Allies' demand for the heirless assets, the Nazi loot, the gold and the German property. For all sides, it was the moment of truth, the moment of reckoning. Stucki, the self-admiring patriot, was steeling himself for a showdown to save his country from the demands of the Anglo-Americans, a breed for whom he felt little affection or respect.

Switzerland faced serious problems. Stocks of coal, grain and raw materials were running low. The freeze on Swiss assets in the United States and the Allies' blacklist of 1,500 Swiss companies had crippled some manufacturers and caused unemployment. Safehaven, the Allies' demand for the heirless assets, the Nazi loot, the gold and the German property, could damage the Swiss economy. During their preparatory discussions, Professor William Rappard, the American-educated economist at Geneva University, cautioned Stucki, "We should resist the Allies on everything." That, Stucki felt, was self-evident. Defiance was his maxim.

Stucki's instructions, formulated under his own influence, were to negotiate the end of the Allies' controls, to protect the Swiss economy and to prevent Switzerland from bearing any burden arising from the war. Banking secrecy was to be defended. The heirless assets, the Nazi loot and the gold were not to be surrendered, and he was to defy every demand to liquidate the German assets. Switzerland, Stucki was told, would never recognize the Allies' claims to German assets. "We are not tolerating the confiscation of property belonging to people who have trusted Switzerland," the traditionalists told him. Swiss sovereignty and neutrality could not be infringed. He would even refuse to distinguish between genuine German property and loot, stolen by Nazi thugs and squirreled away by Swiss accomplices.

There was, Stucki was assured by the government's lawyers, "no legal basis for the Allied demands," especially since the Finance Ministry had produced evidence that Switzerland had not been enriched by the war. For that purpose, statistics were being compiled to give the false impression that Switzerland had imported from Germany more than it had exported to Germany. No one in Bern had mentioned, however, that Switzerland had, unlike its neighbors, not become poorer. That reality did not interest Stucki. Anticipating a good fight, he brusquely rejected the idea of offering compensation voluntarily to the Allies. Only as a last resort would he draw on the government's authority to offer as a goodwill gesture between SF200 million and SF250 million toward Europe's reconstruction. But that would be offered, he insisted, only after he had staged a dramatic breakdown in the negotiations.

Until the last moment, Stucki had resisted pressure from the Bankers Association to include a banker in his delegation. "The bankers don't have a good reputation in America," he told Schwab, "and their mission in 1944 didn't have an outstandingly good result." Having secured government support for his disdain, Stucki refused to meet a delegation of bankers before his departure. That chore was to be assigned to others. Schwab endorsed his friend's antipathy. "It's amazing. The bankers now say that they've got 'important information' about the German assets. They've never said a word until now!" But Stucki was warned by Alfred Hirs, the central banker: "We're always going to be Germany's neighbor and we shouldn't allow ourselves to become a tool of the Allies." The bankers, said Hirs, should be included in the delegation. Stucki was contemptuous. The banks, he snapped, refused to obey the government. "Only 400 out of 2,200 safes have so far been opened. We've got to force this issue." But in the hours before his departure, Stucki had been reminded of his status, and Eberhard Reinhardt of Crédit Suisse and another banker had decided to travel to Washington. The banker had little cause to fear Stucki's ambitions. Shortly before flying to Washington, Stucki had been approached by a German who had lived in Switzerland for many years. "If you can protect our fortune," said the German, "then Switzerland would be entitled to one quarter of it." He intended to oblige.

The eleven Swiss delegates, led by Stucki, flew from Zurich, leaving a country that seemed as prosperous as ever. The landscape was unaltered by war, and the shops sold food and luxuries that had still not reappeared across the frontier. Having brilliantly resisted the overwhelming demands of both sides during the war, Switzerland had no intention of succumbing to any threats or of sacrificing its profitable interests—at least not without a bitter fight.

Stucki was greeted in the United States by the *Washington Post*'s description of him as "Al Capone." Randolph Paul, the American representative, a former assistant secretary at the Treasury, was more polite.

Born in upstate New York, Paul, a short, humorless man, was one of America's most prominent tax lawyers who relaxed by chopping wood on his small Maryland estate. He was famous for winning remarkable tax breaks for rich clients and then petitioning Congress to close the loophole he had just exploited. As a tax lawyer Paul had had no experience of negotiating a governmental agreement, although he took comfort from the State Department's briefing—

which was mistaken—that Stucki was "strongly pro-American and pro-British." Paul's guard was also lowered when he found that, contrary to a Foreign Office brief, Stucki also spoke English and French—and by the visitor's opening expressions of humility.

Calculating how to soften Paul's instinctive antagonism, Stucki conceded during their introductory meeting at the State Department that there had been mistrust of Switzerland for the "crime" of not fighting in the war. Disparaging the malicious critics who alleged that Switzerland "harbored sympathies for the Germans," Stucki pleaded that the Allies should recognize Switzerland as the world's "oldest and most freedom-loving democracy." With rising emotion, the Swiss expressed his "dismay" that the Allies mistrusted a "small and economically helpless country" that had not succumbed to Nazism or to any Nazi decree to hand over the property of the nationals of the occupied countries. The law was sacrosanct, he said, and just as Switzerland defied the Nazis to protect foreign-owned property, it was obliged to resist the Allies despite the Allies' good intentions. "Switzerland is a keeper of right and of morality," he concluded. In no way could it be bound by the laws and demands of a foreign country, whether Nazi Germany or the United States. Switzerland's economic survival depended upon protecting those who had faith in the country and invested their assets in it.

"Thank you," replied Paul politely. America could effortlessly suffocate Switzerland's economy, and his two colleagues, Sy Rubin and Orvis Schmidt, were eager to utter such harsh threats in order to extract the loot and the heirless assets. A note to Paul from Fred Vinson, the Treasury secretary, Morgenthau's successor, advocating the threat of sanctions, strengthened their resolve. "It is our view," wrote Vinson, "that without sanctions, no matter how tough we talk, they will know that it is really a bluff and will act accordingly." The only constraints on Paul and the two crusaders were the State Department, unenthusiastic about even threatening sanctions, whose silence was ominous, and the two other Allied negotiators.

Paul Charguéraud, France's temperamental representative, had limited sympathy for the Swiss and especially for Stucki, the friend of

Pétain and Vichy, who symbolized the pro-Nazi inclinations of the Swiss-Germans. Swiss solidarity with the Germans had, in the Frenchman's opinion, never disappeared and was confirmed by Switzerland's concealment of Nazi loot taken from France and traced to Switzerland, transiting occasionally to South America. But the French diplomat knew that, while Stucki would evince similar contempt toward Frenchmen who had opposed Vichy or who posed as brave members of the resistance, his own championing of French interests would be undermined by Paul, whose distaste for France sneaked out in caustic comments.

Paul's animus was not as evident against Francis McCombe, the minor British civil servant from the Economic Warfare Department, whose appointment signaled Britain's lack of interest. The selection of McCombe, an expert on the administration of charities and a passionate tennis player, but no celebrity, was Whitehall's insult to the crusaders. To Rubin's irritation, in their preliminary meetings McCombe emphasized that since Britain's paramount concern was to increase world trade, the remaining restrictions on Switzerland would have to be removed by the end of June. The Labor government's opposition to any sanctions against Switzerland, he said, had been decided "at the very highest level." Sanctions, the British embassy had earlier told the State Department, were "not an appropriate weapon." Those State Department officials who were sympathetic to the crusaders had wanted to summon Lord Halifax, the British ambassador, "and give him a good dressing-down." Their wish was disregarded. Rubin, nevertheless, was aghast. Switzerland had been dragged to Washington only because of the freeze, the blacklist and the threats, and now the British were unapologetically proposing to demolish the armory. An urgent telegram from the American embassy in Bern explained McCombe's instructions. The Swiss government had just agreed that Britain could buy Swiss francs for sterling rather than gold, an important concession for a bankrupt nation. McCombe's only interest, Rubin realized, was to terminate the negotiations promptly with the promise of reparations for Britain from the German assets.

Naturally, Stucki took comfort from the hint of divisions among the Allies, but Paul's introductory remarks raised the tension in the room. Regardless of the principles of neutrality, said the American, it could not be used to "shield the aggressor or his property." America's claim—"rigidly fixed," asserted Paul—was that Germany's assets should be used to "repair the injuries" it had caused. German assets in Switzerland were German, not Swiss, and the only issue was whether the Swiss would cooperate in finding and selling those assets. "The Allies," continued Paul, "are paying millions for food imports to keep the Germans alive. That's a real sacrifice. There is no reason why German assets in Switzerland should not be used to pay for the food."

"We propose," said Paul, "a joint commission to enforce sales and inspect Switzerland's banks and vaults for looted property and gold." Paul was demanding nothing less than direct interference by the Allies in Switzerland's most sacred internal affairs. "Until then," concluded Paul, "sanctions will remain and, if necessary, new ones will be imposed."

Stucki's digestion of Paul's warning was interrupted by McCombe's coos about Britain's "admiration and gratitude" for the Swiss Red Cross and recollections of Britain's "many friends in Switzerland." Charguéraud limited his welcome to similar gratitude for Swiss help during the war. Stucki seized the cue. "Switzerland," he replied, "fully recognizes a great moral obligation toward the innocent victims of this war; she does not deny furthermore that she owes an immeasurable debt of gratitude to the Allies for their victorious efforts." Stressing the humanitarian endeavors already undertaken, he pledged the country to spend more, "although there is no legal but only a moral obligation." The signal of defiance had been given. Feelings of unease had been heightened.

Formal negotiations started on March 22 in the austere, functional atmosphere of Room 1009 in the State Department. To the waiting press, Paul spoke of being "greatly impressed with the cooperative attitude" of Stucki and with his willingness to "get on with the business." Once the doors had closed, the fate of the German assets ignited the first row.

Switzerland's "enormous losses" during the war, said Stucki, totalled SF4 billion, including SF501 million for "war damages" suffered by Swiss nationals. Against that staggering sum, Switzerland claimed all the German assets in Switzerland, worth SF1 billion, including the "contents of safe-deposit boxes" valued at SF76.600.

Paul was convinced of Swiss perfidy, and his reply was abrupt: "Switzerland's claims are most uncertain and of doubtful value." McCombe agreed: "These proposals are not adequate and are unacceptable." Even in the smallest detail, Stucki's declaration was untrue. The contents of the 2,663 safes that had been opened contained SF84 million in cash, and in addition the investigators had found valuable jewelry and paintings whose value had not yet been assessed. Although the dishonesty of Stucki's claim was still unknown to Paul and McCombe, both dubbed the Swiss diplomat with a more appropriate name: "Sticky."

Undeterred, Stucki replayed his emotional lament: "I do not want to hide our great disappointment with the Allied attitude. The miserably strong Allies have various ways of making life difficult for us and eventually we will be forced to concede to any demands. But do not forget Roosevelt's message in Christmas 1943: 'The doctrine that the strong shall dominate the weak is the doctrine of our enemies—and we reject it.'"

"Switzerland's claims," replied Paul sternly, unaffected by the sentimental reference to the president, "must be greatly scaled down." Switzerland was entitled, he conceded, to repayment of some debts, but it would not be allowed to profit from the war. Realizing that agreement would not after all be easy, he saw an advantage in exposing Switzerland's weaknesses: the gold and the loot. "At least $200 million of gold transferred by Germany to Switzerland," he told Stucki, "was looted, although we believe that the real figure is much larger."

Investigations of the Reichsbank's incomplete records by American and French groups had failed to establish precise statistics about the bank's genuine reserves and its loot, but the evidence of Swiss dishonesty was nevertheless conclusive.

In Berlin, William Dunkel, an American attached to the Financial Intelligence Branch of the U.S. military government, had recovered some of the Reichsbank's ledgers. With the help of Albert Thoms, the head of the Reichbank's Precious Metals Department, Dunkel tried to discover the fate of the Belgian gold. Pages from the ledgers had been removed, but he soon established that the gold, delivered to the Reichsbank in twenty-four shipments, had been resmelted over eighteen months. When that chore had been completed in August 1944, with all the ingots date-stamped 1937, their destination was recorded as Switzerland. Dunkel had, however, been unable to establish precisely how much gold had been seized by the Nazis from Austria and Czechoslovakia, or how much gold remained in Germany at the end of the war—in the Reichsbank's vaults and in hiding places. The British estimate was $252 million, while the American estimate was $293 million. But in preparing for the Washington conference the Allies produced credible calculations. Having assumed that at the outbreak of war Germany's gold reserves were worth at most $160 million (although the more likely amount was $120 million), they believed that Reichsbank had acquired during the war between $579 million and $661 million of looted gold: from Belgium $223 million, Holland $161 million, Italy $84 million, Czechoslovakia $50 million, Austria $46 million, Russia $23 million, Poland $12 million, Luxembourg $5 million, and Danzig $4 million, and "large amounts" from private safes and from the Balkan countries, including Yugoslavia.

According to the Reichsbank records, between $398 million and $410 million of gold had been shipped to Switzerland. From Bern, gold worth $138 million had been reexported to Spain and Portugal. On the most conservative estimate—and thus the estimate "most favorable to Switzerland," the National Bank in Bern had accepted "an absolute minimum" of $185 million in looted gold and more probably $296 million.

Included in the looted gold sold to Switzerland was Belgian gold worth $223 million and Dutch gold worth $100 million. Some of that gold was shipped on by the Swiss to Turkey, Spain and Portugal. Of the 3,859 ingots that arrived in Lisbon from Bern, including at least 1,180 Dutch and 673 Belgian bars, 318 were still stored in their original Dutch wrappers. The Portuguese, reported one British investigator, were "visibly worried" because the looted gold lay in the vaults "as if the bank held the Mona Lisa itself without even retouching it." The Portuguese government was adamant in its claim that the gold had been obtained from Switzerland in good faith and refused to approve its return. By contrast, the Spanish government handed over one ton of gold to the U.S. government in December 1945 to be flown immediately to Frankfurt, and kept the remaining seventy-three tons. The Swiss National Bank admitted nothing.

Three flaws had undermined the Allied investigation. First, all the Reichsbank's gold shipments to Liechtenstein were ignored. Second, the Reichsbank's shipment of Dutch gold to Switzerland was wrongly estimated to be $100 million instead of $161 million because the Dutch government was unaware of the facts and the Swiss did not reveal that clearly marked Dutch gold had arrived in Bern. Third, the French investigation was poor. After overlooking some files about the fate of the Belgian gold, the French investigators had ignored the German records describing the conversion of the Dutch gold.

The mistakes and the divergent motives of the three Allied negotiators were sensed by Stucki. The British, uninterested in the gold, caused little anxiety. The French, having compensated the Belgians for the loss of their gold, were obviously troublesome. The Americans, motivated by anger, were campaigning for justice—theirs was the most difficult argument to deflect.

One cause of the Americans' anger was Rappard's broken promise to Currie on March 8, 1945, to restore the looted gold, especially the 110 tons of Belgian gold accepted by Switzerland in 1943 after its rejection by Sweden. Angered by that dishonesty, the U.S. Treasury had wanted to dispatch experts to Bern in December to investigate the National Bank's records and inspect the vaults. The British were appalled by the suggestion. W. A. Brandt had warned John Winant, the American ambassador in London, that approaching the Swiss at that stage would be "a great mistake." The Swiss would never allow foreigners to pry into their secrets. Surprise, he said, would be an "important weapon" in the future negotiations to defeat Switzerland's "incontestable ground that they acquired the gold in good faith as an ordinary business transaction before the allies made their looted-gold declaration." Winant persuaded the Treasury in Washington to agree. Three months later, Paul and Rubin eagerly awaited the chance to expose Switzerland's chicanery.

The Swiss officials arrived in Washington with different degrees of knowledge. Stucki disbelieved allegations that the National Bank had knowingly accepted looted gold. Rappard suspected that it had but was prepared to reject any such allegation by the Allies. The implication that, by melting the looted gold, the Germans must have known that their possession was illegal was ignored. Alfred Hirs knew the truth, not least after a recent detailed briefing from Maurice Frère, the director of the Belgian central bank, but he presented himself as a nonspeaking technician, present merely to give advice. Hirs's position was inflexible: his bank was not guilty and its directors refused even to consider admitting an error. Just before the start of the session on gold, Paul buttonholed Stucki in a corner of the conference room. "Take care," advised the American lawyer. "We can prove that Switzerland knew the gold was stolen." Stucki shrugged. His dislike of Americans and their way of life encouraged him in his skepticism.

Stucki opened with one concession: "We agree that gold worth SF7 million was tainted." The ingots had arrived, following the agreement with Emil Puhl, just before the collapse of Germany. But in reply to Paul's allegation that Switzerland had knowingly accepted over $200 million of looted gold, Stucki was adamant. The gold that the Swiss had accepted during the war from the Reichsbank, worth $376 million (SF1,638 million), was not looted. "Those statistics are wrong," answered Paul dismissively, suspecting a deliberate falsification of Swiss records and a bogus interpretation of the Reichsbank's reserves.

Brushing that riposte aside, Stucki glared at Charguéraud, always sensitive about France's wartime record. Switzerland, said Stucki, did not believe that the Belgian gold had been looted by Germany. France, he charged, had "stolen" Belgium's gold. "We will not recognize," he added, "that a legal or moral obligation is incumbent upon Switzerland or the Swiss National Bank to restore any of that gold." Inflamed by Stucki's fanciful tale, Charguéraud countered, "The Swiss National Bank did not seem to have taken the most elementary precautions before accepting the gold offered by the financial authorities of the Third Reich."

All eyes shifted toward Hirs. Uncomfortable in the spotlight, he mumbled, "I'm not here to defend the National Bank. However, we have never handled looted gold."

The questioning was delegated to Marcel Vaidie of France, the finance attaché in Bern. "Well, how much gold did Switzerland receive, and how did you try to establish its provenance?" he asked.

"I have no evidence that we accepted looted gold, and we have numerous assurances that the gold we received was not looted."

"From whom?" asked Vaidie.

"From Poland, Norway, Yugoslavia and Denmark."

Noticeably unimpressed, Vaidie recited the history of the Belgian gold.

"We didn't know that," said Hirs.

"We've gone through all the German records and we've concluded that Switzerland received at least $200 million of looted gold from Germany. We need details of Switzerland's transactions with Germany."

Stung by the challenge, Hirs dropped the pretense of the humble technician and recounted the statistics of Switzerland's gold trade, adding, "I admit that the Allied warning in 1943 made no particular impression on me." After Morgenthau's February 1944 declaration, warning Switzerland and the neutrals not to buy gold from Germany, Hirs continued, Puhl had been questioned and had "assured us that Germany was not supplying looted gold but was using hidden reserves." Belying the traditional image of a hard Swiss banker, Hirs presented himself as an honest but gullible broker who believed Puhl's estimate that the Reichsbank's "hidden gold reserves" were

worth SF2 billion. But his parting shot displayed remarkable insensi-
tivity and arrogance. The Belgian gold, Hirs speculated, might well
be stored in the United States or France. The atmosphere soured.
The meeting broke up. The Allied negotiators were outraged, but at
the Swiss embassy that evening no one discussed the effect of Hirs's
flippancy. Instead, the conversation reflected the resentment that had
developed among the Swiss about the number of Jews in the
American delegation. Rubin; Oscar Fletcher, the State Department's
gold expert; Walter Surrey; and Warren Silver, also from the State
Department, were all Jewish. "Why do I have to negotiate with Jew-
boy?" exclaimed Stucki, referring to Rubin. Hirs also had remarked
on the "majority of Jews" in the delegation. The resignation of
Morgenthau, they had believed, would "gradually demobilize the
Jewish lobby" and reduce "the aggression." But the anticipated benefits, namely better relations with the Americans, had not materialized. Realizing how impolitic it would be even to hint at their common distaste for the Americans, Stucki decided that Hirs should, the
following morning, instead attack the French.

Hirs opened with the familiar and tedious assertions of
Switzerland's honesty and neutrality and its services to the Allies. As
he moved on to discuss his personal relations with the Nazis, the
atmosphere became charged. "We always regarded Puhl," stated
Hirs, "as a banker whose integrity was above suspicion. He was never
considered to be a thief or even a Nazi in the usual sense. He laughed
at us for believing enemy propaganda about looted gold and gave us
an absolute guarantee that none of the bars being sent to Switzerland
was loot."

Hirs then switched to an assault on a most sensitive spot.
Accusing the French of expecting others to bear the consequences of
their collaboration with the Nazis, he blamed France for the loss of
the Belgian gold. In particular, he blamed de Boisanger, the president
of France's national bank. "He's a well-known collaborator," he
smirked, deriding de Boisanger's wartime visit to Switzerland,
"whose warnings in 1943 were a few general and sketchy indica-
tions," which were rightly discounted as "tactics of deception [when]

practiced by the Germans." Looking at Vaidie, he concluded coolly, "After all our checks during the war and recently, the bank has a clear conscience. The blame is on France and its negligence."

Vaidie's fury was redoubled by the presence of Stucki, the impassioned admirer of Marshal Pétain, whose signed photograph the Swiss official had accepted at the end of France's occupation. The silver-framed photograph now stood on his piano in his home in Bern. Such hypocrisy! Only his secret knowledge prevented Vaidie's anger from exploding. James Mann's interrogation of Puhl was still unknown to the Swiss; and the Swiss were likewise unaware of the discovery of Puhl's letters to Walther Funk, the Reichsbank's president, written during the March 1945 negotiations. Both revealed Switzerland's eager collaboration with the Nazis.

The moment for revealing those secrets had now come. "Just look at the Puhl letters to Funk," Vaidie said. "Look how you collaborated with the Germans." Calming the Frenchman, Albert Robbins, a British lawyer, revealed Puhl's interrogation. Holding out a page to Rappard and Hirs, he read the Reichsbank deputy president's confession that Weber and Hirs—"The second man after Weber," was Puhl's description—had been informed that Germany would include looted gold in the shipments to Switzerland. "You didn't act in good faith," snapped Robbins. "Puhl warned you that some of the gold was looted. You didn't take enough care." A pause was allowed for dramatic effect. "Here's a man who you have repeatedly said was honest."

Taken aback, Hirs nonetheless brushed aside Rappard's request for an adjournment. "Puhl was a decent and honest man," he proclaimed. "Anything he now says should not be believed. Believing Puhl means disbelieving the Swiss." Stony, distrusting faces stared at Hirs. The banker, unaccustomed to any confrontation outside his citadel in Bern, understood what they were accusing him of: that he and his government had reneged on their solemn agreement with Currie.

"Do you want to take 500 million Swiss francs of gold," blurted out Hirs, "and ruin my bank?" That outburst, unexpected and unexplained, caused the atmosphere to freeze. Hirs seemed on the verge of tears. The eight Allied representatives stared across the table in amazement. Until then, no one had suggested that Switzerland should return as much as SF500 million of looted gold. Hirs's anguish only increased his colleagues' embarrassment. Robbins broke the silence. "Your concern about your bank," he said to Hirs with studied gravity, "must be weighed against the suffering of many nations under the greatest tyranny in history."

"We won't need another meeting," interrupted Rappard. "Please supply us with other examples of looted gold."

"You won't need me anymore," muttered Hirs, his eyes now filled with tears. Crestfallen and humiliated, the banker shuffled from the room.

That night, Stucki's rage exploded across the embassy. Even for Paul Jolles, a junior diplomat well used to the official's uncontrolled tempers, the violence of his anger was fearful. "You lied!" Stucki screamed at Hirs.

The banker cowered: "I did lie. I did it to protect you."

The following morning, March 29, Stucki seemed to Paul "badly shaken." An Allied memorandum, delivered during the night, listed Switzerland's receipt of looted gold. "How much gold do you actually want?" asked Stucki. "Just tell us what you think is the correct amount."

"On any hypothesis, at least $200 million of the gold transferred by Germany during the war to institutions in Switzerland was loot," replied Paul. "And that's the most favorable interpretation."

That night, Stucki received another memorandum from Paul. Dressing his speech up with polite acknowledgments of Switzerland's uniqueness, Paul threatened that if there was no agreement the Allies could destroy the Swiss economy and might launch a worldwide propaganda campaign exposing Swiss misdeeds. "This is an arrogance we cannot accept," Stucki ranted to his aides. Jolles stood quietly, realizing the dangers. No American was prepared to speak to the Swiss anymore. "I will not negotiate under threat," shouted Stucki, ignoring the refusal of the Americans to continue the talks until the

Swiss capitulated. Quietly, he had ordered his legal team to seek the advice of Sullivan and Cromwell in New York, where the Dulles brothers were senior partners. Knowing that the Americans derided any notion of Swiss legality, he needed help. The Dulles brothers were proven friends of both the Germans and the Swiss, and their advice would be valuable. But no advice could rescue Stucki from his predicament. It was the moment, he decided, to stage a breakdown of the negotiations.

Some would speculate that Stucki conjured up the crisis in order to stage a return to Bern so that he could write his own instructions. Others would claim that he sincerely needed to obtain a fresh brief from the government. Both ideas were partly right. Stucki returned to Switzerland on March 30 carrying a stinging memorandum from Paul alleging Swiss greed. The crisis was real.

Restrictions on reporting by Switzerland's newspapers meant that few Swiss understood that the three Allies were negotiating on behalf of eighteen nations and that all of them were critical of Switzerland. To the uninformed, Stucki was fighting to protect Switzerland's sovereignty and the sanctity of private property—whatever the sacrifice. Only insiders realized that the deadlock was caused not just by the dispute over the fate of German property but by allegations over the Nazi gold. Even Petitpierre, Marcel Vaidie would later reflect, was probably unaware of the full facts. "The Swiss delegation," he judged, "was not being frank with Bern about the negotiations." The Anglo-Americans were simply bewildered by Stucki's antics.

"We are isolated," Stucki groaned to his colleagues.

"Do you really think a rich man is ever isolated?" responded Hans Schaffner, a government economist, puzzled by Stucki's fear of the Americans. "The National Bank was naive but acted in good faith. The Allies are not very friendly. They don't understand how hard it has been for us. Their behavior is an insult because they're jealous that we survived and they don't acknowledge our bravery." Instructed to tell lies on his own initiative to liquidate the past, Stucki returned to Washington on April 11. Unknown to him, his legacy in Bern was fomenting dissatisfaction.

Soon after Stucki's arrival in Washington, a telegram from Petitpierre announced his demotion. His functions would be reallocated to six sections. The Swiss, as Stucki knew, bore a deep dislike for anyone who enjoyed wielding excessive power. But the more serious mark against Stucki was his distrust of bankers. His principal successor, Alfred Zehnder, was like Petitpierre, sympathetic to the requirements of Switzerland's financiers and less likely to dictate his own terms. The personal humiliation was not reflected in Stucki's performance when he resumed the negotiations.

During the break, reminded by the British that the restrictions on Switzerland would have to be removed within seven weeks, Paul and Rubin became uncertain about their tactics. While the State Department's long silence since the negotiations began confirmed its indifference, some Treasury officials had also become noticeably concerned. Inexperienced in the wiles of diplomacy, Paul had not considered asking the FBI to tap the Swiss telephones to glean an insight into their opponents' strategy—although Stucki would become convinced that his rooms were bugged. As lawyers, Paul and Rubin were motivated only to argue and win their case. Success would be to deliver a deal. The difference between deals among individuals and deals among governments was barely grasped. The two Americans, driven by the conviction that the Swiss had been dishonest, believed that incontrovertible truth would deliver justice. Under pressure, they embarked on a countdown.

At the outset of their next meeting, Stucki resumed his customary defiance. "No blame can justifiably be placed on the Swiss National Bank in connection with its purchases of gold," Stucki told Paul. "Switzerland," he said, had not knowingly accepted looted gold, and any restoration of looted gold would be "solely decided by the Swiss Federal Tribunal," the country's supreme court.

Paul pushed a bundle of papers toward Stucki. "The same gold which Switzerland accepted from Germany had been rejected as suspicious by the Swedes," said Paul softly. Startled, Stucki remained silent. That night, Rappard produced a four-page questionnaire for the Allies to explain in detail the fate of the looted gold. The many details he requested were clearly intended to daunt the Allies and complicate the argument. The answers, explicit and damning, were placed on Stucki's desk within twenty-four hours. His hopes for room to maneuver were disappearing.

Soon after resuming his seat in the conference room on April 13, Stucki uttered a confession. Switzerland, he said, had been mistaken in its belief that Puhl was "a decent and honest man." But even that admission revealed feigned naïveté. Why, asked Stucki, had the Germans gone to such lengths to conceal the origins of the Belgian gold? Paul did not trouble to answer the rhetorical question. He smelled blood. Academic issues were of no interest, he told Stucki: "It's imperative to come to conclusions quickly." Stucki, the realist, suggested an offer. Concessions, he said, like giving the Allies a share of the German assets and "a part of the gold" acquired from Germany after February 1943, depended upon an end to discrimination against Switzerland. Paul nodded. The breakthrough was in sight. But then it disappeared. Switzerland, added Stucki, did not "recognize any legal or moral obligation for the restitution of gold [and] Switzerland has never recognized and is not now prepared to recognize that the Belgian gold was looted by Germany."

Fearing a new deadlock and the disintegration of the Allies' unity, Paul pitched the Allied claim low, just $130 million compensation for the traceable Belgian gold. "This is much more than we expected," said Stucki with puzzling sincerity. His counteroffer, $25 million, was accompanied by a refusal to answer any questions about the movement of gold through Switzerland during the war. "Only Swiss law and the Swiss courts have any jurisdiction over the gold," he muttered as he rose to his feet. "There's no purpose in continuing." The Allies' moderation and their sincere wish to reach an amicable settlement had failed to achieve anything. A leak to American newspapers reported the deadlock. From London, McCombe was instructed, "Half a loaf is better than no bread and you are authorized to agree to any concession which the Americans and French are ready to grant in order to avoid a breakdown."

That night, Rubin sensed for the first time the increasing criticism of the crusaders around Washington, "the fire-eaters in the American agencies angered by any conciliatory spirit." State Department officials were complaining about the crusaders' lust for vengeance. In particular, there were suspicions about the motives of Sam Klaus and others who were expressing their indignation that the American negotiators had not squeezed the Swiss into submission. Influential voices in Washington were hinting that the United States was pushing just a bit too hard. Any discomfort Rubin felt evaporated when, on April 30, he read Switzerland's latest offer, described by Stucki as an "extremely generous . . . voluntary payment." Insisting that there could be "no question" about the National Bank's "good faith" over the Belgian gold, the Swiss admitted liability only for SF150 million ($34 million) of the gold, because that was identifiable and in Switzerland's possession. "Rejected," said Paul, pushed by Rubin into a cliff-hanger. Stucki did not spot the stress or the cracks. Cut off from support in Bern and isolated among his delegation, he had no alternative but to bow and offer something a little more substantial.

The following day, May 1, Switzerland's lofty declarations about the sanctity of private property and its good faith to all nations evaporated. Stucki offered to liquidate all the German assets in Switzerland and divide the proceeds equally with Allies. Paul was attracted by that offer. His official State Department instructions suggested that the United States expected to obtain "a large portion" of Germany's assets for itself, especially from the Nazi loot, and the whole of IG Farben's subsidiary in the United States. Paul merely nodded as Stucki turned to the question of gold. His new offer was $50 million, double his first proposal. Again Paul said nothing. McCombe and Charguéraud agreed to wait. Rightly, they expected rising tension in the Swiss embassy. On May 2, Stucki called personally: "SF250 million. On my honor, that is our final offer." That represented $58.14 million.

"We've got a good case for $88 million," countered Paul. "Let's compromise at $75 million."

"No," said Stucki. He had reached his own limit.

The Allies were split. Charguéraud was against any compromise, while McCombe wanted to accept.

"What about $70 million?" asked Paul on his next meeting with Stucki.

"No," replied Stucki. "$58 million or nothing. And we want a 2 percent collection fee."

Paul gasped. Swiss greed was unique: "That's chiseling! No way!"

Stucki retreated, but only on the collection fee.

The talks were stalled. In London, Paul Rügger, the Swiss ambassador, called at 3:30 P.M. on May 3 to ask Sir Orme Sargent, the senior Foreign Office official, to prevent "a complete rupture of negotiations," which would be "deplorable." In an obvious ploy to discover whether the Allies were divided, Rügger added, "We need conciliation not least because Stucki's temperament is too rigid to get around the difficulties he faced." Bemused, Sargent remained non-committal.

From Washington, McCombe reported that the Swiss were "kicking violently" in a bid to keep their gold. Stucki was hinting to Allied diplomats that a bitter struggle had erupted among the members of his delegation. Paying any compensation to the Allies, argued Hirs, ignoring Puhl's confession and fighting for his reputation, was an admission that he had either closed his eyes to Germany's use of looted gold or had accepted assurances without any proof. On both interpretations, compensation suggested Swiss complicity with the Reichsbank. Stucki should argue either the disingenuous—that Belgian gold had been willingly deposited in Berlin—or the outrageous: that Swiss ignorance had been genuine. Six weeks in Washington had only made the delegates more stubborn. Profoundly isolated, they remained immune to the world's condemnation of Swiss morality.

In Bern, on May 6, Petitpierre summoned the U.S. ambassador. Sitting in the west "sunny" wing of the Bundeshaus, Petitpierre, the son of a lawyer who had represented Switzerland's watchmakers, enjoyed a spectacular view across the meadows toward the Alps. Below his office in summer, hundreds of local citizens swam in the

River Aare, giving a somewhat unreal atmosphere to any discussions in the foreign minister's office, especially when the topic was Switzerland's secret relationship with the Nazis and the Allies' irritating demand for explanations about the looted gold. Any compensation payments for the gold, the foreign minister explained, would impose a "heavy burden" on Switzerland. To anyone traveling through the wasteland of Europe, Switzerland's quest for understanding would find little sympathy, but it seemed that Petitpierre actually believed his plea would evoke sympathy.

Chargueraud was resigned to the fact that Switzerland could exert pressure. Ordered by Paris not to accept the Swiss offer but to seek more, Chargueraud reported his fears that Switzerland possessed enough "clout" to cause trouble and "bring out influential big guns in America." His evidence was the appearance of favorable articles about Switzerland in the *Wall Street Journal*. Somewhere in New York and Washington, Switzerland's American friends were moving levers. Some would suspect the Dulles brothers.

Unknown to Chargueraud, later that day, before the report of Petitpierre's plea had reached Washington, Paul and Rubin traveled to the Washington home of Senator Harley Kilgore. In widely publicized hearings in the Senate, Kilgore had stressed the importance of controlling any renewed threats posed by Germany to world peace. The politician's support for any deal, Paul and Rubin recognized, was indispensable. Seated in the senator's spacious living room, Paul explained how investigators had established that $223 million of the Belgian gold had been transported to Switzerland: $88 million was still in Swiss hands; the rest had been transferred to other countries. "By any reckoning," said Paul, "Switzerland is proposing to keep one third of the loot."

"Only continued sanctions can work," said Kilgore.

"The British won't," explained Rubin. "Not beyond June 30. The pressure for relaxing controls is increasing all the time."

Kilgore nodded: "I'm getting a lot of letters on that." He added, "We've done the best we can. I never thought we'd get more from the Swiss."

For two more days Paul fenced with Stucki. On the afternoon of May 8, he sat with Rubin; Fred Vinson, the distinguished economic warrior; and William Clayton, the assistant secretary of state, formerly the United States' biggest cotton broker. "That was Stucki's last offer," said Paul. Poker games, staking the reputation of nations, were not his normal line of business. Above all, he wanted a deal. "We're risking losing everything," he told Clayton. Sanctions, everyone agreed, were proving less effective.

"It's a lot of cash," said Clayton.

"It's probably as good as we can get," argued Paul.

"If we say no, we might be left with nothing," added Rubin.

From the State Department came the message that rejection of Stucki's offer would stoke international recrimination about the United States' bullying of "a small democratic country." The French, suggested Paul, should be "pressed" to accept. "Agreed," said Clayton.

But Charguéraud was not eager to succumb. In a telegram to Paris marked "Urgent," he reported that the State Department "insists [that] rapid action is necessary" for acceptance. His own recommendation was to "suspend the negotiations." His advice was instantly rejected. Tiny Switzerland had won an astonishing deal, paying back $58,140,000, one fifth of the $296 million of looted gold it had accepted. Most would be given to France to repay Belgium. Charguéraud was livid. Stucki, he believed, was a calculating liar who, among many deceptions, had deliberately concealed the shipment of seventy-four tons of gold from Switzerland to Spain.

Stucki did not reveal any delight when told of the Allies' acceptance of the deal, despite the end both of the blacklists and of the freeze on Switzerland's assets in the United States. Instead, on May 21 he insisted that the announcement of the agreement be postponed while a list of complaints and definitions was negotiated. Under pressure from bankers and industrialists, he was ordered to prevent any further payments beyond the SF250 million for the gold. To allow the Allies to seize a share of German property, Nazi loot and the heirless assets would violate Switzerland's citadel. Sensing the waning motivation among the Allied negotiators, Stucki planned to exploit the unwary. Words are the armory of lawyers and diplomats, and Stucki insisted on the inclusion and exclusion of apparently innocuous words in the agreement. Paul, Rubin and McCombe incautiously agreed.

On German assets, Stucki committed Switzerland to agree to sell the "property of every description ... owned or controlled by Germans in Germany" and "the property of any German who was to be repatriated to Germany." The agreement applied to German nationals resident in Germany. Believing that Switzerland was therefore obliged to seize and sell all German assets, Paul agreed to include the private property of all "Germans in Germany," and to divide the proceeds equally between Switzerland and the Allies as reparations. Only Stucki appreciated the loopholes he had introduced. Effectively, the Allies had forsaken any power to implement the accord. Only the Swiss had any rights to investigate, seize and sell the German property and, since refusal to implement the accord bore no sanctions, Stucki had ensured that, legally, Switzerland had no need to do anything.

Some would later accuse the two American negotiators of naïveté, but they convinced themselves they were securing the best deal. "We relied upon an assumption that it would be in Switzerland's interest to live up to the agreement, even if compliance was not 100 percent," Rubin would recall later. But, in their rush to close the deal, Paul and Rubin had also failed to include in the agreement a distinction between Germans and German Jews, the vexed issue still causing such misery to survivors. Rubin believed it was unnecessary. During his discussions with the Swiss, he had been assured that the Jews would not suffer, not least because Stucki had been told that Allied Law No. 5, seizing all German assets in neutral countries, "specifically excluded Jews." Assuming that an "informal agreement" had been reached with Stucki that excluded Jewish property from the compulsory sale, Rubin did not insist on a specific clause. Stucki and his lawyers were delighted. All that mattered, they knew, was the words, and by omission the agreement was explicit: the persecuted and their persecutors, Jew and Nazi, would continue to be treated alike.

Rubin was less sanguine about the fate of the heirless assets. Four

days before the formal signing of the agreement, he insisted that the
Swiss should commit themselves to their recovery in Switzerland and
their distribution to the Jews. Stucki resisted. "I cannot," he said,
"commit the government to break the banking secrecy laws." The
Swiss parliament, he explained, would never ratify an accord with that
provision. Yet he understood that the State Department, "under the
pressure of the Jewish organizations," would insist that he sign a public declaration about heirless assets. "We could not resist," he
explained later, "so I agreed to accept but put Switzerland under no
obligation except to consider the question." Urged to end the negotiations, Rubin and Paul agreed with Stucki to a formula of words.
While Stucki would "recommend to the Swiss government that procedures should be established" to distribute the heirless assets, he in
turn would sign a letter to accompany what would be known as the
Washington Accord. The words seemed impressive: "My government
will examine sympathetically the question of seeking means whereby
they might put at the disposal of the three Allied governments, for the
purposes of relief and rehabilitation, the proceeds of property found in
Switzerland which belonged to victims of recent acts of violence of the
late government of Germany, who have died without heirs."

To Rubin, it seemed a suitable if not perfect solution. Stucki
would personally help claimants recover identified looted property
found in Switzerland and hand over the heirless assets to the survivors. Even though the assurance was unenforceable, Rubin reasoned, the Swiss would not want to appear to be enriching themselves
at the expense of the victims of the Holocaust. Neither Rubin nor
Stucki considered that the letter did not mention the nationality of
the Jews whose savings were deposited in Switzerland. "No distinction was made," acknowledged Stucki, "and it was not discussed."
Since the letter was not legally binding, there seemed no reason to be
concerned. Indeed, none of the five notes signed by the Swiss official
were more than promises. As a sideshow to the negotiations, they had
been approved by the State Department but not even shown to
McCombe or Charguéraud. If either man was irritated, he never
complained to Rubin. In truth, neither the British nor the French

government was concerned about the Jews. Each was interested in securing reparations for its own nation, and both failed to understand that the German assets, the loot and the heirless assets, all depending upon Swiss goodwill, were intertwined.

Rubin understood that interrelationship. During the last days of the negotiations, he extricated from Stucki the promised contribution to Europe's reconstruction. In the Washington Accord, Switzerland undertook to advance $12.5 million to the Inter-Governmental Committee on Refugees established under Article 8 of the Paris Agreement in 1945. The money was "to be devoted to the rehabilitation and resettlement of non-repatriable victims of German actions." On Stucki's insistence, the payment was mentioned in a lofty promise expressing Switzerland's "desire to contribute its share to the pacification and the reconstruction of Europe."

For the crusaders, Switzerland's promise of $12.5 million was a crowning success that was to be matched, according to the Paris Agreement, by the Allies out of the sale of German assets in the neutral countries. When all this was combined with the heirless assets and further contributions from Sweden and Portugal, there was finally money to relieve the suffering of the Jews in the camps in Europe.

The accord was formally signed on May 25, 1946. No champagne was poured to toast an agreement tainted by suspicion. Paul and Rubin were anxious to complete the formalities; this was a contrast to the relaxed enjoyment they had experienced at a celebratory dinner with the Swedes. "It was always sour with the Swiss," recalled Rubin, "and the gold turned it worse." After the formal documents were quickly signed, there were brief nods and muted farewells. The accord, it was feared, might merely be the prelude to further problems. That sentiment was confirmed soon after Stucki arrived home.

Thanks to the prism through which the Swiss had followed the Washington negotiations, the truth had been distorted and the Allies' position misrepresented. In near unanimity, Switzerland's newspapers and politicians publicly lambasted Stucki for humiliating Switzerland, comparing the Allies, especially the United States, unfavorably with Hitler. At least the Nazis, cried Stucki's critics, had been polite and had acknowledged Swiss neutrality and sovereignty. Decent Switzerland, bayed the chorus, had become the victim of gangsters hustled by Jews. Sensing his vulnerability, Stucki magnified the distortions by bemoaning his personal misfortune. Unable to resist demands for an unjustified admission of guilt as the price for removing the economic sanctions, he complained, Switzerland had yielded to "relentless pressure" to sign an agreement whose terms had been dictated by the Allies.

Bureaucrats, appreciating that a smoke screen of anger and grief would obscure Switzerland's embarrassing exposure for dishonestly accepting looted gold, concocted a revised version of history. "The Allies," scoffed Ernst Nobs, the director of the Ministry of Finance, "are entitled to fight their own wars, but we're not returning the stolen Belgian gold. We're just making a generous contribution for the reconstruction of Europe." Newspapers and gullible politicians were briefed by Nobs and ministers that the Belgian government was suing the French government for compensation in the U.S. courts. "A Swiss lie," fumed Marcel Vaidie, "just as they lied that they had accepted Reichsmarks from the Germans and not gold." The Swiss, he said, wanted to "shunt off on to France the entire responsibility for the acquisition of gold looted by the Germans."

Although publicly the French collaborators were blamed for the German acquisition of looted gold, internally Ernst Weber, the president of the National Bank, and Hirs were criticized for being "completely taken in by Puhl" and for not being honest with Stucki about the Belgian gold. Their real sin was causing an embarrassment by allowing the exposure to take place. Both were forced to retire. That fate, Stucki determined, would not befall him, despite the unusually high opposition vote when parliament ratified the accord on June 27, 1946—by 142 votes to 29.

Stucki's reward from Petitpierre for having negotiated the accord was to be given the task of supervising its implementation, harangued from one side by irate bankers and industrialists, and from the other by the United States and Jewish groups. The first draft of his poisoned chalice was being prepared in Paris.

10

THE HIDDEN
MILLIONS

One day after Walter Stucki had agreed the essentials of the
Washington Accord, on May 13, 1946, Eli Ginzberg, a thirty-five-
year-old fast-talking Jewish New Yorker with a doctorate in economics from Columbia University, sailed to England in comfort on
the *Queen Mary*, the world's most celebrated luxury liner, as the State
Department representative for a conference destined to distribute the
$25 million and the heirless assets to the refugees. In 1944, as the
chief of the logistical office of the Surgeon of the U.S. Army,
Ginzberg had read the reports about the extermination camps and,
influenced by Moses Abramovitz, had assumed "an obligation to care
for the Holocaust victims." His voyage to London was the fulfillment
of that obligation.

Ginzberg's progress had not been smooth. In the weeks before
his departure, the State Department had resisted his appointment.
Tinged with anti-Semitism and ambivalent about refugees as "a losing card," State Department officials knew that the British Foreign
Office opposed any conference, while the French were lukewarm.
But the department's opposition collapsed under the onslaught of the
crusaders in the Treasury and White House. "We had to push the
State Department," Ginzberg told his friends just three days before
his departure. Despite those difficulties, the letter of appointment

157

from John Hildring, an assistant secretary of state, included a ringing exhortation: "This government feels that it has a particular moral obligation to these unfortunate victims of Hitlerite aggression." Few, however, expected any results. Although Article 8 of the Paris Agreement had established an Inter-Governmental Committee on Refugees, Ginzberg arrived in London knowing that Britain's "delaying tactics ... by raising a host of extraneous issues" reflected its "deep antagonism" to the very idea of such a committee. Five months had elapsed since the original reparation agreement had been signed, and while the condition of the Jewish refugees deteriorated, the French government had failed to convene the five-nation conference in Paris. After his first meetings with the British, the Allies' lack of interest was confirmed. Ginzberg sought the advice of Sam Burger, the labor attaché at the American embassy. The solution, suggested Burger, was to meet "my good friend Hector McNeil." McNeil, a junior minister at the Foreign Office, was preparing for a visit to Washington. "It's all about big prices, " Burger told Ginzberg as they drove at night to McNeil's home in north London. "The Brits need us." "I'll offer him a deal," laughed Ginzberg, who that day had met David Ben Gurion, the Zionist leader. "None of the Allies," Ben Gurion had moaned, "want to help us." Unlike conventional diplomats, Ginzberg was motivated to help his people.

While smoking Ginzberg's Chesterfields, McNeil was candid about the obstacles: "We don't want to complicate the Palestinian problem." Giving money to Jewish refugees to emigrate to Palestine, admitted the minister, would cause extra headaches. Even Ginzberg's request that 600 children be allowed to emigrate to Palestine was excessive. "Look," offered Ginzberg in his affable, fast-talking New Yorker manner, "my government wants this settled. If you help me, I'll help you in your mission to Washington. I'll write to Hildring and sort you out." The minister believed him. "That sounds very acceptable," he replied, speculating that perhaps 250 children could be admitted every month. "You've been unnecessarily handsome in understanding our position. We'll support the conference." McNeil's only condition was that the original term in the Paris

Agreement—that the money would "be devoted to the rehabilitation and resettlement of non-repatriable victims of German action"— should remain unaltered. Neither Palestine nor the Jewish distribution agencies would be mentioned.

Elated, Ginzberg sought out the three other representatives delegated by the eighteen-nation conference with responsibility for settling the issue: Czech, Yugoslav and French. During an expensive lunch, Kilvana, the Czech, revealed to Ginzberg, "I do everything the Yugoslav tells me." Over another "fancy" meal, Bartos, the Yugoslav diplomat, explained, "So long as there's no money for Tito's enemies, we'll support you." The French, Ginzberg decided, would not be a problem: "We'd just given them a big slice of money." Shuttling between the diplomats in London, Ginzberg, invoking the "deep interest of my government," had negotiated by June 7 the draft agreement that would be formally considered by the conference in Paris on June 11. The money, it was agreed, would be used not for compensation but for "rehabilitation and resettlement." Anticipating that he would be able to "guide" Philippe Pérrier's chairmanship, Ginzberg congratulated himself and traveled to France.

In London, Douglas Mackillop, a Treasury official nominated as the British representative, was irritated by Jewish agitation and complaints. Jewish groups had protested to British officials about their "grievous disappointment" that no special mention had been made in the original Paris Agreement about their plight. Nor, they complained, was there an explicit promise to compensate Jews for the Nazis' theft of Jewish property worth billions of dollars or an explicit statement of the right of the Jews to administer their own funds. To Mackillop's annoyance, Jewish petitions and meetings had urged politicians to recognize that "most of the 'heirless' property of Nazi victims in neutral countries consists of property belonging to Jews" and it should be secured for their benefit. Now, capping all that irritation, came the arrival of American zeal in the person of Ginzberg. "The United States delegate," Mackillop noted to his colleagues, "will be a very active-minded young Jew who is by all accounts anxious to secure the handling of all the moneys allocated to Jewish beneficiaries by the Jewish Agency for Palestine and the American Joint Distribution Committee." Allowing those agencies to administer the funds, he grumbled, was distinctly "unwelcome in view of the record of these organizations in connection with illegal immigration into Palestine." Worst of all, Ginzberg was guilty of seeking money for Austrian and German Jews and his proposed agreement would distinguish between Jewish and non-Jewish victims.

Mackillop's proposal, to find a Jewish group who opposed Ginzberg and manipulate them in Britain's favor, aroused Waley's concern. On the eve of Mackillop's departure to Paris, he was urged by Waley to bear in mind American passion for the idea that the money should be used to resettle Jews, especially in Palestine. Unimpressed, Mackillop coldly ignored the advice.

In Paris, Ginzberg enthusiastically introduced himself to Mackillop. The Scotsman, he decided, was "unexciting" and clearly burdened by the eight children he had fathered. For his part, the British representative was depressed by Ginzberg's news. The three delegates from France, Czechoslovakia and Yugoslavia, chortled Ginzberg, supported his plan, and so did Hector McNeil, the British Foreign Office minister. "McNeil did not tell me he supported you," intoned Mackillop, proffering a piece of paper. "Here's my proposal. Somewhat different from yours." Ginzberg's ire was palpable. "Let's settle our differences in private this evening," suggested Mackillop in retreat.

That evening Ginzberg confronted the prejudice of the Foreign Office. There could be no mention of the Jews as beneficiaries, insisted Mackillop, nor could the agreement support their resettlement in Palestine, nor could the money be distributed by Jewish organizations. "The money should be distributed by governments," said Mackillop.

At once excited and furious, Ginzberg bluffed: "My instructions from Washington are to formally withdraw from the conference if any attempt is made to delay distributing the money." Staggered by the American's ultimatum, the British official sat quietly as Ginzberg continued, "Involving governments as the distributors means delay, and the Swiss have agreed to advance the money explicitly for those beneficiaries." Uneasy and acknowledging that he was isolated, Mackillop scrambled together a compromise: the American Joint Distribution Committee and the Jewish Agency would not be mentioned in the formal agreement as administering 90 percent of the fund but could be nominated in associated letters of instruction to the Inter-Governmental Committee on Refugees as the agencies to distribute the money. However, the funds would not be released until there was an approved resettlement program; and, although Palestine would not be mentioned, there could be a phrase indicating that the money was to help the Jews "in finding new and permanent homes." "Agreed," Ginzberg said with a smile.

In his report to London, Mackillop would boast that Ginzberg's plan had been partially sabotaged, but that did not prevent his acceptance of the American's generosity. Just before signing the agreement on June 14, Ginzberg visited the American embassy's commissary and brought a box of chocolate bars. "These are for your eight children," Ginzberg told Mackillop. "But you can have them only after you've signed. Otherwise it'll be seen as a bribe." Without embarrassment, Mackillop accepted the gift. Later that day he successfully won postponement of a plan to help the Hungarian Jews on the ground that it was "awkward." The Swiss, commented the Scotsman on his return to London, deserve sympathy for the problems that beckoned. Untroubled, Ginzberg returned to New York content that he had contributed toward the survivors' relief. All that remained was to secure the money from the neutrals.

Under the Paris Agreement, Philippe Pérrier, the French chairman, had been nominated by the five governments to recover the $25 million and the heirless assets. On the assumption that all of the assets were Jewish in origin, 95 percent, it had been agreed, would be used for Jewish rehabilitation and resettlement. Pérrier's letter to Bern was dispatched on August 20. Switzerland, like the other neutral countries, was asked to "take all necessary action to facilitate the identification, collection and distribution of these assets which have arisen out of a unique condition in international law and morality." The Swiss were invited to act with "understanding and energy."

Choosing France as the representative was in the circumstances not astute. Ever since the Washington Accord had been signed, Swiss politicians had denigrated the French, accusing them of stealing Belgium's gold, for which Switzerland had had to pay compensation. Outraged by Swiss deceit, Henri Hoppenot, the French ambassador in Switzerland, urged his government to release a dossier proving the Swiss dishonesty. "The present cowardice of the Finance Ministry," he exclaimed in a coded telegram to Paris, "is a disservice to our prestige and ensures that no one will take our work seriously." The silence from Paris, Hoppenot knew, was related to the continuing negotiations for loans. By 1949, Switzerland would have loaned SF790 million to European countries and France would receive by far the largest share, SF340 million. Hoppenot's complaint about the "finance administration's desire to coddle the powers in the Swiss National Bank" was ignored.

While the British had deliberately remained silent about heirless assets, convinced that "the atmosphere might not be particularly favorable," Irwin Mason, a U.S. diplomat, was dispatched to Bern to negotiate the speedy release of the heirless assets. "Moral pressure," he was told, was the only weapon available.

Max Gottschalk, a foreign affairs consultant for the American Jewish Committee, had discovered during his visit to Switzerland in May 1946 the limitations of moral pressure as a means of obtaining the heirless assets. Meeting Armand Braunschvig, the vice-president of the Swiss Federation of Jewish Associations, Gottschalk was struck by the timidity of the Jewish leaders. Cowed by native anti-Semitism and shamed by the association's wartime failure to protest more vigorously about the expulsion of foreign Jews, Braunschvig had in 1945 unquestioningly repeated gossip from fellow Jews and Swiss bankers: "There's not a large amount of heirless assets." One year after the war, as reports accumulated about missing Jews, Braunschvig revised his assessment. One Swiss shoe manufacturer reported that no word had been heard from any of his Jewish representatives, who were known to control seventy-five bank accounts in Switzerland. Another Swiss reported that the owner of property worth SF2 million had disappeared and his possessions were being administered by a bank. The heirless assets were now estimated to be worth $38 million. Gottschalk questioned whether Swiss law would allow their transfer to the survivors. The Swiss courts, he was initially told, could declare victims dead and authorize the transfer of their assets to survivors. But in May 1946 he heard that under Swiss law the heirless assets would revert to the government of the depositor's nation.

That unforeseen advice was also sent to Eli Ginzberg by Mason of the State Department. Under Article 22 of a Swiss law of 1891, reported Mason, the Swiss government did not control the "ultimate disposition of assets in Switzerland of foreigners who died without heirs." However, he said, Switzerland's secrecy laws would prevent any foreign government from claiming the heirless assets. The only solution would be to secure the agreement of the other countries to waive their claims and call the money "unclaimed funds" rather than heirless assets. Ginzberg's recommendation was artless: if the other governments refused to oblige, the Swiss government should change its laws.

Ginzberg's solution seemed unexceptionable to the lawyers in Washington. Pressured by the Jewish lobby, Congress had recently amended the Trading with the Enemy Act to allow European Jews to recover possessions that had been seized as enemy property in the United States by the Alien Property Custodian. No one in the State Department doubted that, with goodwill, the Swiss could find a satisfactory legal remedy, especially after Stucki's signed promise to "examine the question sympathetically." With that hope, the State Department wrote to Stucki on July 10. By then, Stucki's department had received a succession of letters from U.S. diplomats protesting about the plight of former German citizens who were unable to obtain their money from Swiss bank accounts, insurance policies and trusts blocked by the Compensation Office. The latest letter sought an explanation of why the Compensation Office was continuing to demand that claimants produce documentary proof of their loss of German nationality or that a relative had died in the gas chambers. That proof, submitted the State Department, did not exist. Stressing the "entirely unprecedented situation," Stucki was asked to "recognize the urgent and immediate necessity" of devising procedures to transfer the heirless assets to the survivors.

Regardless of his own difficulties after his return from Washington, Stucki did not dispute Switzerland's obligation toward the Jews. "There is a moral obligation and I believe that the problem must be pursued with energy," he noted, proposing that the government introduce a new law to secure and transfer the heirless assets. By then, Stucki was considering a thirteen-page proposal delivered by Dr. F. Bienenfeld, a British lawyer representing the World Jewish Congress. Some heirless assets, he suggested, should be immediately freed to help 9,500 Jewish refugees in Switzerland, and the Swiss banks should be protected by a new law from penalization from any future claims for handing over the heirless assets.

Franz Kappeler, a senior official in the Political Department, unquestioningly accepted the need for a solution despite obstacles and conflicting claims. While the Allies expected the neutral countries to give $25 million and the heirless assets to the Jews, he noted, the Polish and Czech governments had asked the Swiss earlier in the year for the assets deposited in Switzerland by their citizens who had died during the war. In summary, Kappeler identified the major obstacle: while the banks needed to establish the amount of heirless assets, they had difficulties in establishing whether or not a depositor was actually dead because so many foreigners had given instructions that they were not to be contacted. Any investigation by the banks to discover whether their customers had survived the war might endanger those people, he wrote. One solution, he suggested, was to retain some of the heirless assets to pay those who reappeared. In the meantime, he expected the amount of heirless assets to be established soon because most of the inheritors of other accounts would claim their deposits. That summary was incontrovertible and fair. Since there was no predetermined legal solution, any settlement required careful thought. Yet in his conclusions, Kappeler, a pro-Nazi during the war, revealed disdain for the Allies' plan: "It should not be assumed that just because a depositor was Jewish he would have desired that his legacy would be used for repatriable refugees." Nevertheless, he suggested that a conference of banks, lawyers, notaries, trustees and their associations be summoned for discussions that would lead to legislation.

Four days later, on August 3, all of Switzerland's banks, lawyers, notaries and trustees were asked by the Political Department to estimate the amount of heirless assets. While appreciating the work involved, the department added, "It is vital to acknowledge the undertakings given in Washington and the political importance which the Allies attribute to the issue."

Clearly appalled that the government contemplated a breach of their secrecy, the Bankers Association reacted with a mixture of artful ingenuity and defiance. Mentioning their "surprise" about Stucki's undertaking on heirless assets—"which we were unaware of until now"—the association curtly listed the legal requirements to establish an heirless asset: namely, documentary proof that the depositor was dead and that there were no heirs. "No," scribbled the Political Department official, criticizing the association's conditions as too restrictive. In their counterproposal, the association suggested that the government should ask the Allies what they were doing to discover heirless assets in their countries. "It seems to us that the neutral states cannot do more than the signatories at the reparations conference."

"That's true," commented the official at the Political Department, understanding Switzerland's position—that the country should implement the accord to the same extent as the Allies. The idea of shifting the fate of the heirless assets onto the Allies shone with advantages.

The Swiss reply on the heirless assets was handed to the French embassy on September 11, 1946. The government, wrote Petitpierre, had studied the Allies' request "sympathetically" and would consult the federal authorities about the legal issues. In the meantime, the government was undertaking inquiries to discover "the approximate number and amounts of heirless estates in question."

Guy de Rahm, Stucki's assistant, approached the banks, the insurance companies and the Swiss Lawyers Association for information. The banks and insurance companies were expected to produce estimates of the amount of heirless assets, although the lawyers had instantly refused to breach the confidentiality of their clients. That, followed by the notaries' similar refusal to cooperate, looked suspicious. In private, Schwab and Stucki had heard whispers that not only banks and corporations but also Swiss individuals—lawyers, business associates, notaries and accountants—had diverted into their own or specially created accounts money held in trust for Jews who had disappeared. By its inaction, de Rahm feared, the Swiss government was encouraging more people to steal those dormant accounts. Deciding the fate of the heirless assets had become embroiled with Switzerland's attitude toward the Jews and the Germans.

On November 1, 1946, Robert Meyer, a respected lawyer in Zurich, called at the Political Department to propose using the heirless assets, which he estimated were worth between SF40 and SF50 million, to help 5,000 Jewish refugees settle in Switzerland. The respect that Meyer's plan generated outraged lawyers close to Heinrich Rothmund, the director of the Police Department. They were anxious that all foreign Jews should leave the country. Police representatives rushed to de Rahm to denounce Meyer as a mere mouthpiece of the World Jewish Congress. His estimate of heirless assets, they said decisively, was too high. "He wants 5,000 to 6,000 Jews to stay in Switzerland out of political rather than humanitarian motives," Rothmund's emissaries told de Rahm, adding that there was unhealthy competition among Jewish groups to control the heirless assets. The police offered an alternative proposal. To save public funds, the heirless assets should be used, until their removal from Switzerland, to alleviate the "big problem" of caring for the refugees in the spartan camps. Just as they had been during the war, the Jews should be self-financing. Since "the money belonged to the same type of people who would now benefit," submitted the police, the financial problem at least would be solved.

Four months had elapsed since the accord was signed and the crusaders in the Treasury and State Departments, under pressure from Jewish groups highlighting Swiss obstruction, urged action. Intelligence reports from Europe revealed that, in contrast to the

Jews, the 72,000 Germans resident in Switzerland were enjoying uninterrupted Swiss hospitality. Despite American demands that 24,000 suspected Nazis be expelled, only 3,000 incriminated Germans—all political and intelligence operatives—had been ordered to return to Germany. On Swiss criteria, only those who were undesirable to Switzerland were expelled. The Allies' interest in the German financiers and industrialists was ignored.

Freed from the Allies' restrictions, Eduard von Steiger, the minister of justice and the police, had also quietly altered the conditions for Germans' entry into Switzerland, a particular help for former Nazis forbidden by the Allies to travel. Swiss officials, accepting bribes of SF200,000, provided temporary residence permits and "Ersatz Passes" for former Nazis to move clandestinely through Switzerland and disappear beyond the Allies' control. Among the most favored routes was the regular KLM flight, booked in Swissair offices, to Argentina and Brazil. "The Swiss government," noted Tom Caruth, the assistant military attaché in Bern, "made a considerable profit getting rid of [the Germans and ensured] that too many questions were not asked."

Other privileged Germans, allowed to remain in Switzerland, were enjoying such relaxed conditions that the country was condemned in the House of Commons as a refuge for former Nazis. In Lugano's luxury hotels and villas, Nazi Germany's former diplomats, arms dealers and SS officers, pampered by newly recruited staff, paraded in expensive cars. In Davos, the location of the German-owned Catholic sanatoria that in wartime had been centers of German espionage, former Nazis who had crossed the border looking impoverished soon tapped into their protected bank deposits to buy new clothes, eat well and rejoin "the anti-Semitic movement." In their conversations, none voiced any contrition about the past. Rather, they spoke of vengeance against the Americans for the injustice they had suffered. Among the many sources of suspected income were 15 tons of gold bullion, mostly in coins, missing from a Berlin bunker controlled by von Ribbentrop's Foreign Ministry and 3 tons that had been smuggled across the border into Switzerland at Lake

Constance. None of those Germans was pursued as the Jews had been by von Steiger's police or was subjected to investigation by Compensation Office officials, who were preventing Jews from gaining access to their funds. The accumulation of those reports even persuaded the British and French governments in September to send protest letters to Bern about the Swiss failure to fulfill their promises. The instinctive reaction in Bern was to ignore any criticism, although German influence was beginning to encroach on Switzerland's attitude toward the accord.

On September 13, Stucki chaired the first meeting of the Swiss commission to implement the accord. Two antagonists faced him across the conference table. Robert Dunant, representing the Bankers Association, was upset and determined to forestall the transfer of 50 percent of the German property, the loot and the heirless assets to the Allies and Jews. Having warned Petitpierre since March that the Currie agreement was dangerous, Dunant, the son of a prominent Swiss diplomat, had ever since unloaded his fellow members' complaints onto the minister, attacking the government's opinion that "the Swiss people would not understand if the German assets were left untouched." In funereal tones, the bankers' representative expressed his "exceptional regret," as a Swiss patriot, that the accord had been signed. "It's contrary to Switzerland's constitution," he insisted, "it will undermine Switzerland's sovereignty, and, most seriously, it will be exploited by the Allies to allow Switzerland's competitors to discover our commercial secrets." Stucki understood that the bankers were declaring war on the accord, expecting Switzerland to renege on the agreement.

The second antagonist facing Stucki was Heinrich Homberger of the industrialists' Vorort, the representative of Switzerland's most powerful clan. Homberger's influence was only too evident: he was provided with an office in the Ministry of Economics to facilitate his access to civil servants and ministers in the shaping of Switzerland's policies.

Stucki's opening remarks, which ruffled his adversaries' feathers, showed that he was not easily manipulated: "There's resistance to the implementation of the accord. We're getting reports that some financial groups are causing problems in the freeze on private German assets." Dunant and Homberger knew that the reality was worse than Stucki and Schwab could imagine. Swiss companies that had agreed to become protectors of German companies at the outbreak of the war were refusing to transfer property back to the Germans—either to protect it from seizure or purely for profit. Other Swiss displayed outright greed. "It's shameful," said Max Ott of his countrymen's avarice, "how many people think that they can just take these German assets."

Unknown to Homberger and Dunant, Schwab's suspicions about their activities had prompted the Compensation Office to tap a number of telephones. Schwab's motives were laudable. He was deluged by rumors and unsubstantiated reports, and his only chance of discovering loot and hidden fortunes held by those known to be working closely with the Germans was by taps. Those suspicions nonetheless reinforced the antagonism in the room, signaling to Stucki, whose approach would increasingly reveal his Jekyll-and-Hyde character, that to avoid isolation and allay the financiers' fears he should switch direction. So, with a hint of skepticism, he began explaining how the implementation of the accord could be delayed. The principal ruse, he suggested, was to argue with the Allies about the exchange rate for calculating the value of the German assets. "We fought like lions in Washington over the exchange rate," Stucki told Homberger and Dunant. "The Allies are obviously very interested in selling off the German assets as fast as possible, not least because the first SF50 million is to be used for the Nazis' victims. But so long as the sale hasn't started, they can't have the money. So we've got a bargaining counter which we shouldn't waste."

Homberger warmed to Stucki's new defiant tone. In cryptic terms understood by everyone present he declared: "I'm pleased with that report. I've always wondered whether the accord could ever be implemented. I've always believed that fixing the exchange rate will determine everything." Left unspoken, however, was his anger with Stucki. Germany's assets in Switzerland, he believed, should not be shared with the Allies but should be used to pay off Germany's debts to the Swiss state.

Nine days later, at the second meeting, Homberger raised a new demand. German assets in Switzerland, he told Stucki, should also be used to pay off private debts owed to Swiss nationals. "That's impossible," protested Stucki, clearly disliking the industrialist's motives. "The Allies insist on using the money for reconstruction and we must hand over some money to the victims of the Nazis. There'll be a huge argument with the Allies if we do what Herr Homberger wants." Homberger was unimpressed: "Your arguments are political and everything will change." Stucki disagreed. "The accord may be crude; but if it looks as if we are breaking the agreement and representing German interests, it would do us no good and we'd be giving the Allies the chance to take everything." Stucki knew how to interpret Homberger's silence. Switzerland's industrialists were untroubled by the Allies' feelings or threats.

Toward the end of that second meeting, Dunant asked about the fate of the heirless assets. Stucki's reply was encouraging. Their fate, said the official, would be determined by those sitting around the table. There was no mention of asking Switzerland's financial community to deliver the results of its investigation initiated by Petitpierre. The subject would not be formally discussed for another two years.

Stucki's resolute indifference was prompted by the sudden turmoil across the border. News reports were describing a major break in relations between the Western Allies and the Soviet Union on the question of Germany's economic future. For the first time a permanent division of Germany was being discussed. In the developing struggle to establish Europe's fate, Switzerland was too unimportant to attract much attention from the Allies.

The reply to the Foreign Office's mild protest in September had been a question from Stucki calculated to deter any further interest. Britain was asked to supply any information about the heirless assets in Switzerland and to explain how the British government intended to discover the heirless assets deposited in Britain. Gerry Villiers was perplexed. There was no mention of any Allied responsibility in the Paris Agreement, and naturally the British government had not contemplated searching the British banks for those assets—nor did it consider such a search possible. In the absence of banking secrecy laws, inquiries by Jewish survivors without any information were routinely circulated among Britain's banks, and if the names matched, the bank immediately admitted the existence of an account. All that was required was for the claimants to prove their right to the inheritance. The Swiss, it was clear to Villiers, were "just fishing." The British could not suggest to the Swiss how else to trace the assets. The best solution, Villiers decided, was to "throw the ball back" to the Americans, such passionate supporters of the cause: "I'll be interested to see what the result will be." Six months had elapsed since the Swiss had promised to explain their proposals for the heirless assets. Selous, the commercial secretary in Bern, wanted to know whether he should formally inquire about progress. The consensus in London was to ignore the Swiss query and to remain silent.

In Paris, a similar Swiss inquiry received an obfuscatory reply. Since the nonmonetary gold found in Germany, replied the Quai d'Orsay, had been given to the Jews, the French government was not obliged to introduce legislation to discover and hand over to the victims of Nazism any property deposited in France. This evasion concealed France's refusal, in contrast to the behavior of the British and U.S. armies, to hand over to the Allied depository all the gold and other valuables whose ownership was now unknown but that had been confiscated from the Jews. Among the valuables shipped to Paris, allegedly for the compilation of an inventory, were 2,500 kilos of gold belonging to Hungary, and cases of jewelry and paintings, seized from Jews, discovered in the Austrian Tyrol. Their fate in France remained unknown.

The Swiss letter to the State Department was cunning: "It would be helpful to the Swiss authorities to know the basis for the allegation of the Allied governments that a considerable number of the victims of the Nazi persecution died without heirs and had their estates in Switzerland." At the end of the short, polite note was a reference to

Poland's claims to the heirless assets of Polish citizens. In their struggle to find an answer to the main question, State Department officials
neither pondered the mention of Poland nor contemplated any
amendment of the law to discover the heirless assets in U.S. banks.
There were no secrecy laws to prevent a bank's disclosure of a
deposit, and if an account was dormant for ten or more years, it was
automatically disclosed in public advertisements. To increasingly
beleaguered State Department officials, the minutiae of small sums of
money and wartime principles were becoming irrelevant compared
with the fate of Europe. Paul Culberston, head of the State
Department's Western European division, shared the British lack of
interest in Safehaven. Irreconcilable difficulties with the Soviet government relegated the differences with Switzerland to the status of an
unwelcome irritation. Western Europe's survival depended upon a
unity of purpose. Chasing Nazi war criminals and Nazi loot was
interfering with the bewildering skirmishes being fought over the
evolution of a strategy. The crusaders had become an embarrassment. The United States, Culbertson told William Clayton, assistant
secretary of state, in October, was viewed by the Swiss as the "big bad
wolf," not least because too many staff members in the State and
Treasury Departments considered the Swiss "a bunch of crooks."
Culbertson wanted to remove the "running sore" with the Swiss and
withdraw all but one of the Safehaven personnel in Switzerland. The
Swiss should be allowed, he concluded, to run Safehaven. Clayton
agreed.

Without telling Rubin, Culbertson dispatched Benjamin
Kittridge, a State Department official, to visit Albert Nussbaumer in
Zurich. Kittridge confided to the Swiss banker, Petitpierre's roving
ambassador, that his department was "fed up with postwar animosity"
and wanted to reestablish a normal relationship with Switzerland.
The problems, admitted Kittridge, were caused by "certain personalities among the American delegation in Bern whom he would investigate." Nussbaumer immediately advised Petitpierre to respond to
the "indisputably" pro-Swiss State Department, "who do not agree
with the Treasury." To the minister it appeared that Safehaven was

all but dead, not least because the Treasury representatives in Bern were failing to block the sieve as loot disappeared and German property became harder to expropriate. The quest for the heirless assets was suffering in the retreat.

Placed in the front line of the dragnet for the plunder and the Jewish money, Max Schwab and Max Ott of the Conservation Office were handicapped. Confronted by the overwhelming hostility of the bankers and industrialists, they could no longer rely on the Political Department for support. Despite his honest but confused intentions, Schwab could not untangle the myriad interlocking local relationships between German and Swiss companies, nor could he penetrate through the secrecy laws to discover the heirless assets or the German assets.

Schwab's failures to seize German property for the Allies were frequently picked up by Allied intelligence officers in Germany intercepting the mail with Switzerland. Letters addressed to Swiss banks, often coded, revealed Germans illegally entering Switzerland to manage their assets, which should have been sold, or using their funds in blocked accounts to offset debts to each other; other intercepts revealed how Germans were transferring their fortunes out of Switzerland by using Chinese or South American businessmen to buy Swiss products with the Germans' money. Inside Switzerland—unlike the situation during the war—neither MI6 nor two American intelligence officers, Harvey Ginsberg and James Kronthal, had replicated the Allies' wartime successes by comprehensively penetrating the Swiss banks, the industrialists' boardrooms, the Compensation Office or Stucki's office. Inconsequential intelligence reports to London and Washington mentioned an increase in food parcels sent to Germany, the suspicious activities of a Christian relief organization and the continued presence of suspected Germans, but in total it amounted to ignorance. Schwab and his staff, dubbed "uncooperative" by Selous, revealed nothing. Whenever American or British diplomats submitted examples of undisclosed German assets, Schwab merely replied, "We know about that already."

Schwab was lying, yet out of the Allies' sight he was fighting with the banks to reveal the truth about the Allies' reports. In one case, he had inquired about a German account. The bank replied that on February 16, 1945, the day the freeze was declared, the account did not exist. After persistent questioning, Schwab discovered that just days before February 16, in anticipation of the freeze, the account had been transferred into the name of an Englishwoman living in China and the German had continued drawing on his money by using blank checks signed by the woman. "It is," admitted Schwab, "a typical case of cloaking." Although the bank was liable to prosecution and a fine, no action was taken. Even the bank's refusal to reveal its client's name remained unpunished. Switzerland's prosecutors were refusing to administer a law denounced by bankers and their clients as unjust and ridiculous. "We're not finding much understanding in the courts," Ott told Stucki. "If the courts refuse to do their job properly," replied Stucki, "that's their problem. That must not prevent us from prosecuting." Ott was not persuaded. His feeling was that "the Germans should be grateful to the Swiss for using the freeze to protect their assets." Their irreconcilable struggle remained unknown to Allied diplomats in Bern, who witnessed only Stucki's aggressive defense in the national interest of what he privately condemned.

To denigrate the Allies, Stucki called a press conference in January 1947 to announce that, although the Allies had reported one thousand cases of hidden German assets, only five were unknown to the Swiss government. In Sweden, Rubin had swiftly negotiated an agreement that 74 percent of German assets would be sold and the proceeds handed to the Allies and thence the refugees; by contrast, the Swiss vigorously disputed the value of German assets. Instead of the $1 billion estimated by Allies, the Compensation Office's valuation was $120 million. Stucki's department, cajoled by bankers and industrialists, was seeking ruses to avoid implementing the accord and to manifest exemplary fairness toward the Germans as proof of Switzerland's reliability: "We cannot allow the world to think that the German owners did not get fair compensation."

Within their closed sanctum, Switzerland's bankers and industrialists had persuaded themselves that their country was under siege.

"Look at the American press reports," Ernst Speiser, a director of Brown Boveri, the engineering giant, told Stucki and Homberger. "They're even suggesting that we are trying to sabotage the Washington Accord." Stucki growled, "We'll have to hold on to our nerve." The blame, he said, to general agreement, lay with the American Safehaven team, who were feeding Michael Hoffman, the local *New York Times* correspondent, with malicious gossip. "It's all about money, companies and the expansion of American cartels," Speiser complained. Schwab agreed. Reagan, Conover and Mann were condemned together for sharing anti-Swiss sentiment—motivated solely by the desire to help U.S. corporations seize German assets. Schwab's misconceptions were mixed with a modicum of reality. The Safehaven team in Bern, he told everyone, was "isolated and cannot count on any support from Washington." "We'll go on the offensive soon and deal with them," snapped Stucki. "Reagan isn't strong and we're not helpless." Homberger's prediction about the diminution of the Allies' aggression was turning out to have been correct, weakening the effectiveness of the Compensation Office and presenting an omen for Stucki as his misgivings about the bankers' honesty were sustained.

In spring 1947, Stucki became disquieted by the discovery that the Kantonalbank, one of Switzerland's biggest banking chains, had furtively ceased paying interest on foreign accounts ten years earlier. Believing it to be an isolated case, he told Dunant, the Bankers Association's representative, "I believe we have a duty not to allow the banks' enrichment to pass unnoticed." Irritated by Stucki's moral fervor and keen to minimize the revelation, Dunant soothed, "Only twenty-seven Kantonalbank branches according to the Compensation Office are involved. Very few Germans deposited money in that chain. At most we talking about repaying SF1 million." The Compensation Office, he suggested, was exaggerating the problem associated with controlling "hot money" in 1937. Yet the implications of Dunant's limited admission were considerable. Unclaimed deposits in the twenty-seven banks, probably belonging to non-German Jews, were worth, according to the Compensation Office, SF6 million. Among the thousands of individual branches of Swiss banks, the unclaimed deposits could amount to hundreds of millions of francs.

Suspicious of Dunant, Stucki proposed that the question should be referred to a court. Dunant was appalled by that prospect. There were serious disadvantages the banks might suffer, he told Stucki, if that course were pursued. The two agreed to a compromise: a new investigation would be undertaken by the Compensation Office staff. Weeks later, the new investigation revealed an even more distasteful scenario. Swiss banks, discovering that a dormant account belonged to a German or a foreign Jew, had retrospectively deducted the interest paid over many years on savings accounts, anticipating that there would not be a complaint because the depositor could well have been murdered. By any measure, the banks were guilty of a crude theft. Stucki was shocked.

Dunant was forced into the defensive. In a meeting with Stucki on September 9, the bankers' representative explained, "This wasn't done only to the Germans but to everyone except Swiss nationals living abroad." His explanation exposed his loss of contact with reality: "Swiss banks informed all their foreign customers. They all knew what we had done and none of them protested." The idea that a German or Polish Jew living in the fear of the Gestapo who received a letter about interest payments from a Swiss bank might protest about it was inconceivable to everyone except Dunant and the members of his association. No one pointed out that, to avoid risk, the instructions accompanying practically every foreign account in the Swiss bank forbade the dispatch of any correspondence to the depositor. Letters to the banks' clients would therefore have been sent to mailboxes inside the bank itself. Stucki's inveterate suspicions about banks were being reinforced as Dunant's explanations unfolded.

"There's clearly a misunderstanding," said Schwab, interrupting Dunant. "I was present at the National Bank when it was agreed to suspend paying interest to stop 'hot money' from coming into Switzerland. It was never the intention to punish savers. The small banks have actually continued paying interest. And it's particularly crass that interest was retrospectively deducted."

"We are trustees for the Germans," insisted Stucki. "We must care for their interests."

Dunant was nonplussed. His association had confiscated the money from every foreign deposit account, and here was Stucki, with his narrow, legalistic, bureaucratic mind, wanting to make distinctions. "But we can't make an exception for the Germans," he exclaimed.

The confusion was compounded in a written report compiled by the Bankers Association. Most interest payments, explained Dunant, were stopped only in May 1946, after the Washington Accord had been signed. His earlier explanation about controlling "hot money" in 1937 had become incomprehensible. Three weeks later, the Compensation Office's own investigation exposed Dunant's lies. In a survey of all bank accounts, it was found that the interest payments had varied widely. Only 16.5 percent of all savings accounts, Stucki's staff reported, were fairly administered, while 35.2 percent of the foreign accounts and 38.9 percent of German accounts were "badly" administered. The discrepancies exposed how the banks were exploiting foreign savers for their own profit.

"The banks acted unscrupulously," Stucki pointedly told Homberger as they read the report. "I just don't understand why the Bankers Association uncritically defends a minority of banks." Dunant, conveniently, was absent. Schwab added his support: "The association swore that all the banks had behaved with absolute honesty. At the last meeting Dunant said he'd shoot this one down." Even Ott was outspoken: "The banks clearly thought that it was all a theoretical discussion."

Disdainful of that unanimity, Homberger defended the banks. "Most Germans left their money here for security, not for the interest. Surely we can't force the banks to pay interest?" Amazed, Stucki replied, "We must protect the Germans. We'll let a court decide." Homberger, not to be outflanked as a protector of German interests, also cared for the banks. He spoke on behalf of all of Switzerland's industrialists, and his solution was unchallengeable by a mere government official: "There's no hurry. Let's postpone taking any action." Stucki accepted defeat. Schwab uttered a cry of despair: "I always tell everyone that we protect the Germans. But I don't understand why interest should not be paid just because it suits the banks." Schwab, of course, knew the answer to his own outburst. The banks enjoyed influence and protection among the nation's power brokers. And there was now a unity of purpose among Dunant, Homberger and most government officials to champion Switzerland's interests, reassure the Germans, rebut the Allies and ignore the Jews.

11

PERFIDIOUS SWISS

A Jewish conspiracy, Walter Stucki was convinced, challenged and menaced Switzerland. As Switzerland's relationship with the Allies improved, he became obsessed with the fear that his country's recovery was hindered by malicious threats and criticism published in British and American newspapers. The conspirators, he believed, were members of the Committee Against the Third World War, whose chairman, he was sure, was Lord Vansittart, the mouthpiece for the Jews.

In fact, Vansittart, an outstanding senior British civil servant, had led the prewar campaign against appeasement and Hitler and in the postwar years was an equally passionate anticommunist. He was not Jewish but a devout churchman, not anti-Swiss, and not associated with the committee. But Stucki's paranoia, common among his countrymen, effortlessly fed his delusions. "The committee is 80 percent Jewish," Stucki told Homberger and the bankers. "Its guiding spirit is a French Jew." Hirsch, identified as a Frenchman involved in its work, had been banned from entering Switzerland. "We've got to defend ourselves against dollar imperialism," agreed the industrialist Ernst Speiser solemnly. Unembarrassed by his articulation of the Nazis' doctrine associating Jews, Americans and communists, he added, "The Americans are obstructive." Brazen anti-Semitism and pro-Nazi sentiments had become common within the Compensation Office. Max Ott, in a discussion about the fate of IG Farben, revealed that "a Galacian Jew called Roth has been nominated by the

Americans to receive 25 percent of IG Chemie if he helps them expose the German ownership of the company." In the league table of disparagement, "Galacian Jews" were classed by anti-Semites at the bottom, living among rats in the sewers. The Compensation Office's prejudice was intensified by the appointment in February 1947 of Franz Kappeler as a senior officer. Posted during the war to the Swiss embassy in Berlin, Kappeler had voluntarily joined a pro-Nazi organization and frequently boasted of his pro-German sentiments. That reinforcement of prejudice was evident in the Compensation Office's treatment of the unclaimed possessions of Jews.

Stacked neatly in warehouses across Switzerland lay a mountain of unclaimed luggage and crates, sent by anxious Jews from all over Europe in advance of their uncompleted journeys before and during the war. The aspiring refugees had carefully labeled their possessions for eventual collection. Many undoubtedly contained valuables, pitifully hidden, to finance their owners' survival. Two years after the war, the Jews' fate had been long settled. Officials of the American Joint Distribution Committee (AJDC), in conversations with Max Ott of the Compensation Office and with officials in von Steiger's Ministry of Justice, claimed those possessions as heirless assets to be used for the benefit of the survivors. The response was uniformly negative. Swiss secrecy laws, they were told, prevented anyone but the owners from looking at the labels. No unauthorized person could be allowed access to hunt for a relative's possessions, nor could these possessions be transferred for the communal use of the Jewish refugees. Since the claimants were dead, the AJDC was told, the luggage would be auctioned to pay the outstanding warehouse costs. The contents could be plundered by the storage companies.

For the demoralized Jews, suffering deteriorating health in the camps during the second winter since their release from concentration camps, hopes were dwindling. Sympathetic banks had advanced loans to the AJDC in the expectation that the $25 million promised by Switzerland in Washington in 1946 would soon be received, but that cash had been spent by the two Jewish refugee agencies while

Stucki prevaricated and then refused to advance the first $12.5 million (SF50 million) as agreed. Without funds, the AJDC's task was becoming impossible. On March 28, 1947, Edward Warburg, its chairman, appealed to Dean Acheson, the acting secretary of state, for help: "We've reached the limits of our resources." Acheson was asked to persuade Switzerland to advance at least $5 million to prevent the "demoralization and deterioration of these victims" in the camps.

On April 16, 1947, Acheson protested to the Swiss about the delay in paying the $12.5 million and asked for an immediate payment of at least $5 million, "in full recognition of the urgent needs of those victims." Inevitably, the industrialists' representative Heinrich Homberger was consulted about Switzerland's response. Conscious of the Allies' disarray, Homberger urged the Political Department to ignore their threats. Switzerland "must not rush," he told Stucki. Everything would be solved by playing for time. That policy appealed to Stucki, but realizing that Switzerland's bankers and industrialists wanted to terminate the accord, he feared the consequences. "The government will never go that far," he cautioned Homberger. "We're not strong enough for that. There'd be a huge international press campaign against Switzerland, and that would be very unwelcome." Patiently, the industrialist manipulated the puppet into an appreciation of the realities of power. By the end, the bombastic official was convinced of his own masterful creation of a new policy. "We'll be accused of sabotage," he told Homberger. "We have to work out what alibi we can use."

Stucki rose to the occasion. Adopting his most solemn pose, he expressed to Gerald Selous, the British commercial secretary, his "deep sympathy" for the refugees, reaffirmed his eagerness to help the victims of Nazism—and regretted that nothing could be done. His excuse had been carefully plotted by officials in Bern. The Jewish refugees, Petitpierre's department had decided, would be exploited as a bargaining ploy to secure Switzerland's own claim for German assets.

Stucki's expression did not betray any cynicism as he unfolded

Switzerland's dilemma to the Englishman. Before any sale of the German assets could begin, so that money could be collected for reparations, he told Selous, a rate of exchange needed to be fixed between the Swiss franc and the Reichsmark. Otherwise, he continued, the German owners might not receive fair compensation for their confiscated property. In the meantime, he concluded regretfully, "nothing can be done."

The Foreign Office's reaction to the "bombshell" was to convince itself that Stucki was personally to blame for Switzerland's gymnastics. "I have been wondering," commented Villiers, "whether the Swiss political authorities are aware of the tangle that we have got into. Monsieur Stucki is a notoriously obstinate man and may have been keeping the whole business to himself."

James Mann, still employed in the American embassy's Safehaven team and the regular butt of Stucki's complaints as "obstructive" and guilty of "endless puerilities," knew that Stucki was simply the front for a cabal. "The Swiss," he declared, "are going to have to be defeated. We're going to kick them down." Eagerly, Mann had responded to an invitation from the American and Canadian delegates at the Inter-Allied Reparations Agency (IARA) in Brussels to discuss how the money could be extracted from Switzerland. To Stucki's relief, the West's deteriorating relations with the Soviet Union had paralyzed that initiative. "We could rely on the support of the British and French governments," Stucki said with a smile, "to block that move."

By then, although German assets in Switzerland were, according to the Allies, worth $1 billion, only $2.6 million (SF11.5 million) had been raised by the Compensation Office through the sale of houses, cars, machinery and a trout farm. A meeting at the Foreign Office to consider "suggestions for turning the heat on the Swiss" debated the question whether Washington should be asked to refreeze Swiss assets and deny Swiss businessmen visas. Instead, influenced by British diplomats in Bern who, easily seduced by their hosts, excused the Compensation Office's "admirable work" despite the slow "running in" of a reluctant staff employed in a "blind-alley job," Villiers reflected that any action would be "likely to stiffen the Swiss in their present attitude." The State Department's counterproposal—that Switzerland either sell the property pending agreement on an exchange rate or hand over SF250 million immediately and sell the German property at its own pace—was also dismissed: "We regard the American proposals as altogether impossible."

Thanks to the British, the Swiss had achieved their purpose—to delay any sale of German property for reparations until Germany's fate was established. In the meantime, to increase the pressure on the Allies, the Compensation Office's discrimination against the German Jews was intensified. While Max Ott insisted that all Germans must be treated identically—ordering that the assets of German Jews should be sold off in common with other German property—his decrees were sharply discriminatory. To help Germans secure their property in Switzerland, he proposed that any German who had served in Hitler's armed forces should be deemed not to have lived in Germany. Yet simultaneously he tightened the regulations preventing German Jews who had returned to Germany from using their money and property. Unashamedly, Stucki endorsed the reinterpretation of the letter he had signed in Washington committing Switzerland to help Jewish refugees. To match the new mood in Bern, he insisted that no distinction in favor of Jews was intended in the confiscation and sale of German assets. "It seems to me that the letter must have equally referred to German Jews," he told his Compensation Office colleagues. In Washington, Rubin was appalled: "It never crossed the minds of the Allied negotiators to discriminate against those persecuted in Germany. The Swiss are being difficult." Swiss lawyers were using the Jews as pawns.

On March 26, 1947, a test case was presented to Stucki. Maria Wilcke, a German Jew who had survived an extermination camp, had found on reaching Switzerland that her bank refused to hand over her savings and was threatening to confiscate the money for reparations. In reply to the State Department's appeal for help, Stucki wrote: "I must concede that it would be obnoxious if Mrs. Wilcke's Swiss assets were liquidated, considering her suffering in Germany." But his words were not matched by any rectification of the grievance.

In justification of the misery Swiss discrimination was causing, Stucki pointed to the Allies' conduct toward Jews in Germany. In May 1945 Germany had been divided by the four wartime Allies into four zones. Each zone was ruled by an Allied military government, making its own laws by decree. While the three Western Allies increasingly coordinated the economies of their zones, their disagreements over less important issues—such as the restitution of property—delighted Stucki. In the American zone, the military government had decreed that the property of the 100,000 Jews who had lived in the area until 1933 should be restored to the survivors or their heirs. But, despite American pressure, both Britain and France had refused to enact similar legislation in their own zones. The British, controlling a zone where over 100,000 Jews had lived until 1933, had reneged on their earlier support for the Jews. Their military government refused to issue a decree allowing Jews to claim damages from Germans, to use the heirless assets for the relief of survivors, or to allow Jews to recover their own property from the Nazis, who had expelled them from their homes, casting them penniless into the streets. British policy caused the American Jewish Committee (AJC) "deep regret," but British Jewry had failed to persuade the Labor government to acknowledge the immorality of allowing the survivors, often sick from incarceration in concentration camps, to remain destitute while their tormentors tranquilly enjoyed the benefits of their crime. Whitehall's agenda was consistent: the Jews should not be allowed even to recover their own money because it might finance their cause in Palestine.

The AJC's efforts in Paris had proved equally "futile." Not surprising, perhaps, since French police had deported over 100,000 Jews to concentration camps during the war. The French government had refused to help the survivors and heirs of the 45,000 Jews who had previously lived in their zone. Instead, the Nazis' victims suffered discrimination. With official French encouragement, the Germans authorities established "common funds" to collect the heirless assets of Jews and keep the money for the benefit of the local Germans. Confiscated Jewish property was to remain in the possession of former Nazis, even if, say, the original owner sought to reclaim a home. Penalized by their lack of money, documents and assistance, returning Jews were barred from their own homes by the same Nazis—supported by the French government—who had originally expelled them onto the streets. Protests were deliberately stalled by the French on the ground that assisting Jews "constitutes an act of discrimination." When the French restitution office closed in March 1951, only 2,762 cases had been investigated, leaving 98,675 applications abandoned and undecided.

Since the Allies had at the Paris conference delegated France to bring pressure upon Switzerland to extract the reparations for the Jewish refugee organizations, Stucki satisfactorily drew the inference that the Swiss, following British and French policy, could favor German interests and their own interests instead of the Jews'. But he had reckoned without the passion of the crusaders.

In August 1947, under pressure from Jewish groups to demand an interim payment for the refugees, the State Department again protested to Petitpierre that at least $5 million should be advanced for the refugees. Washington expected the Foreign Office and the French to support that demand. But the U.S. protest was condemned by the Foreign Office as a "bad mistake" because it gave Switzerland "a chance of evading the major issue." Officials feared that the Swiss would make a "beau geste as regards Jewish refugees"—a generous gesture enhancing Switzerland's reputation—while seeking an excuse to prevent the sale of German property. That alarmed the Foreign Office, whose principal motive was to deny the American Joint Distribution Committee the relief money to promote clandestine immigration into Palestine.

In Bern, Selous, always sympathetic toward the Swiss, had deliberately left Stucki with the impression that the British were not too eager for the $5 million to be paid. The British, Stucki understood, supported his official justification for not handing over the money from the sale of German assets. "It's not our fault," smirked the Swiss, "that the sale has not yet begun."

Relishing these exhibitions of Anglo-French prejudice and eager to display his talent for playing the international broker, Stucki seized the opportunity of a regular meeting with Homberger to express his real feelings concerning the pressure upon Switzerland to hand over the SF50 million. "I've no doubt that behind this broad and strong offensive against us are Jewish groups provoking trouble in Washington, in Paris and among the smaller Allies." Unconsciously, Stucki was using the vocabulary familiarly used by the Nazis. When Goebbels had ranted about Jewish provocation, he had used the word *aufhetzen*—just as Stucki was now doing. "Supporting the Jewish attack," continued Stucki, warming to his listener's prejudice, "are commercial interests. After all, the first SF50 million is for the Nazis' victims and 90 percent is going to the Jews." Stucki speculated about the advantages of paying the money immediately: "We'd pacify the 'hunger' of these groups and it would show our goodwill." The Swiss government, he admitted, had agreed to pay the SF50 million if the Allies asked. "But," he added rhetorically, cherishing the opportunity to exploit the Allies' disagreements, "it's not clear whether the Allies would make an approach." Looking at Homberger, he concluded with delight, "The British position in Palestine, it appears, would not be improved if this money falls into Jewish hands. Let's find a discerning Englishman to help us."

Receptive to Stucki's tone, and especially to his criticism of the Jews' "provocation," Homberger lashed out at the Allies' occupation of Germany. "It's absolutely appalling to watch that awful, careless, senseless policy they're pursuing," whined a man who recalled the recent Nazi past with nostalgia and whose contribution to Europe's reconstruction was to propose that "our best policy is to wait and see." The industrialists' leader, irritated by the notion of giving SF50 million to refugees, was unconcerned by the Jews. "The provocation by those organized groups," he told Stucki, also using the Goebbels expression *aufhetzen*, "shouldn't affect us. We've probably made so many concessions to the Allies that they think they can trample all over us." On that issue, there was unanimity. The plight of the Jews was irrelevant, and the fate of the SF50 million depended upon the united force of the Allied demand.

By the end of August, Stucki was confident that the Allies' criticism had been muted and the SF50 million had "become an amusing question." Gerald Selous, his trusted Briton, had confirmed that the British government, anxious to prevent Jews from chartering ships to transport refugees to Palestine, was "in no hurry" for the funds to reach the Jewish groups and was untroubled if Switzerland failed to honor its pledge. All that remained to be done if the Political Department was completely to restore its close relations with the Allies was to persuade the U.S. government that the disagreements about the Washington Accord should be ignored. The policy of stubbornness of little Switzerland drew closer to success by the decision of Vyacheslav Molotov, the Soviet foreign minister, to abandon the summit of the four Allies in Paris on July 2, 1947, and return to Moscow.

Molotov's abrupt departure from Paris shattered the dream of a peaceful postwar settlement in Europe. Two years of political bickering and ideological intrigue about the government of Germany had crippled the continent's economy. In Paris, the three Allied foreign ministers and an army of officials huddled together pondering the outcome of an unpredictable war of nerves. Salvation was delivered by George Marshall, the U.S. secretary of state, the mastermind of a detailed plan to pour billions of dollars into Europe to stave off imminent disaster. To Petitpierre's delight, the State Department invited Switzerland to join the discussions about implementing the plan. Switzerland, crowed the officials in the Political Department, had been readmitted to the European community.

"We can defeat any Allied onslaught," boasted Stucki, "and the French agree with us. Shares in Switzerland are rising. The future of Germany has changed." With satisfaction, he noted that no one was asking about the SF50 million anymore. Like all Swiss, he viewed the American trials in Nuremberg of German industrialists, bankers and former Nazi government officials on charges of international plunder and the employment of slave labor as a contemptible example of victors' vengeance. A request from the United States for information about loot hidden by Austrian and Hungarian war criminals was derided by Ott.

"War criminals" no longer existed, and the Allies lacked the power to crush Swiss obstructions, he chortled. Significantly, the Compensation Office did not draw the same conclusion about the heirless assets. Stucki still seemed bound by his undertaking.

In January 1947, the *Finanz-Revue*, a newspaper representing Switzerland's financial sector, had published an editorial supporting the case, in the name of Switzerland's good reputation, for distributing the heirless assets, on the ground that "it would not be understood if these accounts remained in Swiss banks without the banks' knowing who owned the money." Reflecting the same sentiment, Olivier Long, working in the Political Department, produced in March a draft law requiring banks, insurance companies and others to notify the department of all assets of depositors "of whom there has been no sign of life since May 9, 1945." The punishment for failing to declare the assets was a fine or imprisonment.

Rumors about the draft law aroused anger among the bankers. Telephoning Stucki's office, Alberto Caflisch, the Bankers Association secretary, announced that he was "very annoyed" by the preparations for a census of all assets. His bluster was calculated. Caflisch knew that not only were the bankers unwilling to reveal the unclaimed Jewish assets, but, more important, there were enormous wartime deposits by Nazis and Germans, probably of loot stolen from Jews and others, lying in dormant accounts. Either the depositors had been killed in the war or, quite possibly, they could not safely leave Germany and enter Switzerland in the current circumstances. To care for the Germans' interests, a major concern for the banks, it was vital to sabotage the government's scheme. To avoid the law, Caflisch suggested, the banks would conduct a voluntary census that would be passed to the department in confidence. His offer was accepted at the end of May, but with a warning. If the banks failed to complete a census, said Stucki's assistant de Rahm, the government would be bound to introduce a law requiring a census to "satisfy the undertakings given in Washington."

Eight weeks later, capitalizing on the dramatic change of atmosphere after the breakdown of the Allies' talks in Paris, Caflisch approached the government hoping to persuade ministers to abandon a meaningful census. At a meeting with the Political Department on August 21, he volunteered that the Bankers Association's members would conduct a census but "without any guarantees." Pointedly, the banker told de Rahm, "We are sure that the result will not be a serious basis for any discussions." Adolf Jann, the intimidating managing director of the Union Bank of Switzerland, who had been the wartime secretary of the Bankers Association and was present to support Caflisch, agreed: "If the amount is big, the Allies' appetite will grow bigger; if it's small, they'll doubt its validity." Caflisch nodded. The number of depositors who had died without heirs, he said with remarkable authority, "is between 3 and 5 percent." De Rahm was left in no doubt about the efficacy of the proposed census and why the bankers were no longer inclined to cooperate. "The era when the accord was signed," said Caflisch, "has changed. America is no longer as strong and there's no reason to go down on one's knees because of stupid questions. On the contrary. It's convenient to profit from circumstances and tell them quite clearly that this question must be reconsidered." De Rahm was too insignificant to disagree, especially after Caflisch threatened war if "such a stupid measure" was ordered. Any answer to a census, de Rahm rapidly became disposed to agree, would be satisfactory and there would be no upset if the amount was small.

Any qualms still harbored by de Rahm and his departmental colleagues about Switzerland's promise to find the heirless assets were quashed on receipt of a letter from Paris. In a new reply to Switzerland's letter asking the amount of heirless assets found by the French government, Paris stated that a search among the nation's banks had revealed "no heirless assets." Considering that 83,000 French Jews had been murdered and that the French had been major clients of the Swiss banks, the statement lacked credibility. To the Political Department, the abrupt denial also signaled the Allies' loss of interest in the topic. "I confirm," wrote Walter Hohl from the Ministry of Justice to Stucki, "that, concerning the heirless assets, it is not necessary to take any further action until the Allies raise the matter." The bankers naturally agreed. Switzerland, wrote the association, more as an order to the Political Department than as an opinion, should not take any further initiatives. By then, the association had revised an earlier estimate that the total of heirless assets held by its members was SF208,000 and told the government that its members had found heirless assets worth SF482,000. To suggest that the wealthiest among the six million murdered Jews had deposited just over $100,000 in Swiss banks was less than credible but was the alleged result of a careful search among the association's four hundred members. To terminate the discussion, the association told the government that any future queries from the Allies should be met by repeating the counterquery: asking what those governments were doing to find heirless assets in their own countries. To the bankers and the Political Department that appeared to close the whole matter.

Distraught that, just two years after the horrors of the Holocaust had been exposed, the Allied governments and the Swiss government seemed united in their indifference to the fate of the survivors, the Swiss Federation of Jewish Associations delivered a long plea to the Political Department. Reminding officials of the unprecedented murder of millions of innocents, the federation warned that the heirless assets would disappear, to be kept by those who happened to be entrusted with them. "Millions of Swiss francs are involved," asserted the federation, adding that the deposits were scattered among Swiss corporations, which held the money as a favor for foreigners, and only a law could uncover the truth. The federation requested a meeting with Petitpierre. Within the Political Department, there was no appetite for a meeting with the Jews. The Allies, the foreign minister was told, "do not seem very interested in this question." Even a U.S. diplomat had told the department, "This issue is of no great interest in America." The department's decision was inaction: "We'll leave this dormant and pick it up only if the Allies raise it." The Swiss Jews were told that Petitpierre was unavailable. The next step, carefully contrived within the department, was to test whether Washington would tolerate the unceremonious burial of the accord.

Inspired by a leak from Petitpierre, the *New York Times* published

a dispatch from Bern on September 14, 1947, stating that Swiss officials no longer believed the accord would be implemented and had
"virtually abandoned" their objective of destroying German financial
power in Switzerland. Sowing more mischief, Stucki leaked to a journalist the claim that Washington had rejected a Swiss offer of $11
million for the refugees, which was untrue. Switzerland had not made
an offer but was passively waiting for the Allies' request. As the mis-
information started to gain credibility, Stucki watched the gathering
confusion with delight. Jewish groups attacked the U.S. government
for rejecting an offer and in turn disbelieved the administration's
denials. U.S. diplomats in Bern relayed their suspicions about the
original source of that story to Washington. Cursing British perfidy,
the State Department summoned Lord Inverchapel, the British
ambassador, for a reprimand. The Swiss, he was told, would have to
abide by the accord they had signed and, moreover, the British could
not ignore "the humanitarian principles" to which they also were
committed. Inverchapel departed without comment, "preferring to
let sleeping dogs lie." Foreign Office reaction to the unwarranted
reprimand was truculent. "The Americans, of course," commented
Neal Goodchild, "have been unable to act without us and so nothing
has been done." Unashamedly he described how Britain, anxious not
to "weaken our bargaining position" with Switzerland, would be willing to consider an American proposal only if it was "economically
advantageous to HMG." Smoothing Britain's relations with
Switzerland was the priority, despite the obligations under the
Washington Accord to obtain money for the refugees: "We are
unfortunately committed to . . . this scheme and we can hinder it only
by raising technical objections such as those which have so far held up
the release of the 50 million Swiss francs." Petitpierre was adroitly
exploiting British sympathy.

Since May 1946, the crusaders had gradually become convinced
that Paul's failure to include sanctions in the Washington Accord had
encouraged Swiss obstinacy. Rubin in particular was angry about the
Swiss denial of an "informal agreement" to exclude Jewish property
from the compulsory sale. There had been, Swiss diplomats insisted,

no such conversation. Rubin and his colleagues gathered at a meeting in the State Department on November 25, 1947, and regretted that their only option for securing Swiss cooperation was a diplomatic protest. That admission of weakness was combined with the crusaders' last hope: the appointment of Nat King, a forty-year-old Texan engineer turned lawyer, as the Safehaven diplomat in Bern. Because King had served during the war in Argentina and London as a Safehaven officer, Rubin clung to the hope, as he briefed the diplomat, that the energetic lawyer might succeed in discomfiting the Swiss. But King's personality did not bode well. "A big, bumbling fellow," thought Rubin, "without any emotional commitment." King's singular achievement by the end of his tour was to write a book describing Swiss restaurants.

King was greeted in Bern by James Mann's announcement that his investigation of the Swiss banks' handling of stolen securities had exposed Max Ott's persistent deception. For two years, Ott had assured Mann that the Allies could rely upon the affidavits supplied by banks attesting to the legitimate Swiss ownership of shares. Repeatedly, Ott had assured Mann that "a better system of control could not have been devised." Under threat of prosecution for commercial espionage, the Swiss had forbidden Allied citizens to undertake any investigations while apparently refusing to conduct any of their own. Ott's excuse was that Allied information was invariably wrong. But in a confidential, internal report Stucki had disclosed, "Regrettably, the Compensation Office has discovered that a large number of affidavits were false." His excuse was not for Mann's eyes. "It is understandable that some Swiss, holding assets for German friends, faced a conflict of interests and did not obey the law."

Helped by sympathetic Swiss lawyers, Mann, nevertheless, had in March 1947 received evidence confirming that Ted Hoch of the Swiss Bank Corporation was a "fence for the systematic falsification of affidavits." The SBC, confided a Swiss lawyer, was "notorious for such practices." Swiss lies, Mann told King, "were so convincing." But pursuit of Hoch, he added, was pointless. Not only had the Swiss refused to reopen their wartime investigation, but Hoch, through an anti-

NAZI GOLD ■ 193

Safehaven diplomat in the American embassy, had obtained a visa and traveled to New York. "Looks like a charade," King said, laughing. "Do you think the Swiss officials know what's happening?" King was clearly bewildered by the idea of government-endorsed dishonesty.

Ott did, however, consider the incriminating evidence collated by Mann about the Union Bank's cloaking of share transactions in the Munich Reinsurance Company. Ott had even wanted to tell Mann that the Compensation Office had completed its own investigation, which incriminated Paul Jaberg, the bank's president; and Rudolf Ernst, the bank's honorary president. It would, he told Homberger and Dunant, be "a little dangerous" to conceal the findings of the Compensation Office, since the Americans would eventually discover the truth. Homberger overruled his advice: "There's no reason to hand over this information." Dunant of the Bankers Association agreed. Ott, complained Dunant, had portrayed the bankers in a "disadvantageous manner." Although no one could disagree that the bankers had awkwardly broken the law, the financier conceded, the Americans were using these cases and the accord to further their commercial interests.

While the Swiss wrung their hands, Mann confronted Adolf Jann, the UBS chief with close connections to the insurance companies, about the Munich Reinsurance plot. "Surprised" and "very much embarrassed" by the exposure, Jann gave what Mann considered an odd explanation. The covert transaction, said Jann, had been undertaken only because the German official offering the shares had pleaded that he would be murdered on his return if he failed to accomplish the deal. Jann presented no evidence for that colorful defense and, after receiving the dossier from Mann, Ott did not undertake any further investigation. Ott's lack of interest was consistent with the Compensation Office's failure to investigate Crédit Suisse and the Julius Baer banks after Walter Ostrow's complaints that three U.S. servicemen were selling stolen Dutch securities through the two banks. The cause of the inactivity was not just prejudice. Rather, Compensation Office officials had unearthed much more serious falsification cases relating to the theft of foreign shares.

One investigation incriminated both of Petitpierre's brothers—the banker and the speculator.

The Compensation Office's investigation of the Petitpierres had been commenced after inquiries by Mann and Ostrow. Although the Americans were dissatisfied by the Compensation Office's response, by August 1948 the investigators had compiled a damaging exposé of corruption, and their report was due to be considered on August 8 by the seven ministers of the Bundesrat, Switzerland's cabinet. Unusually, an announcement in the *Bund* newspaper predicted that the council would be making a statement about "a very serious and sensitive affair involving gold, valuables and affidavits."

The short statement shocked Eberhard Reinhardt, who was the director of Crédit Suisse and an observer at the Washington negotiations. A short, intelligent man with a squeaky voice, Reinhardt, the son of a priest, was very good at seeming reasonable and winning the trust of U.S. diplomats in Bern while actively scheming against the Allies' interests. Reinhardt knew that besides Alexander Petitpierre, the speculator, senior government officials and businessmen in Geneva, Lausanne and the Valais were also implicated in procuring and selling the false affidavits during and after the war. That morning, Reinhardt's first call from his holiday home in the mountains was to the minister of defense—a personal friend and one of the seven who would meet later that day. Begging that the affair be handled with utmost discretion, Reinhardt urged his friend to prevent at all costs any sensational disclosures. Publicity about the regrettable affair, he told the minister, would cause "immense" and "irreparable damage" to Switzerland's banks and the whole country. To foreign countries it would confirm all the accusations of "corruption" directed at Swiss banks in the previous years: "Outsiders will not realize that this is a one-off mistake by individuals who forgot their responsibilities." Instead of "finding alibis," Reinhardt went on, "we would all be under constant suspicion, just like over the looted gold. . . . Everyone will think that the whole of Switzerland is rotten."

The following day, Reinhardt's plea was endorsed in a telephone call by Albert Nussbaumer, the trusted director of the Union Bank, to

Franz Kappeler at the Compensation Office. The banker, expecting the official to pass his message on to Petitpierre, repeated that the "bankers were very worried by the rumor" of the Bundersrat's meeting and about a draft communiqué, which named not only the suspects but also the banks involved. Nussbaumer was well informed. The secret communiqué mentioned, among others, Alexander Petitpierre. "Have you considered," asked Nussbaumer, spelling out the bankers' fear of the United States, "the effect on Swiss financial interests abroad?" The communiqué should be withheld, he urged, and Petitpierre should agree to meet Bernhard Sarasin, the president of the Bankers Association. Personal discussions with politicians, the bankers reassured themselves, always guaranteed their influence. The lobbying was apparently successful, although the formal decision taken by the seven ministers at the Bundesrat meeting on August 8 was, as usual, never officially disclosed, but it could be inferred from its consequences.

By the time Sarasin met Petitpierre, another Compensation Office investigation had discovered that false affidavits for securities and residence permits had also been traded in the canton of Fribourg. Max Schwab's advice to Petitpierre was to suppress the new revelation. Two days later, on August 26, Petitpierre rejected the proposal. The Americans, replied the foreign minister, had already been told. That, Petitpierre knew, was untrue, but he had no intention of leaving an incriminating paper trail. Nevertheless, mindful of Reinhardt's request for secrecy, Petitpierre read with benevolence a submission from the Bankers Association justifying the false affidavits as a legitimate self-defense against the illegal freeze on Swiss assets in the United States. Nothing more, the minister decided, needed to be done. With evident relief, Caflisch and Dunant assured the possessors of the stolen shares that, since the statute of limitations for recovering stolen property had expired, any future attempt to retrieve the looted shares would be hampered by the procedures of the normal civil courts. In the annual report of the Bankers Association, both men naturally concealed the scandal. "Our experience has confirmed," they informed their members, "our earlier opinion that the existence of stolen share certificates in Switzerland was greatly exaggerated." Concealing embarrassments was, as the Safehaven team discovered, an effortless chore for Swiss officials.

Nat King quickly grasped, after sitting with Ott and the two other Allied representatives through just two sessions, the institutionalized masquerade of the Compensation Office and of the Joint Commission established under the accord to sell German assets. In strictly legal terms, the Nazis' victims could rely only upon adoption by the Swiss of "principles of morality and fairness," and the Swiss showed "no intention of doing much." The "charade," King reported to Washington about the Joint Commission, was "entirely unworkable and the quicker it is abolished the better." The blame for that condition, King believed, lay not only with the Swiss, who regarded the Compensation Office "as only an impotent consultative body and somewhat of a nuisance," but with the "servile attitude of the French member of the Commission" and the "complacency of the British member."

The attitudes that infuriated King manifested themselves in the two diplomats' reports. While the French representative uncritically supported Swiss policy, Hugh Legg, the British representative, had described the Compensation Office to London as "satisfactory" and its rules as sufficiently "elastic" for each case and claim to be decided on its merits. For their part, the British had become exasperated by the Americans.

Ever since the Washington Accord was signed, British and U.S. officials had, with disparate enthusiasm, sought to negotiate its implementation. But the mood in Washington had changed, however. Having frozen, confiscated or sold German assets in the United States, officials in the State Department and Treasury cared little about extracting reparations from the German assets in Switzerland. All that remained of interest in Washington was the IG Chemie interests located in the United States, which were worth over $100 million. Washington insisted that IG Chemie was German, but the Swiss government, covertly protecting German interests, claimed that the company was legitimately and entirely owned by Swiss shareholders. In retaliation for the continued American sequestration, the Swiss refused to transfer the promised SF50 million to the refugees or help the Jews to recover either their deposits in Switzerland or the heirless assets. The battle between Washington and Bern had poisoned the implementation of the accord.

One year earlier Villiers had been convinced of the Allies' strength: "The Swiss are rattled and Stucki knows that he is on the spot." But now, in 1948, the British official blasted the "American intention . . . to smash the accord." The Justice Department's obsession about IG Farben, he complained, was "the nigger in the woodpile." That obsession was typical of the "ignorance and crass stupidity which the Americans have always shown in Safehaven matters."

Petitpierre was content with the "slow tempo of the operation," and his interest in the accord had "long since dwindled to a quiescent distaste." His policy was to do practically nothing other than wait for the Allies to come around to Switzerland's point of view. Deriding the Allies' request for SF50 million, and irritated that the government should consider honoring the accord, Heinrich Homberger growled, "We mustn't throw money out of the window." He added, in reference to the gold payment, "We've already given the Allies SF250 million. I wouldn't like to bet that the accord will be implemented." Doing nothing also suited the industrialists and the bankers. In the meantime, the bookkeepers in the Compensation Office diligently reduced their estimate of available German assets from SF581 million to SF371 million—a far cry from Washington's estimate of SF4 billion ($1 billion). "I'm not displeased about these figures," Dunant had said to Max Ott with measured cynicism. "It just shows the weakness of the old press campaign against Switzerland." Fear of the crusaders now seemed a dim memory.

On the eve of his resignation from the State Department, Seymour Rubin was sensitive about his original gullibility regarding Swiss promises. Unlike the ever-skeptical Sam Klaus, who was single-handedly fighting the Pentagon to prevent incriminated German scientists, many guilty of war crimes, from settling permanently in the United States, Rubin had trusted some colleagues. Officially, the State Department had accepted that there was nothing in the Washington Accord to help claims by anti-Nazi Germans and the persecutees, but as a parting gesture Rubin persuaded Willard Thorp, the assistant secretary of state for economic affairs, to invite Stucki to Washington and to protest formally to him about Switzerland's failure to honor its commitments to the Jews.

Among the last crusaders still serving in the government, Rubin had developed close social relations with the Swiss diplomats in Washington but was unable, despite tennis and dinner parties, to gain a closer understanding of their endgame. His Swiss hosts, however, had accurately gauged the declining support for his cause in the department and, in their reports to Bern, had encouraged their government's instinctive resort to self-interest. Then, on March 24, 1948, Thorp's invitation to Stucki arrived.

Nineteen days earlier, General Lucius Clay, the American military governor of the United States zone in Germany, had cabled to the Pentagon warning that war with the Soviet Union "may come with dramatic suddenness." Six days after Thorp's invitation had been sent to Stucki, the Red Army imposed a blockade around Berlin in a bid to drive the Allies out of Eastern Europe, isolating the western part of the city and heralding the Cold War. Affected by the tension now pervading Washington, Thorp perceived no advantage in continuing to irritate Switzerland and contemplated renegotiating the Washington Accord. But that notion would arouse British anger. The State Department, complained the Foreign Office, is "wasting time [and will] only [make] the Allies look ridiculous [by] virtually repudiating their signature. . . . We have too often in the past given way to the State Department against our better judgment."

Thwarted by London, Thorp adhered to the agreed-on script when Stucki arrived. "We're worried about the lack of progress," said Thorp.

"We refuse to allow history to brand us as thieves," replied Stucki brazenly. "The Germans must receive fair compensation for their property." The issue, he said, was the rate of exchange between the Swiss franc and the German mark.

"Is that the only problem?" asked Rubin, exhausted by the Himalayan proportions of the disagreement.

"Yes," replied Stucki. "We are interested in a speedy solution. After all, we will receive 50 percent of the proceeds." The Swiss was unmoved by the news that, to prevent the sale of Jewish assets in Switzerland, Congress had passed a law preventing the government from accepting as reparations any property in Switzerland belonging to persecutees. That, he said smoothly, smacked of interference in Switzerland's sovereignty.

Depressed, Rubin cast a glance at Thorp. There was not a hint of emotion. Shortly afterward, Rubin resigned from the department to join a private law firm.

Stucki meanwhile returned to Bern to reassure his colleagues that Thorp was markedly different from the crusaders. He was a man who sympathized with the Swiss.

Stucki's self-congratulation was brief. Over the previous year, Swiss stubbornness had split the Allies, but new evidence of Bern's duplicity, compiled as officials from the three Allied countries planned a new approach to finalize the accord settlement, quickly healed their disagreement. Switzerland, the officials realized, was making fools of the Allies.

Unraveling Switzerland's relationship with Germany had exposed the fact that Swiss wartime collaboration had been more profitable than previously imagined. Switzerland's claims that it had imported from Germany more than it had exported to Germany had camouflaged the truth. Careful examination of slick accounting had shown that Switzerland had earned extra profits by accepting looted gold to pay for financial services and for Swiss francs used in payment of imports from other countries. Clever accounting had also disguised Switzerland's imports of German coal as repayment of Germany's prewar debts. Switzerland was now demanding, in addition to those wartime profits, 50 percent of German property in Switzerland— which it still refused to seize and sell—to repay the SF1 billion in Swiss loans that had helped the Germans wage ware against the Allies. Considering Europe's continuing dire economic plight—widespread war damage, industrial dislocation and chronic shortage of fuel, food and medicines—Switzerland's contribution to the continent's recovery rested immobile at zero.

On May 5, 1948, the Allies protested to Bern about the "untenable position." The German assets in Switzerland, they complained, "make no contribution whatsoever to the common effort" of rebuilding Europe. Considering that the "urgency of the circumstances cannot be exaggerated," the Swiss were asked for an immediate SF100 million for the Allies and SF20 million for the refugees and a promise of negotiations to settle the implementation of the accord.

Alfred Escher, the Swiss chargé d'affaires in London, was summoned to the Foreign Office to explain Switzerland's stubbornness. By then, Britain's economy had seriously deteriorated—devaluation of sterling was for the first time being discussed—and the government's enthusiasm for a share of German property in Switzerland had grown after it had been calculated that, while the United States could expect 15 percent and France 20 percent, Britain would obtain over 40 percent of the proceeds. Britain's predicament did nothing to change Escher's cheerful attitude or his lack of contrition. Justifying Swiss obduracy, he recited a list of reasons why Switzerland could not comply with the accord—the Allies' slowness in replying to Swiss notes, the failure to agree on a rate of exchange, the status of the Swiss as trustees for German assets, and the claim that Switzerland had signed the accord "under duress." Escher added that the Allies' criticism of Switzerland was "unhelpful." Having completed his long condemnation, the diplomat departed. "As monstrous a piece of hypocrisy as we have come across," exclaimed the Foreign Office official subjected to Escher's reprimand.

The Allies' attempt to extract some money from the German property would end disastrously. Neal Goodchild had predicted that the Swiss had become "fed up with waiting and we will lose all advantage from the conciliatory attitude they have shown over the past three months." In the event, Stucki, the bulldozer, had scattered the Allies during the discussions. "He was as tricky, pompous and difficult as ever," Goodchild groaned, "and made himself thoroughly unpopular, particularly with the Swiss delegation." Condemning Swiss behavior as "abominable," Gerry Villiers had resigned himself to perpetual defeat: "It would not advance matters one whit to make a protest at Berne . . . but it would be no small satisfaction to tell the Swiss in blunt language what we think of them."

In Bern, Petitpierre and von Steiger gladly accepted their lawyers' advice that the government could continue to ignore the commitments signed in Washington. The Allies' renewed interest was clearly motivated by Switzerland's enemies. "I've no doubt," said Stucki, identifying the culprits, "that the Allies' initiative wasn't their own idea. The string goes back to the Committee Against the Third World War. That means, the strings go back to Jewish groups."

Under Stucki's supervision, the Compensation Office had become pitiless in its discrimination against the Jews. Allowing concentration-camp survivors use of their savings deposited in Swiss banks, Max Ott told Nat King's assistant, "would create insurmountable administrative difficulties" and "a very dangerous precedent." Poker-faced, Ott added, "We know that all Germans were victims of the Nazis." Stucki's officials in the Compensation Office had forgotten the Holocaust. Contrary to the decision on December 17, 1945, there had been prac-tically no exceptions to the freeze, not least because the Compensation Office "did not want to rely on dubious foreign documents."

Among Ott's victims was Jorg Heyd, a German-Jewish engineer who had fled to Switzerland in 1933. During an ill-timed visit to France in 1940, Heyd was arrested by the Germans. After miracu-lously surviving the war, Heyd was consistently denied reentry to Switzerland, and Ott denied him access to the substantial balance in his American Express bank account. Otto Mendelssohn-Bartholdy, the grandson of the German Jewish composer Felix Mendelssohn-Bartholdy, had survived a concentration camp and was also denied access to his savings in Swiss banks, in particular to shares worth SF1 million that had been confiscated by the Germans and deposited with UBS in Basel. The Compensation Office's justification for denying Mendelssohn-Bartholdy his money was his presence on February 16, 1945, when the freeze started, in a concentration camp in Germany—he was therefore "a German resident in Germany" on that date. With proof of his individual statelessness, Mendelssohn-Bartholdy had sought the help of Hans Frölicher, the official at the DIV appointed to care for Germans' interests. But in Frölicher's opinion, Mendelssohn-Bartholdy was a Jew, not a German. Referred by Frölicher to the Compensation Office, Mendelssohn-Bartholdy was told by Ott, unwilling to peek at the number tattooed on his visitor's arm, "The Swiss government would find it extremely difficult, having been a neutral, to distinguish between persecutees and other residents of Germany."

In private, Ott admitted that his real motive for discriminating against the Jews was to sabotage the Allies' freeze on German property. "When the Allies' influence in Germany diminishes," he agreed with Homberger, "then Germans will turn up here and accuse us of stealing their property." Not only Jews but also anti-Nazis would be used as Switzerland's pawns to help former Nazis. Members of the German resistance who had spied for the Allies against the Reich were, Ott decreed, forbidden to use their wartime payments deposited in Swiss banks by the Allies. "I'm against exceptions," Ott was told by Armin Daeniker, a Political Department official whose brother, Heinrich Daeniker, was a senior member of the Bankers Association. "It would weaken our position in the accord." Ernst Speiser, the industrialist, in blunt language, also supported the official: "I strongly warn you against allowing any exceptions. We mustn't allow that under any circumstances." Anti-Semitism and pro-Nazism had unashamedly resurfaced in Bern; yet paradoxically their manifestations were controlled by Stucki's sense of honor.

The creation of Israel in May 1948 (after Britain had ignominiously surrendered its mandate in Palestine and admitted defeat against the Arabs and Zionists) had altered Foreign Office policy toward helping the Jewish refugees. Now united, the Allied diplomats in Bern persuaded Stucki that Switzerland was finally bound to pay an interim SF20 million to the refugees. Stucki's concession infuriated Heinrich Homberger, who was certain that the creation of a new German state was inevitable. "I think it's a shame for those good Swiss francs," he told Stucki. "It's a loss for Switzerland," Dunant agreed. Goaded, Stucki lost his temper. The dual character of the official, pure Jekyll and Hyde, was displayed once again before his persistent critics: "It's about Switzerland's honor! The payment was agreed on in Washington!" But the moment passed and Stucki relaxed. So much, he conceded, had changed since 1946. Perhaps, he sighed, lamenting Britain's unreliability, he might remind the British about their confidential requests to withhold the money. "We thought that the British didn't want the Jews to get the money, but we didn't know that they would withdraw from Palestine." Reluctantly, on July 1, 1948, Stucki scribbled a note pledging that Switzerland would finally advance SF20 million "in view of the IRO's financial difficulties and out of compassion for the Nazis' victims." Four weeks later, just as the money was deposited in the International Refugee Organization's account, an earthquake struck the foundations of the crusade.

In a hot congressional committee room on July 31, 1948, Elizabeth Bentley, a well-educated New Englander who was a graduate of Vassar, confessed that while posing as a librarian she had been a full-time courier shuttling between Soviet intelligence officers based in New York and Washington and senior U.S. government officials. Her admission, in the midst of the blockade of Berlin and the mobilization for war, that Americans were traitors destabilized the United States and offered a reprieve to Switzerland's bankers. In particular, Bentley accused Lauchlin Currie and Harry Dexter White of membership in a communist spy ring, taking orders from Moscow to sabotage the West German economy and using, among other weapons, the Safehaven program. Currency reforms in western zones of Germany and negotiations for a new constitution anticipated the permanent division of Germany by the creation of a West German state in 1949. Although Currie and White strongly denied the accusations and the evidence was questionable, to those American officials long opposed to Safehaven, Bentley's testimony not only was credible but explained and justified their antagonism. In Switzerland, the resentment against the Washington Accord and the Jews hardened. Currie and the freeze were a communist plot, the Swiss agreed. Overnight, Abba Schwartz, an easygoing AJDC executive, sensed that the Swiss attitude had become intolerable.

In 1945, Schwartz had found two gas cannisters filled with wedding rings and gold teeth near a liberated German concentration camp. With special permission, he had exchanged the gold for cash in Switzerland to help the survivors. Ever since, he had worked ceaselessly to persuade the Swiss to release the heirless assets, but in July 1948 the negotiations for the promised census to identify the heirless assets had first soured and then halted. "The Swiss government," wrote Jean Brunschvig from Geneva, "is determined not to initiate any legislation with regard to Jewish heirless property before some of the Allied nations have done the same."

Six months later, stirred by his conscience, Rubin lunched with former colleagues at the State Department. To his "amazement," he heard that the problems of the German Jews and the heirless assets remained unresolved. "This is a thorough perversion of the terms and the intent of the accord," he told Schwartz and volunteered to negotiate with the Swiss government on the AJDC's behalf. Rubin arrived in Bern in April 1949 aware that the Allied and Jewish negotiating position was "hopeless." Stucki was suffering from "diplomatic illness" and had withdrawn from the endless negotiations about implementing the accord. Both the British and the French delegations had told Nat King that their governments opposed giving any further money to the Jewish refugees and would not press the Swiss to unblock the German Jews' assets. The Allies' indifference had encouraged Swiss greed and unscrupulousness: ignoring Jewish claimants' pleas for their own money, the Swiss government had just released $47 million to Germans.

To secure Switzerland as an ally in the cold war, Washington had agreed to pay $69 million in compensation for the mistaken bombing in 1944 of Schaffhausen, a small town close to the German border. Switzerland had also demanded interest on the compensation. The damaged property, the Swiss argued, had not earned any money since the bombing. That bookkeeper demand had been rejected. France had also been presented by Switzerland with a bill for SF164,950 and 75 centimes for violations of the Swiss frontier and Swiss neutrality when stray machine-gun bullets crossed into Switzerland and French pilots made forced landings at Swiss airports. Switzerland's additional demand for 5 percent interest was rejected when the Quai d'Orsay handed over SF150,000. "I leave it to your imagination," the French finance minister wrote to the defense minister, "under what heading you classify these expenses."

In his discussions with Max Ott, Rubin heard familiar expressions of bookkeepers' mentality and irritating sentiments about the Third Reich, added this time to an audacious initiative to penalize the Jews still further. To seize more property owned by German Jews as reparations, Ott proposed to define as "residents of Germany" any Jew who had traveled from a concentration camp through Germany before settling in Displaced Persons camps in other countries. Although that Swiss initiative would be scotched by the Allies, Rubin concluded in a letter to New York on June 6, 1949, that "the negotiations are in a state of advanced collapse." Looking through the window of his bedroom in the Bellevue Palace Hotel at the Jungfrau towering among the Alpine peaks in the distance and at the River Aare flowing gently below, Rubin was bemused by this idyllic background to such unpleasant events. It was as hard as ever to get a handle on the Swiss.

The initiative passed to Max "Moose" Isenbergh, a thirty-six-year-old lawyer trained at Harvard, Columbia and Yale, who had recently been recruited by the AJC from the Department of Justice as the counsel for European operations. Born in Albany, New York, Isenbergh had spent the previous three years helping German Jews in the United States. His negotiations for the AJC to recover Jewish property in Austria had proved intensely depressing. Fearful of losing votes, Austrian politicians had refused to order loyal Nazis to return Jewish property distributed by the former regime. Only the threat of sanctions by Congress had compelled the Austrian government to offer $17 million compensation. "Peanuts," cried Isenbergh. He was convinced that the heirless assets in Switzerland were worth between $50 million and $70 million, but he was conscious that Congress was preoccupied with other issues. The crusade now depended entirely on Jewish lobbyists in Europe.

To resolve the Swiss crisis, Isenbergh asked Petitpierre to meet a delegation representing the principal Jewish organizations to discuss the heirless assets. Instead, at the minister's suggestion, the delegation was directed to Eduard von Steiger, the minister of justice. Isenbergh could not have anticipated the outcome.

12

THE POLISH CONSPIRACY

The patrician Eduard von Steiger, the minister of justice and the police, was an accomplished actor and a cunning survivor. During the war, while masterminding Switzerland's anti-Jewish policies, he had allowed the spotlight to fall on Heinrich Rothmund, his loyal police chief, and in the aftermath he had evaded blame by sheltering in shadows. After hearing that a delegation of Jews would be visiting his office, he trusted his instincts as an ultraconservative lawyer and asked Emil Alexander, his colorless legal adviser, to act as spokesman. Although he would naturally greet the delegation in his office, von Steiger planned to remain silent, avoiding participation in the pantomime.

Unsuspecting, at 3 P.M. on July 8, 1949, Max Isenbergh, Seymour Rubin and Dr. Bienenfeld, representing the World Jewish Congress, entered von Steiger's wood-paneled office. They were given coffee. Speaking English in his contrived, fawning manner, von Steiger explained, "The Political Department have asked us to prepare a report on the heirless assets because complex legal questions are involved." Nodding toward Jakob Burckhardt, the minister explained that Petitpierre's representative would report their discussions to the Political Department.

"Fine," replied Isenbergh, settling into a chair. The Swiss, he believed, understood the history of the heirless assets, had calculated the sums involved, and were prepared to transfer the money to the Jews. He still trusted the Swiss despite the secrecy imposed by the bankers.

Since the Bankers Association had given the Political Department its estimate, in late 1947, that its members had traced heirless assets worth SF482,000, lawyers representing the Swiss Federation of Jewish Associations had met Guy de Rahm and other minor Political Department officials. Under instructions not to reveal the Bankers Association's census, de Rahm had listened to the Jewish lawyers' detailed submissions and uttered polite reassurances that the department was struggling with "the difficulties of definitions" and awaiting other contingencies. To de Rahm's relief, the delegation had departed without mishap. After self-congratulations, Walter Hohl, an official in the Ministry of Justice, minuted his colleagues, "The amount of goods which comes under this account appears to be so minimal that no formal census is justified." Unaware of that decision, Isenbergh now addressed von Steiger with misplaced optimism: "All we ask of you is to comply with your promise made in Washington in 1946."

Von Steiger remained silent. Government files confirmed that the Allies had been uninterested in the fate of the heirless assets since 1946, and the silence from Washington had encouraged Swiss bankers to dismiss the issue as nonexistent. But von Steiger preferred to allow Alexander to justify the paralysis in uncontroversial, legal terms. "We cannot assume that all dormant accounts are heirless," Alexander told the delegation, "because there may be heirs who do not know the existence of the assets." Those who had not communicated since May 5, 1945, said the adviser, needed to register.

"But if they're all dead," said Isenbergh, pulling the discussion back from the world of Alice in Wonderland, "they can't claim."

"Yes," agreed Alexander, barely acknowledging the logic. "The Compensation Office will investigate, but under our law we must deal with heirless assets on the basis of the inheritance laws of the deceased's country of origin."

"We strongly oppose that," countered Bienenfeld. The thought of transferring the savings of German Jews back to Germany was truly appalling. "The Jews brought their property to Switzerland because they did not want it to fall into the hands of their own governments. Switzerland encouraged the view that it would defend that intention."

"We will consider that," Alexander agreed, "but everything must be settled by the laws passed by our parliament."

Disquieted by this reliance upon legalities, Bienenfeld switched to morality: "Those governments often persecuted the very people whose murder made the assets heirless. They have no moral claim over the deceased's property." As Rubin and Isenbergh nodded in agreement, Bienenfeld resorted to an absurdity in the hope of winning support: "If any nation could claim the property, it is Switzerland, and clearly Switzerland does not want to enrich itself unjustly by taking ownership of this property." Thinking that the murmurs of his audience showed how persuasive he was being, Bienenfeld outlined the legal options Switzerland could adopt to overcome the unprecedented situation.

When Bienenfeld's monologue ended, Rubin added, "You could use the 1945 decrees ordering the banks to break their secrecy laws to disclose German and Japanese assets to discover the heirless assets."

"No," replied von Steiger firmly, in his only intervention. "Those decrees were revoked by parliament in December 1945."

"But the precedent has been established," said Rubin. "You could pass new legislation." Other European countries—Greece, Italy and Holland—had introduced such laws, he pointed out, not mentioning his disappointment that Britain and France had refused discreet requests by the State Department to do the same. On one issue the two sides agreed. To find the heirless assets, Switzerland's bank secrecy laws would need to be amended. The meeting had ended. Everyone agreed that the discussion would continue in the near future.

Outside, in the cobbled street surrounded by Bern's sunlit stone buildings, the delegation commented on the friendly atmosphere.

In May 1945, Allied soldiers discovered the first evidence of "the greatest robbery in the history of mankind": stacks of gold ingots looted by the Nazis from Europe's central banks. *(Courtesy of the Hulton Getty Picture Collection)*

They also found wedding rings and dental fillings yanked from Jews murdered in extermination camps. *(Courtesy of the Hulton Getty Picture Collection)*

Investigators established that Switzerland's National Bank had accepted from the Nazis gold and ingots manufactured from the rings and fillings taken from Jewish victims. *(Courtesy of the Hulton Getty Picture Collection)*

In 1942, Charles Sonabend, shown above with his parents and sister, and his family were smuggled into Switzerland from France to escape the Nazis. Deported by the Swiss police into the hands of the waiting Gestapo, the children were placed in a French orphanage while the parents were shipped to Auschwitz, where they perished. *(Courtesy of the Sonabend family)*

Fifty-five years later Charles Sonabend found evidence in a Swiss police file that his father had had a Swiss bank account. The Berner Kanontalbank denied having any records. *(Courtesy of the Daily Mail/Skinner)*

Estelle Sapir, seeking her murdered father's account, presented a deposit slip to Swiss bankers. "The bankers were rude and arrogant," she complained. "They wanted a death certificate." Greta Beer, above, and Gizella Weisshaus, who were both told by their fathers of Swiss accounts, received no help from Switzerland's bankers. *(Photograph of Greta Beer courtesy of Uimonen-Sygma; photograph of Gizella Weisshaus courtesy of Lichtenstein-Sygma)*

Condemned by the British as the Crusaders, a group of American government officials masterminded the plan to seize German loot and recover money from Switzerland for Jews. Shown above is the James Angell delegation. Angell is the tall man in the last row, fourth from the right. Moses Abramovitz, who negotiated the reparations agreement in Potsdam, is in the back row, third from the left.

Eli Ginzberg outwitted British prejudice to secure an Allied commitment for Jewish refugees.

Sam Klaus invented the Safehaven Program.

James Mann fumed about
Swiss duplicity.

Seymour Rubin negotiated with the
Swiss government for many years
to extract the money for Jewish
survivors.

Max Isenbergh exposed
Switzerland's secret deal
with Poland in 1949.

Heinrich Rothmund, Switzerland's wartime police chief, forcibly expelled all Jews entering Switzerland. That anti-Semitic policy, supported by Eduard von Steiger, the minister for justice and the police, continued after the war. *(Courtesy of the Keystone Press Agency)*

In 1949, von Steiger, seated, and Max Petitpierre, the foreign minister, standing beside him, agreed to a secret deal to use the deposits of murdered Jews in Switzerland's banks for the benefit of the Swiss. *(Courtesy of the Keystone Press Agency)*

After negotiating the Washington Accord in 1946, Walter Stucki, left, Max Schwab, center, and Max Ott, encouraged by Heinrich Homberger, below, leader of Switzerland's industrialists, protected Swiss and German loot and spurned Jewish claims. *(Courtesy of the Keystone Press Agency)*

In 1952, Stucki, second from right, lied to Sir Patrick Scrivener, far left, Britain's diplomat, and John Carter Vincent, right, the American ambassador, that there were no heirless Jewish deposits in Switzerland. Seven years later Stucki confessed, "There are several hundred million" in the banks. *(Courtesy of the Keystone Press Agency)*

Petitpierre, left, having tea with Churchill. Petitpierre's dishonesty was encouraged by British policies. Winston Churchill, extreme right, had endorsed Switzerland's wartime conduct as winning "the greatest right to distinction," while Britain's anti-Zionist policies and requests for Swiss loans reassured Petitpierre that Switzerland could resist demands by Jewish groups that Switzerland honor its undertakings to transfer the heirless deposits in Swiss banks to Jewish refugees. *(Courtesy of the Keystone Press Agency)*

Edgar Bronfman, left, of the World Jewish Congress, was outraged when George Krayer, right, chairman of the Swiss Bankers Association, reneged on his promise in February 1996 not to reveal a survey of unclaimed Jewish deposits in Swiss banks. The failure of Hanspeter Häni, below, the ombudsman of the Swiss Bankers Association, to find more than $8,750 in unclaimed Jewish deposits in the banks convinced Senator Alfonse D'Amato, on the opposite page, to shame Switzerland by holding hearings in Washington, D.C. *(Courtesy of the Associated Press/Richard Drew)*

(Courtesy of the Associated Press)

Thomas Borer, left, the head of the Swiss Task Force, sought to defuse the onslaught of Senator D'Amato's "war of documents" by pleading for understanding to Israel Singer, center, of the World Jewish Congress, and Stuart Eizenstadt, right, President Clinton's special envoy. Borer failed. By spring 1997, Switzerland's banks were wounded, retreating and confessing. *(Courtesy of the Associated Press/Ron Edwards)*

The report to Abba Schwartz would mention how the Swiss were "seriously trying to find a legal basis to dispose of the assets" but would want to avoid breaking international laws and annoying certain countries. Rubin voiced the only serious note of caution. Switzerland, he warned, would continue to stall until other countries adopted similar laws. Looking up at the snowcapped Alps, he again cursed the incongruity of conducting business as sordid as this amid such beautiful scenery.

Two hours later Max Isenbergh arrived in Zurich. Walking near the leafy Bahnhofstrasse in the city center, he met by chance Adolf Jann, the heavy UBS banker renowned for his booming voice. Over the past months, Isenbergh, an avuncular hedonist, had developed friendly relations with the former secretary of the Bankers Association. Enjoying the last rays of the summer sunshine, Isenbergh recounted his meeting in Bern that afternoon. Pensive and obviously troubled, Jann stood momentarily silent. "You won't get your money," he breathed in an unusually low tone. Puzzled, Isenbergh waited for an explanation. "You won't get your money," repeated Jann, wondering whether to say more.

Jann's unsolicited revelation was not motivated by generosity or sympathy toward the innocent and murdered Jews who had trusted Swiss banks. The unusual indiscretion reflected Jann's fury, common to all Swiss bankers who were privy to Petitpierre's latest machination. Inexcusably, two weeks earlier, the Swiss government had interfered in the banks' affairs. Exposure of the state secret, he hoped, would embarrass the minister and safeguard the inalienable rights of banking secrecy. After glancing at Isenbergh, the banker continued. As a member of the Bankers Association's Polish Committee, explained Jann, he had been told of a trade agreement between Switzerland and Poland. "Within that agreement"—the banker was speaking slowly—"is a secret clause transferring the heirless assets of Polish Jews to the Polish government."

Isenbergh stood, frozen. "Did von Steiger and the other officials whom I just met in Bern know about that?" he asked.

"I am late," replied the banker. "*Aufwiedersehen*, Herr Isenbergh."

Isenbergh's news devastated Rubin. "This is a serious blow to our efforts," he reported to New York. "Either von Steiger was a knave or uninformed." Their trust had been abused and their naïveté exposed. Burdened by the secret, the small group despaired about what to do. Publicity, they feared, might so antagonize the Swiss that everything would be lost.

Eduard von Steiger naturally knew the truth. Just hours before he had greeted the Jewish delegation, at the morning meeting of ministers, Petitpierre had presented the Polish agreement to the Bundesrat and had disclosed the secret clause concerning the heirless assets. Von Steiger, in common with his colleagues, had approved the result of secret negotiations conducted over the previous months. Their incentive had been a lust for profits from war-ravaged Europe, and a need to relieve Switzerland's persistent shortage of coal.

In 1945 and 1946, Europe had been starved of fuel. With Germany's coal mines still severely disrupted and Europe's roads and railways unrepaired, Switzerland relied upon the Allies' generosity for supplies. Simultaneously, Swiss industrialists, denied their German markets, were manufacturing in plentiful quantities products that its bankrupt neighbors could not afford. To solve that combined problem, Max Troendle, the hyperactive trade minister, embarked upon an extraordinary blitzkrieg across Europe. Ceaselessly crisscrossing the continent at a time when travel was difficult, Troendle sought markets for Switzerland's manufacturers and sources of coal. On February 2, 1946, he opened negotiations in Poland, one of Europe's most plundered nations but also one possessing abundant supplies of fuel. During those early discussions, Poland's communist officials mentioned that many of the rich among the nation's two million murdered Jews must have deposited money in Switzerland or have invested in life assurance policies. That money, insisted the Poles, belonged to their motherland. Troendle had little reason to dispute that claim, except that the Swiss government could not simply seize the Jewish money. On the other hand, the Polish communists had confiscated property owned by Swiss nationals and his countrymen were aggrieved about their own losses.

On June 8, 1946, Troendle outlined to ministers in the Bundesrat the elements of a deal. "The Poles have requested the assets of missing Poles deposited in Swiss banks and insurance companies," he wrote, "and in a compensation deal, the Swiss debtors [the banks and insurance companies] would be obliged, after a presumption of death, to hand over that money to the Polish government in the form of bilateral compensation. But the Poles would have to promise to repay the money to any depositor or his heirs should there be a claim."

Although attractive to ministers, Troendle's proposal arrived just seventeen days after the Washington Accord had been signed, and the government still felt bound to honor Stucki's undertakings. Troendle's recommendation was filed along with a letter sent by the Polish government to Bern on April 4 formally requesting the heirless assets. Six months later, Switzerland's stance had not changed. In a conversation with Franz Kappeler on January 24, 1947, the Polish ambassador's request for the heirless assets was rejected. Poland, he was told, could not expect "special treatment." The ambassador was advised to seek help from the Bankers Association, where the result was a foregone conclusion.

Two years later, in April 1949, the issue resurfaced. In Warsaw, Troendle was negotiating a new trade agreement to sell Swiss products in return for coal. Once again, the Poles asked for the heirless assets. "Many Poles who died," said the negotiators, "deposited funds in Switzerland." Despite the cold war and the Soviet blockade of Berlin, the incentive for the Swiss to satisfy the communists had grown. To those Swiss eager to earn profits, the tension as Western Europe once more fought for democracy was irrelevant. Ingrained among Switzerland's rulers was the satisfying belief that their country had protected itself from the Nazis and that neutrality would now save the nation from the communists. Morality, scoffed those Swiss industrialists and politicians urging acceptance of Troendle's latest deal, was the argument deployed and distorted by interfering foreigners. The balance, said Troendle, had tilted in favor of satisfying the Poles. The Allies' interest in the heirless assets had evaporated, the feeble Jewish protest could be ignored, Swiss nationals were still pressing their claims for compensation, and Poland offered profits and coal. There was every reason to please the Poles and satisfy the Swiss. "At the appropriate time," the Finance and Political Departments suggested to the government, "we should examine whether the Polish heirless assets could be used to set against Polish compensation for nationalizing Swiss property." The only outstanding issue was to calculate the amount of Polish deposits that were heirless.

During the negotiations, Rudolph Speich, the chairman of the Swiss Bank Corporation accompanying Troendle, had told the Poles that the banks held "at least SF2 million" in Polish heirless assets. The origin of Speich's estimate—an important benchmark in the dispute—was a survey conducted by the Bankers Association and the insurance companies. Speich told Troendle that the bankers had reluctantly agreed to reveal the amount on condition that the heirless assets clause in the agreement remain secret. That request, Petitpierre decided, was unobjectionable. On formally signing the agreement on June 25, 1949, the Swiss government undertook in a secret clause that after July 1, 1954, Switzerland's banks and insurance companies would release the assets of Polish nationals whose accounts had remained unclaimed and dormant for five years since the end of the war. In return for transferring that money to Account N (for "Nationalization Compensation"), specially opened in Poland's name at the Swiss National Bank, Poland agreed to pay SF53.5 million in compensation to Swiss nationals for the loss of their property. In effect, Swiss property owners would receive compensation only because the heirless assets of Polish Jews deposited in Switzerland were transfered to Warsaw, although a fig leaf was cleverly provided. The Polish government was required to promise compensation to any Poles who subsequently made claims. Since the Poles would not be given the names of the account holders, the provision was included merely to bestow some legality on the deal.

Grubby deals did not trouble Adolf Jann, but to the government's misfortune he did not believe that the Bankers Association had ever approved breaching the secrecy rules to reveal the Polish heirless assets. The government and Speich, he fumed, had deliberately misconstrued the bankers' opinion to secure the trade agreement. Telling Isenbergh about the secret clause, the banker calculated, might frustrate parliament's ratification of the agreement, and in the meantime the banks would refuse to cooperate with the government.

Unaware that the secret was now known to the Jews, Petitpierre's officials were soon pondering how to overcome the bankers' intransigence and discover the amount of Polish heirless assets. Alfred Zehnder, the Political Department's senior official, appointed in 1946 because of his affinity to the bankers, admitted to Stucki, "There are complications." To avoid jeopardizing the whole agreement, Stucki was ordered to conceal the truth. The Poles were to be told that the heirless assets would be transferred "as soon as the checks were completed." A carrot would be offered but nothing else.

Knowing of the deception and of the government's intention of concluding similar agreements with other communist countries, Stucki was slightly troubled about transferring the Jews' money to the Poles, but, considering that Swiss law provided for that contingency, he remained silent. The deceit was also bothering von Steiger. The minister was naturally concerned neither by the Jews nor by the subterfuge, but he was aroused by the dissent of others in his department, especially that of Emil Alexander, his legal adviser. Alexander had sent Petitpierre a note, attached to the minutes of the meeting with the Jewish delegation, stating that when he had spoken to the Jewish delegation he had been unaware of the deceit. Although that was probably untrue, Alexander also sent a copy of a note written before the meeting, recommending that there should be no special treatment for the Polish heirless assets or any transfer of those funds to a foreign state before the Swiss government had ordered the banks and others to conduct a proper census of foreign deposits established before the end of the war. Alexander had also minuted Petitpierre to the effect that a trustee should be appointed to transfer any unclaimed money to a committee so that it could be used for humanitarian purposes.

Alexander's disquiet was shared by Felix Schnyder, an official in

Petitpierre's own department. Jewish groups, Schnyder told Troendle at the same time as Alexander was protesting to Petitpierre, were justified in seeking the heirless assets, not least because of Stucki's commitment in Washington and because the Polish communists had encouraged renewed persecution of the Jews after the war, forcing more Jews to flee. "Your spontaneous solution based on trade negotiations," wrote Schnyder, "risks breaking Swiss law, and we might run into similar difficulties with the Washington Accord." Troendle was also, warned Schnyder, ignoring the real possibility that Poles who were still living in Poland, but were too afraid to contact their Swiss banks, might find that their money had been confiscated as heirless.

Naturally cautious, Eduard von Steiger was disturbed by the unusual opposition to a simple trade agreement. True or false, Alexander's alibi was, von Steiger saw, pretty watertight; and, disconcertingly, Felix Schnyder's objections echoed the complaints of Jann and other bankers. Eight weeks after the meeting with Isenbergh and Rubin, the minister of justice decided it would be politic to distance himself from the secret diplomacy and establish an official alibi. The mechanics he adopted were crass.

In a letter to Petitpierre, von Steiger recited the established facts. First, he informed his colleague, he had discussed with representatives of Jewish groups their demand for the heirless assets. Second, he defined the consequences of Switzerland's secret agreement with Poland, which had not been revealed to the Jews: "Swiss nationals will receive compensation for the nationalization of their property [from the heirless assets]." Von Steiger asked Petitpierre for confirmation of those facts and for an explanation.

In a reply the following day, August 4, the minister received his alibi. Petitpierre wrote that he was taking responsibility for the "confidential exchange of letters on compensation which are not to be published" and concluded by saying that similar agreements might be signed with other governments. Three weeks later, von Steiger's caution was itself proved to have been justified.

In a short letter to von Steiger dated August 26, 1949, Max

Isenbergh denounced the Polish agreement. "It is incompatible with the principles of justice," he railed, mentioning the transfer of the heirless assets but without revealing his explicit knowledge of a secret clause. To von Steiger, the Jews were worse than irritants. An earlier letter from Bienenfeld pleading that Switzerland should neither forget the mass murder of Jews nor allow the murderers to profit from their crime had prompted the minister's scoffs about the naïveté of the lawyer. The implications behind Bienenfeld's concluding speculation—"I am sure that there can be no suspicion that Switzerland would ever want to take any advantage for itself from ... the assets"—had scarcely registered. But now Isenbergh's letter clarified Bienenfeld's conjecture. Those Jews! thought the minister. After reflection, von Steiger merely acknowledged Isenbergh's letter and passed the correspondence to Petitpierre with the message that in the future the foreign minister should deal with "this American Jewish Committee."

Not only was the secret disclosed, but Petitpierre's officials knew that they had been exposed as dishonest. "The agreement contradicts what von Steiger told the Jewish delegation," Franz Kappeler admitted. But even that confession did not inhibit Kappeler's recommendation that, while there was no choice but to admit that there had been an agreement with Poland, the details should be suppressed. That advice was accepted, but, as a precaution in the event of any questions, the Political Department briefed certain Swiss ambassadors about the background of the agreement.

In a dispatch to Switzerland's ambassador in Paris, the department stated that the Allies had placed "no great importance" on the issue of heirless assets and that their ambition to "grab a huge fortune in Switzerland has been abandoned." Despite the bankers' opposition, the government, acknowledging that the Poles "placed the greatest importance" on the issue, had signed a secret agreement. "We want to avoid if possible," the ambassador was told, "any direct contact with international Jewish groups." Nevertheless, the ambassador was instructed to contact Isenbergh privately and pacify his anger. Six days later, in an urgent telegram, the Political

Department's instructions were canceled. To avoid confirming the secret, ordered Bern, Isenbergh was not to be approached. The Swiss government's policy had been overturned by Max Oetterli, the aggressive new secretary of the Bankers Association responsible for internal affairs.

Alerted by Jann and other bankers, Oetterli had raised the alarm in Bern. Any suggestion, warned the secretary, that heirless assets could be surrendered would set a dangerous precedent. To reverse government policy, he had telephoned Troendle during the minister's visit to Vienna. The agreement, demanded Oetterli, must remain secret. In a crude demonstration of the bankers' potency, Troendle had instantly telephoned back to Bern demanding that Oetterli's request be obeyed. At that moment, the secret agreement was known to a handful of politicians and their officials, some senior bankers and industrialists, and the Jews. Parliament was unaware of the secret, and it was Petitpierre's intention, after withdrawing the messages to the ambassadors, to preserve the politicians' ignorance. "The agreement with Poland," the Swiss ambassador in Paris was told, "will not be revealed to parliament." Adhering to that strategy, on October 7 the government sent an official message to parliament announcing that the trade agreement with Poland emphasized the importance of Polish coal. The secret clause on heirless assets remained unmentioned.

On the same day in Washington, Rubin appealed to the State Department to stop the "tragic travesty of the principles of humanity." Switzerland's anti-Jewish policy was supported, Rubin knew, by Britain and France. Beggared by the economic crisis and the humiliating 30 percent devaluation of sterling in September 1949, the British were even prepared to demand a share of unclaimed valuables, probably belonging to murdered Jews, found by Allied armies in 1945 in Italy. The U.S. plan, either to transfer the valuables to the Italian authorities or to hold an auction and give the proceeds to charity, was partially opposed by a British suggestion that any sterling notes discovered among the property should be returned to the British treasury. Rubin protested that Britain's "attitude on this issue is unconscionable," although his only solution was further discussions.

In Bern, Stucki reveled in the reflection that the division among the Allies was playing into Switzerland's hands. "The British," he told Petitpierre, "don't like American dominance." He boasted about his humbling of a British diplomat who had accused Switzerland of "breaking agreements" and had complained of the Swiss government's "unreasonableness." "I put him in his place," bragged Stucki to his master. Likening the atmosphere of 1949 to that of 1946, he laughed, "was like comparing a sunny June day with a gloomy day in December. The old troublemakers don't bother us anymore." Pompously, he refused to advance the remaining SF30 million promised by Switzerland for the Jewish refugees in 1946 (SF20 million had been paid in 1948), dangling the possibility of payment only if the Americans agreed to implement the accord on Swiss terms. "Switzerland," he crowed, "has done everything to expedite the negotiations with the Allies. Any delays are not our fault." Giving any further money, he reckoned, would lessen the Allies' interest in agreeing on a final settlement.

Sharing Stucki's delight, Max Ott refined what Isenbergh and other Jewish lobbyists later interpreted as blackmail. "We see the Washington Accord," Ott told a delegation from the American Jewish Congress, "as an economic, not a political, agreement. Any measures to help the Jews would need a formal amendment to the agreement, approved by all the parties, and ratification by the Swiss parliament." Since it was next to impossible for such a scenario to be realized, Ott spelled out Switzerland's solution. The property of German Jews, he said unapologetically, even those who had emerged from concentration camps, would be sold to fund the repayment of Nazi Germany's debt to Switzerland. Hearing those sentiments, actually spoken in German at a time when so many victims of the Holocaust were still suffering, provoked a shudder among Ott's visitors. Appealing against such morality was pointless. "Moose" Isenbergh was planning a more combative strategy.

Five days after Switzerland's politicians had been misled,

Isenbergh approached what he thought were sympathetic Swiss government officials for an explanation. By then, Petitpierre's plot to divert Isenbergh by encouraging him to pursue his case through the Federation of Swiss Jews—an easy group for Petitpierre's officials to manipulate—had misfired and, at 10 A.M. on October 15, Isenbergh was greeted by Felix Schnyder and Denise Robert of the Political Department. Schnyder's criticism of the secret agreement was unknown to Isenbergh, but he suspected that the official was uneasy.

"You gave assurances that the heirless assets would be used for humanitarian purposes for the survivors," opened Isenbergh, swallowing his anger but challenging the officials to justify the deceit. "Von Steiger told us emphatically that disposing of the heirless assets would need legislation."

"But Poland might use the money for reconstruction," countered Schnyder impassively. "After all, the country was badly damaged in the war."

"To use the money of the victims of persecution for general reconstruction," replied Isenbergh, "is offensive to our ideas of public morality."

"But you don't know how much of the heirless assets belonged to Jews," said Schnyder, retaining his professional detachment.

"But you can find out," objected Isenbergh. "Under your deal with Poland you will know just that." Slicing through the Swiss defense and exposing its contradictions was a pleasure for the New York lawyer. Accusingly, he continued, "Switzerland is the only country in Western Europe using the heirless assets in this way. The owners sent their money here to put it beyond the reach of the Polish government. They trusted the reliability of the Swiss banks. This is a failure of the admirable banking standards for which Switzerland is renowned—and falling short of your usual standards of public morality."

Schnyder missed the irony in Isenbergh's voice. Instead, the official, suppressing his personal opinion, bemoaned Switzerland's predicament with Poland. "We were pressed into accepting the agreement by the Poles," sighed Schnyder, suggesting a helplessness that Allied negotiators had never discovered.

"It's a cruel irony that the Poles who persecuted the Jews should receive the Jews' money," mocked Isenbergh, understanding the simplicity and duplicity of the Swiss character. Behind the appearance of civility was a layer of obstinacy, and beyond that was solid egoistical incomprehension of anyone else's opinion.

Inevitably, Schnyder offered his own agenda. If the secret was exposed, he said quietly to Isenbergh, Switzerland would have no alternative but to treat all heirless assets in the same way: "You would have the moral satisfaction but nothing more." However, if Isenbergh stayed discreet, the remaining heirless assets would be used for resettlement as the committee wanted. "I've been working on a plan for the heirless assets along the lines you desire. It will be complete in a matter of months." Only silence could ensure its success, confided the official. For a moment Isenbergh was silent. If Schnyder's offer was genuine, there were advantages, but joining Switzerland's damage-limitation exercise was an unattractive option, especially since Schnyder's plan bore traces of eyewash. And, even if he was honest, one official could not change Switzerland's policies. "It'll all come out in the end," Isenbergh said, "and all the other governments will want the same deal." Public opposition and a negative vote in the Swiss parliament, he now believed, were the only chance of forestalling ratification. That required the exposure of the secret clauses. "Publicity will be harmful," cautioned Schnyder as Isenbergh departed at the end of their ninety-minute meeting.

Schnyder's report to Petitpierre was accurate. His warning, he admitted, had been unsuccessful. Isenbergh, he predicted, would publicize the secret clause. Recognizing his predicament, Petitpierre launched a final—and to him distasteful—ploy to limit the damage. The minister agreed to meet George Brunschvig and Paul Guggenheim, representatives of Switzerland's Jewish community. In July, Brunschvig had timidly declined to attend the meeting with von Steiger and subsequently, to avoid provoking new anti-Semitism, he had opposed any public protest. Yet even Brunschvig had been appalled by the duplicity of his countrymen, especially by the Political Department's subsequent request for his "discreet handling of that affair." Petitpierre's patience as his two visitors recounted their anger concealed his contempt, especially for von Steiger. The minister of justice, scribbled Petitpierre in a memorandum, had foolishly promised the Jews that the heirless assets would be used for humanitarian purposes "on the same day as he agreed to the [Polish] agreement." Von Steiger was evidently careless and, to Petitpierre's further annoyance, had become critical of the agreement. Now, his two Jewish visitors were irritatingly unmoved by his blandishments. Petitpierre could not understand why he was fighting old battles. The attitude toward Switzerland in Washington and New York, as Paul Keller, the trusted new president of Switzerland's National Bank, had reported, was "respectful and understanding." After speaking to American bankers and economists, Keller, a former professor of economics, had written that the "malaise" was history and the anti-Swiss antagonists had "disappeared." Willard Thorp, the assistant secretary of state for economic affairs, had agreed with Keller that "a healthy Switzerland in central Europe" helped the United States. Yet the Jews, thought Petitpierre angrily, were still interfering and causing trouble. That aroused the minister's hostility. Having listened to his visitors' protest, he blandly bade them farewell.

Isenbergh, undeterred by the threats and scornful of the courtesies, had begun lobbying the handful of potentially sympathetic Swiss parliamentarians—all of them, until his approach, unaware of the secret clause. All foresaw how Petitpierre would justify his agreement. Referring to the 1891 law, the foreign minister would rightly insist that under Swiss private international law an heirless inheritance belongs to the country of last domicile or nationality. "But that would mean," cried Isenbergh, "that Germany could claim the heirless assets of the citizens its predecessor had murdered." Not even the immorality of allowing murderers to profit from their crimes could prompt many Swiss politicians to criticize Petitpierre. Only pressure from the State Department could help. Rubin hoped to win his old department's sympathy.

Theodore Achilles, the policy officer responsible for relations with Switzerland, was Rubin's first call on December 6, 1949.

Elsewhere in the building, anxious officials were still reeling from the disclosure ten weeks earlier that the Soviet Union had tested an atomic bomb. The balance of power had tilted away from Washington, and the department was faced with constant crisis sparked by widespread communist agitation in Europe, the final victory of the communists in China, and the demagogic denunciations of "communist" officials in the department itself by Senator Joseph McCarthy. Compared with that bedlam, Rubin's complaint about Switzerland could make little impression on Achilles. Nevertheless Rubin persisted: "Their obvious double-dealing is jeopardizing all the other heirless assets in Switzerland." Starkly unhelpful, Achilles declared, "The department will not issue further instructions to protest." Warning against any public protests by the American Jewish organizations, which would "make the Swiss more recalcitrant," Achilles suggested that the only course was to rely upon the Jewish groups in Switzerland.

Rubin's frosty reception was followed by a shock. His regular access to confidential State Department memoranda and even diplomatic messages from European governments about Jewish affairs suddenly ceased. The Jewish groups, victims of McCarthyism and innuendo, were now unwelcome. In Bern, Isenbergh decided that the policy of self-imposed silence had run its course. Bereft of allies, he turned to Michael Hoffman, the local *New York Times* correspondent. A telephone call to the journalist seemed to be his last chance of mobilizing an international protest. Hoffman's article, published on December 7, exposed the secret clause and reported that the heirless assets of two million Polish Jews were allegedly only worth SF500,000. Within days, outrage spread among the Jewish groups in New York. The Poles and the State Department speculated in public that between $5 million and $50 million of Polish heirless assets were deposited in Switzerland. Objections from Bern that those estimates were "absurdly high"—Swiss bankers were already whispering to ministers that the true figure was $150,000 (SF645,000), markedly reduced from the original SF2 million—inflamed the anger.

Galvanized by the deception, James Rice, a lawyer employed by

the American Jewish Distribution Committee, appealed to Willard
Thorp, the assistant secretary of state, to raise the fate of the heirless
assets with Switzerland. Thorp had no appetite for the subject.
During the summer, he had led an American delegation in the disas-
trous negotiations with Stucki to settle the differences about the
Washington Accord. Disagreements with the Allies had flustered
him. In Neal Goodchild's opinion, Thorp's conduct was "excessively
feeble" and, compared with the "vigorous and intelligent" de
Panafieu, the senior French delegate, Thorp had noticeably wilted
before Stucki. Wounded and confused in the aftermath, Thorp
sought to rescue his reputation by inaction. Any thought of the Jews'
interfering was anathema. "The situation is very delicate," warned
Thorp. The Jewish organizations, he told Rice, should resist publicly
and privately criticizing the Swiss because it would upset the Allied
negotiations on reparations. Recovering the heirless assets, he
directed, was no longer important, and irritating the Swiss might
jeopardize their final contribution of SF30 million to the IRO. "The
State Department will not criticize the Polish agreement," he
declared. "It may be immoral but it's not illegal."

"But you've sent instructions to the Bern legation to protest,"
countered Rice, disclosing information gleaned by Isenbergh.

"Those were sent in haste and ill-considered," snapped Thorp.
"The legation has already replied that it would take no action. Those
instructions have been withdrawn."

Rubin was aghast. Without State Department support, the
Jewish organizations were practically impotent. He telephoned State
Department officials who might understand that justice and respect
for obligations accepted by the United States demanded further
efforts despite the complications. The replies were not encouraging.
In New York, Jerome Jacobson and others in the AJDC suspected
that Rubin's loyalty to his old department had blinded him to its dishonesty. Thorp's warnings about the "delicacy" of the Allies' negotiations with Switzerland for reparations sounded suspicious, because
the U.S. diplomats had deliberately not been sent instructions from
Washington. Although it was unknown except to a few senior offi-

cials, Washington had decided that the negotiations with Switzerland were pointless and should end. "The British," wrote Jacobson about the stalemate, "apparently were correct in their insistence that the department was dragging its feet. All this is, indeed, a very sad business."

Nevertheless, fearing that if the reparations negotiations did collapse, American Jewery would be blamed, Isenbergh was told to "encourage the Swiss [Jews] to take the initiative" in organizing a protest, but he was "not to get carried away and become directly involved with the Swiss." New York was determined "to keep our own hands out." Acting on those instructions, Isenbergh's approach to George Brunschvig was more unsettling than usual. Convinced that his telephones were being tapped and fearing the Swiss police, Brunschvig had in the previous months employed unusually guarded and excessively polite language in his public statements. Now he resisted Isenbergh's notion of publicly lobbying Swiss politicians. "There is no real hope of stopping the agreement," he objected. Yet, subjected to Isenbergh's persistence, he reluctantly agreed to make a quiet approach to sympathetic politicians. All would eventually remain silent.

Isenbergh's last hope was Jacques Salmonovitz, the Jewish owner of the Société Générale de Surveillance, a notary and trust company in Geneva with connections to the Balkan countries. Since the 1920s, Salmonovitz had discreetly cared for his clients' gold, jewelry and cash by undertaking to deposit the valuables—in numbered accounts or under SGS's name—in banks and safe-deposit boxes. During the war, Salmonowitz had been hailed by OSS as "our great friend" for providing information, not least a list of Jewish clients who had entrusted SF8.4 million and about $90,000 to the notary pending their arrival from the Balkans. Yet Salmonovitz, to Isenbergh's surprise, was inexplicably unwilling to join a public protest. The Swiss Jews, fearing anti-Semitism, had no vested interest in embarrassing Switzerland's financial community into releasing the heirless assets. Salmonovitz's personal interest was unknown to Isenbergh. Many Balkan Jews whose money Salmonovitz held on trust had still failed to reclaim their money. Like all the other heirless assets, these remained undeclared.

Denied the support of Swiss Jews, Isenbergh and James Rice, arriving from New York, approached John Vincent, the new minister at the American legation in Bern. Intolerant of the willful insincerity he had encountered in Bern, Vincent, unlike his languid predecessor, was anxious to protest about the secret clause. The difficulty, he confided, was not the hoary fear that criticism made the Swiss more stubborn, but the absence of enthusiastic support from the two Allies. The British were still piqued about the creation of Israel, while France's ambivalence had only recently been reconverted into lukewarm interest. "I'll try my best," Vincent promised his visitors, "to persuade the Allies to join a protest."

The French Foreign Ministry was embarrassed. Over the previous two years, despite their responsibilities, French diplomats in Bern had remained silent. But since the creation of Israel the Quai had sought reconciliation with the Jewish lobby, so the department now bowed to Vincent's initiative. The protest, personally delivered on December 20, 1949, by Henri Hoppenot, the French ambassador, asked Switzerland what measures had been taken to discover the heirless assets and whether the Polish agreement contained a secret clause on heirless assets. To Hoppenot's delight, Alfred Zehnder, the Swiss official who accepted the letter, "not without a degree of embarrassment," confirmed that Swiss citizens would benefit from the heirless assets but confided, in Switzerland's defense, that the total of heirless assets, "would not exceed SF500,000."

The American note two days later was more precise. "If the agreement," wrote Vincent, "does in fact contain such a provision, it would not appear to be consistent with the declarations previously made by the Swiss authorities regarding the disposition of heirless assets found in Switzerland."

Petitpierre was unconcerned by the protests. Two years had passed since the Allies had last mentioned heirless assets, and he had little doubt that the resurrection of the question had been inspired by Jewish groups. The protest from Paris contained a colorful concoction explaining France's silence for two years. "We did not take any measures on heirless assets," stated the Quai d'Orsay provocatively, "partly because there are no heirless assets on our territory and partly because the Paris Agreement of June 14, 1946, applied only to neutral countries." Unlike Switzerland, according to the Quai, France had not sequestered property belonging to others: "France has sacrificed much for the victims of Germany, has handed over all the gold it found in Germany, and has refused to accept the German assets found in the neutral countries." Petitpierre was not impressed. In the margin of the French letter, the reader had scrawled heavy exclamation marks. The Allies' interest, the Swiss foreign minister was sure, would soon pass. Even the prospect of that day's parliamentary debate and vote about the agreement aroused little disquiet. Other ministers at that day's council meeting had agreed that "bending the rules" was justified, although it should be done "only in exceptional circumstances." Rather than tell the truth, Petitpierre would obfuscate and rely upon the customary obedience of members of parliament.

Just as planned, later that morning, Petitpierre denied in the parliament that there had been "a secret letter." Concealing his own recent attempts to suppress the secret, he told the two members who asked about heirless assets that the clause was merely "confidential" and that the failure of disclosure had been an unfortunate "error, a blunder of a subordinate." Within two hours, despite more serious criticism about Switzerland's relations with the communists, the agreement was ratified by 98 to 18 votes. One aspect of Petitpierre's secret was still safe. The connection between the heirless assets and compensation for Swiss property remained shrouded.

Hours later, the British minister delivered a protest note similar to Vincent's. The crusaders were not grateful. Ignoring the waning interest in Washington, Rubin said that the "unfriendly attitude" of the British and French had been "a great encouragement to Swiss selfishness." The Polish agreement, he feared, would be a precedent for similar agreements with other countries. Isenbergh agreed. The prospect of extracting any money from the Swiss was "by no means good. Yet we must try." Both still seriously underestimated the prejudice infecting Bern.

Thomas Tull, a British diplomat trusted by Alfred Zehnder, heard the unvarnished parochialism on December 29, 1949. That morning, the *New York Times* reported a leak from Zehnder that the Polish heirless assets were not worth more than SF500,000. Odd, thought Tull, to include a secret clause in an international agreement for such a small sum. Seated in Zehnder's office, Tull heard the Political Department's senior official contrive a scenario to justify the secret clause that even the Briton, in his report to London, decided was absurd. "The Polish heirless assets," pronounced Zehnder, "had belonged for the most part to members of the former ruling classes in Poland who had been liquidated, so far as we know, by the Polish communist government and not by the Nazis." Switzerland, he said, could not hand out money on the basis of religion or race to Jewish organizations.

Shortly after Tull's report reached London, the Foreign Office telegraphed a copy to the State Department. Rubin was allowed to read the confidential message. "That point about the Jews," he exclaimed, "is particularly nasty." Zehnder seemed to be infected with anti-Semitism. Reading further down the report, Rubin came upon a piece of unexpected candor. After parliament had ratified the Polish agreement, Zehnder had told Tull, the Swiss government would have authority to compel the banks to disclose the relevant heirless assets. If, contrary to expectation, the assets belonged to victims of the Nazis, there would still be time to take it up with the Polish government. That admission, Rubin saw at once, contradicted everything the Swiss had pleaded over the past four years about banking secrecy. The odor of rottenness, unwittingly revealed to Tull, was intolerable. And finally there was Zehnder's hand-wringing, hand-on-heart, deep-felt compassion. The Political Department director, reported the British diplomat, felt "uneasy" about the Polish agreement, as did Petitpierre, who "had been much concerned" in case there was a breach of "a gentleman's agreement" made by Stucki in 1946. The hypocrisy was breathtaking. In public, to reassure the Polish communist government, Petitpierre's officials were saying precisely the opposite.

In a press release issued in early 1950, the department dismissed the 1946 letters as "not binding" and the Jews' "sentimental arguments" for receiving the heirless assets as "not convincing." Poland, said Petitpierre, "can argue the same [as the Jews], since it was invaded by the Germans, needs money for reconstruction, and suffered Nazi occupation." To confirm Troendle's assurances in Warsaw, the department also contradicted Zehnder's leak. Polish heirless assets, announced the official statement, were worth a maximum of SF2 million. Any estimate above that figure was a "gross fantasy" because the number of heirless deposits was "very small." To Rubin it seemed clear that the banks were protecting their secrets. Unknown to outsiders, Oetterli was aggressively lobbying Petitpierre's officials.

In early 1950, the bankers heard that the government was negotiating a trade treaty with Czechoslovakia. The worst fears of the Bankers Association were being realized. Suspecting that the agreement would also include an heirless-assets clause, the association warned the government not to interfere in their business or endanger their clients' privacy. In anticipation of pressure by other foreign governments for answers to a question that had lain satisfactorily dormant, it was agreed that a delegation of bankers should meet Rudolf Bindschedler, the Political Department's lawyer, on January 10, 1950.

Meetings between bankers and government officials were rarely more than cordial. Despite their constitutional position, the civil servants understood that their status in the country was a purely servile one. Bindschedler nevertheless tried on this occasion to retain some dignity. "Before we can take the necessary legal measures," announced the lawyer regarding the Polish agreement, "we must have a census to know the size of the heirless assets." Instinctively, Max Oetterli, sitting beside Adolf Jann, sprang to attack the proposed breach of the banks' secrets, but he soon relented, to allow Heinrich Daeniker, a director of the Kantonalbank, which had unilaterally ceased paying interest to the refugees, to explain the bankers' new grievance. Besides all the familiar problems, said Daeniker, the bankers feared that any announcement of a census would arouse "unrealistic expectations of a large sum." But worse, he continued, the bankers disliked the proposed involvement of the Compensation Office. Their unspoken anxiety was that Compensation Office officials were difficult to manage and understood the bankers' ploys. "Don't worry," promised Bindschedler; "the Compensation Office will not be involved. The census will be handled by a trustee who will be appointed only after a discussion between ourselves." With that reassurance, the atmosphere became relaxed. Any census would be conducted on the bankers' terms. The lawyer's dignity had been compromised.

Bolstered by the bankers' success, the insurance companies also proclaimed their reluctance to become involved in a census. The sums, Bindschedler was informed, were minuscule. A limited inquiry by Swiss insurance companies had unearthed only eight policies worth SF29,000 that might be heirless and to continue the investigation posed a serious risk of fraud and worse. Masquerading as the protector of its clients, the insurance association told the Political Department, "In previous years we have successfully resisted the attempts of confiscation by foreign states and will not succumb now to any other direct or indirect measures of forced expropriation. Experience shows that to tolerate that would cause great damage—moral and financial—to Switzerland." The hundreds of complaints by German Jews whose policies had been surrendered against their wishes by the insurance companies to the Nazis, or who had been offered repayment after the war in worthless Reichmarks although they had regularly paid their premiums in dollars, were self-servingly ignored. No one in Switzerland would champion the foreigners' cause as victims of dishonesty. Yet the pressure did not lessen. Political groups, dismayed that in the midst of Stalinist oppression in Moscow Petitpierre should have made concessions to the communists, demanded more information about the Polish agreement.

Reluctantly, the minister was compelled on March 14 to return to parliament to explain the government's trade policy with communist Europe. Naturally, he did not intend to offer a full confession. Instead, in a coarse display of legal evasion and bravado, he performed a remarkable somersault—finally admitting the existence of the secret clause, conceding that the secrecy had been "a wrong deci-

sion," but declaring that "there is no question of secret diplomacy."
Toward the Allies and the Jews, however, Petitpierre betrayed not a
hint of regret. His countrymen, he was convinced, despised any concessions to those groups. The Jewish issue, for the Swiss, was irrelevant. Subtly changing tack, the minister claimed insouciantly, "The
declaration made in Washington contains only a promise to examine
the question [of the heirless assets] and does not indicate a solution."
Stucki's promise to examine the issue "sympathetically," he continued, obliged Switzerland only to consider the heirless assets of
German Jews; and on the question of the remaining Jews the
Washington Accord was silent. Since Poland was not a party to the
accord and Switzerland was not a party to the Paris Agreement on
heirless assets, there was no reason why Switzerland was not justified
in transferring the heirless assets to Poland under international law.
None of Petitpierre's audience contradicted his interpretation of history, which just happened to suit Swiss interests. The issue, so far as
he was concerned, was once again closed. Even the sums involved
were irrelevant. According to the Swiss banks, he declared, the
amount of heirless assets was "probably less" than the estimated
SF2 million. No one in his audience challenged that figure, although
Petitpierre knew that the banks had not conducted a proper census.

Unwillingly and unannounced, Petitpierre had in fact made one
concession. Realizing that Switzerland could not risk another row
with foreign governments, he had jettisoned in February a similar
secret clause in the trade agreement with Czechoslovakia. To
inquiries from the Israelis, the Americans and the local Jewish
groups, Petitpierre could honestly promise that Switzerland had not
offered any heirless assets to Prague. Since the inquiries did not ask
about a secret undertaking to Hungary, he did not volunteer that
Switzerland would on July 19, 1950, sign an agreement with the communist government in Budapest, trading the heirless assets of
Hungarian Jews for compensation to those Swiss whose property had
been confiscated. The only refinement was the requirement imposed
on the Hungarians to produce evidence about the existence of heirless assets in Switzerland. That clause was not published, but to avoid

future accusations of a "secret deal" Troendle dispatched a letter to the Hungarians stating, "The understanding concerning the heirless assets is not to be regarded as secret." It was "confidential" but not to be published. Both sides understood that Troendle's letter was a safeguard if the need for an alibi arose.

"A whitewash," commented officials of the World Jewish Congress in New York, after reading Petitpierre's statement about Poland, even though they were unaware of the hectic renegotiations with the Czechs and Hungarians. Rubin despaired of ever trouncing the "extremely stubborn man in control on the other side." Even Dean Acheson, the acting secretary of state, unaware of the truth, was anxious that Petitpierre might have signed an heirless-assets agreement with Hungary, whose 600,000 Jews exterminated by the Nazis were "known to have substantial assets in Switzerland." But Acheson's passing interest vanished after South Korea was suddenly invaded by 175,000 communist troops on June 25.

The Jewish organizations seemed more bereft of Allied support than ever. Although the French government had complained that Switzerland was "guilty of a grave breach of diplomatic etiquette" in its secret diplomacy, the Quai's renewed involvement was terminated. In the Foreign Office, Neal Goodchild was "more than content to leave such a delicate subject" in American hands. Reflecting with satisfaction that the Swiss and Swedish governments had privately assured British diplomats that "no such assets have yet come to light," Goodchild concluded, "I am afraid that, whatever answer they give, there is unlikely to be any cash." Without deliberate sarcasm, he commented, "We have achieved nothing, but we have done what we can." He had, however, successfully suppressed the issue in Britain. Asked by the *Jewish Chronicle* for information because the Swiss government was ignoring its inquiries, he thought that if John Shaftesley, the editor, was "reliable" he could be privately briefed. Goodchild's intention was "to keep him quiet and show that we are doing something." After meeting the editor, Goodchild congratulated himself. Shaftesley had been persuaded "to drop the subject." But other Jews were unwilling to be cajoled.

13

NEW HOPE

In March 1950, the government of Israel politely asked the State Department and the Foreign Office to allow the new Jewish state to approach Switzerland concerning the fate of the heirless assets. The initiative, encouraged by all the Jewish groups, was also supported by the International Refugee Organization, which was destined to receive the funds. Dean Acheson promptly welcomed the idea. But the news did not please the British. The initiative "needs watching," complained a British official, suspicious of Israel's "hunger for foreign exchange." For the Foreign Office, the irritation of Israel's meddling in an agreement to which it was not a signatory was compounded by its assumption of the right to represent the world's Jews when only 117,000 had migrated there since 1947, as compared with 80,000 who had arrived in Britain. Given British policies over the years, cooler heads would have understood the illogicality of those complaints, but Britain's exclusive concern was to recoup some of the £200 million spent supporting Germany after the war and to forestall any diminution of its share of reparations. That desire for money and Britain's certainty that the Swiss would eventually pay had prompted Goodchild to dissuade the State Department from breaking off negotiations with Switzerland on the grounds that the accord had proved "unworkable." One price for that perseverance, to Goodchild's distaste, was the State Department's past and occasional present references to the heirless assets. The Americans, Goodchild said bitterly, wanted to "fan the flames" of an "insignificant controversy" that should be dropped. Yet if Britain was to share in the reparations, Goodchild admitted, there was no alternative but to follow the U.S. lead, despite the "rather barren argument."

Swiss officials were bemused by the notion of dealing with Jews on equal terms. Only a few years earlier, the very officials who received the formal letter from the Israeli Foreign Ministry in Tel Aviv had rejected hysterical pleas by the same kind of people to enter their country or had thrown them wailing across the frontier into the hands of the Gestapo. It was not easy to accept that ghetto inhabitants had been transformed into diplomats who had to be treated with respect. It was especially difficult for Paul Ritter, the first Swiss consul in Tel Aviv. Ritter had been summoned at the end of December 1949 to the Israeli Foreign Ministry to receive an "angry" protest about the Polish agreement. In his report to Petitpierre, Ritter, a sharp critic in 1944 of Carl Lutz's issue of letters of protection to the Hungarian Jews, could not resist sneering that the head of the Ministry's West European division, Herr Avner, was "formerly called Hirsch."

Since Israel was a signatory of neither the Washington nor the Paris agreement, a protest from Tel Aviv could have only limited impact. But the Swiss could not reject the Israeli government's right to represent its citizens in their bid to find their families' assets in Switzerland. Long letters naming murdered fathers, brothers and uncles who had lived in Eastern Europe and had regularly traveled before the war to Switzerland to deposit money there had accumulated in the Israeli Foreign Ministry. Impoverished and isolated from Europe, the survivors relied upon Moshe Sharett, the foreign minister, to seek assistance from the Swiss government.

In July 1950, Gershon Meron, who was the Israeli representative in Bern and a former banker, met Alfred Zehnder to find out what help the Jews might expect. Appreciating that Switzerland's lawyers could create loopholes within loopholes, Meron adopted a placatory approach that surprised the Swiss official. To Zehnder's delight, Meron refrained from criticizing the Polish agreement and said that most Israeli claims involved money entrusted to friends and business associates in Switzerland, not to banks. Meron's admission was as encouraging as his unexpected acceptance that any estimate by the Swiss banks of the Polish heirless assets would be honest. The Israeli was unaware that the banks had progressively reduced their estimate of SF2 million in 1949 to "less than SF1 million" in April 1950 and were proposing to "reveal" the figure as SF598,000 in their bid to persuade the government that a formal census was unnecessary. Meron's only request was that the Swiss approve a public appeal to find the heirless assets. Since this scheme posed no danger, Ritter was ordered to place an advertisement in Israeli newspapers asking claimants to send information to the Israeli Ministry of Justice.

In Washington, the "argument" had become the responsibility of Roswell McClelland, the State Department's Swiss desk officer, who had been the representative of the War Refugee Board in Bern in 1945. As the latest official to read through the old departmental files, and recalling the frustration caused by Switzerland's endless stalling tactics and the Swiss newspaper commentaries vilifying Stucki as a traitor, McClelland was inclined to join his predecessors and damn the whole business, until he realized that Switzerland's protection of German interests had assumed a new dimension. The government of the new West German republic, McClelland appreciated, was covertly influencing Switzerland's attitude toward the fate of the German and heirless property in Switzerland. The cause of the intrigue master-minded by industrialists and bankers was the indisputable risk that over $1 billion of German property might be confiscated under the Washington Accord. Quietly, German diplomats were warning not only the Swiss government, but also the Portuguese and Spanish governments, that the seizure of German property for reparations would be regarded as unfriendly and would be contested. Even the return of property identified as Nazi loot was forbidden by Bonn.

Stucki, perpetually under pressure from the Swiss-German interests, was powerless in the face of the sudden and unexpected demands from Bonn. At risk was not only Switzerland's own property in Germany, worth between SF5 and SF6 billion, but also its 50 percent share of the German property in Switzerland, marked to repay the wartime loans to the Nazis. McClelland's uncertainty about

Switzerland's new predicament as a victim or perhaps a puppet of Bonn contrasted with the Foreign Office's wry amusement: it was an "embarrassing" position, commented an official. Neal Goodchild had received an unexpected confession from Victor Umbricht, a first secretary in the Swiss embassy, who, fuming about West Germany's latest moves, recounted events that had taken place since 1946. After negotiating the best deal in Washington, revealed Umbricht, Stucki had devoted himself to discovering or inventing any reason not to sell German property. Now the Swiss were aggrieved by the Germans' ingratitude. "It has for some time been obvious," summarized Goodchild, "that Switzerland is torn between two conflicting instincts: on the one hand political fear of Germany; on the other, native financial greed whetted by the knowledge that only the [Washington] Accord gives them any hope of salvaging any part of this milliard credit. The Swiss are sufficiently hardheaded to contrive to serve both these (not too admirable) instincts simultaneously, and sufficiently hypocritical to believe that by doing so they will emerge with flying moral (and financial) colors." Switzerland's "German experts," formerly pro-Nazi, were victorious. "I find the action of the Swiss depressing," agreed a weary colleague.

Max Schwab also found his position depressing. His secret had emerged. Under attack from bankers and lawyers for tapping telephones as if he were the Gestapo, he lamented that the Compensation Office had dealt with dishonest bankers and lawyers who, despite falsifying documents and lying, had escaped any punishment by the courts. Stucki acknowledged the dishonesty but was reconciled to the new realities in Bern. "Gangsters" was the epithet being used in Zurich and Bern by the pro-Germans against the Americans. Offered renewed reason to swagger by the resurrection of a German state and the rout in South Korea, where communist troops had occupied practically the whole country, the former Nazi sympathizers were challenging Washington to listen to some straight talk from Swiss "cowboys." Retreating, Stucki resorted to his standard defense: "We're not defending the Germans but fighting for a just solution. That's the strength of our position."

Rubin detected something worse. The Germans, he suspected, were reckoning that the Allies would tolerate the evasion of their moral and legal obligations. The U.S. government's release of major Nazi war criminals, including famous incriminated industrialists and bankers, and the commutation of death sentences on mass murderers as calculated gestures to win German support in the cold war, had encouraged the regeneration of the familiar brazenness. "Now that they have Korea on their hands, the Americans are a lot more friendly," quipped a German industrialist as he prematurely emerged from prison despite his conviction for participating in atrocities. The Germans, enjoying increasing prosperity as a result of the Marshall Plan, showed every intention of taking the profits, recouping their foreign and looted property and giving nothing in return. Included in Bonn's shopping list were the heirless assets of the German Jews in Switzerland, a request that Petitpierre was sympathetically considering.

Repaying the assets of the Nazis' victims to Germany was increasingly troubling Stucki as much as Switzerland's policy of returning the heirless assets to East European countries. His signature was on the letter signed in Washington in 1946, and Petitpierre's self-interested ambiguities about Switzerland's commitment offended his sense of honor. "It's a question of interpretation whether non-German victims were included," Stucki told Zehnder, "and since nothing was mentioned during the Washington negotiations, I'll leave the decision to you so that you can pursue what is in Switzerland's best interest." Stucki's withdrawal from involvement with the heirless assets coincided with the Compensation Office's establishing that at least SF16.5 million of the frozen German property in Switzerland was heirless. Considering how limited that classified survey must have been, Stucki grasped that the repeated assertions by the banks and Petitpierre that the amounts were "small" were simply untrue. But any fear among the secret trustees that their illegal inheritance would be exposed seemed to have no basis after the Congress in Washington rejected legislation transferring to refugee organizations the heirless assets found in the United States. Bill 603, introduced by Senator Taft, to authorize the transfer of heirless assets to Jewish organizations had been approved by the Senate, only to be rejected by the House of Representatives. That decision, the work of a vocal pro-German lobby in Congress, persuaded Max Oetterli, the secretary of the Bankers Association, that governments and individuals could be ignored. But his relief was short-lived. To his irritation, a serious challenge arose in Switzerland itself.

On March 14, 1950, Werner Schmid, a liberal politician, asked if the government planned to transfer Hungarian heirless assets to the regime in Budapest. To conceal the truth, Petitpierre promised to give an answer sometime in the future. The sensitivity of Schmid's question and his promise of permanent vigilance stirred Max Schwab, under constant pressure from Oetterli, to rewrite history and add confusion to the problem of the heirless assets, the claims by survivors for unidentified accounts, and the continuing freeze on German property. "The Allies never mentioned that the Nazis' victims should be specially treated," Schwab wrote to Stucki and the Political Department. "Even if the Americans wanted special treatment, the British and French would not be so eager." Aligning himself with the government and the banks, Schwab dismissed the credibility of all Jewish demands. "Ninety percent of the applicants say they've been persecuted," he said, reciting the familiar mantra, "and we can't check." Schwab's certainty, however, was soon shaken by the unexpected response to the Swiss government's public appeal in Israel, which encouraged more claims from the new Diaspora around the world. Reading that cascade of letters evoked cynicism in Bern rather than sympathy, but it also aroused trepidation.

Relating pitiful tales of escape while whole families were murdered, survivors pleaded for help in finding an unknown numbered account opened by a father or an uncle in Switzerland. Lydia Wohlin, writing from New York, described how her family from Bialystok, Poland, had been murdered. Struggling in postwar Europe, Wohlin met an old Polish friend who recalled that her father had opened an account in Switzerland. "Could you be so kind," asked Wohlin, "to find the bank? I understand it is a very hard thing to do." Similarly,

Hanna Milkowska, living in London, had heard from a friend of her dead husband that there was an account, although she too did not know the details.

Penniless in a kibbutz near Haifa, Israel, Diamant Schimshohn knew precisely the name of the Swiss company to which his father had entrusted his money in 1939. Schimshohn asked the Swiss president for help, explaining that his entire family had later been deported to Auschwitz: He escaped while all of the others died. "During the whole war and afterward," he wrote to the president, "I just dreamed of completing my medical studies. . . . My father said that the money was for his children's education. Could you please help me find it and satisfy my innate desire to study medicine? . . . I hope, your Excellency, that you will understand the human purpose of my request and will relieve so much of my tragedy as is possible by supporting myself." The reply from the president's office, the response given in identical terms to hundreds of similar pleas, was short: "Please write to the Swiss Bankers Association, who may be able to help you."

Seymour Rubin, representing claimants, had experienced the Bankers Association's customary answer to inquiries: "A number of legal and practical problems arise." The "problems," condemned by Rubin as "completely impossible requirements," were the need for the depositor's authenticated death certificate, proof of heirship and—an "indispensable" stipulation—the precise identification of the bank account. "Proof of death in a gas chamber is extremely difficult," complained Rubin. "All we know is that the deceased was last seen entering a concentration camp and is not known to have ever emerged." Requiring the claimants to provide "exact details about the banks in which the accounts in question exist" was unrealistic and illogical. The Jews had chosen to deposit their money in Switzerland because anonymity was guaranteed. They were unlikely to reveal the details of the secret to their families. Rubin had pursued the case of Izak Goldwasser, whose heirs had asked the Bankers Association for help in finding his bank account. The Bankers Association's initial response had been encouraging. Rubin was convinced that the account had been found. But suddenly the door was firmly closed with the excuse that the banks' secrecy rules precluded the release of any information. Rubin suspected that a bank, a member of the association, wanted to conceal the existence of Goldwasser's account, but the terse assertion of ignorance by the association, regretting its inability to find "any trace" of an account, could not be disproved. In the face of deceit, the outsider was helpless.

Erwin Haymann, a Genevan lawyer, was confounded by the same problem. Haymann had been retained by the widow of an Italian Jew murdered by the Germans; he had good evidence that SF1 million had been deposited in a Crédit Suisse account in Geneva. The bank, pleading secrecy, refused to help the widow regain her money. In desperation, the lawyer appealed to the Bankers Association for help, but the bankers, Haymann protested, "do nothing to help the inheritors." Even inheritors with authentic documents were unwelcome.

Lydia Reginek's husband Hans had been murdered in Auschwitz soon after arriving on July 14, 1941. Unusually, the following day, the widow received a telegram from the camp commander announcing his death. Before the end of the war, Lydia Reginek had obtained from the Polish courts an official death certificate and an order declaring that she was the inheritor of her husband's wealth in Switzerland. Yet in Switzerland, seeking possession of his estate, Reginek was told that the authorities did not recognize the validity of the Polish documents. The new communist Polish government, explained the bank, had declared that everything committed during the Nazi occupation was invalid. The bank's objection was supported by a Swiss court. The banks justified their caution by stories of fraud. Too often, the association claimed, they had responded to a pitiful tale of survival and, discovering that an account did exist in the survivor's name, had released money—only to welcome at the bank, once the first claimant had disappeared, another member of the same family who stated a better claim.

Amid the confusion, emotion and recrimination, the Israeli diplomat Gershon Meron had, after weeks of searching through dozens of claims, identified two compelling cases that he believed,

properly pursued, would strip the bankers of their sanctimony.
Hirschel Bragowski, who was the uncle of Anna Merlinski, and Julius
Spira had been gassed in extermination camps and were known by
their relatives to have deposited money in Swiss bank accounts. Since
their own application for information had been stonewalled, Meron
asked Zehnder for assistance. Meron's inquiries were passed to the
Bankers Association. In reply, the association recited its obligations
under the secrecy laws, its strict requirements for the precise location
of the account and legal proof that Bragowski and Spira had died and
that the claimants were entitled to their estates. Thereafter, declared
the association, "we would be very glad to undertake a new search for
the account." As a dutiful messenger, Zehnder passed on the news to
Meron. Unlike previous inquirers, the Israeli enjoyed sufficient status
to reject Swiss guile. "Be more cooperative," he bluntly threatened
Zehnder, "or I will seek a more legal solution." Unaccustomed to
undiplomatic language and appreciative of power, Zehnder warned
the Bankers Association that Meron would demand special regulations in the absence of an unsatisfactory reply. "We agree," Zehnder
wrote to the Association, "that this sort of solution should be avoided
if possible. We can achieve that only if we compromise with the
Israelis."

Zehnder's sober appeal for good sense was read by Max Oetterli.
He was confident that everything was under control and that the
chance of special legislation was remote, and so his instinct was to
retaliate. Unlike Robert Dunant, who had gradually softened his
stance toward the Jewish question, Oetterli was vigorously antagonistic to the Jews. Zehnder's letter provoked him into blasting the
Political Department for the suggestion that the association should
dispatch a circular to its members. "Don't expect any response to
your letter," he cursed Maurice Jaccard, one of Zehnder's subordinates, in a telephone call. "The Israelis' constant protests are quite
simply fallacious." Attempting to reason with the excited Oetterli,
Jaccard explained, "I can't prevent your association from adopting
that attitude, but the Israelis won't be satisfied with your 'solution.'
They'll just double their efforts and even demand a decree in court to

obtain the documents." Oetterli was implacable. In a message to Zehnder, Jaccard reported, "Herr Oetterli was rather excited and spoke in despicable words about "'Jewish propaganda.'"

The following day, Oetterli telephoned Rudolf Bindschedler, the Political Department's senior lawyer. Renowned for his long silences, Bindschedler had been affected by the letters of complaint from Jewish survivors seeking help. Now he was listening to an excited bankers' spokesman cajoling the department: "Don't simply collapse because of a demand from Tel Aviv. Fight the Israelis." Damning the Washington Accord and the "famous exchange of let-ters," Oetterli warned that the bankers would not tolerate any change in the existing laws. Trying to calm him, Bindschedler explained, "When the existing laws were introduced, there hadn't been an heir-less assets problem. The Israeli request is not based on the accord." Then the lawyer issued an unexpected counterwarning: If the associ-ation remained unhelpful, new legislation might be necessary. Deaf to that caution, Oetterli defiantly terminated the conversation. After reading his typed record of the exchange, Bindschedler wrote in pen-cil in the margin, "Glaringly exposes the Bankers Association and Oetterli."

For one month, Switzerland's senior bankers contemplated the Political Department's attitude. Given the sympathy they could rely upon from Petitpierre, the bankers considered, Bindschedler's com-ments could be ignored, but it might be worthwhile to nudge the department toward a greater understanding of the realities of Israel and the Jews. The immediate difficulty was Meron's request for information about the Spira and Bragowski accounts. The best response, the association believed, was to cast suspicion on the Israeli government's motives. "Israel needs foreign currency," the associa-tion wrote to the Political Department, "and forces its citizens to exchange that currency into Israeli pounds at huge losses." The new instruction to Swiss banks receiving queries from current Israeli clients was to send no letters to Israel. Slyly, the association added that if the Swiss banks transferred any money to Israel it would effec-tively be confiscated. "We doubt," wrote the association, "that the

Israeli request was freely supported by the named inheritors."
Unwittingly, by acknowledging that money would be transferred to
Israel, the bankers had implied that the claimants were genuine. That
nuance was missed by Zehnder, who marked the letter's comments
about Israel's alleged motives "correct."

Unsure whether others in the department understood that the
Bankers Association opposed any changes in the law that would release
the heirless assets or disclose bank accounts, Oetterli started bullying
officials. "With despicable words," commented Jaccard, "he talks
about the Israeli requests." Oetterli's uncontrolled anti-Semitism provoked him into a contemptuous assertion that the department's officials were unwilling to understand that the term "heirless assets" was
meaningless. Too many complainants, he said, uneasy that support for
the banks was not universal, were approaching the Department.
Among the complainants was Erwin Haymann, the lawyer in Geneva
specializing in such claims whose inquiries concerning the bank
account of Max Reiser, a murdered Polish Jew, had been stalled. "You
advised me," he wrote to the Political Department, "to ask the Bankers
Association for information . . . the same advice as in previous cases. I
have followed that advice scrupulously, but I never receive any information from the Bankers Association and sometimes not even a
reply." Politely, Haymann warned the department: "It seems to me
absolutely vital, in the interests of both Switzerland and the settlement
of this business, that a solution is found to this problem." The department did not respond. Then in autumn 1951, Oetterli's anger
reignited.

Philip Schmid, another member of the Swiss parliament, was
criticizing the government for failing to donate the heirless assets to
the Nazis' victims; and officials in the Political Department had, in a
lukewarm, noncommittal manner, assured George Brunschvig of the
Swiss Federation of Jewish Communities that they would consider
legislation compelling banks and other financial institutions to register all dormant accounts. To Oetterli, even these insignificant expressions of intent amounted to a crisis. Apoplectic, he shouted at
Maurice Jaccard that the department should show him any proposed

reply to Schmid before it was published. Shaken by Oetterli's assumption that the government was merely an agency serving the banks' interests, Jaccard made a mental note to ignore that demand, but his manner did not betray any disdain. The official had, however, come to share with Alexander and Bindschedler, the two senior lawyers, a sense of outrage at the iniquity of the banks' behavior. To strengthen their case for a law, they dispatched an inquiry to Switzerland's embassies in Washington and Western Europe asking for information about their host government's treatment of heirless assets. Switzerland, they knew, would react only to foreign pressure.

Oetterli understood the same. In its annual report, the Bankers Association prominently complained that foreign governments were applying "pressure" on the banks, implicitly reproaching the Political Department for failing to provide protection. The association's next step, since it was fearful that the government might bow to foreign influence and change the law, was a public offensive. Under the headline "German assets in Switzerland," the Swiss Bank Corporation published a bulletin asserting: "Charges have been made that Switzerland allowed her territory to be used by Nazi organizations to hide looted property. An official census of German Assets in Switzerland has shown that these suspicions are entirely unfounded and that the total value of German assets in Switzerland is far below what irresponsible quarters had alleged." Another statement, issued by the Bankers Association, warned against "special legislation introduced because of pressure by foreign organizations," which would constitute a "severe violation and change of our system of justice."

Oetterli's frenzy was not inexplicable. Seven years after the war, the banks, insurance companies and other trustees were better able to gauge the amounts in dormant and unclaimed accounts. At stake was a gigantic, unmonitored windfall. In addition, as tax rates soared across Europe, secret accounts in Switzerland had become increasingly attractive to the rich. Protecting German property and Nazi loot and defending the secrecy laws acted as a magnet for potential customers seeking a safe refuge for their undeclared income. Any threat to the secrecy laws, Oetterli understood, threatened his members' fortunes. Suppression of information was crucial for the banks' profits, and any exposure of their illegal activities was to be ruthlessly resisted. The history of one scandal, suppressed over the previous months, indicated the trouble that would befall his profession if Oetterli's tactics failed.

Rumors of the bankers' success in preventing an investigation had reached Dr. Lüthy, a government lawyer. The subject was the official investigation into the provision of false affidavits offered with stolen securities during the war. Appalled by the bankers' obstructionism, Lüthy wrote to Minister of Justice von Steiger asking him to consider the circumstances. The Bankers Association—"a state within a state," according to Lüthy—had been aware of the illegalities before the authorities had; and the bankers had profitably exploited the public's trust to avoid punishment. Lüthy wanted the culprits imprisoned. Among those Lüthy named as culpable was Henri Grandjean, a director of Crédit Suisse who had purchased stolen French bonds attached to false affidavits. According to Lüthy, Grandjean, as a member of the French Committee of the Bankers Association, had abused his position. "His profits were huge," declared the lawyer. Yet at the end of his eighteen-page letter, Lüthy performed a remarkable about-face and reconsidered his earlier request for exposure and punishment. "These facts," he concluded, "are not known to the public. Happily!"

At the end of 1950, Lüthy's recommendation that the scandal should remain secret was overridden. Revelations by communists and social democrats about other falsifications and dishonesties had compelled Petitpierre to make a statement to parliament about the Bankers Association's conduct. By then, the foreign minister's loyalty toward all bankers, including those who had profited from the false affidavits, was so intense that a confidential tip about shares, offered to him by a Volksbank director, did not even evoke a written reply that could officially distance him from the suggestion. In an uninterrupted one-hour speech to Switzerland's politicians, Petitpierre adhered to the gospel that the government could not interfere in the banks' internal affairs. He selectively admitted known mistakes while protecting the association from demands for state control. His solution, adroitly legal, was a cover-up. The responsibility for further investigation and any prosecutions, he announced, was to be dispersed among all the cantons. In a confidential letter, he justified this maneuver by explaining that any personal culpability had to be subordinated to "important external considerations. . . . A trial in a canton court would arouse much less attention than one in a federal court." The anonymous victims—those whose shares had been stolen and who were unable to obtain their recovery—won no sympathy from Petitpierre. As a precaution, in January 1952 the Ministry of Justice was ordered to draft legislation requiring banks to declare unclaimed deposits, but that was a perfunctory detail. Ignoring the suffering of the innocent was a consistent policy, passed down from the minister to the Compensation Office. In rare cases, though, such as that of the Mendelssohn-Bartholdy family, the victims were unwilling to succumb.

By 1952, Otto Mendelssohn-Bartholdy, the grandson of the composer, had died and his son Hugo, living in Switzerland, was urging Hans Frölicher, the director of the Political Department's German Interests Section, to assist his campaign to gain access to the family's Bodenkreditbank shares, worth SF1 million, confiscated during the war by the Nazis. A complication had already robbed the family of a considerable amount. In 1948, the Bodenkreditbank had made a call on shareholders for extra cash. Those who failed to pay lost a significant slice of their investment, and the Compensation Office had refused to release any of Mendelssohn-Bartholdy's money to maintain the value of his shares—a fate shared by all those who suffered the Compensation Office's discrimination against German Jews. More persistent than others, Hugo Mendelssohn-Bartholdy had obtained from the new communist government in East Berlin a document testifying that the family was stateless. But the document was discounted by the Compensation Office on the ground that it was not the original individual decree issued by the Nazis. Similarly, the Compensation Office rejected a document issued by the Nazi Reichsbank showing that the shares had been confiscated from their stateless owners. The Compensation Office explained that the Reichsbank's declaration did not specify whether the stateless person was Otto or Hugo Mendelssohn-Bartholdy. "The Compensation Office is looking for any pretext to avoid releasing my money," Mendelssohn-Bartholdy wrote to Frölicher.

Initially, the Compensation Office had denied Otto Mendelssohn-Bartholdy his money because his incarceration in a German concentration camp proved that he was "a German resident in Germany." Hugo was also trapped. Between 1940 and 1946, he had lived in Austria, which the Compensation Office, having unquestioningly accepted the Nazis' rather than the Allies' definition, had deemed to be part of the German Reich. So he too was "a German resident in Germany." By chance, in 1951 Mendelssohn-Bartholdy discovered that three years earlier the Compensation Office had finally accepted the Allies' version of history: that Austria had been militarily occupied by the Nazis. Mendelssohn-Bartholdy was after all entitled to his assets and would have saved his one million francs if only the Compensation Office's officials or Frölicher had cared to tell him earlier.

Frölicher's concern was to care only for the assets of Aryan Germans. Finding an old violin abandoned in the deserted German embassy in 1946, he had made considerable efforts over the years to find its owner, Paul Sachs. His hunt, with the help of former embassy employees and German diplomats across Europe, followed Sachs's travels via a convent in Florence and a hotel in Milan to the home of Baroness Münchenhausen, where he discovered that Sachs was a Jew who had died either of a heart attack in 1944 or during deportation to a death camp. Had Frölicher realized at the outset that the violin belonged to a stateless Jew rather than a German, he would not have pursued the owner. But by then his very office had become academic. German diplomats and bankers, with the Swiss government in tow, had established the framework for the final settlement of the Washington Accord. German and Swiss satisfaction with the terms inevitably implied the dissatisfaction of others, including the Jews.

The agreed intermediary in the settlement of the triangular dispute was Hermann Abs, Germany's most prominent banker, the managing director of the Deutsche Bank, who had been arrested in 1945 as a suspected war criminal for plundering foreign corporations and for sanctioning, as a director, IG Farben's investment in collaboration with the SS in a factory sited in Auschwitz. Protected by British officers against the Treasury crusaders, Abs had become an architect of West Germany's economic regeneration.

Over twelve months, Abs, a consummate diplomat, shuttled between the European capitals brokering a deal to match German interests against Switzerland's refusal to dilute its claims against Germany, all the while soothing the Americans' suspicions of Stucki. The State Department had tried to have the venue moved to Washington, because "we are on unfavorable ground in Bern," where Stucki could be subjected to "the influence of those Swiss who are closely linked with Germany"; but the attempt failed. "The Swiss," commented Robert Swann, a British diplomat in Bern, "appear far more ready to cooperate with the Germans than they were with us." In Stucki's opinion, he was capitulating rather than cooperating. Although his continuing refusal to advance the promised SF30 million ($7 million), or even a reduced sum of SF17 million, for the refugees until the Washington Accord was satisfactorily completed suggested that he was continuing to protect German property, in private he was enraged.

"We're in a grotesque situation," cried Stucki. He was objecting to Bonn's "sabotage" in forbidding the Swiss to use the German property in Switzerland to pay reparations to the Allies, or to repay Switzerland's wartime loans to Germany, or as compensation for the $58 million paid to the Allies for the looted gold. The Germans should "do something about their debt" to Switzerland, he shouted. Sidelined, the Allies could now read the awful truth about the previous decade in *Der Bund*, an influential Swiss newspaper: "Switzerland stood up for a just handling of German interests after the signing of the Washington Accord. . . . We have always protected German interests, and it has not always been easy."

Protecting Germany's looted gold had certainly been fraught with difficulty. During 1947, investigators in Germany had discovered that the real amount of Dutch gold being shipped to Switzerland had been $161 million rather than $100 million. Dutch anger was shared by the State Department. Although the accord was a final, legal settlement, Rubin had appealed to Charles Bruggmann, the Swiss ambassador, more in embarrassment than anger, hoping that the Swiss would not take advantage of the disarray in Holland after the war. "On grounds of morality, Mr. Ambassador," Rubin had urged, "surely you can see from the documentary evidence that the Dutch case is watertight." Rubin was being polite. The evidence suggested that officials at Switzerland's National Bank must have seen Dutch markings on the ingots. Corroboration was provided by the Reichsbank's delivery of 722 bars of Dutch gold to Sweden. Because the Germans had been pressed for time, 217 of those bars had arrived in their original Dutch wrappers, with documents showing their history and true ownership. Rubin had every reason to believe that the German shipments of Dutch gold to Switzerland were similarly mixed, not least because other unsmelted Dutch ingots had been sent to Portugal from Bern. During the Washington negotiations, Hirs had concealed that knowledge.

But Bruggmann had been unmoved by Rubin's appeal. The Dutch government had also formally asked Petitpierre to consider reopening negotiations. Bern had scoffed at the suggestion, repeating old excuses: "Switzerland has already paid a very considerable amount under the 1946 accord in the absence of any legal obligation." The government had added that "only a negligible fraction" of the gold received from Germany "bore a Dutch marking."

Observing the State Department's similar inability to recover looted gold from Portugal (Lisbon had offered to return 9 tons of looted gold despite having received 32 tons) and from Sweden (which returned only 7 tons of looted Dutch gold and eventually offered 301 bars as a settlement for a further looted 722 bars—16 tons), the Swiss saw that there would be no reprisals if they likewise protected other German loot. Included in that loot were the bags of gold coins worth $1.5 million found in the German embassy's safe in May 1945, which, although plainly stolen, were declared by the Political Department to be "state property" belonging to Germany. Yet, despite all those efforts, neither Abs nor any other West German offered his country's gratitude to Stucki.

"It's time for the Germans to make a sacrifice," Stucki told Homberger. Serenely, the industrialist sought to pacify the official: "The accord took us dangerously near to illegality. The Allies were threatening us, but today we don't need to be intimidated. We've got to make sure that in one hundred years' time, history will justify what we've done as proper for a neutral, law-abiding country." Stucki was not easily assuaged. Implementing the accord would complete his official service to Switzerland, yet reports from everywhere threatened that ambition. Swiss nationalists were demanding that all the money be used to repay the wartime loans; Swiss industrialists, who had earned fortunes by collaborating with the Germans, were submitting arrogant complaints full of lies to Petitpierre; while German industrialists and bankers were badgering Switzerland not to pay any compensation.

"They say the accord is dead," Ott, his deputy, told Stucki, "and their Swiss lawyers and trustees are telling them just to be patient." Ott deplored the widespread ingratitude. Neither the Germans nor even the Swiss realized how effectively Compensation Office employees had used the freeze and delaying tactics to protect German interests. Instead they were attacked for obeying the law. Stucki agreed. Though he had not been acting "on behalf of Bahnhofstrasse," he flattered himself, deriding the Swiss bankers he so much distrusted, "American suspicions about Switzerland's attitude toward the accord were not completely unjustified."

In parallel agreements initiated on August 28, 1952, symbolizing West Germany's status as an accepted European power: The Allies, grateful to receive anything, signed a new agreement with Switzerland, while the Swiss concluded a separate arrangement with the new West German government. The Allies, abandoning their original demand for SF250 million, accepted Switzerland's "final" offer of SF121.5 million, minus a 10 percent deduction for payment in cash, and minus SF17 million (negotiated down by the Swiss from SF30 million) to be paid to the International Refugee Organization. Under the latter agreement, Germany undertook to pay SF121.5 million to Switzerland and SF121.5 million to the Allies to cover Allied claims under the accord. No German assets in Switzerland were sold. In total, Switzerland recovered SF650 million of its loans to Germany, including the SF121.5 million. Homberger hailed the settlement as a victory for Switzerland. "It was a triumph for justice," he told Stucki. Switzerland had retained all its assets in Germany, had recovered half the debt owed by Nazi Germany that seven years earlier had been written off, and had proved that its bankers cared for their clients' interests regardless of pressure. "We saved what we could," replied Stucki. "The Germans will be grateful to us." André François-Poncet, the French high commissioner in Germany, concurred. The agreement, he wrote to Paris, would secure German "gratitude" toward Switzerland, "whose epithet as a 'safe haven country' is thus, as ever, well deserved."

To prove Switzerland's reliability, Max Ott traveled to Bonn shortly after the treaty was signed to discuss the fate of the deposits of the German Jews. Anxious to win favor, Ott regaled Benninghaus, a German government official, with a flavored version of history. Boasting about the Compensation Office's battle against the Allies to protect German interests, he proudly explained his tactics. While the Allies, he emphasized, had been concerned only about the Jews, "we opposed them saying that not only Jews were persecuted but others were too." Then, remembering Bonn's new version of history, Ott added that his staff had also keenly protected anti-Nazis. Not surprisingly, he forgot his own refusal to help the anti-Nazis during a conversation with bankers and industrialists on January 13, 1948. After all, as he well knew, history belongs to the victors—in this instance the Germans. Ott would later be employed by IG Chemie in Switzerland, as a reward for safeguarding its interests.

On April 7, 1953, the Swiss government deposited SF101.5 million ($23.3 million) in a special account opened in the Swiss National Bank for the three Allied embassies. In London, Foreign Office officials complained that the Americans, having received $34 million from the sale of German property in the United States, "have done very well out of the reparation program and are bored with the whole business." By contrast, the Europeans received very little. "Every effort," ordered the Foreign Office, "should be made to minimize such deductions" especially of the money owed to the IRO. "As the United Kingdom's entitlement to receipt from IARA is higher than [that of] any other country, we stand to lose more than anybody else by these deductions." The most Britain would receive, it was calculated, would be SF34.5 million, but more likely SF22.5 million. France would receive half that amount. Both countries resolved to resist the Americans' demand that SF17 million be handed over to the IRO, a decision that echoed the consistent antagonism toward the Jewish claims throughout the negotiations.

On that issue, however, Britain's and France's defeat was swift. Under pressure from the Jewish organizations, the State Department demanded that the accord be implemented. After loans were deducted, SF12.8 million was to be deposited in the IRO account, of which the American Jewish Distribution Committee and the Jewish Agency were to receive $1.4 million each. For Rubin, the success was sweeter because some State Department officials had until the very last months proposed to "abandon entirely" negotiations with Switzerland. But his elation that his persistence on behalf of the Jews had been rewarded was dampened by a press release issued by the World Jewish Congress claiming credit for the settlement. "As usual the WJC in London is manufacturing press releases," complained Eugene Hevesi. "One of those outrageous things the World Jewish Congress does," agreed a colleague. But worse than this bitching was the crusaders' failure in the final settlement to trounce Switzerland's banks and insurance companies and extract the heirless assets. Both Swiss groups had successfully prevented encroachment on their secrecy. They still controlled the heirless assets and the unidentifiable bank deposits.

On January 24, 1952, Max Oetterli had been spitting with fury. Despite his demand, Maurice Jaccard in the Political Department had given no forewarning about Petitpierre's answer to Philip Schmid's allegations nine weeks earlier in parliament about the heirless assets. Schmid had accused the Bankers Association of apparently intending to "retain" that money rather than transfer it to the rightful owners. Unwilling to sustain a complete deceit, Petitpierre had announced on January 22 that the government would order compulsory notification of heirless assets. "I am astonished," Oetterli screeched at Jaccard, "that the government took this action without first consulting the Bankers Association." The banker would not be calmed. "I want to meet Zehnder," he demanded, referring to the senior official sympathetic to the bankers' requirements. "Herr Alexander at the Ministry of Justice is responsible for the legislation," replied Jaccard. But Oetterli's relations with those officials were not as close.

Surveying the Bankers Association's attitude over the previous years, Emil Alexander, the director of the Justice Division, noticed suspicious variations. In 1947 the association had reported that the identifiable heirless assets amounted to SF208,000. Two years later in Warsaw, the Polish assets were assessed to be SF2 million. Later that had fallen to SF600,000 and then to "less than SF500,000." The department had proposed to issue a special decree to compel the banks to declare the true amount, but the bankers had successfully argued that the issue was not urgent and that any change in the law would damage Switzerland. In 1952, an uncompleted survey by the Bankers Association among twenty-one members had identified heirless assets worth SF36,580, with an overall total estimate of SF825,000. The insurance companies estimated a figure of SF29,000. Alexander's dissatisfaction was mild compared with Rubin's. After conversations with sympathetic Swiss bankers, he estimated the heirless assets to be worth at least SF14 million. Alexander and Rubin were agreed on one fact. Despite all the disparities, heirless assets certainly existed in Switzerland's banks. That assessment had been unwelcome to the British and French governments.

To secure more money for Britain, Neal Goodchild had sought to prevent heirless assets from contaminating the negotiations. In a visit to Bern, he had been persuaded that the amount of heirless assets and the money belonging to the persecutees was so small that the subject was not worth discussing. With little difficulty, he converted the Quai d'Orsay and the State Department to the same opinion. The subject, Rubin was told by Avery Paterson, was "a most difficult one to settle at this time." There were more pressing issues. Rubin's only success had been to inveigle the State Department into securing British and French support to prevent Switzerland from including the assets of persecutees as German property to be used for reparations. Germany's bid during the negotiations for the final agreement to inherit the heirless assets of the German Jews had also been foiled—a victory dubiously shared with the Swiss banks. But in the months before the final settlement, the Jewish organizations had failed to prevent Germany from inheriting other heirless assets of the victims of Nazism.

In the French zone of Germany, the military government had allowed the Germans to keep the heirless assets and deny the Jews any benefit and had even stipulated that any remaining money should be used for the benefit of France, despite the plight of destitute Jews in Germany. "Unfortunately," commented a guilt-ridden official in the French Foreign Ministry, "the existing French zone law allows assets, the majority of which are of Jewish origin, to be used for the profit of groups of people who are mostly not Jewish." Wanting to improve France's image, Robert Schuman, the French foreign minister, had asked the German government to behave more benignly toward the Jews and Israel and suggested rebuilding synagogues in France. Reports from the French ambassador in Bonn confirmed that Germany, still anti-Semitic and mirroring France's lack of interest, was searching for legal reasons to avoid paying reparations to Israel by arguing that the new government in Tel Aviv was not legally entitled to represent the dead, who were not Israeli citizens when they were murdered. "While it is not surprising that the Germans themselves could resort to this kind of immoral and undignified duplicity," Eli Rock of the Jewish Restitution Successor Organization wrote in a memorandum to Ross McClelland in the State Department, "the willingness of the French to go along with such a program ... is beyond comprehension." French complicity with the Germans, complained Rock, even in the midst of international tension, not only undermined the Allies' position but represented an unacceptable "act of immorality and injustice," overturning all the ideals and reasons for destroying Nazism. It was, he wrote, a "fraud" perpetuated by the Germans to evade all responsibility.

McClelland had ignored Rock's letter, but an inquiry by Israel on April 10, 1951, about progress in settling the issue of heirless assets required a personal response from the secretary of state. Drafting the answer, McClelland sought to defuse any protests: "The American delegation is under instruction to seek a solution to this question along the lines of the proposals advanced by the government of Israel on June 15, 1950." McClelland added that while the negotiations in Bern were under way, the outcome was uncertain. His caution was advisable. The department's negotiators in Bern had been instructed not to contest the Swiss on the subject. For their part, the Swiss had long anticipated the Allies' attitude. Ever since Switzerland had rejected the Allies' protest about the Polish agreement, Jaccard noted, "The Americans, British and French have not been very interested." That assessment was vindicated at a preliminary meeting in Bern in April 1951. No diplomat representing the three Allied governments had challenged a memorandum submitted by the Swiss government to the Allies reporting that an investigation by the Bankers Association and the Swiss Association of Life Insurance Companies had "revealed no (rpt no) assets of heirless German victims of Nazi action." The pertinent inclusion of the word "German" was not questioned and the fate of the non-German heirless assets remained undiscussed. The briefing paper on heirless assets for Sir Patrick Scrivener, the British delegate, instructed, "The memorandum ... by the Swiss delegation suggests that the matter may now be dropped."

On April 20, 1951, all three of the Allies consented to drop the issue, subject to a letter signed by the three Allied representatives and Stucki. Formally, the Allied governments noted that the new agreement did not mention heirless assets because the Swiss government had stated, "there exist in Switzerland no assets of this nature." If such money was found in the future, the letter continued, "the Swiss government will study with forbearance the possibility of donating these assets to the assistance and aid of victims of Nazism." Petitpierre dispatched a statement to the Allied diplomats confirming, "There are no heirless assets in Switzerland." The minister promised that if in the future any heirless assets were found, the money would be used for refugees. In his own letter, Stucki confirmed that during the negotiations the Swiss government had "declared that there are no heirless assets," and he too promised that if any were found they would be donated for reconstruction.

The Bankers Association had good reason to believe that, if Petitpierre was prepared to repeat an untruth to the three Allies, its victory was complete. To underline the futility of the crusaders' continuing their campaign, the association handed the American Jewish Committee a survey conducted among its members about dormant accounts. For all practical purposes, the Bankers Association concluded, such accounts "do not exist." In a final riposte, the association damned most claimants who alleged an inheritance in Switzerland's banks as relying on nothing more than their imagination. The crusade had again suffered a defeat.

14

KEEPERS OF
THE FLAME

Occasionally, Rudolf Bindschedler suffered spasms of conscience about the heirless assets. Disdainful of Max Oetterli and suspicious of the banks, the legal adviser in the Political Department heard troubling rumors and read reports that aroused his concern. In April 1953, one case in particular was, with customary understatement, underlined in the department's file as "informative."

The case involved Otto Trachsel, a German who nearly forty years earlier had opened a savings account in a remote Swiss Alpine village bank. Trachsel had died and in 1949, by chance, his son found his father's savings book. In 1953, the son asked the bank for his inheritance. The bank replied that in 1935, after his father had not been heard from for twenty years, the account had been closed and the bank had assumed ownership of the money. Without any apology, the bank admitted that it did not believe it was legally obliged to hand over the money. Bindschedler, to his disquiet, discovered that the bank had no other object than self-enrichment. In 1935, it had placed an advertisement in a local and little read newspaper, listing seventy-seven names of depositors whose dormant accounts would be closed if there was no contact within ten years. In the meantime, the bank had made no effort to contact Trachsel or any of the other depositors. Once the period had passed, the bank transferred all the money to its own reserves and, as permitted by Swiss law, destroyed the records.

Trachsel's letter, accompanied by irrefutable evidence of the deposit, could not be ignored, but the bank's reply revealed, in Bindschedler's opinion, an unfortunate attitude. The son was offered the SF3,430.65 that had been on deposit in 1935, but without any interest on the capital. The lawyer was concerned that the Swiss Banking Commission had failed to protect innocent depositors. Moreover, the bank's behavior undermined Oetterli's ceaseless claim that secrecy was necessary to protect the clients' interest. "This case," Bindschedler wrote to Oetterli, "is particularly shocking and will rekindle the interest in the laws on heirless assets." Oetterli, as usual, scoffed. Bindschedler, he believed, represented a tiny minority influenced by Israel. The reports from Swiss diplomats in Tel Aviv were to blame for the Political Department's nervousness. "The Israelis' imagination about the so-called Jewish heirless assets," reported Karl Seifert, the Swiss ambassador in Tel Aviv, "has grown intensively." Blaming "emotional motives" and the need for foreign exchange for fueling "demagogic interpretations," Seifert warned that relations could be damaged. That prediction suited Oetterli perfectly.

Oetterli's stance depressed the crusaders. "Our prospect of getting anything out of Switzerland," noted Jerome Jacobson of the AJDC, "on the strength of the Five Power Agreement (negotiated in Paris in 1946) alone is pretty hopeless." Eight years after the war, the stalemate appeared complete. On one side, the Swiss government refused to honor Stucki's promise and resisted invitations for discussions from the Jewish organizations. On the other, the State Department ignored pleas to bring pressure on the Swiss. Without allies, Rubin and other representatives kept a forlorn vigil, anticipating Switzerland's unanswerable rhetoric: "What is the United States doing about heirless assets in American banks?" Congress, Rubin lamented, was considering legislation that undermined all the Jewish organizations' work since 1944. But, unseen, the worm was turning.

The minutes of the ferocious encounter on November 17, 1952, between Oetterli and two leaders of Switzerland's Jewish community in the office of Markus Feldmann, the new minister of justice, had been filed in a growing collection of government papers. Oetterli's blustering attempts to stop the ministry from drafting a law on heirless assets—work that had started on January 22, 1952—had failed. Honest in his commitment to George Brunschvig, Emil Alexander, the ministry's legal adviser, was still considering legislation that would compel banks and other financial institutions to register all dormant accounts and deposits. Subordinates were preparing drafts for his consideration. Alexander sensed that, with the exception of the bankers, those without a vested interest deplored the uncertainty as intolerable and damaging. Oetterli's opposition, however, handicapped Alexander. Some justification for the bankers' opposition had surfaced during the year. The Hungarian government, asserting its entitlement to the heirless assets of its nationals, had submitted the names of allegedly dead citizens to Swiss banks to retrieve their deposits. The banks had discovered that some of those listed were, unknown to the communists, living in the West. Even replying to the Hungarian regime could endanger those clients' relatives. Noncooperation was the only safe policy. In contrast, even Stucki had been heard saying to Petitpierre, "There must be cases where no inheritors are alive." After all, the Compensation Office had discovered that SF16.5 million of frozen German assets were heirless. Anxious to distance himself from von Steiger's policy, Feldmann sympathized with those who suspected that the bankers were motivated simply by a desire to keep the money, but his opinion was tilted more by developments in West Germany.

Without moral qualms, Konrad Adenauer's government had in its early days denied any responsibility for the crimes of the Third Reich and ridiculed the notion that the new republic should bear any responsibility for the debts of its predecessor. Flouting international opinion, the new chancellor had recruited close advisers whose previous loyalty to Nazism was unexamined and unmentioned. In return for securing the Nazis' support after 1949, Adenauer had honored the pension allowances of former SS officers, regardless of their murderous service, while refusing help to destitute German Jews. A polite protest from the Allies noting that Germany "has taken no measures

affording significant compensation to the victims of Nazi persecution" was roundly rebuffed by Adenauer. "Most Germans," he told
the Bundestag, "had resisted the Nazis." The country, he added, pos-
sessed only "limited resources" and could not afford restitution.
Under pressure from the Americans, Adenauer slightly modified his
defiance, at least in public. In 1953, after emotional negotiations, the
West German government had finally agreed to pay reparations to
Israel. Markus Feldmann appreciated the inevitable repercussions.
"Undoubtedly this will activate the question of heirless assets in
Switzerland," he told Alexander. Others, especially Oetterli and
Homberger, were unconvinced.

With increasing confidence, German industrialists and other former Nazis began pressurizing the chancellor to recover their confiscated assets, especially in the United States, estimated to be worth
$500 million. Adenauer's appeal to President Eisenhower in
February 1954 for the return of German property intentionally coincided with the creation by the Senate Judiciary Committee of a sub-
committee under Senator Everett Dirksen of Illinois to investigate
the Trading with the Enemy Act. Dirksen and Senator William
Langer of North Dakota—Illinois and North Dakota both had large
German-American populations—had already won the support of
John Foster Dulles, the secretary of state, to return the German
property. To encourage West Germany's rapid rearmament and its
participation in the fight against communism, Dulles, dismissing the
international agreements, proclaimed that the United States recognized private property even in wartime and that confiscation of
German (and implicitly Swiss) property had been wrong. Dirksen
and Langer went further. Repudiating the eighteen-nation Paris
Agreement, their report condemned the seizure of German property
as an immoral, un-American communist plot masterminded by
Harry Dexter White. Everyone rightly expected that their bill to
return confiscated German property would be approved by the
House and Senate. (Eisenhower, however, would veto the bill in
August 1954.)

In Bern, Markus Feldmann's attitude toward the heirless assets had gyrated, his position depending on external developments and the bankers' threats. West German rearmament had whetted the appetites of Swiss munitions manufacturers for resuming their lucrative wartime trade with Germany, while the banks, proclaiming themselves as a safe haven for investors worried about another war, issued threats in a bid to protect their lucrative secrecy. For the hyperactive minister, the Jews and their money were an easily forgotten nuisance that unfortunately could not always be ignored. Fourteen months after the confrontation in his office, on February 12, 1954, Feldmann reluctantly summoned a meeting to discuss his department's draft law ordering a census. To prevent an undignified fight, Feldmann had asked Judge Plinio Bolla, representing the Bankers Association, and Professor Paul Guggenheim, of the Jewish community, to present memoranda outlining their cases.

Bolla's case was predictably uncompromising. Reciting the bankers' gospel, he pronounced the existing legislation to be adequate and predicted that special legislation would undermine the secrecy laws and the Swiss constitution and would legalize confiscation. While disputing the size of the heirless assets, he argued that, should any exist, they would be subject to international law just like the assets of the Polish Jews. In the code that implied that Switzerland had been victimized by foreign and Jewish interests, Bolla urged the government not to succumb to the same political blackmail as had operated in Washington six years earlier.

Guggenheim's submission was equally predictable. Switzerland, he wrote, remained "isolationist and lacked understanding" about the uniqueness of the Holocaust, adopting a "business-as-usual" attitude while the banks were hiding large sums of money. The banks' behavior since 1945, he continued, and the Polish treaty were hardly reassuring: "Passivity is not suitable to protect private property." The only solution, he concluded, was to compile a register based on an external investigation of dormant accounts and missing people.

Bolla's written reply reeked of contempt. There was, he declared, no problem. Dismissing any notion that banking secrecy could be infringed, the judge derided independent investigation as impossible because there could be no agreement about what was to be registered, and any dishonest bank or fiduciary could easily evade the requirement. Any heirs, he continued, had already staked their claims, and the amounts of heirless assets were so "trivial" that no bank would ever keep those unclaimed deposits. "Why," asked Bolla in familiar and false rhetoric, "should the Swiss be required to compromise their principles and not the American banks?"

In the face of such irreconcilable opinions, Feldmann's options were limited. Without any obvious compromise, either he could compel the banks to disclose the heirless assets or he could retreat. The invitation to Bolla and Guggenheim to meet personally in his office signaled the minister's retreat. In contrast to the invitation in November 1952, when the ministry had declared that there would be a law, Feldmann's present invitation suggested that the new talks would discover "whether it is possible to solve the problem of heirless assets without changing the law." Yet, in the days before they met, Feldmann retreated even further. Persuaded by the bankers, the minister told George Brunschvig that his request for legislation was still delayed by "some preliminary work." Nevertheless, the minister would agree to chair a meeting.

Five bankers and two representatives of Switzerland's Jewish community, Paul Guggenheim and George Brunschvig, faced each other in Feldmann's office. Brunschvig was always disquieted by these confrontations, but his courage had grown as his anger increased. Over the past months he had received anonymous denunciations claiming that bankers had enriched themselves by diverting into their own accounts the funds of Jews who had made their deposits before 1939 but had not been heard from since. "An official of American Express in Zurich," one informant had recently written, "has just bought himself a huge flat and comfortable car out of the deposit of a Viennese Jew who died." Other rumors mentioned strange activities in the vaults of banks. Safe-deposit boxes, untouched for more than fifteen years, were being opened for an "inventory." All belonged to foreigners, mostly Jews. Mysteriously, their contents—jewels, cash, paintings and gold—had been stored "for administrative reasons" elsewhere in the bank and had then disappeared. Bank employees later spoke of a "sudden huge inheritance" from a distant relative, but the truth was known. Stories about the wholesale theft in banks of property belonging to murdered Jews were widespread around Switzerland. Not all this property was heirless. In many cases, there were undoubtedly heirs, but they were unaware of the boxes' existence or were denied access by the banks. But the flood of anecdotal evidence, Brunschvig decided, would not convince the bankers. And he feared their hatred of Jews.

Shamelessly, Jakob Diggelmann, the senior director of Bank Leu, who had deigned to express regret for his bank's close cooperation with the Nazis, opened with a threat to Guggenheim: "If, despite our warnings, there is a decree, we will fight for a referendum." Everyone understood. Diggelmann would protect banking secrecy by arousing anti-Semitism, under the veneer of defending Switzerland's sovereignty. But Guggenheim was not as easily intimidated as Brunschvig: "We're speaking a different language from the banks. Six million have died. In many cases there are no heirs to their money. That needs special measures."

"We're certainly speaking two different languages," said Diggelmann brusquely, deliberately ignoring the background of their meeting. For Diggelmann and the other bankers, the Holocaust was in every sense irrelevant. Only self-interest counted: "We'll never agree if there is any suggestion of changing the law. We are protecting the deposits for the legitimate owners."

"The bankers' explanations will never reassure us," repeated Guggenheim, undeterred. "I haven't always received proper answers from the banks about the property of missing people."

Agreement was impossible, and Feldmann refrained from negotiating a compromise. "The opposition by the Bankers Association to any legal measures appears insurmountable," Feldmann told Petitpierre after rejecting, at the bankers' request, a new Israeli approach to discuss the heirless assets. Reading Feldmann's new hard-line stance, Bindschedler, the Political Department's lawyer, commented, "Predictable if the Police Division is involved!"

Max Troendle, the energetic minister of trade, welcomed Feldmann's hard line, but in September 1954 he was irritated to discover that, although five years had passed, the heirless assets had still not been transferred to "Clearing Account N" for the benefit of the Poles. His query to the Political Department was silenced by an admonition to "leave it to the banks." Troendle did not protest. Even the Political Department feared asking the banks for a progress report. "Perhaps the banks have forgotten about the matter," wondered Bindschedler. "It would be the responsibility of the Bankers Association to remind the banks and avoid any public discussion." Even Bindschedler seemed to have forgotten that he was reflecting on an international treaty signed by the government, but he was aware that no one was exactly eager to challenge the power of the banks.

One year later, Feldmann was still procrastinating. A letter from Guggenheim suggesting the appointment of a trustee to care for all the heirless assets had lain unanswered on his desk for six months before he asked the Bankers Association for its comment. Also on Feldmann's desk was a letter from Stucki regarding the case of Chaim Dunajewski, a Russian Jew who, while living in Hamburg in 1930, had deposited SF1.2 million in three Swiss banks as protection from the communists. It had been frozen as a German asset in 1945, and the Compensation Office decided in 1955 that Dunajewski was not German and that his twenty-five-year silence suggested that he had been murdered by the communists after his return to Russia. The Compensation Office therefore unfroze the money, prompting Stucki to write to Feldmann. The banks, he complained, "after the expiry of time for giving notice of unclaimed assets" could behave dishonestly. "There is the possibility, even the probability," he wrote, "that after the expiry of the time limit the banks will quite simply keep the money." Stucki sought the minister's approval for inviting the Compensation Office to ensure that the money was declared as an heirless asset. Rejecting the request, Feldmann ordered that the banks should be allowed to wait until a potential inheritor appeared. Nor, ruled the minister, should the money be transferred to a trustee. Finally, nothing was to be announced or even mentioned that might alert potential claimants. The banks could keep the money, fore-stalling the chance of a claim. Stucki had been ordered to maintain the conspiracy of silence.

Dilatoriness on heirless assets suited Feldmann. The Jewish question had once again become uncomfortable. Researchers of Nazi history working in archives in Berlin had in 1954 discovered the documents dealing with Rothmund's demand that a "J" be stamped in the passport of German Jews to help Swiss police identify those whose entry was banned. The revelation, publicized in Switzerland by SIG, shocked many Swiss. Silently, all the individual files stored in Feldmann's ministry concerning the refugees forcibly returned to occupied Europe and the Gestapo were destroyed. Removing the traces of history suited Feldmann, but the unremitting questions from Tel Aviv continued to disturb him until the sudden and alarming appearance of Samuel Tolkowsky, the Israeli ambassador, in Feldmann's office on March 28, 1955. Seven years after its creation, Israel was no longer just a desolate refuge for escapees from Eastern Europe's ghettos. Supported by the United States, the Israelis had proved themselves economically, politically and militarily against the surrounding Arab states. Tolkowsky, personifying that brand of aggressive self-confidence, now stood in the minister's office reciting the recent revelations by Rothmund and accusing the Ministry of Justice and the Police of the murder of thousands of Jews. Now, thundered the ambassador, Switzerland was constantly replying to charges of injustice relating to the heirless assets with nothing better than "It's being checked" or "It's being worked on." But there were no results, and Tolkowsky wanted results.

"We must solve this problem energetically," Feldmann told his officials after his unwelcome visitor had departed. "This dilatory reaction by the Bankers Association is embarrassing both the government and, particularly, the ministry." Unwilling to risk further trouble in Switzerland or with Israeli's mentors in Washington, Feldmann ordered action: "It is vital energetically to 'put pressure' on the Bankers Association and demand from them a response to proposals." To some it might have seemed that the bankers faced real pressure. "Each delay," Feldmann wrote to Oetterli, "risks creating doubts about Switzerland's intentions and places Switzerland in a delicate situation toward Israel."

But the bankers had heard it all before. Banking secrecy had become elevated to the status of a weapon in the war against communism. Defense of the bankers' interests had become a litany of euphemistic phrases referring to the "extremely exaggerated" amounts, the "so-called heirless assets" and the "casualties of war." Jews were never mentioned.

Oetterli's strategy was to minimize the problem. After a detailed search, he told Feldmann, the total of Polish heirless assets in Switzerland's banks had been established at SF22,300. "The exchange of letters," wrote Oetterli in his brutal style, "which churned up so much dirt, has proven to be unrealistic and is reminiscent of American suspicions that Nazi loot was hidden here." Remembering the original estimate by Rudolph Speich, the banker involved in the 1949 negotiations, that the two million dead Polish Jews would have deposited at least SF2 million in Switzerland, Oetterli knew that the communist government would not be pleased by his announcement that the Swiss had found just one-hundredth of the money. Since Zehnder had insistently told the bankers that "the agreement with Poland cannot be sabotaged. Our signature must be honored," the only feasible tactic, implied Oetterli, was to delay, conceal and deceive. "We've told [the Poles] that the investigation is not yet completed," he informed Zehnder. The bankers were once again dictating the government's policy.

Individual ministers and officials of the Swiss government were confounded by the bankers' audacity. But, since Feldmann had accepted the banks' assurance that the heirless assets were "small sums," the chance that a law would be passed to uncover the truth had again diminished. Over the following year, the bankers relaxed.

A chance meeting and a passing remark by Max Oetterli in May 1956 prompted Feldmann yet again to review his attitude. During a conversation with a Department of Justice official, Oetterli mentioned the bankers' willingness to provide more precise information.

Oetterli had not suffered a dramatic conversion. Rather, he was confronted with an embarrassing report from the Compensation Office. Marked "secret," this report had suggested that German heirless assets worth at least SF10 million existed in Switzerland. What was more worrying for Oetterli was that the Compensation Office detailed its inability to handle dozens of inquiries every year from Germans looking for their inheritance who, like the Compensation Office, were stonewalled by the banks. Unable to ignore that revelation, Feldmann had urged an informal approach to the Bankers Association to encourage it to conduct a proper census. Grateful that Oetterli had not responded violently, the minister implored the banker to comply. Otherwise a law could not be delayed for much longer.

Oetterli and Diggelmann well understood how to play the minister. By the end of a meeting on June 4, 1956, Feldmann was willing to say precisely what the bankers required. There would be no law, he announced, if the bankers' census revealed "a clear picture" that the property involved was "small" and "irrelevant." His benchmark for inaction was SF4 million to SF5 million. The bankers departed satisfied that the government, relying on their census, would not introduce a law if they reported that the heirless assets were worth less than SF4 million.

In their headquarters in Basel, Oetterli and the association's lawyers composed the questionnaire to be sent to their members. Just two words, judiciously placed within their long letter, nullified the questionnaire's purpose. Bankers were asked whether they "knew" or had "assumed" that any of their clients had been murdered by the Nazis. Allowing the bankers the discretion to decide whether indisputable facts were "known" or whether they cared to "assume" a client was dead merely because of his or her silence could have only one result.

Three months later, Oetterli supplied Feldmann with the results. Three banks had declared that they "knew" a client was dead. Those assets amounted to SF36,580. Twenty-one banks had "assumed" that clients were dead. Those assets were valued at SF825,832. Oetterli delighted in offering his conclusions: "The importance of the 'so-called heirless assets' is not as great as the opposition always tries to allege." Since the amount was less than SF4 million, Oetterli asked Feldman to "confirm in writing" that the government would "drop" the proposed law.

The minister was not quite convinced. Too many authenticated complaints aroused his officials' unease. A letter from Dr. Lothar Dessauer, a Swiss trustee who was a lawyer specializing in Jewish claims, was particularly bewildering. A Polish client, explained Dessauer, who had fled to Britain, had in 1956 written to her Swiss bank requesting her deposited savings. The bank had replied, "Your money has been transferred to the Polish government." Since no money had been yet paid to Poland, wrote Dessauer, he was puzzled. Officials in the Political Department were not puzzled. The bank's dishonesty was patent, although it would be later excused by the department as a "misunderstanding." To forestall future complaints and to silence the critics, Feldmann suggested to his officials a solution. SIG, he proposed, should be offered "a sum of money" to be used for the Nazis' victims. His "solution" evoked only mirth. Buying off the Jews with a lump sum without admitting any responsibility was universally rejected as "absurd." Either there was an injustice and legislation was necessary, or there was no substance to the complaint. "It would look as if the country was paying out 'silence money,'" noted one official, "so that the banks can keep money that does not belong to them." Hans Streuli, the minister of finance, agreed: "It would be a paradox if the country actually paid for private interests to enrich themselves from money entrusted to them." Feldmann retreated, hoping he might return to a state of inactivity. It was left to Bindschedler to catch the mood. The Ministry of Justice, he carped, "has simply capitulated to the banks." Oetterli, the lawyer knew, enjoyed considerable access to politicians, and his influence was substantial. Indeed, soon after, Oetterli visited Petitpierre, who afterward noted approvingly that the banker "hoped that there was no question of a new law."

The Polish government was less easily placated. In 1958, new trade negotiations with Poland were under way and the past tactic of politely stalling inquiries from Warsaw about the amount of heirless assets was no longer straightforward. The Bankers Association's latest census had revealed that the Polish heirless assets in the banks amounted to just SF17,550, while the insurance companies reported SF849. That disclosure, admitted the Political Department with marked understatement, would be "a disappointment" to the Poles. "We can hardly say that since 1949 most of the Polish clients have shown signs of life," Robert Kohli, the new chief of the Political Department, was told. Yet this was precisely what the bankers were urging the government to believe. In the midst of the 1956 revolt in Poland, many anticommunists had escaped to the West and some, according to Oetterli, had contacted their banks for the first time in twenty years. Whether that was credible was beyond Kohli's judgment. To avoid embarrassment, the department's officials had initially wanted the Bankers Association to explain the small amounts to the Poles, but Kohli opted for silence. "Delay telling anything to the Poles," the Swiss embassy in Warsaw was instructed. Pondering the matter, Kohli decided in 1958 that when the truth was finally revealed the Swiss negotiators should blame the Poles for their own high expectations: "Switzerland has always been skeptical of the Polish estimate of the deposits." Israel, on Petitpierre's direction, was to be treated with similar slyness.

The Israeli ambassador's occasional request to assist the Swiss government irritated the Political Department, already concerned because of speculation in Israel that the heirless assets could be worth $500 million. His latest inquiry, with Israel emboldened by victory in the Suez war, sounded more vigorous than before. Consistent with the Swiss paradox, the greater the threat, the more stubborn was Petitpierre's reaction.

Still believing the banks' assurances that the heirless assets did not exceed SF1 million, Petitpierre approved their demand for protection. "We will not allow Israel any involvement or discussion in this question," he insisted. "We just do not know how much money is at stake." On Petitpierre's initiative, in reply to the ambassador's query whether a census would be ordered to discover the heirless assets, the Federal Council repudiated the interference of a foreign government: "The Swiss Confederation has assumed no obligation to take any definite steps in this matter."

Too many Swiss, however, had become uneasy about the banks' conduct. Fourteen years after the war, anger about the Nazi era had grown rather than waned. Gradually, ignorance and prejudice about those years were yielding to unpalatable revelations. West German prosecutors were, for the first time, seeking to remedy the Allies' failure to investigate more than a handful of the Nazi war criminals. Their first major success in 1959—a trial in Ulm of former SS officers stationed in Auschwitz—caused a major shock in all German communities, including Switzerland. The authenticity of the evidence presented by Germans prosecuting Germans for their crimes against the Jews was unchallengeable, shedding a new light on the Nazi period. The previous year, the public expression of "deep disappointment" by Heinrich von Brentano, West Germany's foreign minister, after the U.S. government's refusal to return Germany's property, thereby allegedly causing "unjust and inhuman suffering," had aroused sympathy in Switzerland. But, in light of the Ulm trial, the raw statistics—that West Germans including former Nazis had received DM90 billion compensation for their wartime suffering while the victims of Nazism had received only DM5 billion— reflected a merciless degree of self-interest. As the facts about the Holocaust—heard for the first time by most Swiss—unfolded, Dr. Harald Huber, who was a prominent Swiss lawyer from St. Gall and a social democrat member of parliament, became uneasy about Swiss banks' retaining money deposited by the victims of Auschwitz.

Motivated neither by affection for Jews nor by dislike of the banks, Huber contacted Friedrich Wahlen, the new and popular minister of justice and the police, in March 1959 to recount a disturbing conversation. "A specialist banker, a member of a long-established Swiss family," Huber wrote, "told me that, on the basis of his experience across the industry, he knows that lying in the banks there are assets worth hundreds of millions belonging to the missing people." The letter was a bombshell. Huber, as Wahlen knew, was neither a fantasist nor a sensationalist. On the contrary, he was a respected politician and staid lawyer who would become the president of Switzerland's federal court. Huber's estimate of "hundreds of millions" of francs was the first time any Swiss had mentioned a sum that was not "small," and the source—who appeared to be interested only in truth and justice—could not be dismissed as lacking credibility. More pertinently, Huber was actually accusing the banks of deliberate fraud.

According to Huber's informant, many of the accounts containing the "hundreds of millions" of francs deposited by murdered Jews had been closed by bank employees aware of the circumstances—particularly the fact that no outsider knew the details about these accounts. Unmonitored, explained Huber's informant, the funds had been transferred to specially created corporations. "The banks," he wrote, "are naturally interested in using those interest-free assets as long as possible, even if they do not contemplate appropriating the money for themselves." Although that was legally tolerable, the banker also disclosed that unscrupulous employees were transferring the deposits of dormant accounts into other, unsupervised accounts from which the money could disappear. Thefts, Huber added, were not unusual: "My banking informant is aware of that happening." Huber did not mention his personal suspicion of a fiduciary who had accepted money from two Jews who had not reappeared since the war. The fiduciary's denials of the allegations were unconvincing, but—as was usual in these cases—Huber lacked specific proof.

Huber hoped that the minister would be more inclined to respond to the damaging allegations than Markus Feldmann had been. (Feldmann had since died of a heart attack in his office.) "I assume that this information, which confirms my own suspicions, will interest you." In the restrained language that is beloved of lawyers but nevertheless can reveal their excitement, he concluded, "It is clear that the banks, in order to deny the need for special legislation, are deliberately minimizing the amount of money involved. For me, the special law is obviously vital."

Four years earlier, Huber had asked the government for a law to compel the banks to reveal any heirless assets, but the government, wary of "misunderstandings" and "criticism" and fearful of arousing controversy and international speculation about "unquantifiable" millions in Switzerland, had dithered over a reply. But maintaining the silence demanded by the banks had become difficult. Not only was Switzerland increasingly vulnerable to external pressure from Israel, but the publication of a damning book by Carl Ludwig, a Swiss historian, commissioned after Rothmund's exposure in 1954 and describing the country's wartime treatment of the Jews, had stirred some consciences. To reduce the sense of guilt, an unidentified government propagandist shone a spotlight on the activities of Carl Lutz, the Swiss vice-consul in Budapest in 1944, to glorify a brave Swiss patriot who had saved thousands of Jews. Even Lutz had been surprised by the sudden attention. Over the past thirteen years, he had been not so much ignored as criticized on the ground that saving Jews had been unneutral behavior. Overnight he was hauled from obscurity and transformed into a hero, to end what Feldmann had called "the masochistic wallowing in one's own guilt." Feldmann's carping irony had been influenced by a confidential report from Rothmund. In unrepentant tones, the retired police chief justified his wartime policies. The responsibility for Switzerland's policies toward the Jews, wrote Rothmund, must be borne by Switzerland's Jews. It was their fear that anti-Semitism would be aroused by the impending flood of foreign Jews that compelled him to introduce the restrictions at the Jews' request. The fate of the Jewish refugees, he insisted, was the responsibility of the Jews themselves. It was an argument that appealed to Feldmann and other Swiss who suspected that the search through the Berlin archives was motivated by malicious revenge—an unwise tactic, Feldmann had thought, because Switzerland's Jewish leaders had certainly not protested against Rothmund's policies. Using Lutz as a diversion had been effective—only Huber was not so easily placated. Convinced that the heirless assets amounted to "much more" than the one million francs suggested by the banks, he told Wahlen, "We must end this uncertainty and remove the danger that the money will remain in the hands of people who are not entitled to keep it."

The existing law, Huber told the minister, was seriously flawed. Either a frustrated administrator of a fund did not know whether his client and the client's heirs were alive, or dishonest trustees were encouraged to keep quiet, hoping that the owner was dead and that the heirs would fail to find the funds before the statute of limitations annulled the inheritance. Huber's solution was to order the compulsory registration of all dormant accounts and to simplify the procedures for heirs to prove a death and their claims. Any unclaimed or heirless assets, he proposed, would be transferred to a special fund.

Unexpected support for the new law was offered by a prominent government official. Winding up the Compensation Office's affairs and transferring the staff to other departments, Walter Stucki wanted to embarrass the man who had savagely curtailed his career thirteen years earlier. On May 22, 1959, eight weeks after Huber's letter to the minister of justice, Stucki invited himself to the same ministry. Insisting that what followed should be classified "top secret," the veteran castigated Switzerland's lawyers for "shamelessly" earning a fortune representing Jewish claimants searching for their money. He then moved on to an unforeseen disclosure. Over past years, he growled, it had always been possible to establish whether Jews were the owners of unclaimed assets. The banks, Stucki had discovered, had entered the detail of their new clients' religion when the accounts were originally opened. And, most important, officials of the Compensation Office reviewing the records had discovered that in "very many cases" the owners of the unclaimed German assets were labeled as Jews. By itself, that astonishing revelation was most damaging to the banks. Warming to his theme, Stucki continued unburdening himself, recounting his conversations with two bankers based in west Switzerland. Independently, both bankers had admitted to him that "several hundred million Swiss francs" which belonged to French nationals "whose fate is today unknown" was deposited in their banks. Appreciating the effect of his revelation, he said, "This all shines a strange spotlight on the Bankers Association's insistence that the heirless assets are worth less than one million Swiss francs."

Unrecorded in the secret minutes of that meeting was the two men's common suspicion that most private people, including lawyers and notaries, entrusted with money by foreign Jews would long ago have quietly assigned that fortune to themselves, leaving no trace of their perfidy. Even the banks, paying no interest on diminishing amounts as they regularly deducted costs, could legally begin destroying some records. Under Swiss law, financial institutions were not obliged to maintain the records of dormant accounts beyond ten years after the last "activity," provided they gave notice of their intention to close the account. To fulfill their legal obligations, banks were required to serve only six months' notification of their intention by writing to the depositor's address. Since, to maintain discretion, foreign clients invariably stipulated that their address should be a mailbox within the bank, there was no opportunity for heirs to become aware that the process of legally eradicating any evidence of an account had begun. The alternative illegal scenario considered by Stucki and government lawyers was the traceless transfer by bank employees of dormant accounts into accounts under their own names.

The unrecorded discussion of that unpalatable probability coincided with a rash of Nazi attacks on Jewish cemeteries across Germany. The international uproar caused by the desecrations impelled Wahlen—skeptical that more than SF1 million would be found—to ask his officials in 1959, "When can a final version of the law be presented?" The banks, it seemed, finally had cause to fear a decree ordering disclosure of the untouched millions. Their counterattack began within days.

Still convinced that there was no serious foreign interest, the Bankers Association dispatched to Wahlen a list of "reservations" about any draft legislation. Unintentionally, the bankers' long submission revealed embarrassing somersaults. First, the so-called heirless assets, the minister was told, were not "heirless" but belonged to living persons. Yet the bankers failed to explain why those "non-heirless assets" had not been transferred to the "living persons." Second, reversing its opposition to the Polish agreement, the Bankers Association justified not releasing the "few" existing heirless assets—

at most SF1 million—by explaining that the money did after all belong to the country of the depositor. Third, in an unusual twist of logic, the Bankers Association resisted handing over the heirless assets to a charity because that would violate the "principles of trust" under which they were originally deposited and would be tantamount to confiscation, damaging worldwide confidence in Swiss trustees. To threaten that confidence in Swiss banks, pleaded the Bankers Association, by introducing special legislation for such trivial, inconsequential amounts of money was self-destructive. But the minister seemed disinclined to listen.

Cherishing that breakthrough, on November 2, 1959 Rubin flew to Zurich to consult Eberhard Reinhardt, a director of Crédit Suisse who in 1946 had been a member of the Swiss delegation to Washington. Rubin believed that the Bankers Association's anger, and the Swiss government's concession, confirmed that there were hidden heirless assets. "The Bankers Association's protests have an unpleasant look," he told Reinhardt. Hoping that with "goodwill on all sides" an agreement to release the money could be reached, he urged the banker to accept that "ways can be found to conduct a census which do not infringe Swiss secrecy laws or the rights of depositors." As usual, the banker nodded politely, agreed that a solution could be found, and bade his visitor a fond farewell with no intention of helping the Jews. Although Rubin did not know it, the Bankers Association's pressure on Wahlen was proving successful. By early 1960, Huber's initiative had been stymied.

In June 1960, the silence from Israel and Poland persuaded Petitpierre that there was after all a lack of foreign concern about the "small amount" involved. Noting the minister's eagerness to find an excuse so that the issue could slip off the agenda, Bindschedler had advised that "we cannot renege on our decision" to introduce a law. Petitpierre easily ignored this advice. The minister was also undisturbed by a note from the American embassy. Reminding the Swiss government of an assurance in 1952 that it would give "sympathetic consideration" to the use of heirless assets, Petitpierre was asked how he intended to locate and dispose of that money in Switzerland.

Petitpierre's officials assumed that the letter had been prompted by the Jewish lobby, and they were given ammunition by Stucki's recollection of the 1952 statements. "Besides the fact that no one on either side was really serious about this issue," explained Stucki in a Jekyll-and-Hyde transformation of his stance, "the Americans said cynically that they had been persuaded by the American Jews to present something. After all this time, we don't need to do anything any more." Stucki's dishonesty—claiming in 1952 that there were no heirless assets when he knew the contrary to be the truth—was ignored. Petitpierre, after all, had committed the same sin. "No exchange of letters took place in 1952," replied the Political Department curtly and inaccurately to Washington, adding, "Investigations have shown that the sums in question are quite small." The minister did not care to predict "the result . . . of the work currently in progress." Days later, Petitpierre's mood changed dramatically.

A visit to the foreign minister by Joseph Linton, the Israeli ambassador, was deliberately timed to coincide with international excitement following the announcement that Israeli intelligence officers had kidnapped Adolf Eichmann from Argentina. As expected, the diplomat could see that Petitpierre was not immune to the worldwide passion and accusations aroused by the capture of the former SS colonel, an architect of the Holocaust. Unaccustomed to criticism in Switzerland, the minister was plainly disquieted by the negative publicity orchestrated by Tel Aviv against his country. Unlike the previous eight visits by Israeli diplomats, Linton's visit was accompanied with the threat of mighty Israel's displeasure if the heirless assets were again ignored by tiny Switzerland. Petitpierre's hauteur gave way.

"It would be irresponsible to drop the problem now," Petitpierre announced to parliament in October 1960 as he hastened to introduce the law, first drafted in 1952. "Switzerland is expected to produce a solution." The mood had changed. Even a single remark to Ludwig von Moos, the new minister of justice, by Anthony Mann, a journalist writing for the *Sunday Telegraph* of London, made Petitpierre wince. Mann had mentioned that he expected assistance from the Israeli embassy in the writing of an article about heirless assets. "The matter must be ended soon," von Moos instructed his officials, responding to Petitpierre's wish that a draft law be swiftly published.

The news dismayed Max Oetterli, who was already agitated by the prospect of Petitpierre's retirement on July 1, 1961, and his replacement by the less sympathetic Friedrich Wahlen. To help the bankers, even on his last day in office, Petitpierre was urging the minister of justice to grant concessions. Since von Moos had edited a Catholic newspaper during the war that published anti-Semitic articles, he was not averse to Petitpierre's request, nor was he unreceptive to Oetterli's plain language. "Israeli exaggerations," the bankers' representative told von Moos's officials, had been spread across Europe by the governor of the Bank of Israel, who was personally responsible for "drafting" the Swiss government's law. Oetterli's last card, fanning anti-Semitism by conjuring the specter of the manipulation of sovereign, neutral Switzerland by the Jews and Israel, terrified George Brunschvig. Naively confessing his apprehension to von Moos's officials, Brunschvig reassured the successors of Rothmund's ministry, "My organization always represents Swiss interests and has kept its distance from both the Israeli embassy and foreign pressure groups." The officials were delighted to hear Brunschvig's complaint that Nahum Goldmann, the president of the World Jewish Congress, had "stirred up unpleasantness" after his publicized arrival in Switzerland and his claim to have masterminded the introduction of the new law. And they loved the protest from Jews in the United States, angry that Jews in Israel might receive a major share of the heirless assets when the money should properly be distributed among the refugees in the United States. But that was a pleasant sideshow to the prospect of future difficulties.

Friedrich Wahlen, Switzerland's president that year, was treated to an exhibition of anti-Semitism when a large delegation of bankers arrived in Bern in September 1961. "We are against giving the money to Jewish groups and especially Israel," Albert Matter, a director of the Basler Kantonalbank, warned the politician. "That would be against the intentions and traditions of the banks." If the heirless assets were to be distributed, the banker suggested, the ideal charity was the Winkelried-Stiftung, which cared for the distressed families of Swiss soldiers. The prospective newspaper headline "Holocaust Victims Fund Swiss Soldiers" might well have tickled Wahlen's earthy humor, but his reply was restrained: "The Jewish groups will criticize us. You cannot deny that those groups have legitimate interests?" Oetterli naturally disagreed. Anger blinded him to the implications of his new demand. If the government insisted that the banks pay out the heirless assets, said the Bankers Association secretary, then ministers should promise an indemnity in case a claimant should later appear. Wahlen smiled. If the amount of heirless assets was as small as the banks claimed, the risk was surely irrelevant.

The inevitability of the law was shaking out the truth. "Just on the basis of all the claims which have arrived in my office," Dr. Lothar Dessauer, the Swiss lawyer specializing in claims by Jews, told the Ministry of Justice, "many hundreds of millions [of francs] are at stake." A similarly pertinent complaint from Rolf Frei—a lawyer and director of a major trust corporation (Treuhand AG)—pointed at the bankers' dishonesty. "From my own experience," he wrote, "in many actual cases the banks have sold the assets." The claimants were simply denied their money.

Anticipating an investigation, the insurance companies admitted for the first time that their members had obeyed the Nazi "special law," paying out money to the Nazi government under policies subscribed by Jews. Even surviving Jews, admitted the insurance association, had been deprived of their money. But there was no prospect of an apology or of compensation.

Yet a milestone had been passed. Abandoning sixteen years of claims that the amounts were trivial, the government was finally prepared to acknowledge that the outstanding heirless assets "may still represent a substantial sum"; that, since not all banks were members of the association, there were certainly more unclaimed deposits in numbered and pseudonym accounts and in safe-deposit boxes; and that undoubtedly some money had been stolen. However, in the months before von Moos rose in the parliament on May 4, 1962, to introduce the draft law, Oetterli and the insurance companies had persuaded him to insert loopholes into the law to neutralize its effect.

"To speak of reparations is a diversion," the minister of justice told parliament, specifically denying that the country owed a moral obligation to the Jews. "Switzerland has a duty of reparations neither toward the victims of Nazism nor toward Israel. That must be absolutely clear." To acquit himself of any accusation that he was a puppet of the Jews, Harald Huber agreed with the minister: "Switzerland really does not have to apologize for anything, and we don't owe any country anything." Having cleansed his reputation, he added, "Critics have rightly said that the law does not go far enough. This is the most minimal measure possible." No one disagreed. The flaw was glaring and deliberate.

Under the proposed law, the banks' obligations to maintain secrecy were removed in relation to heirless assets. Banks, insurance companies and lawyers were ordered to compile an inventory of any unclaimed money, valuables and jewelery: "All property in Switzerland whose last owners were foreign nationals or stateless persons, in respect of whom no reliable information has been available since May 9, 1945, and of whom it is known or believed that they were the victims of racial, religious or political persecution, must be registered within six months of the law's coming into force." The maximum penalty for failure to register or for giving false information was SF10,000 or imprisonment.

Ostensibly, the legal obligation was watertight but, succumbing to the demands of the banks and insurance companies, the government had weakened the law. The banks and insurance companies were given discretion to decide whether a client was "known" or "could be assumed" to have been murdered. To avoid the obligation to surrender any money, bankers needed only to say to themselves, "The client may be alive, perhaps in a communist country." To block that obvious loophole, the government was urged to adopt a presumption of death if nothing had been heard from a client since May 8, 1945. Oetterli had successfully resisted that provision.

One hundred and sixty-six members of both houses of parliament voted on December 20, 1962, in favor of the law. None voted against it. Declaring their opposition, the critics understood, was unnecessary. Huber's belief that the new law would "achieve as complete a settlement as possible of the assets in question in Switzerland" depended on the attitude of Hans Weber, the official at the Ministry of Justice appointed to administer the inquiries under the new law. The law's opponents confidently relied on Weber's loyalty.

15

COMPLICATING
THE RIDDLE

Hans Weber, a sullen bureaucrat in the Ministry of Justice, readily agreed to perform his functions in an appropriate manner. As the director of the Office for the Property of Missing Foreigners, Weber was to assist Jews searching for their inheritance; and, under the new law, he and his staff of twelve enjoyed considerable powers to demand information from the financial community, to open bank vaults and safe-deposit boxes, and to order the transfer of any money and valuables.

Help to the Jews, Weber knew, could be offered in two guises. During the eighteen years since the war, the bankers, insurance companies and lawyers had enjoyed ample opportunity to squirrel the heirless assets and other unclaimed deposits into a maze of untraceable accounts. Either he could energetically search for dormant accounts by harassing the banks for information, or he could interpret the law restrictively and rely on the banks' own initiative whether to declare the existence of a dormant account. To the satisfaction of the Bankers Association, Weber chose to be unhelpful. As he explained to colleagues, under the new law he was not "explicitly charged to search for the rightful owners of assets." Within weeks, his prejudices were reinforced.

Dispatches from the Swiss consulates in Tel Aviv and New York described thousands of Jews besieging their buildings, demanding application forms. Newspaper reports around the world publicizing the new law had encouraged Jews to rush to register claims for their lost inheritance. Hans Gasser, the normally sober consul in New York, reported in May that "tens of thousands" of Jews were contacting his office. Weber was horrified. His initial hopes that few would be troubled to apply were dashed. Panicky Jews evoked nightmarish images, but he was convinced that they were unaware of the rigid criteria under the law, which restricted his duty to find any money. After consulting his superiors, Weber decided that his strategy would be to interpret in the narrowest way the restrictions on the numbers who could apply.

Hans Gasser's report in May 1963 from New York had included a request for application forms. Weber procrastinated until March 1964. Then, carefully sealing the envelope, he dispatched just ten forms to New York—by sea mail. To complicate matters further, each application form was printed in German, French and Italian, but not English. Inside the package, now moving at a snail's pace across the Atlantic, was a note from Weber, urging his colleagues in New York, "Do not waste the forms." Impatient Jews had by then invented an alternative. A brisk trade, nurtured by rogue lawyers, was offering claimants improvised forms at $2 each, and the lawyers' services as intermediaries with Weber's office. But the resulting confusion and acrimony did not disturb Weber.

The ten application forms arrived in New York in April 1964. Appalled, Gasser dispatched a telegram asking for another 1,000 forms and stipulating: "Send by airmail." Unwilling to succumb to the pressure, Weber dispatched 200 forms with the message that they should be issued only "with restraint" to people who could first prove the strength of their claim. The explanation of that policy was minuted by Emmanuel Diez, a lawyer in the Political Department supervising Weber. The diplomats in the United States, commented Diez, were starting from "false premises. We don't really want any registration process for those entitled. The opposite problem is much simpler." Facing complainants who could not submit an application at all was easier than laboriously examining each claim.

Consular officials, realizing that their masters in Bern were unaware of the turmoil, offered their advice. The consulate in New York, reported Hans Lacher, had for some years come under "strong pressure" from "hundreds of people" claiming property that had disappeared. "I am afraid that I have been unable to persuade the overwhelming numbers of these people about the Swiss position," he pleaded. Switzerland's image was not improved, he added, by the lack of personnel to cope with the rush, nor by the belated dispatch of just 500 more forms. To emphasize to those isolated in the mountains in Bern the reality of Manhattan, Lacher added that the demands were presented by the Jews in a "tough and aggressive nature" and that "even the slightest appearance of a restrictive attitude must be avoided." His bid to introduce "calm" and reality was ignored by Weber. Clearly the consul had less understanding of the policy than the U.S. State Department, which had been persuaded not to provide any information for applicants.

Weber had adopted the same tactics in Israel. One hundred forms had been sent to Tel Aviv, arousing the ridicule of Israeli newspapers and a campaign against Switzerland. "That's all we need," cried a Bern official. But the Political Department refused all offers of help from other countries. The process, explained officials, was strictly an internal Swiss affair. Their motive was not solely to defend Switzerland's sovereignty. Few claimants, they believed, were genuine. Officials of the same departments who twenty years earlier had encouraged Gestapo and Nazi Party officials to deposit their loot in Switzerland suspected all Jews of being dishonest. The officials believed that if they delayed the process, those dubious Jews would be discouraged from submitting application forms.

Weber's attitude was not properly appreciated by the major banks at the outset. Initially, the senior lawyer of the Swiss Bank Corporation asked for 200 forms and then increased his request to 4,650 forms, explaining that "a very high number of assets have been discovered." The lawyer of the Union Bank of Switzerland, also mentioning the large number of dormant accounts, requested 3,240 forms. In total, Weber's office dispatched 7,112 forms to banks and other financial institutions. But by the end of the year the institutions had understood his policy. Free of any sanctions, the banks began limiting their search to Jewish-sounding surnames, ignoring the use of pseudonyms or special numbered accounts. The results were spectacular. SBC, which had requested 4,650 forms, registered only seventy-seven accounts, while the Union Bank, having requested 3,240 forms, registered 251 accounts. In early 1964, Weber had been notified of just 1,048 dormant accounts belonging to either foreigners or stateless citizens. The total amount was SF9,469,882, or $2.5 million. Considering that the banks in the late 1940s and thereafter had declared that the heirless assets were either "trivial" or worth "at most SF1 million," the new disclosure should have aroused Weber's skepticism. He might also have asked how many of the association's member banks had responded. He would probably have been surprised to discover that of 400 banks, only twenty-six had replied to the questionnaire.

Above all, Weber might have read the very detailed eleven-page protest to the Ministry of Justice from Eric Mehnert-Frey, a retired deputy director of the Compensation Office. After more than twenty years of experience, Mehnert-Frey was familiar with the banks' dishonesty. He had seen how the banks had illegally transferred Jewish deposits to foreign countries or camouflaged them within anonymous corporations that were excluded from Weber's responsibility. Mehnert-Frey had also seen Jewish deposits surreptitiously transferred to Liechtenstein—but that adjunct of Switzerland had been skillfully ignored by the lawmakers. Unless Weber pursued those leads, wrote the expert, the law was pointless. To Mehnert-Frey's disappointment, Weber and government ministers ignored his letter and instead congratulated themselves. Contrary to the allegations by the Jewish organizations that "hundreds of millions" of dollars lay unclaimed in the country, the banks' search had revealed just $2.5 million.

The self-congratulation threw the Jewish organizations into disarray. While Switzerland's Jewish organization believed that all the banks had complied strictly with the law, Jews in New York and Israel doubted that all the trustees and banks had been honest and had obeyed the law.

In the face of that criticism, Weber remained entirely passive. He neither challenged the bank's responses nor sought to investigate whether there were any undeclared deposits. No banks were requested to produce any records, and none was even threatened with prosecution for failing to comply with the law. Despite Weber's inertia, over 7,000 claims had arrived at his office. All were indexed and compared with the banks' disclosures. If the two matched, Weber considered whether under the law he was obliged to inform the claimant. For the official, that task implied seeking an excuse not to reveal the existence of the account. No lists of rightful owners were to be published, and no inquiries were answered beyond acknowledging receipt of the claim. The casualties of Weber's edict were usually powerless.

Mrs. Ortar-Zabludowsky, writing from Jerusalem on April 7, 1964, was one of many applicants who became victims of Weber's ploy of avoiding giving help. Seven months after receiving her letter asking for information about the property of L. Kronstein, a relative, Weber replied that his office was too busy to discover whether the property was registered. In 1966, Weber dispatched a short duplicated letter that no registration had been found. Ortar-Zabludowsky's inquiries were stopped dead.

Anna Hoerhager, living in Vienna, complained that Crédit Suisse had knowingly handed over her mother's account, opened in 1914, to the Gestapo. "It was not a fortune," wrote Hoerhager, "but the bank handed over the money to Nazi Germany without any legal authority . . . and without her signature." Her problem was that pursuing the bank would be too expensive. But her appeal to the government to investigate how a bank could break the law was waved aside. Her only recourse, replied the Political Department, was the Swiss courts. Weber's office offered no help.

The heirs of Friede Lindemann, a German Jew, applied to Weber for her estate in Switzerland, unaware that the Schaffhausen branch of the Union Bank had already identified her account and had disclosed to Weber's office that it contained SF14,000. The death certificate submitted to Weber by the heirs stated that Lindemann had died near Danzig, Germany, in January 1941 from natural causes. Weber denied their right to use his office to seek their inheritance. According to his interpretation, the 1962 law applied only to "victims" of the Nazis who died "violently." In fact the law did not mention "violent death," but Weber refused to take into account the conditions under which Lindemann had lived as a Jew in Nazi Germany or to consider that the cause of death on the certificate might have been false. Weber's readiness to trust the Germans contrasted with his disparagement of those Jews who died in ghettos or from bombing, hunger, sickness or lack of medical attention. Those Jews, he agreed with his fellow officials, were not "victims" because there was no obvious Nazi violence. Lindemann's heirs, according to Weber's edict, and at least 223 other claimants, were precluded from using his office to search for their money. The Union Bank was allowed to keep Lindemann's estate, and the family, kept completely in the dark, were told that Weber could not help; they were then charged for the costs of the investigation.

Weber's treatment of the Israeli heirs of Chaim Dunajewski, a Russian Jew who had lived in Hamburg, was similarly restrictive. During the 1930s, Dunajewski had deposited SF1.2 million in three Swiss banks—the Union Bank, the Swiss Volksbank and the Zurich Kantonal Bank. Knowing that Dunajewski was dead, his relations had sought the money in the 1950s, but in 1955 Markus Feldmann had ordered that the money should remain in the banks' custody and no attempt should be undertaken to trace the heirs. The survivors' claim to Weber revealed that Dunajewski had died in Moscow in 1948. Clearly fearing the Stalinist authorities, the Russian had not dared to contact the banks or his family. Weber's office had received information about Dunajewski's accounts from three Swiss banks and was in no doubt that the Russian was dead and that the heirs were genuine. Yet Weber refused to give the family any information. Under the 1962 law, he recorded, he was empowered only to help the heirs of persecutees whose death was caused by Nazi violence; he could not

help the victims of Soviet persecution or the families of people who
had died from natural causes. Acting on Weber's criteria, the banks
refused to transfer Dunajewski's fortune to his heirs and kept the
money.

Weber's propensity to help the banks and deny the transfer of
any money that could be deemed heirless assets—and should therefore have been transferred to refugee organizations—embraced the
savings of Betha Jacobsohn, a German Jew who had probably been
murdered in a concentration camp. She had no heirs. A bank had
declared the dormant account to Weber's office and, under Swiss
law, Jacobsohn's money should have been returned to the German
state, a solution supported by Stucki. Weber disagreed. Since they
were heirless assets, he decided, he was not competent to determine
the fate of the money. Always inclined to favor the banks, he decided
that the money should remain in the institution.

Weber's cozy alliance with the banks was finally challenged in
late 1964 by Hanusch Weigl, a lawyer in Tel Aviv specializing in
claims. Irritated by Weber's behavior in successive cases, Weigl
appealed to Golda Meir, then the country's foreign minister, for help
in the case of Ernestine Steinhardt, who had, in unknown circumstances, disappeared during the Holocaust.

In the years before the 1962 law, Weigl had written on behalf of
Steinhardt's relatives to all the major Swiss banks, including the Swiss
Bank Corporation seeking information about the existence of an
account. SBC's formal reply gave no hint that the lawyer's request
had been successful. Relying on a client's right to secrecy, the bank
justified its refusal to help by pointing to Weigl's failure to provide
valid documents proving that his clients were entitled to inherit the
deposit. Unaware of the truth, Weigl had in 1963 submitted a routine
application to Weber's office. Weber's reply was unsatisfactory and,
certain that the persistent silence was suspicious, Weigl recruited
Golda Meir to protest and ask the Political Department to intervene.

The government officials soon established the facts and, without
telling Weigl, asked for an explanation. The problem, the bank
replied, was uncomplicated: Steinhardt had an account, but there

were no proven heirs. Weber endorsed the bank's defense. Weigl's clients had not proved that they were genuine heirs. On the other hand, Weigl's application did not fall within the terms of the 1962 law, because the account was no longer dormant. The "activity," explained Weber, consisted of the original letter sent by Weigl before the 1962 Act! Even officials in the Political Department were stunned by that tortured logic. The new law, protested the Political Department, was intended to facilitate applications for these sorts of accounts. But the bankers were adamant. Without proof of Steinhardt's death and proof of the claimants' right to inherit her money, Weigl should not be even told that an account existed. Weber even criticized Weigl's behavior and insisted that "unfounded emotional and self-opinionated arguments; even unobjective and uncalled-for threats by claimants or their legal representatives" would not prevent the Claims Office from faithfully adhering to the law. Despite protests that it was wrong that Weigl should be required to prove the claimants' authenticity to the bank's satisfaction rather than to Weber's, the bankers' position prevailed. The money was not released.

After the first year of Weber's activities, Israeli diplomats had become concerned. Many banks, they told officials in the Political Department, might not have declared dormant accounts. Their fear was dismissed by Edgar Mottier, the director of the Justice Division. "I can't believe that, given the horrors," he replied, "anyone could live with his conscience by not declaring any assets." Mottier's remark reached Weber, who disagreed. Many assets, Weber volunteered, had not been declared, but the blame lay elsewhere: not among the banks but among those "many private and small banks" who had failed to declare any deposited assets or whose declaration was untrue. On the basis of "innumerable letters and conversations," Weber would later tell George Brunschvig, the leader of Switzerland's Jewish community, "it has been established that there are people without conscience, frequently Jews, who withhold property from their coreligionists." Accusing Jews of stealing from Jews was unlikely to endear Weber to those seeking their money or to win the trust of those looking for an unspecified inheritance. But Weber didn't care. He had no intention of substantiating his assertion, least of all by ordering an audit of the banks and the other institutions.

In 1966, three years after the Office opened, 824 unclaimed dormant accounts remained registered in Weber's files. Neither the depositors nor their heirs had been found. Among the new casualties were the German heirless assets valued at SF16.5 million that Stucki had reported eight years earlier. In 1963, Stucki had suggested that those heirless assets should be the subject of the new law. Weber had reacted coolly and begun searching for an excuse to forestall any accusation of misappropriation. His salvation was a small announcement published in 1958 by the Compensation Office in the *Bundesblatt*, the Swiss government's official gazette, listing all previously frozen accounts that could be claimed. Included in that advertisement was the SF16.5 million that, to the banks' satisfaction, had remained unnoticed by everyone. Legally, nothing more was required to find the heirs. The banks rather than the charities would inherit the money. Weber's only remaining chore was to rid himself of the 824 unclaimed accounts. That drudgery he gratefully delegated to Heinz Häberlin, a retired lawyer appointed as a public trustee to search for the inheritors.

Häberlin's task was eased by the unilateral decision taken by Ludwig von Moos, the minister of justice, to abandon any search if the deposit was less than SF500. Four years later, von Moos raised the limit to SF1,000. Those 325 excluded deposits, worth about SF111,000, were to be transferred to a fund labeled "unclaimed assets." The lawyer's task was further eased by Weber's decision to exclude Eastern Europe from his search.

Despite the thawing of the cold war, the risk of endangering Eastern Europeans persuaded Weber and Häberlin to search only for owners and heirs in the West. Proudly, Weber confirmed that he had refused even to send letters to Eastern Europe. At least a hundred application forms asking for information had arrived from Eastern Europe, but Weber kept those requests secret, even from officials in the Political Department. The profits of that self-denial accrued to the banks. Despite that restriction, fifteen account holders, whose money had been written off on the ground that they lived in communist countries, were matched with reported dormant accounts. In Hungary, one family told Häberlin's discreet emissary they preferred their money to remain in the West. Häberlin passed their new addresses to the banks, but the banks, invoking the secrecy laws, resisted contacting the clients and their heirs and used the case to reinforce their contention that the amount of "so-called heirless assets" was much less than alleged.

By 1969, Häberlin had successfully traced 132 heirs (19 percent of the accounts), entitled to SF1.6 million, in the United States and Israel. But SF4.8 million, nearly half the money declared under the 1962 law, identified as "Eastern European" in origin, remained undispersed. Since its owners had not been contacted, and since there was turmoil in the communist countries in the wake of the Soviet invasion of Czechoslovakia in August 1968, Weber wanted the money to be declared heirless and placed in a fund for charities. Without any legal authority, the money would be effectively confiscated. Von Moos was uncomfortable about this and suggested that the money remain with a custodian. Weber became agitated. There would be protests, he warned, from "the bankers in particular." His solution, pursued successfully and with uncharacteristic fervor, was to divert all the money into the "unclaimed fund," avoiding an official declaration that the Jews were missing. Soon after completing that ruse, Weber suddenly—and still inexplicably—died.

Weber's successor, Edgar Mottier, the retired director of the Justice Division, did not approve of Weber's ruse. But in 1972 Kurt Furgler, the newly appointed minister of justice, overruled his officials and his predecessor. Having negotiated a change in implementing the law, he ordered that, without any further checks, all the Eastern European money should be transferred to the "unclaimed fund." That solution was welcomed by Häberlin, the public trustee, who after six years was eager to return to retirement and be rid of the thankless task. The money to be transferred to the "unclaimed fund" involved 200 accounts. One blip threatened Furgler's policy. A trustee company in Basel undertaking similar tracing work for the local canton reported that his officials had discovered the heirs of accounts, previously declared by Häberlin to be untraceable in Eastern Europe, to be living in the West, and had also traced other living heirs in Eastern Europe. Furgler, the minister, was unconcerned. The search, he decided, ignoring the law and the morality of the cause, should be abandoned. The final decision was greeted with "great relief and gratitude" by Häberlin. Wanting to share Häberlin's relief, Furgler ordered his officials to rid him of the problem as fast as possible.

By 1972, the original SF9.4 million declared by banks had increased to SF10.8 million. Exactly half, SF5.4 million, was declared to be "unclaimed" and returned to the banks and other institutions to be kept for their own benefit. The files of those 1,048 accounts opened by Eastern European Jews were neatly stored in the archives. Each file revealed that inadequate research had been undertaken to discover whether the owners or their inheritors were alive and denied future claimants any method to discover the money. Of the remaining half of the money, heirs and claimants received SF1.4 million. The rest of the "unclaimed" money came, after expenses, to SF2.4 million, and was declared to be genuinely heirless and available to charities. In 1946, Stucki had pledged to transfer all the heirless assets to Jewish relief organizations. Twenty years later, the Swiss government intended to renege on that promise and transfer the whole amount to a Swiss charity. After protests, two charities were chosen. One-third was given to a Swiss charity (not the Red Cross, because of its failure to help the Jews), and the remainder, SF1.5 million, to the Swiss Federation of Jewish Communities. All that remained of the declared dormant accounts was SF789,000. That money was subject to special treatment to finalize the secret agreements with Poland and Hungary.

In May 1949, before the Polish agreement was signed, Swiss officials had wanted to use the heirless assets of Polish Jews as compensation for the loss of Swiss property in Poland. One year later, after the international protests and the arguments within Switzerland,

Petitpierre had notionally retreated from that idea, although the principle was unchanged. After a survey, the total of Polish heirless assets was fixed by Switzerland's financial community at SF541,000. Five years later, the banks revised their figure to SF23,300. After another three years, in 1958, the figure had fallen to SF17,550, plus SF849 for insurance policies. By 1963, the strategy behind the original agreement had collapsed. Deliveries of Polish coal were less than anticipated and only half the SF53.5 million compensation to Swiss property owners had been paid. Negotiations resolved the breakdown. Sufficient Polish money was paid into Account N in the National Bank to satisfy all Switzerland's claims. The Poles now demanded that the heirless assets be transferred to the account.

In 1965, Swiss ministers agreed that Polish and Hungarian heirless assets should be kept separate from the "unclaimed fund." Weber's office disregarded that direction by paying all the deposits that were less than SF1,000 into that fund, allowing the banks to retain the money. Ten years passed. Sporadically, the Polish government inquired about the heirless assets and received unrevealing replies. Embarrassed by the agreement, the Swiss, who always preached about their passionate adherence to the law and to legal obligations, had decided unilaterally to reduce sharply the amount to be transferred and also to vary the terms by refusing to name the depositors, to prevent any unpleasant recrimination. The result for the Polish government was disagreeable. Despite the original agreement, it was unable to fulfill its legal obligations to transfer the money to the survivors or their heirs. That consequence was precisely what the Swiss government had intended. On August 6, 1975, SF463,954 was transferred to Account N, the Polish government's account at the National Bank. No explanation was provided for how the banks had arrived at such a precise figure. The Swiss government merely hoped that the subject was closed.

Settling the payment to Hungary under the terms of the agreement on July 19, 1950, was more complicated. Six hundred thousand Hungarians in 1939 had been Jews, and the government in Budapest was now convinced that thousands of rich Jews had deposited hundreds of millions of francs in Switzerland's banks. Under the "confidential" agreement that was successfully kept secret, Switzerland had agreed to help the Hungarian government find the assets of any person named by the Budapest authorities. Shortly after the agreement was signed, the Hungarian government submitted names of those suspected of having accounts who had died without heirs. One name proved to be accurate, but the depositor was actually alive and had settled in the West. Other names and deposit details were also accurate, but the Political Department, acting on the banks' instructions, resisted confirming any information. Weber's own list of thirty Hungarian dormant accounts was not even passed to the Political Department. That money, Weber had decided, should be transferred into the "unclaimed fund," even if the heirs could have been identified. Discussions were abruptly halted soon afterward by the uprising in Hungary in 1956 and political upheaval elsewhere in Europe.

Talks resumed in 1963, as the Hungarians, expecting a windfall, urged the Swiss to hand over the heirless assets to fund Hungary's repayment of its own debts to Switzerland. Simultaneously, the Hungarians also demanded the names of the account holders to allow them to trace the heirs. That request sparked a row among the competing Trade, Political, and Justice Departments in Switzerland. The resolution favored the banks. No names would be provided to the Hungarian government.

The Hungarian negotiators were baffled. Not only was Switzerland refusing to trace the rightful owners of the money, but it was also protecting those Nazis and their collaborators who might have transferred to Switzerland money that was stolen or extracted through blackmail from Hungarians. Altogether, Swiss policy was a deliberate injustice that would enrich the wrong people. Unfazed by that possibility, Diez, the lawyer in the Political Department, replied that Switzerland's policy would not be dictated by Hungary. "We have already defended ourselves against more powerful opponents," the lawyer told the Hungarian ambassador. "The claims and demands you insist on are so exaggerated and wide ranging that it's not even worth discussing them."

Ignoring the Hungarians was nevertheless impossible. Under the pressure of Swiss exporters, the government needed to satisfy the Hungarians, who could threaten to make compensation for Swiss property owners dependent on the transfer of the heirless assets. The solution, proposed the Political Department, was to offer Hungary a lump sum without admitting any obligations or identifying the owners of the accounts. The object, explained Diez, was to avoid setting a precedent that would allow Israel to establish its own claims. To obviate legal complications in Switzerland, Diez declared that the unclaimed Hungarian assets would be "confiscated" from the banks. That, decided the official, was a legally acceptable way to avoid telling parliament about the deal and would deflect the Hungarians' demand for the names of the original depositors.

The Hungarians were no longer just baffled but angered. Switzerland's solution, said their negotiators, was "painful" and "completely negative." The proposal tilted the settlement in Switzerland's favor, awarding it "unjustified enrichment."

The Claims Office in 1964 had calculated how much of the heirless assets belonged to Hungarians. Its first report on December 7 stated that fifty-three depositors had owned SF460,500 and there were nine unopened safe-deposit boxes. One year later, the sum registered had not altered but the safe-deposit boxes were no longer mentioned. By 1971, the office reported that the amount of Hungarian heirless assets had fallen to "half the amount"—SF217,000—because the heirs had been traced. That might have been true, but more likely the office had allowed the banks to retain the money, which had been the fate of all but two of the cases presented by the Hungarian government. "This is a thin result," Diez conceded after refraining from giving the Hungarians any information beyond those two cases. "There are limits to everything."

In Hungary, there were no illusions about the behavior of the Swiss. While Switzerland still bemoaned its failure to resist U.S. pressure in Washington in 1946, the legitimate demands of the Eastern European countries were, according to cynics in Budapest, being "heroically resisted" by Bern to allow self-enrichment with the unclaimed assets.

That criticism suited Switzerland. Faced with similar demands for heirless assets from other Eastern European countries and Israel, Swiss politicians and bankers were anxious to appear unyielding. Any settlement with Hungary that transferred heirless assets threatened that image. Diez proposed outright deceit. Having agreed that Hungary should be given without explanation SF325,000 withdrawn from the "unclaimed fund," Diez proposed to conceal the payment. It would simply be subtracted from the compensation paid by Hungary to Switzerland for the confiscated property. Nothing in the published documents would reveal that Hungary had received any heirless assets. No announcement would be made to the Swiss parliament, nor would the necessary parliamentary approval be sought to withdraw the compensation from the fund. To sugar the pill, SF400,000 was deducted from Hungary's debts in 1973, and nothing more was said. The Swiss government had used the Jewish heirless assets for its own purposes, and for the next twenty-three years, as the conspirators died one by one, it seemed that the nation could draw a final veil over its collaboration and deception.

16

THE DEAL

Edgar Bronfman does not appreciate infidelity. Blessed with a billion-dollar fortune, the stylish heir to the Canadian Seagram distillery empire is accustomed to compliance and obedience from others. But as a businessman Bronfman likes and is accustomed to making deals. Unfortunately for Switzerland, when George Krayer, the chairman of the Swiss Bankers Association, met the president of the World Jewish Congress in September 1995, he misjudged the new crusader. Krayer believed that Bronfman, as a professional dealmaker, would regard his offer to pay a lump sum in final settlement of Jewish grievances as an attractive deal. The banker did not contemplate that a businessman might be troubled by questions of morality.

Ever since his election as president in 1981, Edgar Bronfman, sixty-eight, had gradually jettisoned his playboy lifestyle. Besides managing the world's biggest liquor manufacturer, he had transformed himself into a notable personality among world Jewry. From his unique office in the Seagram Building in central Manhattan, surrounded by Rodin sculptures, a Miró tapestry, and other master-pieces, he had saved the moribund World Jewish Congress—cofounded in 1936 by Nahum Goldmann to crusade against Nazism—from bankruptcy and in 1991 had tasted the success of his first crusade. With energy, gusto and skill, the three senior executives employed by the World Jewish Congress in New York had captured universal attention by establishing that Kurt Waldheim, the president of Austria and the respected former secretary general of the

United Nations, was a liar and had been associated with Nazi war crimes. Singlehandedly, the WJC had destroyed the politician's reputation and had tarnished Austria forever. Four years later, Bronfman arrived on his private jet in Bern with two members of the Waldheim team to reactivate the cause of the heirless assets and dormant accounts.

Israel Singer, the WJC's general secretary, an orthodox Jew and graduate of a rabbinical seminary, was an experienced strategist with a good understanding of history and twenty years of experience in negotiating on behalf of the Jews with foreign governments. Renowned for his volatile temperament, Singer was the logistician on whom Bronfman relied. The mouthpiece was Elan Steinberg, the executive director, who shared Singer's aggressive energy and his courage to shout when others might shy away out of embarrassment; he would prove to be a shrewd propagandist. The level of noise generated by these two men suggested an enormous organization, but in reality the two were the complete executive staff of the World Jewish Congress. That truth was understood by the Swiss bankers.

Bronfman had flown to Bern at the suggestion of Rolf Bloch, the president of the Swiss Federation of Jewish Communities. Over the previous four months, Bloch had noticed a significant change of mood in Switzerland. The collapse of communism and the restitution of confiscated property to Jews in the former East Germany had encouraged Kaspar Villiger, the Swiss president, to choose the fiftieth anniversary of the end of World War II as the occasion for an emotional appeal. A new study of Switzerland's wartime treatment of the Jews by Jacques Picard, a Swiss historian, based on newly released archives had recently exposed the wartime government's anti-Semitism as much worse than previously thought. Speaking in parliament, Villiger had told his countrymen that Switzerland must apologize to the Jewish community for its behavior toward the refugees during the war. "We can only bow our heads in silence before those whom we led into suffering and captivity, even death," he had intoned. "We can only bow our heads before the family members and descendants."

Bloch reported to Bronfman that the discussions he had started with the Bankers Association in March had progressed substantially. "The bankers are showing a new sensitivity," said the representative of Switzerland's small Jewish community. "They are aware of the new attitude in Switzerland. There's anger that Switzerland deceived foreign governments about its relations with the Nazis and that the Swiss lied about their handling of the property of the Jews." The Bankers Association had agreed with Bloch that their members should be asked to produce a final account on the heirless assets and unclaimed accounts. After six months of preparatory discussions, Bloch had arranged a meeting with Bronfman that, everyone agreed, would remain strictly private.

George Krayer, the chairman of the Bankers Association, was waiting for the three Americans on September 12 in a private room at La Grande Société, a club near the parliament building. Standing with the chairman were Hans Baer, an affable Jewish banker who had spent his childhood during the war in the United States; and two association officials: Jean-Paul Chapuis, the secretary general, and Heinrich Schneider, his deputy responsible for internal matters. Standing in the background were several lawyers and Hanspeter Häni, recently appointed as the Bankers Association's ombudsman to help Jews find dormant accounts in Swiss banks. Since Häni was overtly pessimistic about finding "much for the heirs of the Holocaust," his presence was a warning that the association could not be trusted.

None failed to be impressed as Bronfman, a tall, imposing figure, entered the room. As president of both the WJC and the World Jewish Restitution Organization, Bronfman had received the endorsement of Yitzhak Rabin, the prime minister of Israel, as the representative of world Jewry in Switzerland. On the other hand, the two swarthy men peering through thick glasses who accompanied the tycoon struck the waiting bankers as men who, like their predecessors over the previous fifty years, required reluctant toleration but could eventually be ignored.

After shaking hands, Bronfman rapidly became irritated. They were standing in a small room without tables or chairs, and the mood was frosty, in marked contrast to the warmth they had encountered in meetings earlier that day with the Swiss president and the chairman of the Swiss Bankers Commission. "They are pledged to negotiate in good faith and in secrecy," Kaspar Villiger had told Bronfman, "until you reach a just solution." Yet the bankers were exuding unfriendliness. Pompously, Krayer announced to Bronfman that a survey conducted by the Bankers Association had found dormant accounts with a total value of SF38 million ($32 million). Although not all the SF38 million was identified as originally deposited by Jews, the sharp increase from SF9.4 million disclosed after the 1962 law should have alerted the association that suspicions would be aroused. Instead, the Swiss bankers believed the contrary: that the Jews would be satisfied and grateful that more money had been discovered. For Krayer and the Bankers Association, that money was the solution to the historical problem. Bronfman, they judged, would shake on the deal, eat the lunch offered and depart forever.

"Will you take this as a final settlement?" asked Krayer.

Bronfman and Singer were shocked. "I don't like the 'take it or leave it' attitude," replied Bronfman. "I haven't come here to discuss money. I'm here to discuss a process." Krayer retreated. The tension lifted.

As the party sat down for lunch, the Jews' optimism returned. Two historic obstacles had been removed. Recently, under pressure from Washington, Switzerland's banking secrecy laws had been weakened to prevent deposits of drug money and, while Krayer had said in the past that he had "no knowledge" of dormant accounts, he was now volunteering to the visitors that "the banks had not behaved well." Since the survey among the association's 440 members had revealed the existence of dormant accounts, the banker remedied the introductory insult by promising, "We will certainly return the money, every penny, which belongs to the Jews."

Bronfman had no reason to disbelieve the banker. "We're not here to talk about the amounts of money," repeated Bronfman, "just about the procedure." Krayer nodded. By the end of the meal, an agreement had been reached. The association would conduct another comprehensive survey among its members for all dormant accounts and—Bronfman emphasized that "this is most impor- tant"—there would in the meantime be absolute secrecy. Publicity, it was agreed, would suggest that a final sum had been discovered, and that would provoke controversy and demands for payment. To smooth the presentation, the two sides agreed that their best course was to aim for unanimity before any announcement was made. Until an agreement on the final sum had been reached, they decided, their discussions should remain secret. It'll be a rare occasion that we stick to a pact of silence, thought Steinberg as they drove to the hotel. Pleased with the meeting, Bronfman and the two executives flew to Belgium to attend another meeting at the European parliament about restitution. The secrets of the Swiss banks, it appeared, would be finally revealed.

Over the next ten weeks, Israel Singer returned three times to Bern to meet Krayer and discuss progress. As Singer sat in a suite at the Schweizerhof Hotel, his mood varied. The bankers, he said, tele- phoning Bronfman, were suspiciously slow. In particular, Heinrich Schneider, the Bankers Association's secretary responsible for inte- rior affairs, was hostile. Parochial and antiforeigner, Schneider was also hampered by his intellect. Like Max Oetterli, his understanding was limited to Swiss politics and prejudices. Singer believed the deci- sion to meet in Bern rather than in the association's own buildings in Basel reflected a distaste for allowing Jews into the association's head- quarters. Although Singer had become immune to slights, by the time of his return to New York in December he suspected that the Swiss bankers were intent on breaking their undertaking. A threshold had been passed. A telephone call sealed the fate of Krayer's strategy. Bronfman struck out for an alliance with an unlikely partner— Senator Alfonse D'Amato.

Ever since D'Amato's election to the Senate in 1980, Bronfman had had no reason to meet "Senator Pothole." Not only was Bronfman a lifelong contributor to the Democrats, but he had little personal affection for the fifty-nine-year-old Republican, who had recently held hearings in the Senate to embarrass President Clinton over his association with the illegal finances of the Whitewater development in Arkansas. But, to his credit, D'Amato was a self-made, independent man with a feisty record of public campaigning for the underdog. As a street fighter with a rottweiler's compassion for his target's sensitivities, he was the ideal politician to challenge the Swiss banks, particularly as he was the chairman of the Senate Banking Committee. Past disagreements were ignored by the two rugged personalities as, over lunch in the Senate dining room on December 7, 1995, Bronfman outlined, with Singer by his side, his unease about the bankers and his grief for the handful of surviving Jewish victims. "We want you to know what's happening," said Bronfman. "This is an information trip." Revenge would be uppermost in his mind if he was betrayed by the same breed who had outwitted the disarmed Sam Klaus and Sy Rubin.

"They're taking you for a ride," said D'Amato. Bronfman was still unsure.

D'Amato was not blind to the political advantage of supporting Bronfman, the representative of the largest Jewish population in the world, but he was genuinely outraged by the compounded dishonesty. "We'll hold hearings," he told Bronfman, sealing a pact whose consequences George Krayer could never have imagined. As he walked from the dining room, D'Amato said to Gregg Rickman, his diligent thirty-three-year-old legislative director, "This sounds great. Let's do it."

Compared with other politicians, the one hundred United States senators enjoy extraordinary power, veneration and resources, and over the years their targets have suffered mixed fortunes depending on their vulnerability. Switzerland's bankers, D'Amato and Bronfman agreed, were particularly unprotected. Judged against U.S. banks, Switzerland's financial institutions were puny and their fortunes depended upon their business activities in the United States. Withdrawing their licenses to trade in the United States would destroy their prospects. Beginning the lengthy process to deprive them of those licenses rested with D'Amato's Banking Committee;

and his announcement of "hearings," a euphemism for a public trial or a kangaroo court, would undoubtedly terrify the Swiss banks. To prepare those hearings, D'Amato needed evidence and witnesses to prove to the public the validity of Bronfman's complaint. But for the moment he was cautioned to remain silent until Bronfman's suspicions had been confirmed. On no account, Bronfman repeated, would the WJC break the Bern agreement.

In January 1996, the WJC held its annual conference in Jerusalem. Carefully Bronfman avoided questions about the heirless assets. "We have met the Swiss bankers," he told inquirers, "but I don't want to make any further comment." As he deflected the questions, the Bankers Association, in Basel, was veering toward a different policy. Krayer, with the encouragement of Heinrich Schneider, had become convinced that, to satisfy Swiss opinion and the increasing interest of parliamentarians, it would be politic to announce the results of the association's 1996 survey at the regular half-yearly press conference to be held on February 7. News of that decision, picked up by local journalists, reached Singer in New York the day before.

Excitedly, Singer telephoned Schneider. "What's going on?" he yelled. "If you break the agreement to keep the negotiations silent, we'll confront you. In no uncertain terms." By nightfall in Europe, no association official had bothered to reassure Singer. The Jews, thought Schneider, were powerless. Their threats were empty. Even if Bronfman was rich, he was no different from thousands of other rich men who regularly passed through Switzerland's banks. The Jews were as irrelevant as they had been fifty years earlier. The following morning, Krayer formally announced the association's survey: 775 accounts had been discovered that had been dormant since 1945. Their total value was SF38 million ($32 million), and not all had been deposited by Jews. The impression Krayer left among his audience was precisely that which Bronfman and Singer had feared. Beyond that amount, the association had declared, there was no more money owing to the Jews in the Swiss banks.

Bronfman, Singer and Steinberg were fuming. Fifty years after Klaus and Rubin had complained about Swiss dishonesty, the pattern had not changed. Nor had the association's self-delusion about the Jews. The following morning, February 8, Singer flew down to Washington to brief Gregg Rickman.

Tucked away in the corner of D'Amato's suite of Senate offices, surrounded by files, Rickman, a specialist in Middle East and Jewish affairs, was naturally as aware as most Jews about the generalities of the Holocaust, but he knew nothing about Switzerland, Safehaven, and the heirless assets. Since the lunch with Bronfman two months earlier, he had waited for an explanation to a problem that no one else in Washington understood. At the end of Singer's briefing, the two agreed, "There might be some evidence in the archives."

Among the advantages of recruiting D'Amato to the cause was the alacrity of government departments' responses to a senator's requests. The National Archives, which stored the records of all government departments and agencies, were eager to help the politician, although he was required to supply the researchers. The WJC provided Rickman with Willi Korte and Miriam Kleiman. "It'll only take a couple of days," the two researchers were assured.

Eleven government departments and agencies had been involved in the saga since 1944. Not only the Departments of State, Treasury, Justice and Army had touched Switzerland's activities, but also intelligence agencies and humanitarian groups. Their accumulated records between 1940 and 1962, scattered across the capital, amounted to incalculable millions of sheets of paper. Only a few of the government documents were properly indexed, and although some had been available since 1972 many remained classified. Even twenty well-briefed researchers would need at least one year to compose the history of an issue that was hardly mentioned in textbooks and had been practically forgotten even before the death of most of the participants. Yet, within the first weeks, luck and diligence provided a nugget that confirmed the validity of Bronfman's complaint.

An intelligence report from Switzerland in July 1945 stated that Jacques Salmonovitz, the owner of the Société Générale de Surveillance, a notary and trust company in Geneva with links to the Balkan countries, possessed a list of 182 Jewish clients who had entrusted SF8.4 million and about $90,000 to the notary pending their arrival from the Balkans. The report added that the Jews had still not claimed their possessions. Rickman and D'Amato were ecstatic. Here was historical proof that unclaimed heirless assets were retained by Swiss financial institutions. Still unaware of the background, complexity and dimension of the question, D'Amato submitted the report for publication in the *Congressional Record* on March 27. Dramatically, he accused the Bankers Association of a cover-up, and asked it to explain the failure of its recent survey to account for that SF8.4 million worth $20 million in 1996 values.

George Krayer was worried. The association was unaware of the Salmonovitz account—because the SGS was not a bank—but the existence of such confidential information in the U.S. archives promised a succession of horribly embarrassing revelations. More sensational reports from New York and Washington about public accusations by D'Amato and Steinberg against the Swiss bankers added to Krayer's concern; they were followed by notice of the first hearing to be held in the Senate on April 23.

In organizing the hearing, Rickman had written to Mark Cohen, a lawyer at Wilmer, Cutler, Pickering representing the Bankers Association, asking whether the Swiss bankers would provide a witness. The association's retention of the firm in 1994 had followed the dismissal of its previous lobbyist, Bob Royer, the casualty of an internal dispute. That decision, in retrospect, was not astute. While Royer enjoyed especially close relations with D'Amato and his staff, Cohen and his superior Roger Whitten were outsiders without any contacts in D'Amato's office and ignorant of the sentiments and strategy driving the new crusade. Unquestioning, and unversed in the politics and the history, they accepted their client's professions of innocence and thus misjudged the threat presented by D'Amato. One immediate misguided decision was to allow Hans Baer, the Jewish banker involved in the Bern meeting in 1995, to represent the association at D'Amato's hearings.

In preparing for the hearing, D'Amato and Bronfman agreed on one fundamental principle. Since most of the beneficiaries were dead,

they were anxious not to appear to be mercenary. Bronfman's carefully considered public approach would be to insist that his cause was
moral, not financial. Taking the same ground, D'Amato spoke about
an "accounting." Elan Steinberg referred to the "last chapter of the
Holocaust." Emotions rose. Overnight, the irrepressible mystery of
the swastika, with its drumbeat overtones of brutality, war and genocide, attracted every newspaper to an untold story of hidden fortunes
and greedy, criminal bankers. There was even a living victim.

Greta Beer, an attractive seventy-five-year-old former
Romanian who had settled in Queens, New York, to become a tour
guide, was introduced to the packed committee room near the
Capitol by D'Amato just after 10:05 on April 23. The senator's
opening words were a declaration of war against the Swiss banks.
Greta Beer, proclaimed D'Amato, was a casualty of "the systematic
victimization of people . . . started by the oppression of the Nazis"
and then by the Swiss banks. The "broken trust" perpetuated by the
Swiss banks, he continued, "with the evasions and excuses for over
fifty years," meant that "the Greta Beers have been denied justice."
Emotive references to "deliberate cover-up" and "callousness"
established the accusation. Fifty-one years after Sam Klaus had
drafted the Safehaven proposal one mile from the Capitol, the trial
of Switzerland was under way.

Greta Beer's story was heartrending. Shortly before his death in
1940, her father Siegfried Deligdisch, a Romanian textile manufacturer employing over 1,000 people, revealed that there was a Swiss
bank account for his wife and two children, but he did not disclose
either the identity of the bank or the account number. After surviving
the war, Beer emigrated to the United States and, after the enactment
of the 1962 law, traveled with her mother to Switzerland to seek
information from banks in Bern, Zurich and Lausanne. All denied
any knowledge of an account. "My mother did not have an easy life,"
said Beer, her voice breaking, "and my own life would have been
totally different if we had access to that money. I am bitter about
being deprived." The committee room was silent as the old woman
recounted the last words that she, as a young girl had heard from her

father: "Don't worry. You will be provided for. The money is safely deposited in Switzerland."

The story was a damning one, and Edgar Bronfman's testimony, delivered soon after, encapsulated the moral assault: "Our collective mission here is nothing short of bringing about justice. We are here to help write the last chapter of the bitter legacy of the Second World War and the Holocaust." Condemning Switzerland's banks for "their repeated failure of integrity," for earning a "profit from the ashes of man's greatest inhumanity to man," and accusing Switzerland of breaching its neutral status during the Nazi era in ways that cost a "staggering [number] of American lives," Bronfman demanded "a proper accounting."

For years, the Swiss had enjoyed a cozy niche in the world's consciousness as a tiny, decent, wealthy community associated with Toblerone chocolate, Swatch watches, Alpine ski resorts and at worst boredom. Suddenly cast into the spotlight by D'Amato and Bronfman, the Swiss were no longer just a peculiarly charmless people who had produced no artists, no heroes since William Tell and no statesman, but were dishonest Nazi collaborators who had profited from genocide. "We cannot rest," agreed D'Amato after accepting Bronfman's praise for holding the hearings, "while unnamed individuals profit from the deaths of the six million."

Selecting Hans Baer, a decent, upright man—the chairman of a private bank and a member of the Bankers Association's executive board—as spokesman had seemed a sensible move. His carefully drafted statement to the committee sounded ingenuous. "The SBA," he explained, "has been pained by the accusations that have appeared recently in the press that the SBA is not sensitive to the interests of the Holocaust victims." Old history had recorded that defense but, as Baer knew, history was being rewritten. Anticipating the antagonism, he had arrived with a gesture and a solution. His gesture was an offer to pay for Greta Beer to visit Switzerland to find her missing account. His solution was to establish an independent audit commission with members nominated by the Bankers Association and the WJC who would, under an agreed-on chairman, retain auditors to comb through the banks' records and find any remaining dormant accounts.

Over the previous weeks, Baer and Singer and others had been discreetly "unscrambling the egg and returning the parts into a complete shell." Reminding the Swiss bankers of the Waldheim precedent, Baer had proposed a six-man international committee of eminent persons—three Jews and three Swiss—to supervise an audit and defuse the crisis. Switzerland's banks would assure the auditors, agreed Krayer, "unfettered access to all the relevant files in banking institutions regarding dormant accounts and other assets and financial instruments deposited before, during and after the war." President Kaspar Villiger had agreed to introduce legislation to amend the banking secrecy laws to allow the investigation. The final requirement was an impeccable chairman. The committee, Baer believed, could defuse the tension, but he rightly feared D'Amato's skepticism about the solution. "I'm suggesting that it is a problem," the senator told the banker, suspicious of any committee, especially one funded by Swiss bankers. Nevertheless, by the end of the hearing Baer felt relieved. With goodwill, he was convinced, Bronfman's demand for a full accounting would be satisfied.

The banker was deluding himself. His appearance, despite his sincerity, had made a poor impression and, before he had even walked outside into the lunchtime sun, Bronfman's limousine had swept down Pennsylvania Avenue toward the White House. Distrustful of any Swiss banker, Bronfman was seeking allies, and the most important was the president of the United States. The previous day, at a lunch he hosted in New York, Bronfman had persuaded Hillary Rodham Clinton of the importance of the issue. Thanks to her intervention, he was now seated with Clinton for thirty minutes. Bronfman sought endorsement for his campaign against Switzerland and the president's assurance that Alfonse D'Amato's involvement would not be an obstacle. "I'll work with D'Amato," promised the president and, to prove his commitment, he appointed Stuart Eizenstadt, the government's special envoy for property restitution in Central and Eastern Europe, to conduct an interagency investigation to discover the archival evidence against Switzerland.

In Bern, Basel and Zurich, politicians and bankers were at once bewildered and indignant as they read the reports from Washington. Switzerland, it seemed, had been targeted at the behest of the Jews. The old conspiracy had been resurrected and was proved by the appointment of Madeleine Kunin, a Jewish Democrat, as the new U.S. ambassador to Switzerland. The country, already mortified by recession and unemployment, was under siege by Americans plotting to undermine Switzerland as a financial center. No doubt that was the ultimate sanction available to D'Amato and Bronfman, and the older Swiss knew there was good reason to fear those two men. There was so much history to expose, and the politician and the tycoon were too independent and too powerful to be bothered with Swiss excuses.

Speaking to each other regularly, Bronfman's and D'Amato's staffs agreed that relentless pressure and a diet of embarrassments would eventually defeat their foe. In D'Amato's office, Gregg Rickman was urging the two researchers at the National Archives to "find more stuff that we can hit 'em with." Cleared to read classified material, Rickman disappeared into the sealed rooms, searching in the United States' "secret" archives for more incriminating material. To his chagrin, nothing remotely similar to the Salmonovitz report emerged. But there was compensation. The researchers were photo-copying intelligence, Safehaven, and diplomatic reports about Switzerland—many declassified fifteen years earlier and already read by historians, but all resoundingly accusing Switzerland of perfidy.

Elan Steinberg was not bothered by this flood of detail. The Washington hearings had stirred journalists' appetites for information about Switzerland's crimes. Telephone callers to the WJC demanded more information. Steinberg was happy to oblige. Creating a potent image of an army of researchers in Washington digging up untold secrets of Switzerland's collaboration with the Third Reich, the executive director invited callers to enter his office and catch a glimpse of documents marked "secret" and reeking of authenticity.

Patently ignorant about the history but eager to accept that any facts unearthed in the archives were new and true, European newspapers during May and June 1996 published a series of increasingly prominent "bombshells" about Switzerland's connections to "Odessa documents," the "secrets of Safehaven," Adolf Hitler's "secret Swiss bank account," and Göring's looted art, and about Switzerland's betrayal of the Jews. Terror by embarrassment was Steinberg's weapon, as he uttered a string of accusations designed to cause discomfort and shock. OSS reports, often based on rumor and uncorroborated sources and disregarded for years by historians as hearsay, suddenly assumed uncritical credibility and widespread publicity. European readers enjoyed Switzerland's embarrassment, yet frustratingly for the WJC and Rickman, that interest was not mirrored in the United States.

The WJC needed an emotive issue to link the Holocaust and Switzerland. Documents arriving from Washington mentioned the looted gold and the Washington Accord, about which Singer and Steinberg had known nothing. But they did know that, among the catalog of horrors, few images were more searing than the methodical extraction in the extermination camps of gold dental fillings from the mouths of Jewish corpses dragged from the gas chambers. Bags of gold fillings, it had been established at the Nuremberg trials, had been delivered by the SS to the Reichsbank in Berlin. Under Emil Puhl's supervision, the fillings had been smelted and had reappeared as anonymous gold ingots. There was every reason to believe that those ingots, and others manufactured from wedding rings wrenched from the fingers of corpses, had been delivered to the National Bank in Bern.

Neither Steinberg nor Singer understood the complexities of the negotiations in 1946 in Washington, but both grasped the American negotiators' complaint about British betrayal. Since the Europeans were showing more interest in the story than U.S. newspapers, they judged that the waves caused by accusations leveled in London might rebound across the Atlantic.

The maneuver was delegated to Greville Janner, a vice president of the WJC and, most important, a Labor member of parliament with a guaranteed platform for winning international publicity. At the end of a dedicated political career, Janner was credited, as a moderate spokesman for Jewish causes, for his active sponsorship of the bitterly contested War Crimes Act, which had finally, in 1991, allowed the prosecution of alleged Nazi war criminals living in Britain. Janner's lack of knowledge about the Washington Accord did not hinder his widely published and broadcast allegations in July 1996.

Janner claimed that government documents, recently declassified in Washington, proved that a secret deal had been hatched in 1946 between the Allies and Switzerland allowing the Swiss to return only a fraction of the looted gold. In particular, Janner accused the British government and MI6, the foreign intelligence service, of conspiring to deprive the survivors of uncalculated millions of pounds owed from the gold stolen from victims of the Holocaust.

Malcolm Rifkind, the British Foreign Secretary, who was Jewish, was understandably baffled and turned to his officials for advice. The politician was let down by the low caliber of those employed by the British government. Instead of looking in the government's own volumes of published agreements or referring to published textbooks, Rifkind rapidly uttered a public denial that the government possessed any information whatsoever—an odd statement, considering that the text of the Washington Accord had been published as a government document in 1946. "We have not heard of the allegations that British intelligence knew of the documents concerning holdings by Swiss banks of seized funds," he said. "None of the intelligence agencies is aware of having such information." Rifkind's promise to launch a serious investigation gave unconditional credibility to Janner's allegations. The hare, to the glee of the World Jewish Congress, was running.

Thanks to researchers in Washington, Janner was provided with another tasty accusation. A 1945 report from Lisbon suggested that the painting *Salome* by Titian, stolen from a Jew, had been smuggled into Britain and deposited in the vault of the National Westminster Bank. In broadcasts across Britain and other countries, the Labor politician demanded an immediate search and the painting's surrender. Overnight, the World Jewish Congress was rewarded with massive publicity. Headlines reporting that Switzerland faced a "£15 billion Nazi art scandal" and sensational accounts of German deposits of looted Jewish property in Switzerland worth between $22.3 billion and $106.4 billion filled London's most respected newspapers. Janner spoke eloquently of Switzerland as an "Aladdin's cave of art stolen by the Nazis" and encouraged reports about Switzerland's criminal pact with Hitler. Steinberg was thrilled; the dam was weakening. One more push and the American media might embrace the campaign. No one imagined that a sloppy Foreign Office historian would provide the "eye-catching figure" to rouse *Newsweek* and *Time* and rattle the Swiss.

After proper reflection, Foreign Office officials had realized that Janner's allegations about secrecy were incorrect. Ninety-one government files, all declassified more than twenty years earlier and available to the public in the British archives, told the true story. With unusual speed, the Foreign Office, anxious to create an image of openness, intended to publish a report absolving the British of any role in the nonexistent conspiracy. After rapid research in the archives, the Foreign Office's historian, absorbing the current hostility toward Switzerland, sought to explain and justify the Allies' frustrations in 1946. Fortunately for the new crusaders in the United States, the historian misunderstood the Washington discussions about gold, particularly Alfred Hirs's quip that the Allies would ruin his bank if they demanded SF500 million.

Entitled "Nazi Gold: Information from the British Archives" the twenty-three-page report, published on September 10 and praised by *The Times* as "a crisp and well-compiled historical survey," was an innocuous publication with one "bombshell." After correctly stating that the Allies "had no clear idea" of the exact amount of looted gold "held in Swiss banks," the historian stated that the Americans estimated the amount to be $200 million. He then added, "M. Hirs let slip during a meeting of the gold committee the figure of $500 million." In simple terms, dollars had erroneously replaced Swiss francs, quadrupling Hirs's alleged estimate of the looted gold. In fact, even perfunctory reading of the American transcript showed that Hirs had denied that any looted gold was stored in the Bern bank. He was referring only to the enormousness of the Allies' demand.

Understandably, the media relied on the Foreign Office's own calculations. If $500 million of Nazi gold was stored in Switzerland in 1946 and only $58 million had been repaid under the Washington Accord, then, it was reasoned, Switzerland had profited by $450 million. With inflation, the horde was worth $4 billion and, according to the *Financial Times*, "could still be in the Swiss banks." After the story had crossed the Atlantic, the front page of the *Washington Post* reported that Switzerland "still holds 90%" of the gold—worth "$6 billion"—"right down to the gold fillings of Holocaust victims that were melted down into bullion." The British government, claimed the *Post*, "has accused the Swiss of refusing to relinquish a cache of billions of dollars of looted gold." With a twist, the British and Americans were also guilty. Five tons of "Nazi gold" were still stored in the vaults of the Bank of England and two tons in the U.S. Federal Reserve, possibly also manufactured from dental fillings.

The interpretation was neat and sensational—but it was totally untrue. Nevertheless, the World Jewish Congress had finally succeeded in winning attention from the mass media. "This is the greatest robbery in the history of mankind," said Steinberg, as Rifkind acknowledged the possibility that the gold in the British vaults should, as Janner demanded, be redistributed to families of Holocaust victims.

Switzerland's reputation was plummeting. Unaccustomed to making fast decisions, Flavio Cotti, the foreign minister, admitted that the issue was causing "serious harm to Switzerland's image," and even conceded that the accord could be renegotiated if "new facts arise." Struggling to limit the damage, he told a crowded press conference on September 16, 1996, "Switzerland never intended taking gold from the Nazis and keeping it for itself." Switzerland's total earnings from the gold trade, the National Bank announced, was a mere SF20 million. The only event that day that stilled the rising furor was the Swiss parliament's debate about amending the banking secrecy laws.

George Krayer and the other members of the Bankers Association were appalled. Rather than controlling events, the government was reeling. "This matter," the association wrote to the government, "should not be constantly thrown into the political arena on the basis of tragic cases, suppositions and documents which in some cases are highly suspect." The bankers asked for "more time to clarify what actually needs to be investigated." One statistic was tormenting the association. While its survey published in February 1996 had reported that SF38 million ($32 million) had been found in the dormant accounts, not all belonging to Holocaust victims, Steinberg was reported to be telling journalists that the Swiss were concealing between $7 billion and $20 billion of property belonging to the Jews. Misreading the situation, Robert Stuber, the chairman of the Union Bank, caustically dismissed those claims. "The amounts we're really talking about are peanuts," he scoffed tactlessly, walking straight into D'Amato's trap.

"Switzerland is blatantly profiting from the Holocaust," D'Amato offered as a succinct soundbite. "How can one have confidence in the Swiss authorities when they have only taken action under pressure from public opinion?" Tirelessly driving his staff to hunt for new angles to cultivate the right publicity, he relished the fight against an unequal opponent whose spokesman could only bleat that the senator was exploiting Switzerland's discomfort to win votes. American-style democracy was alien to the Swiss, and the experience was becoming more unpleasant. By early October, Gregg Rickman had found six new victims and a new grievance to spur on the senator's campaign.

Slipping into the crowded conference room in the New York federal court building on October 16 for the second round of hearings, D'Amato was beaming. Six witnesses, all victims of the Holocaust and Swiss banks, were waiting to tell the world of the misery and humiliation they had suffered. D'Amato was also carrying, tucked inside his folder, the sheet of paper prepared by Rickman as the surprise revelation.

The senator's introductory remarks set the agenda: "We're very concerned that Swiss citizens and corporations blatantly benefited from the Holocaust while the interests of the survivors were totally ignored. . . . We want to know where all the hundreds of millions of dollars of assets that the Nazis deposited in Swiss banks went. . . . It's time for justice. Time to get the truth." In the background, Roger Whitten and Mark Cohen, the Bankers Association lobbyists, squirmed. The Swiss journalists scribbled furiously, accurately guessing their readers' reaction. The witnesses nodded. The senator was speaking their thoughts.

In broken English, her voice choking, Estelle Sapir, a small, withered survivor, was the first victim to speak. Describing her quest to find her father's account, she told D'Amato that the employees of the Swiss banks had been "rude and arrogant." "Yes," nodded the senator, "If you look at the age of those who are being further victimized, it seems to me that they [the Swiss banks] would like to stall this until there is no memory left of the survivors." Pausing for the cameras, he added, "Switzerland is playing the old game of delay."

D'Amato now moved to the revelation, which required careful explanation: Switzerland had signed secret agreements with Poland and Hungary to make use of the heirless assets. "Imagine that," said the Brooklyn-accented senator, "Polish Jews had their assets taken over and paid over to the Swiss. Just unconscionable . . . These assets were looted from victims of the Holocaust." By the end of the ninety-minute hearing, the senator had secured a satisfactory slice of TV airtime and column inches. "A fraud was committed on those people," he told the journalists gathered around, "and it continues today." In the midst of the journalists' scrimmage, the politician repeated his single-line message. In Bern, it was 7 P.M.—too late to find Flavio Cotti and ask for his reply.

The following day, the Swiss foreign minister was visibly angry. D'Amato's allegation about the agreement with Poland, he told inquirers, was "totally without foundation." Sure of his facts, D'Amato dispatched a letter to Bern. "The Swiss government," he wrote, "was actually part of the conspiracy with the communist government of Poland. This dishonesty and deception by any government would be offensive against the background of one of the saddest chapters in human history. It is especially disturbing given Switzerland's reputation for neutrality and compassion." Once again Cotti rebutted the claim as "totally without foundation." In parliament, the minister fumed, "What has been said about Switzerland, especially in the foreign media . . . has been shattering, on the very edge of intolerable." Accusations of Swiss profiteering, he nevertheless conceded, "have gravely undermined our self-esteem and our sense of our own moral value."

Hours later, helped by Peter Hug, a Swiss historian, Cotti's officials were led to the evidence of the secret Polish pact stored neatly on the open shelves of the Swiss national archives. "Jewish money," the Foreign Ministry spokesman sheepishly admitted, "was used to compensate Swiss citizens." Besieged in Washington, a Swiss embassy spokesman snapped that the spokesman in Bern "was misquoted." Events, revelations and admissions were multiplying too fast for officials accustomed to a sedate pace. One telephone call to Bern clarified the contradictions. Switzerland, it was admitted at the embassy in Washington, "bought the goodwill of the Polish regime" but "the agreement was not carried out." Facing both ways, the Swiss now sought to explain the deal in a different manner. Switzerland's citizens had been compensated not by the Swiss government but by the Polish government. In Bern, the government announced the creation of a task force led by Peter Hug to investigate Switzerland's agreements with Eastern Europe. Switzerland's establishment was reeling.

By the end of October 1996, five different investigations were either proposed or under way to dissect Switzerland's past. Besides Hug's, there was a proposed historians' commission to examine Switzerland's entire archives concerning the Nazi and post-Nazi era. That was expected to report in five years.

The third probe was being conducted by Hanspeter Häni, the Bankiers Association's ombudsman. Häni had received claims, as Weber had in 1963, accompanied by a fee of SF100 ($80), which were passed to banks for reply. After eight months he revealed that, despite 2,229 inquiries and 1,055 investigations, not a single dormant account had been reported. But, faced with intensifying pressure, he suddenly announced the discovery of eleven accounts worth SF1.6 million. However, only five were linked to Nazi victims, and their total deposits amounted to SF11,000 ($8,750). "A cruel farce perpetuated on Holocaust survivors by the Swiss banking industry," scoffed the World Jewish Congress. "He's Swiss," carped D'Amato. "How do you expect that he's independent?" The fees Häni had received from Jewish claimants exceeded the few dollars his inquiries had discovered.

The fourth proposed investigation to audit Switzerland's banks, under Paul Volcker, the former chairman of the U.S. Federal Reserve, as yet showed no sign of life. Although the terms of the proposed Swiss legislation to compel banks to disclose their secrets had been broadened to include the "fate of assets which reached Switzerland as a result of National Socialist rule," the representatives of the banks and the Jews had still not agreed on their terms of inquiry. The banks had so astutely prevented a proper investigation in 1962 that every precaution to avoid an exhaustive investigation thirty-five years later required attention. "I'd be disappointed if we don't narrow the difference," said Volcker, resisting attacks by D'Amato—who was questioning Volcker's independence because his committee's expenses were paid by the Swiss banks.

The fifth investigation was under the command of Thomas Borer, an ambitious, self-confident thirty-nine-year-old international lawyer, a former counselor for legal affairs in Washington, who ranked number four in the Swiss Foreign Ministry. Borer's task force was to supervise the country's investigation of the fate of the "assets of the Nazis' victims." As a Swiss traditionalist, Borer had adopted an unexceptional attitude. D'Amato, Borer said, was "unfairly rushing to judgment" against Switzerland.

To irritate the Swiss even more, D'Amato offered more venom. The Swiss, he told reporters, "are trapped in the facts of their predecessors' actions and defend themselves with new denials, half-truths and distortions. They continue to compound the horrible things they did years ago by accusing others of misstatements." To overcome the delays, he suggested that the government also establish a "truth commission" similar to South Africa's. For the racially aware Swiss, it was the ultimate insult. "Comparing Switzerland to South Africa is absurd," said the fair-haired Borer. "His charges that we want to delay the investigations," expostulated Cotti, "or that we are not credible because we are Swiss, are insulting and utterly unacceptable."

Pleas of innocence encouraged a switch to a more sophisticated attack. In New York and Washington, enterprising lawyers organized two class actions against the Union Bank of Switzerland, Crédit Suisse and the Swiss Bank Corporation, claiming damages of over $20 billion. Class actions—unknown in Europe—are used in the United States as battering rams against giant corporations to win vast damages for large groups of individuals. The claims alleged that the banks had refused to return money deposited by Jews and that a colossal amount of wealth stolen by Nazis from Jews, deposited in Swiss banks, should be transferred to the survivors. The quality of proof provided in the two claims was decidedly unimpressive, but the nuisance value was enormous. If the judge allowed one composite case to be heard, the three banks would be immersed in a lengthy saga to defend their wartime relationship with the Nazis. To terrorize the banks further, the Washington case, organized by Martin Mendelsohn of the Simon Wiesenthal Centre, had retained Michael Hausfeld. As proof of his status as the United States' leading advocate in class actions, Hausfeld had just won a $178 million settlement from Texaco in a race discrimination case. The Swiss Bankers Association finally understood the gravity of the threat. To reinforce the propaganda value, one of the law firms produced another victim to demonstrate Swiss dishonesty.

Speaking at her home in Brooklyn with a strong Central European accent, Gizella Weisshaus, a Hasidic Jew, described her fate in the summer of 1944 when, aged fourteen, she was arrested with her parents and six younger brothers and sisters in Sighet, Romania. While the family was forced to remain in the house, her father was held at the rail station awaiting the journey to Auschwitz. By paying his guard a hefty bribe, her father had been allowed to return home and bid farewell to his family. In the midst of a hurried and strained conversation, Gizella Weisshaus's father whispered that some money was hidden in the house and that there was more deposited in a Swiss bank. The father returned to the station and was never seen again. Shortly afterward, the whole family was shipped to Auschwitz. At the railhead inside the camp, an SS officer, jerking his thumb, ordered Gizella Weisshaus's mother and the six younger children to go in one direction, while, ignoring the mother's screams for her child, Gizella was ordered to join another group. No one realized that it was a decision of life and death; while Weisshaus would survive, her mother and her six siblings would be gassed within hours. More than fifty of her relatives would be murdered by the end of the war. Having survived, Weisshaus had returned to her home to discover, as her father had disclosed, $1,500 in dollar bills and some gold hidden in the roof. Shortly afterward, she married and emigrated to the United States.

Sitting in her home in autumn 1996, the sixty-six-year-old Weisshaus, staring at a photograph of herself as a child with her father, decried the results of three unsuccessful visits to Switzerland to find her father's bank account: "That made me really mad. They're just playing for time, waiting for everyone to die. I have to do justice for my parents."

The publicity given to the two class actions persuaded over 3,000 other potential claimants to contact the east coast lawyers to join the case. "This publicity is really killing us," groaned a Foreign Ministry spokesman in Bern. "We're peeling back the layers of the onion," rejoiced Stuart Eizenstadt.

To combat the adverse publicity and correct the mistakes, Carlo Jagmetti, the sixty-four-year-old Swiss ambassador in Washington, was ordered by Bern to host a press conference. A heavy man on the eve of retirement, Jagmetti would clearly have been happier sitting in a mountain café, drinking a glass of cold white wine from the Vaud alongside Lake Geneva—or even lying on a beach in Florida—rather than getting embroiled in unsavory controversy. Prior to his appointment, neither he nor his masters in Bern had anticipated that the son of a long-established Zurich family would ever emerge from the anonymity familiar to the representative of an insignificant country in Washington. Indeed Jagmetti, angry that Clinton had allowed four months to pass before allowing the ambassador to present his credentials, had afterward derided the president to Swiss journalists for "laughing at inappropriate moments" during their interview and had even asked, "Who actually runs the country?" That contempt now gave an extra charge to the anger he shared with most of his generation about the slurs being leveled against noble Switzerland. In consequence, Jagmetti and his staff were floundering as they defended their predecessors only to discover that their loyalty was poorly rewarded by confusion. Accusations by the Jews in New York were denied in Bern only to be reversed and admitted. Assertions by Senator D'Amato were ridiculed and then conceded. Who, wondered Jagmetti, was in charge back home and why did D'Amato refuse his requests to meet? The senator was loathsome, disrespectful and a sensation seeker. The ambassador's fury, however, after he had received some careful briefing, was repressed when, on October 30, he begrudgingly welcomed fifty journalists and a dozen television cameras in the embassy's reception hall.

Christoph Bubb, the embassy's legal counselor, stood aside from the ambassador, not much wiser than he had been two weeks earlier when, at the embassy's reception, he had scorned the notion that Switzerland's banks could have retained any Jewish assets and derided Senator D'Amato's suggestion that Switzerland had made a secret agreement with Poland. But the lawyer was still puzzled. Nothing in his education and training had prepared him for the tumult engulfing his country. Coping with the barrage of assaults was testing his very sanity. The language and the emotion typified war rather than diplomacy—a war for the survival of Switzerland. That concern was shared by Jagmetti. Both men viewed the "war" as a conflict about money, not truth or justice. The Americans, they believed, wanted a deal, but negotiating sums of money with such people was impossible.

The ambassador's brief was to reassure. Blinking nervously at the unusual crowd inside his sanctuary, he opened with a promise: the full truth would be disclosed "as soon as possible," and while the historians' investigation was under way, he urged, even if it lasted five years, "we must avoid the trap of hasty conclusions based on alleged revelations." Referring to his principal enemy's accusation that five years "is too long," he countered that D'Amato's remarks were "a travesty," because the historians would produce "early results." A mention of the senator's name, a red rag to the ambassador, aroused a further attack against "misrepresentations," but recalling his instructions from Bern to appear conciliatory he admitted, "Soul-searching is very much going on in Switzerland. There is fundamental discussion. Opinions are polarized." As the questions became hostile, the ambassador uttered his concession: "Of course the banks made psychological mistakes. From the human point of view some real mistakes have been made."

While no cynical journalist was won over by the ambassador, he had succeeded at the last moment in presenting a human face. But his instinctive feelings could not be contained forever. The rotund Jagmetti—caught up, he believed, in a war to defend his country—committed his own "psychological mistake." Talking about Greta Beer, who had been flown to Switzerland by Hans Baer, the banker, to find her missing account, the ambassador said, "They found her account but discovered that her uncles had taken everything from the account in the past. So this was a very tricky case. Had she the money, she would have gotten it right away." But his statement was inaccurate. Hans Baer had found the records of an account belonging to Greta Beer's uncle, which was empty, but he had not found a trace of the account opened by Beer's father. Jagmetti's mistake revealed his prejudice: One Jew had stolen from another Jew. The Jews cannot be trusted.

In Bern, Thomas Borer, firmly in the seat as the task-force commander, considered the ambassador's "mistake" trivial and was scornful of the resulting uproar contrived by the senator and the World Jewish Congress. In a meeting with Paul Volcker (still battling to establish his own investigation), Borer had shown his own prejudices. To explain his conviction that few Jewish dormant accounts would be found in Swiss banks, Borer had declared, "Rich Jews didn't go to Auschwitz. They cleverly bought their way out." Volcker had suppressed his surprise. No wonder he was having difficulty getting the Jews and the Swiss committee to agree the terms to launch the investigation.

Prejudice, anger and suspicion were pulling the antagonists further apart. Intentionally, D'Amato and the WJC executives were feeding more inflammatory documents to journalists to annoy the enemy. In early December, an official of the Simon Wiesenthal Organization in Buenos Aires obtained the wartime records of gold transfers from Bern. Over one billion dollars of Nazi loot, suggested Elan Steinberg, had flowed to Argentina. Rickman in Washington released recently discovered State Department records reporting that Goebbels and Göring had dispatched diplomatic pouches filled with loot to Switzerland for shipment to Argentina, while another intelligence report indicted Swiss officials for helping wanted Nazis to escape through Switzerland to South America. At the center of the web was Switzerland, protecting the Nazis and harming the Jews.

Thomas Borer could not ignore the latest headlines. Nor was he inclined to disregard the evidence. Unlike Jagmetti, he was not instinctively antagonistic toward Americans, nor did he underestimate the combined influence of a senator, a lobbyists' group and sympathetic media. While disparaging the continuous drip from the archives—"Publishing single documents out of context and without regard to the historical realities constitutes sensationalism," he complained—he understood the need for dialogue, even if D'Amato was reluctant to offer mutual respect. Rather than reject outright the evidence from Argentina—he played down Jagmetti's abrupt dismissal as "pure hearsay"—he tried sweet reason: "It cannot be excluded that at some time a diplomatic pouch was misused." After successive meetings with the Swiss ambassadors to Israel, the United States and most European countries, and with Switzerland's top bankers, he proposed a new strategy to persuade the world that the Swiss had not stolen any money.

The place to launch the charm offensive, Borer calculated, was at the new hearings on Switzerland and the Jewish assets scheduled by James Leach, the chairman of the House of Representatives Banking Committee, to start in Washington on December 11. Borer intended to testify and to use his visit to meet the major antagonists.

The official's flight to Washington was not as pleasant as he might have hoped. Shortly before departing, he had received the rushed historians' 145-page report, exclusively about Switzerland's secret agreements with Poland and Hungary, that had been prompted by Senator D'Amato's accusations. Irritatingly, they had concluded that "a number of serious legal and administrative irregularities had been committed by banks and senior Swiss government officials and politicians." That report, he decided, would not be released as promised during his Washington visit. It required amendment, certainly delay, and he would ensure that its publication would be overshadowed by another event.

With that irritation removed, the ambitious official stepped off the aircraft eager to build bridges at a succession of meetings. The most important was lunch with Edgar Bronfman in the Seagram building. To everyone's satisfaction, their encounter would pass off, in Steinberg's opinion, as "friendly, constructive and encouraging." D'Amato would also amiably describe his meeting with Borer as "okay." There was a suggestion from the WJC that Switzerland should establish a goodwill fund. "We need an interim fund to compensate the survivors," said Bronfman. "So far the pace has been slower than a snail. Not one franc has passed hands." Although no amount was mentioned, Borer was understanding. "The crisis may have passed," said Steinberg as Borer flew south to appear at 9.40 A.M. in the Rayburn House building.

Entering the fevered atmosphere of the committee rooms of the United States Congress is for any non-American a daunting experience. Within those undistinguished rooms, politicians like Joseph McCarthy have destroyed the reputations of hundreds of ordinary

Americans, and other politicians have terminated the ambitions of presidents. For Borer and his entourage, the stakes were just as high. Since the hearings in April 1996, Switzerland's reputation had been shredded. Every attempt to rebut or minimize the damage had been at best futile, at worst counterproductive. Borer hoped that his activities would pacify and reassure. But the opening comments of the politicians on the raised dais were not encouraging.

"To those people who find these hearings annoying and unpleasant," admonished Representative Barney Frank of Massachusetts, "there is an easy way to make them go away: Do the right thing." For the Swiss officials to hear American politicians speak with passion about the "greatest moral blot on mankind's record" was disconcerting, but the warning by Representative Spencer Bachus of Alabama was succinct: "The credibility, the veracity, the very integrity of the entire Swiss banking industry [are] at stake in this matter; and the burden of proof lies entirely with the Swiss banking industry." The gap between the banks' estimate of dormant accounts at $32 million and the claims of the survivors that the figure was "as much as $20 billion," warned Bachus, was "too large a gap for honest error."

Borer—nicknamed "Schwarzenegger" by journalists—flinched as Representative Paul Kanjorski from Pennsylvania, the next speaker, issued a blunt message: "No one can ever be allowed to profit from blood money—not now, not fifty years ago, not fifteen years from now. Never again."

In Borer's opinion, Kanjorski was vicious. Not only did the representative heap praise on D'Amato's grasp of the issues and his unremitting criticism of Switzerland, but he speculated about the use of "sanctions." The other representatives seemed to approve, and likewise to applaud D'Amato. But as Borer settled down to give his testimony, the first Swiss official ever to appear before Congress, D'Amato left the room. The senator failed to hear Borer's opening remarks: "Our government and parliament have repeatedly stressed that only the truth and nothing but the truth would satisfy their pursuit of justice." D'Amato also missed Borer's assertion that

"Switzerland is deeply aware of the pain, mistrust and confusion that surround this issue. . . . We are not afraid of the truth."

Eyewash is familiar to American politicians, and the remark by Bronfman, sitting near Borer, about Switzerland's "stonewalling" caused the scales to fall from the Swiss official's eyes. All his assurances of progress and good faith aroused skepticism rather than sympathy. "We will be back here in a couple of months," warned Frank, "with another hearing. No doubt."

"We view this as a moral imperative," said Borer later. "No penny should stay in Switzerland."

Twenty-four hours later, the afterglow of Borer's appearance had vanished. Most people had been impressed by his statement that before arriving at the hearing he had visited the Holocaust Museum, "to reflect in the surroundings of such an important memorial about whether Switzerland and I am doing enough." The reality was somewhat different. Reports from the museum's staff indicated that Borer had arrived with a television crew. After being filmed entering the building, he departed scarcely fifteen minutes later, leaving the impression that his visit had, some felt, been a photo opportunity. So Borer's fence-mending had been counterproductive. D'Amato and Bronfman sensed no advantage in restraining their campaigns. Behind the bombast, however, attempts were under way to negotiate a settlement among lawyers to avoid the trial of the class action. The possibility of a deal—in Borer's opinion the real reason for the campaign—depended on the sum of money and the accompanying statement that would explain the payment. Progress on both, however, was proving impossible—not least because of dissension in Switzerland.

Although he was too professional to confess as much, Borer's negotiations with politicians, Jewish organizations and lawyers masterminding the class actions had been hampered by divisions and weaknesses among the seven ministers in the Federal Council and by the persistent hostility from the banks.

Consistent with its traditions, the Bankers Association had urged the government not to offer any concessions to the Jews. Agreeing to the Volcker investigation was one concession too many, and attempts were being made to nibble at the terms of reference. Like his fore-runners in the service of the Swiss government, going back as far as 1946, Borer was too weak to challenge the association, especially now that the politicians were stumbling. Instinctively protective of their country and artless about the campaign in the United States, the seven ministers were incapable of agreeing on a policy and issuing a directive to solve the crisis. United in their conviction that Switzerland was the victim of a conspiracy, they stubbornly retreated from a position that might enable them to understand the crisis. Their attitude was well expressed by Jean-Pascal Delamuraz, the eco-nomics minister—Villiger's successor as president.

To Delamuraz, the crisis since February had been not about truth or justice but about money. Switzerland was, he believed, under pressure from the Jews to make a deal. Like Jagmetti and so many others of his party and generation, Delamuraz believed that everyone could be bought and that money would solve all problems. The pres-ident, however, was more than suspicious about the gap between the $32 million offered by the Bankers Association and the $7 billion mentioned by the World Jewish Congress. Never doubting that his opinions would be interpreted as honest and reasonable, the wine-loving head of state summarized the government's attitude toward the controversy in an interview granted to his local newspaper on the eve of his retirement from the rotating presidency. Influenced by a dispatch from Carlo Jagmetti (the unauthorized release of which in January 1997 would cause Jagmetti's resignation) advising that Switzerland should "wage war" against groups in America who "can-not be trusted," Delamuraz was angry. The reported demand by the Jews that the Swiss should establish a $250 million compensation fund, he declared, was "nothing less than extortion and blackmail." The "deal" offered by the Jews was also blackmail and was consistent with the United States' campaign to undermine Switzerland's role as a world financial center. The furor that greeted the president's remarks in the United States encouraged his six ministerial col-leagues to endorse that opinion. Delamuraz's disparagement of the

Jews was unexceptional and was not even noticed by his colleagues. His protests voiced the thoughts of many. The government, said Arnold Koller, the new president, was not planning to apologize for Delamuraz's comments. Letters to Swiss newspapers praised the former president for articulating the majority's outrage about having "suffered in silence." Grievances against the Jews were openly expressed on the streets. Supported by the majority of his countrymen, Delamuraz would later utter a perfunctory apology to appease the U.S. government, but did not retract his opinion.

In early January 1997, Borer's education about the threat to Switzerland was nearing completion. In retaliation for Delamuraz's comments, Avraham Burg, who was the chairman of the Jewish Agency for Israel and a member of the Volcker commission, had threatened a worldwide boycott of Swiss banks and the withdrawal of funds. The Swiss president, Burg accused, was involved in "a conspiracy to destroy negotiations between us in order for the Swiss to avoid taking responsibility for their actions ... during the war." There was talk in New York and two other states of starting proceedings to divest Swiss banks of their licenses to trade. Telephoning around New York and Washington, Borer sought advice on how to defuse the new crisis. Time, he was told, was running out. Waiting five years for a historians' commission to report and more than one year for Volcker's committee to complete its work was playing into the hands of D'Amato and Bronfman. The only solution, he was reminded, was a big compensation fund. Rushing to confer with the Swiss ministers, Borer was met with icy stares. The politicians were unprepared to offer money, which would be interpreted as an admission of guilt, especially before the investigations were completed. The sentiments uttered in New York and Washington had merely reinforced Swiss stubbornness. On the same day as Delamuraz said that he had no need to offer a full apology about his remarks because he had been "misunderstood," Borer was authorized to offer a limited deal.

Borer meant well, but when he announced on January 8, 1997, that his government hoped that Switzerland's banks would establish a

Holocaust memorial fund financed from the dormant accounts, his statement exploded in his face. "They are trying to buy us with money that is not theirs," scoffed Avraham Burg. Thrown off balance and groping for another idea, Borer was stunned the following morning to hear the news that a security guard at Union Bank had, during a routine check in the bank's shredding room, glanced at old ledgers and papers filling three large bins. Leafing through them, the guard saw that the fountain-pen entries referred to property transactions during the Nazi era. Quite clearly, historical material whose destruction was forbidden by Swiss law had been illegally dispatched for destruction. Switzerland's defenses were crumbling fast. Union Bank's chairman, Robert Studer, had derided suggestions that there was unclaimed Jewish money in Switzerland's banks and had dismissed as a "fairytale" the allegation that Switzerland's banks had earned fortunes from the victims of the Holocaust. His bank's admission that, after review by a historian, thousands of other documents had been destroyed, although there was no inventory to identify them, was capped by Studer's dismissal of the guard for revealing the shredding and so breaking the bank's secrecy rules. All Borer's efforts were once more nullified as D'Amato and Steinberg offered excruciating soundbites, all faithfully reported to Switzerland.

Ministers and officials in Bern were once again reeling. Only a Nazi invasion in 1940 could have been more destabilizing. Tormented and searching once again for advice about how to stop the collapse, Delamuraz was prevailed on to apologize again for the "misunderstanding," and Switzerland's bankers were beseeched to cease fifty years of obstruction. A deal was vital.

It fell to Rainer Gut, the chairman of Crédit Suisse and the ambitious elder statesman of Swiss banking, to break the logjam. Only one gesture, he knew, could reduce the tension and save the international reputation of Switzerland's banks. On January 22, Gut broke ranks with his two major competitors to offer a solution. A "well-endowed" compensation fund, he suggested, should be established to help Holocaust victims and their families. He mentioned no figure but eventually offered SF100 million ($72 million). Even triple that sum was condemned by D'Amato as too little, too late, and the WJC stuck to $250 million. Each day, the expectations of Switzerland's adversaries grew. One billion dollars was seriously suggested as the minimum price if the campaign was to be stopped. Nothing, it appeared, that Swiss ministers could say would stem the tide. Even the announcement the following day that the Swiss government and all of Switzerland's leading financial institutions had agreed to cooperate with Gut's plan was greeted with silence.

Switzerland, it seemed, had not quite understood. The conflict could be resolved only by a deal. To the Jews, the deal would require Switzerland to acknowledge its wartime conduct. To the Swiss, the deal was to buy off an irritation and get on with business. Switzerland's agony while it came to terms with its past conduct and world censure was of no concern to the United States. There seemed no alternative other than to wait until the Swiss bowed and offered a humiliating apology and massive compensation. For Switzerland, the cost of its delayed remorse would be truly horrendous.

FINAL WORDS

Switzerland's retreat began in early February, at the famed annual World Economic Forum in Davos. The former Alpine Nazi sanctuary was a fitting location for Switzerland's rulers to confront the consequences of their nation's wartime policies. Unlike previous years, the hosts of the world's leaders were not greeted with unconditional warmth. Instead, the invited politicians, government officials and Jewish leaders, not only from the United States and Israel, cautioned Switzerland's ministers and bankers that their stubborn resistance was untenable. Over canapés and champagne, and at discreet dinners, the once impervious Swiss were repeatedly stung by criticism and advice from their guests. Muttered hopes by the hosts that the Jews could be bought off or even ignored were firmly scotched by those whom the Swiss regarded as friends. Despite their hurt sensitivities and their resolute conviction that they were the victims of an international plot and even blackmail, Swiss ministers and bankers finally collided with the immovable conscience of their adversaries. The cost of their predecessors' moral indifference posturing as neutrality bore unpalatable consequences in the new era of global finance. Sanguine and insensitive for so long to events beyond their frontiers, Switzerland's power brokers were revealed as vulnerable, shamed minnows.

Encouraged by Edgar Bronfman and Israel Singer, Flavio Cotti, Switzerland's foreign minister, accepted that his country's proffered solution to champion delay until all the investigations were completed was self-destructive. The pressure on Switzerland was intense. American politicians, including the governor of New York, spoke eagerly of challenging the licenses of Swiss banks in U.S. courts; and the banks, reporting losses for the first time in recent history, were more dependent than ever on foreign earnings. Testimony of the commitment of the Clinton administration to the campaign was the president's announcement, having secured the agreement of the British and French governments, to freeze the final distribution of looted gold seized in 1945 worth $68 million until Jewish claims that some ingots were manufactured from Jewish jewelry and dental fillings were properly considered. More embarrassing revelations about Switzerland's nefarious trade in looted gold with the Reichsbank were promised in an American historian's report being compiled from classified government documents under the control of Stuart Eizenstadt. Gnawing in Switzerland itself was the audit of the banks under Paul Volcker, who predicted that, despite the banks' protestations of innocence, previously undisclosed accounts would be discovered. Absorbing the cumulative threats posed by the Bronfman-D'Amato campaign, Switzerland's frustrated politicians accepted an invitation to negotiate peace.

The first step was the Swiss government's endorsement of Rainer Gut's "Humanitarian fund for the victims of the Holocaust." The second step was Cotti's agreement to participate in a top-level conference. On February 14, Edgar Bronfman welcomed all of the antagonists to the WJC's headquarters in New York. Senator D'Amato, Paul Volcker, Stuart Eizenstadt and Thomas Borer sat with representatives of Israel to agree to a timetable that satisfied the Jews. Miraculously, the temperature had cooled. The fury generated by D'Amato's vitriol had evaporated as confrontation gave way to cooperation.

Contributions from other Swiss organizations had by then increased the potential Holocaust fund to $110 million. The issue was how much the Swiss government would contribute that would be sufficient to meet the WJC's target of $250 million. Within ninety minutes it was agreed that the Swiss government would be allowed the grace of receiving two reports due in the summer. One report from the Volcker commission and a second from historians investigating the wartime accounts of Switzerland's National Bank. These reports, it was believed, would help Cotti and his colleagues to overcome their countrypeople's increasing antagonism. "It was a profound even," said Eizenstadt at the end of the encounter. "Payments probably will be able to begin this summer," Bronfman said, smiling, giving hope to the Holocaust's impoverished survivors. But he cautioned that the crusade had not been about money. Echoing the spirit of Sam Klaus, the original crusader fifty-three years earlier, Bronfman sought to disarm the anti-Semites: "The issue is the truth. The issue is morality."

Burning with anger, Sam Klaus and the original crusaders had fought a valiant but eventually losing battle to compel the Allied governments to fulfill their wartime pledges, honor the ultimate sacrifice of millions and exact justice from those who had sought to profit from evil. It was a testament to western civilization that even after the passage of half a century, the inheritors of Klaus's mantle had marshaled sufficient strength to peacefully persuade the stubborn Swiss of the moral bankruptcy of retaining blood money.

SOURCES

The principal sources for this book were the American, Swiss, British and French national archives, and archives of the American Jewish Committee (AJC) and the American Joint Distribution Committee (AJDC). I also interviewed about forty people.

American archive sources are identified by RG; the British archives sources are the Foreign Office (FO), Treasury (T) and War Office (WO); references to documents from the Swiss archives start with the letter E; the remainder are from the French archives.

Chapter 1: Confrontation and Tears

1   At the head. E 4110 (A) 1973/85, Bd 1.
6   "the completely impossible." RG 59 1950–4 Box 1013 254.0041/7–1150.

Chapter 2: The Seeds of Crime

20   Some eyewitnesses, such. Alfred Haesler, *The Lifeboat Is Full* (Funk & Wagnalls, 1969), p. 77.
21   "overrun with Jews." Ibid., pp. 8, 10.
     By 1942, just. Ibid., p. 19.
     Unscrupulous Swiss businessmen. RG 131 Foreign Funds Control, Safehaven Report 159, October 30, 1945.
     Weissmann's only comfort. RG 58, 1945–9 Box 4202 April 17, 1946.
     "We must protect." Haesler, *Lifeboat*, p. 9.
22   "His report on." Ibid., p. 110.
24   "Jewish dollars." Jacques Picard, *Die Schweiz und die Juden* (Chronos, 1994), p. 416.
     Even Jews born. Ibid., p. 67
28   "We have fulfilled." Haesler, *Lifeboat*, p. 160.

28 a "wild story." Tom Bower, *Blind Eye to Murder* (Little Brown, 1996), p. 34.

CHAPTER 3: THE CRUSADE

29 "redolent of Dickensian." TB/Ida Klaus.

31 To forestall that. RG 169, FEA, Box 991 Margaret Clarke, Monograph, "The Safehaven Study," p. 25.
On Klaus's initiative. Ibid., p. 83.
"Anticipating defeat, enemy." FO 371/45812.

32 Tellingly, the diplomats. Clarke, "Safehaven Study," p. 93.
"Where voluntary cooperation." Ibid., p. 123.
"would not be." Ibid., p. 124.
"investigate and report." FO 371/40579 August 23 and September 28, 1944.
Seeking out journalists. Clarke, "Safehaven Study," p. 42; FO 371 40579, telegram sent by State Department to foreign legations, August 23, 1944.
Flying from London. FO 371/40579 August 23, 1944.

33 Their reception seemed. TB/Cummings. Cummings says that, contrary to the Clarke report, he and Klaus did visit Switzerland during that trip. See Clarke, "Safehaven Study," p. 48.

34 The Swiss, as. FO 371/49714 March 1, 1945.

37 The country's predominant. FO 192/199 January 31, 1947.
"either German agents." RG 226 Records of the OSS "Enemy Agents and the Red Cross" Box 1.
"finely developed net." RG 260 OMGUS Records of Property Division, German intelligence, Switzerland-German Assets Misc. Box 654.

38 Glad to receive. RG 59 800.515/4–1246, State Department German Safehaven Operations in Switzerland April 22, 1946.
"as thoroughly reliable." RG 131 Foreign Funds Control Safehaven, E 060764 and E 060735 March 5, 1941.
The Germans hoped. FO 371/45812.

38   To protect those. E 7160 (A) i 1968/54 Bd 23 (Nr 1–91) February 6, 1947.

39   The only trace. RG 260 OMGUS Property Control Box 653; RG 59 1945–9 Box 4205 May 6, 1946.
The Swiss lawyer. Safehaven Report, February 1946.
a "patriotic duty." FO 1031/89 page 14.
Thereafter, Iselin was. FO 935/18.
In London and. Other specialist fences identified by the British were Bankhaus Ernst Lochman, Bankhaus J. von Tobel and Bank von Ernst in Zurich. Ruegg's accomplices were paid to swear affidavits that German assets in Sweden had been purchased or were owned by Swiss corporations and nationals since 1940. The bank sold the assets as Swiss property and transferred the proceeds through the Enskilda Bank and Gotsland Bank in Stockholm back to Switzerland. (RG 131 Foreign Funds Control, Safehaven Report, October 15, 1945.) Alternatively, Ruegg transferred German money out of Switzerland by selling sanitized share certificates accompanied by false affidavits to the Enskilda Bank in Sweden. (RG 131 Foreign Funds Control Box 382 Safehaven Report 481, October 15, 1945; Nicholas Faith, *Safety in Numbers* [Hamish Hamilton, 1982], p. 118.)

40   The announcement that. FO 371/45812.
By December 31. SF450 million by the end of 1941 and SF650 million by June 30, 1942; FO 371/49714 March 1, 1945.

41   As the war. RG 260 OMGUS Records of Property Division, German intelligence, Switzerland-German Assets Misc. Box 654.
By the end. U.S. Treasury, Currie Mission File March 22, 1945.
In London, the. FO 371/34875 May 3, 1943.
In Bern, the. FO 192/198 "Swiss trade policy during the war, Zurich 1946."

42   Their subsequent explanation. E 7160 (A) i 1968/54 Sitzung 9.9. 1947.

43   Posing as the. Faith, *Safety in Numbers*, p. 49.
The bankers could. E 2001 (E) 1968/79 Bd 2 September 21, 1948.

43 No one, however, was. E 7160–01 1968/223 Bd 214 April 28, 1947, Stucki's inquiry about Göring's bank deposits.

The more sophisticated. RG 131 Foreign Funds Control, Box 382, State Department, "Types of Financial Operations in Switzerland"; U.S. Control Martin Bronfenbrenner, Memorandum from Delman, November 18, 1943; and "Switzerland, the Reich's foremost supplier of foreign exchange." Economic Warfare (Intelligence) Series 588, December 9, 1942.

44 A Swiss investigation. RG 59 1945–9 Box 4218 Walter Ostrow, Memorandum for the Files, Bern February 25, 1947; and March 4, 1947. U.S. Treasury Dept re Swiss banks and Safehaven. The pressure was from Bundesrat Stampfli.

"a better system." U.S. Treasury, re Swiss banks and Safehaven, Mann memorandum March 5, 1947.

Regularly, Allied intelligence. RG 131 Foreign Funds Control, SHAEF Report November 7, 1944.

Buehrle and other. RG 266 Records of OSS, interview with Meck May 27, 1946.

The Reichsbank's ledgers. RG 266 Records of OSS, interview with Landwehr May 27, 1946.

45 "pro-Fascist financial operators." RG 169 Entry 141A Box 1419 January 5, 1945.

Echoing Sholes and. Clarke, "Safehaven Study." p. 131.

Both banks controlled. U.S. Treasury re Swiss banks and Safehaven June 3, 1947.

46 Passing information to. U.S. Treasury, "Switzerland and the Axis February 1, 1943: Schmidt-Branden file," May 28, 1945.

47 "over-persuaded [by] Swiss. FO 371/34875 April 20, 1943.

Foot's "severe warning." FO 371/34875 April 16, 1943.

48 "our action is." Ibid.

To emphasize its. FO 371/34875 April 21, 1943.

"make agreements with." FO 371/34878 February 18, 1943.

49 Since he had. FO 371/39844 August 28, 1944; FO 371/34875 May 21, 1943.

Allied sanctions were. FO 371/34877 November 18, 1943.

CHAPTER 4: LOOTED GOLD

52 On the eve. FO 371/45749 November 1945; FO 837/1173 June 18, 1949.

53 Asked why the. RG 59 State Department 800.515/12–0942.
That would prove. RG 59 State Department 800.515/1–1845.

54 Identified Swiss traders. RG 59 State Department 800.515/11–2044.
Other Swiss traders. RG 319 Records of the Army Staff reports and Messages, 1918–51 to State Department. Switzerland, 12/2/46–3/31/47 Bx 1062; Hutzler of Spohnhols Bank of Berlin Box 1016.
Sympathetic Swiss customs. RG 131 Foreign Funds Control Box 382, FEA "Looted Art in Occupied Territories, Neutral Countries and Latin America," May 5, 1945 by James Plaut.

55 The Swedish government. FFC report, August 1943.
To the Reichsbank. Werner Rings, *Raubgold aus Deutschland* (Zurich, 1985), pp. 51, 70.
"if the gold." Ibid., p. 52.
"One cannot discover." Ibid., p. 48.

56 Weber chose again. Vogler report, "Der Goldverkehr der Schweizerischen Nationalbank mit der Deutschen Reichsbank 1939/45," September 1984.
"clearly without enthusiasm." FO 371/40579 January 1944.
Spain's had risen. FO 371/65002 April 7, 1947.
"unlawful disposition of." FO 371/40579 February 22, 1944.

57 The only precaution. Vogler report.
Isolated in Bern. RG 59 1945–9 Box 4206 Gold Swiss reaction to February 1944 declaration p. 6.
Considering that over. RG 131 Foreign Funds Control Box 380, Swiss president's speech May 1944.
provide "unchallengeable sanctuaries." FO 371/40579 June 5, 1944.

58 When the prospect. RG 131 1942–0 Box 51 July 1944.
In a series. FO 371/39169 June 20, 1944.

58   Indifferent to the. FO 371/39844 August 28, 1944.
Morgenthau again asked. RG 59 1945–9 Box 4206 Gold Swiss reaction to February 1944 declaration p. 6 August 23, 1944.
"I do not." FO 371/39169 July 7, 1944.
"Tight and capable." TB/Cummings.

Chapter 5: "An Impenetrable Racket"

59   "In their dealings." FO 371/39860 May 18, 1944.
"The Gestapo might." RG 59 State Department to Bern embassy 800.515/8–2544.
60   The flood of. RG 131 1942–0 Box 51 July 27, 1944.
be "very busy." FO 371/40579 September 1944 from Troutbeck; FO 371/40996 September 16, 1944; Clarke, "Safehaven Study," p. 46.
"Deportation means the." Haesler, *Lifeboat*, p. 195.
61   In September 1943. Ibid., p. 202.
Heroically, despite reprimanding. Martin Gilbert, *The Holocaust* (Collins, 1986), pp. 701–2, 752–5.
bore "propaganda value." Haesler, *Lifeboat*, p. 286.
62   In Budapest, Eichmann. Yehuda Baur, *Jews for Sale?* (Yale University Press, 1994), p. 164.
Becher's charm secured. National Zeitung Basel October 13, 1945; Baur, *Jews for Sale?*, p. 164 and passim.
63   Swiss police confided. RG 266 Records of OSS, Eduard von der Heydt report.
"In the past." Allemagne, Régime des biens allemands, série P9713, vol. III, pp. 43–6 bis.
The knowledge that. Allemagne, Régime des biens allemands, série P9713, vol. III, pp. 54–5.
"The Allied governments." FO 371/39844 August 24, 1944.
64   Orvis Schmidt, the. FO 371/39844 August 5, 1944.
65   Endorsing that scheme. RG 131 Foreign Funds Control, Box 369.

65 Blaming the "political." RG 59 State Department 800.515/9–1944.

67 "ready to be." Clarke, "Safehaven Study," p. 15.
In early January. U.S. Treasury re Swiss banks and Safehaven, report on Dr. Ricco Bessola in Latin America August 17, 1943. The neutral was. State Department Instruction No. 4985 based on Executive Committee on Economic Foreign Policy December 8, 1944.

68 "secure the objectives." FO 371/45812 January 16, 1945.
"Any resurgence of." FO 371/45812 January 15, 1945.
"we cannot disinterest." FO 371/45750 February 27, 1945.

69 "the impenetrability of." RG 59 1945–9 Box 3660 800.515/1–1345 January 13, 1945.
"No Swiss banks." State Department U.S. embassy Wellington, New Zealand January 15, 1945, Speech of Dr. Walter Schmidt.
"it is quite." RG 169 Entry 141A Box 1419 January 5, 1945.
In confirmation of. WO 219/1655 January 15, 1945.

70 Similarly defiant, it. RG 260 OMGUS. Property Control Box 653; RG 59 1945–9 Box 4205 May 6, 1946.
carrying "large sums." FEA/Treasury January 15, 1945.
Reports from Sweden. FDR Library February 3, 1945.
of stolen furs. FO 371/45750 February 6, 1945.

71 His ideal solution. RG 56 U.S. Treasury, White to Morgenthau February 1945.
"of utmost importance." RG 59 1945–9 Box 4179 800.515 13/2–1945 Bissell to Lyons February 19, 1945.

72 Under the direction. RG 59 1945–9 Box 4206 Conduct of Swiss Banking Institutions, Interrogation of Walter Schellenberg.
Inevitably, his campaign. RG 59 1945–9 Box 4180 4F11 Bern March 2, 1945.

73 "the sole international." Faith, *Safety in Numbers*, p. 91.

74 "I know in." Roger Sandilands, *The Life and Political Economy of Lauchlin Currie* (Duke University Press, 1990), p. 138.
An urgent recommendation. RG 50 1945–9 Box 3523 740.00112 EA/2–645 February 6, 1945 Huddle to State Department.

75   Throughout the war. Rélations bilatérales Suisse/France, Côte EU 29–8–3, vol. 59, pp. 162–9.

"is a noble." *New York Times*, July 30, 1945, p. 6.

Regularly invited to. Commission permanante de conciliation Franco-Suisse, Côte EU 29–8–3 s/d, vol. 19, pp. 29–33.

"renowned as a." FO 371/55574 January 1946.

76   letter marked "urgent." E 2800(-) 1967/61 Bd 97.

77   Stucki had delegated. 800.515/1–2645.

To secure Currie's. T 236/1602 February 16, 1945.

78   Naturally, the banks. E 7160 (A) i 1968/54 November 12, 1946.

"sure that the." E 7160 (A) i 1968/54 vol. 5 October 28, 1947.

79   The Allied demand. Clarke, "Safehaven Study," p. 143.

In Currie's opinion. FO 371/45750 and Memorandum of Dr. Philippe Rossiez December 15, 1945. RG 319, Records of the Army Staff, Reports and Messages, 1918–51 State Department, Switzerland, Box 1058.

Under the agreement. T 236/1602 March 8, 1945.

all German shipments. FO 371/45812 March 8, 1945. The onus for proving ownership was on the shipper.

80   "The Swiss government." RG 59 1945–9 Box 4206 "Violation by the Swiss of March 1945 Agreement."

eight-page letter. T 236/1602 March 8, 1945.

Currie's euphoric telegram. FRUS 1945 vol. V, p. 782; Linus von Castlemur, *Schweizerisch-Alliierre Finanzbeziehungen im Übergang vom Zweiten Welt Krieg* (Chronos, 1992), p. 24 n. 27.

81   "thwarted the Nazis." Sandilands, *Currie*, p. 139.

practiced "virtual deceit." RG 59 1945–9 Box 4234 September 5, 1947.

"This will have." T 236/1602 March 26, 1945.

"We need to." T 236/1602 February 15, 1945.

"You are not." T 236/1602 February 22, 1945.

as "explosive stuff." T 236/1602 March 2, 1945.

82   "the rich Jew." Vogler report, p. 17.

84   "despite the enemy." "Introduction," *Elimination of German Resources for War: Germany's Relationship with Switzerland.* Report of the Kilcore Committee, United States Senate, 1945.

84 "did not ask." U.S. War Crimes Office, Safehaven Report, Puhl
    statement November 17, 1945.
    his "considerable achievement." Cited, Introduction "Elimination
    of German resources for war": Germany's relationship with
    Switzerland.

85 "very influential in." U.S. Treasury, Currie Mission File March
    22, 1945.
    In the euphoria. RG 226 E183 Box 21; Schmidt to Rubin April
    21, 1945.
    In a continent. RG 131 1942–60 Box 51 Safehaven February
    and March 1945; FO 935 18 June 12, 1945.
    A "sudden increase." FO 837/1285 March 16, 1945.
    "large amounts of." FO 371/49710 February 22, 1945.

86 "The Germans will." FO 371/45750 March 16, 1945.
    Quietly, the more. RG 260 OMGUS Property Control Box
    653; RG 59 1945–9 Box 4205 May 6, 1946

CHAPTER 6: CRACKS

88 "appearance of quiet." RG 56 U.S. Treasury, Mann,
    Memorandum for the files May 29, 1945.
    After two weeks. TB/Morton Bach.

89 "Herman Kasper left." RG 56 U.S. Treasury, Mann,
    Memorandum for the files May 29, 1945.
    Switzerland's "omissions," "disregard." RG 131 1942–50
    Gordon to Schmidt Box 457 May 8, 1945.
    All that remained. Clarke, "Safehaven Study," p. 102.
    Without a unified. Ibid., p. 190.

90 So many senior. RG 226 Records of OSS Entry 90 Box 2 May
    25, 1945.
    "strictly confidential" letter. RG 56 U.S. Treasury, Ostrow and
    Mann to White May 29, 1945.
    The declared deposits. *New York Times* November 25, 1946.
    "hundreds of paintings." Preliminary estimates of the Swiss-
    German Creditor-Debtor position. RG 59 1945–9 Box
    4206.

91   Asked by Safehaven. State Department Swiss Accord February
      23, 1951.
      Rapidly their inventory. U.S. OMGUS Finance branch,
      Currency Div. June 18, 1945.

92   "This question may." FO 371/40579 May 1944.
      Henriques set the. Ibid.

93   "dangerous to do." Ibid.
      Henriques's prejudice appeared. RG 131 1942–60 Entry 74 Box
      784 January 19, 1945.
      Fearing "double odium." FO 371/40579 June 5, 1944.
      "Restitution of identifiable." FO 371/40579 July 1944 Appx A to
      ACAO/P (44) 99 Armistice Administration Official Committee.
      "One thing must." FO 371/40579 July 26, 1944.

94   "Information is so." FO 371/40579 July 22, 1944.
      "We shall doubtless." FO 371/45750 April 13, 1945.
      German property seized. FO 371/45750 March 28, 1945.
      That, he knew. FO 1046/210 May 18, 1945.

95   "to make money." FO 371/45812 May 2, 1945.
      "In my opinion." FO 371/45812 May 18, 1945.
      "to get financial." FO 371/49676; FO 371 45813 August 7,
      1945.
      "If there's no." FO 371/45812.

96   "so inadequate that." RG 131 Foreign Funds Control, Schmidt
      to White June 1945.

97   "They stand," Lubin. T 236/1478 July 11, 1945.

98   Abramovitz had previously. TB/Abramovitz.
      "By treating the." T 236/1478 July 18, 1945.

99   "Switzerland must recognize." FO 371/45813 August 7, 1945.
      "If we take." FO 371/45813 July 31, 1945.
      "It will pay." FO 371/45813 August 7, 1945.

100   In the same. RG 59 1945–9 Box 4183 Telegram 3667 July 24,
      1945.
      "actual reasons for." RG 319, Records of the Army Staff
      Reports and Messages 1918–51 Switzerland Box 1056 July 24,
      1945.

101 "It is galling." Biens et interêts Suisse en France, sept. 1944-jan. 1949, Côte Z428-1-2. Z429-1, vol. 32, February 5, 1948.

103 The obstacle, he. E 7160 (A) a 1968/223 Bd 36 (Direktions-protokolle SVS) April 17, 1945.
"The banks say." E 7160 (A) a 1968/223 Bd 36 (Direktions-protokolle SVS) March 13, 1945.
"If we cannot." E 7160 (A) a 1968/223 Bd 36 (Direktions-protokolle SVS) April 28, 1945.

104 "the role of." E 2800 (-) 1967/61 Bd 88 (Banques Suisse) May 30, 1945.
"I'm astonished," exploded. E 7160 (A) a 1968/223 Bd 36 (Direktionsprotokolle SVS).

105 "We need them." RG 131 Foreign Funds Control, General Corr. Box 382 October 18, 1945.

107 "Switzerland gave the." FO 935/18; FO 1046/210 August 14 and 29, 1945.
"so many and." FO 371/48021 October 6, 1945.
"We cannot simply." FO 371/45813 August 15, 1945.
"The quiet confidence." FO 371/45814 November 1, 1945.

108 "This is the." FO 371/49729 August 30, 1945.
Kaehlitz had emphasized. RG 59 1945-9 800.515 3/8 1945.
Ignoring the Americans' irritation. *Foreign Relations of the United States*, 1945 vol. II, pp. 899–900.

Chapter 7: The Nazis' Friends

109 To combat aggressive. FO 371/46766 September 15, 1945.

110 "permanently [to] escape." FO 371/55574 December 19, 1945.
American investigators in. U.S. Treasury, re: Swiss banks and Safehaven, Mann memorandum for the files June 3, 1947.
Schaefer launched a. *New York Times*, June 24, 1946, p. 35.
a "meaningless gesture." FO 371/45813 September 1945.

111 A case pursued. E 2001 (E) 1967/113 Bd 374 (111) November 6, 1950.
Foreign Office officials. FO 371/50443 September 6, 1945.

111 A Jew like Frederick. RG 58, 1945–9 Box 4202 April 17, 1946.

112 "I personally regard." FO 371/45813 September 20, 1945.

"We'll do it." FO 371/45813 September 25, 1945.

"On what Swiss." FO 371/45814 September 26, 1945.

"They're perfectly correct." FO 371/45813 September 13, 1945.

113 "This will go." FO 371/45814 September 26, 1945.

"It's no different." RG 59 1945–9 Swiss Aide-Mémoire, April 1946 Box 4206; RG 59 1945–9 Box 3527 740.00112 EW/9-1445.

"heavy moral burden." FO 192/198 "Swiss trade policy during the war, Zurich 1946."

The promised census. RG 56 U.S. Treasury Mann to White October 10, 1945.

Compounding the insult. RG 56 U.S. Treasury, re: Swiss banks and Safehaven, Mann memorandum March 5, 1947.

"Switzerland's policy is." RG 56 U.S. Treasury Mann to White October 10, 1945.

114 "guilty of dilatoriness." RG 59 1945 Box 4194 October 4, 1945.

"Swiss violations of." RG 84 1942–9 Box 4194 November 28, 1945.

"little value in." RG 59 1945–9 FW 800.515/8–145 October 5, 1945.

115 The "relaxation on." RG 56 U.S. Treasury Mann to White October 13, 1945.

"an old friend." FO 371/49710 October 18, 1945.

116 Weber approved financial. E 2800 (-) 1967/61 Bd 88 (Société de Banque Suisse).

"to fulfill its." E 7160 (A) i 1968/54 Bd 28 (Korrespondenz AK) November 19, 1947.

117 Summoning journalists, he. RG 131, Dept of Justice, Records of the Office of Alien Property; Foreign Funds Control, General Correspondence 1942–60 Box 446; New York Herald Tribune, October 29, 1945.

"America's terrorizing the neutrals." FO 371/45814 October 1945.

117 Only the property. FO 371/46767 October 20, 1945.

Overnight, dozens of. FO 1031/10 January 25, 1946; Eisenhower agreed to postpone widespread publication of the decree by one month to allow the British to champion Rubin's approach. FO 371/45813 October 12, 1945.

"the world safe." RG 56 U.S. Treasury, re Swiss banks and Safehaven, Mann to White August 2, 1945.

118 Among the victims. U.S. Treasury re Swiss banks and Safehaven December 12, 1945.

Listed for seizure. AJDC, letter October 27, 1947.

119 Insensitively, all individual. E 7160 (A) i 1968/54 Bd 95 (49,11. Verordnung zum dt. Reichsbürgergesetz) August 3, 1945.

120 "It's immoral," he. T 236/1478 October 12, 1945.

"It was never." TB/Rubin.

Surely that fact. E 7160 (A) i 1968/54 Bd 95 (49,11. Verordnung zum dt. Reichsbürgergesetz) July 6, 1945.

121 The pro-Nazi lobby. E 7160 (A) 1 1968/54 Berichtüber die Tätigkeit der Abteilung, 1946/47.

Championing that discrimination. E 2001 (E) 1968/79 Bd 2.

122 "That prevents any." Ibid.

123 "should adopt a." E 7160 (A) i 1968/54 Bd 95 (49, 11. Verordnung zum dt. Reichsbürgergesetz) September 29 and October 12, 1945.

124 "Never rely on." E 7160 (A) i 1968/54 Bd 95 (49, 11. Verordnung zum dt. Reichsbürgergesetz) November 25, 1945.

Jews and Nazis. E 9500.193, 1969/150 Bd 2 December 17, 1945.

Chapter 8: The Pawns

125 "We're doing our." TB/Abramovitz

126 To that money. T 236/1478 December 24, 1945; T 236/1479 April 20 and 22, 1947.

There were, Waley. T 236/1478 November 5, 1945.

"obviously attach considerable." T 236/1478 November 8, 1945.

126 Still unaware that. T 236/1478 December 28, 1945.

127 "over £2 billion. T 236/1478 September 20, 1945.
     "I feel little." FO 371/45814 November 3, 1945.
     "It corresponds," Playfair. T 236/1478 November 10, 1945.

128 Weizmann's "monstrous suggestions." T 236/1478 November 8, 1945.
     New submissions to. T 236/1478 September 25, 1945.
     "has no logical." T 236/1478 November 5, 1945.
     Jack Coulson argued. T 236/1478 November 27, 1945.
     Troutbeck's replies to. T 236/1478 November 7, 1945.
     Nothing was publicly. RG 59 State Department Paris Conf. Final Report Box 2 p. 67.
     Accordingly, a request. T 236/1478 October 30, 1945.

129 "It would be." T 236/1478 November 29, 1945.
     "funds deposited . . . by." T 236/1478 December 7, 1945.
     Faced with isolation. T 236/1478 December 6, 1945.

130 "blackmail from the." T 236/1478 December 13, 1945.
     raised "concern" about. FO 371/60479 February 16, 1946.
     Vieli spoke eloquently. RG 56 U.S. Treasury, Swiss banks and Safehaven. Ostrow letter to White February 1, 1946. Lunch was held on January 23, 1946.
     Gerald Selous, the. FO 192/198 February 12, 1946.

131 For example, Bernard. E 2800 (-) 1967/61 Bd 88 (Banques Suisse) July 15, 1947.
     The exemptions from. AJDC memorandum March 18, 1946.

Chapter 9: Washington Showdown

133 "Should resist the Allies." E 2001 (E) 1968/79 Bd 2 (DIV).
     Stucki's instructions, formulated. Admitted to British by Victor Umbricht, First Secretary in Swiss legation in 1951 FO 837/1304 September 5, 1951.
     "We are not." FO 192/198 April 18, 1946.
     "no legal basis." Castlemur, *Schweizerisch-Alliierte Finanzbeziehungen*, p. 41

133 especially since the. Ibid., p. 43.

For that purpose. FO 192/198 April 18, 1946.

But that would. Castlemur, *Schweizerisch-Alliierte Finanzbeziehungen*, p. 41.

"The bankers don't." E 2001 (E) 1968/79 Bd 2 (DIV).

134 But in the hours. Ibid.

"If you can." E 7160 (A) 1 1968/54 November 12, 1946.

Having brilliantly resisted. FO 371 60479 February 16, 1946.

135 "strongly pro-American and." RG 59 1945–9 Box 4206.

"harbored sympathies for." RG 260 OMGUS Property Control Box 653.

"It is our." RG 59, 800.515, 4200; Castlemur, *Schweizerisch-Alliierte Finanzbeziehungen*, p. 27.

The only constraints. TB/Rubin.

136 Swiss solidarity with. Droit International Public, pillages allemands, Côte Y–10–1, vol. 48, p. 2.

"and give him." RG 59 800.515.4199; Castlemur, *Schweizerisch-Alliierte Finanzbeziehungen*, p. 29.

McCombe's only interest. RG 260 OMGUS Property Control Box 653 Rubin to Randolph March 8, 1946.

137 "shield the aggressor." RG 260 OMGUS Property Control, Memorandum A, March 19, 1946, Washington Accord negotiations.

"We propose," said. RG 59 1945–9 Box 4206.

"admiration and gratitude." RG 260 OMGUS Property Control, Memorandum B, March 21, 1946, Washington Accord negotiations.

"greatly impressed with." *New York Times*, March 22, 1946, p. 10.

138 Switzerland's "enormous losses." FO 371/60479 April 5, 1946; RG 59 1945–9 Box 4206 March 26, 1946.

"Switzerland's claims are." E 7160 (A) 1 1968/54 Bericht über die Tätigkeit der Abteilung, 1946/47.

"I do not." FO 371/60479 March 29, 1946.

139 Dunkel had, however. FO 837/1173 September 10, 1948.

139 The British estimate. FO 371/60479 February 1946, of which
      $32 million was identified as Belgian.
      while the American. RG 59 1945–9 Box 4206 German Gold
      Movements February 5, 1946. American estimate included
      $18.5 million assigned to Sweden and $32.5 million to
      Romania.
      On the most. Senator D'Amato in 1996 suggested that up to
      $398 million was looted.

140 The 3,859 ingots. FO 837/1159 February 13, 1947.
      By contrast, the. FO 371/45749 December 13, 1945.
      First, all the. State Department Memorandum June 12, 1946.
      Second, the Reichsbank's. FO 837/1159 January 25, 1947.
      Third, the French. FO 192/200 Pt 3 December 10, 1946.
      Angered by that. FO 371/45749 December 4, 1945.
      "a great mistake." FO 371 45749 December 15, 1945; U.S.
      State Department 20.12.45 B1.

141 Alfred Hirs knew. Castlemur, *Schweizerisch-Alliierte Finanzbezie-
      hungen*, p. 40.
      "We agree that." FO 371 60479 February 1946.
      "Those statistics are." RG 59 1945–9 Box 4206 Gold
      Memorandum April 17, 1946.

142 "stolen" Belgium's gold. Rélations Bilatérales Suisse/France,
      Côte EU 29–8–3, vol. 18.
      "the Swiss National." RG 59 1945–9 Box 4206 Gold
      Memorandum March 15, 1946.
      After Morgenthau's February. RG 59 1945–9 Box 4206 Gold
      Mtg March 26, 1946.

143 "Why do I." E. Schneeberger, *Wirtschaftskrieg auch in Frieden*
      (Bern, 1984), p. 185.
      Hirs also had. Vogler report, p. 16.
      "gradually demobilize the." Peter Hug and Marc Perrenound,
      *Assets in Switzerland of Victims of Nazism and the Compensation
      Agreements with East Block Countries* (Swiss Foreign Affairs
      Department, December 1996; English version, January 1997),
      p. xx.

143 "He's a well-known." RG 59 1945–9 Box 4206 Swiss Observations on Gold Memorandum March 27 and April 13, 1946.

144 "Puhl was a." RG 59 1945–9 Box 4206 Swiss Observations on Gold Memorandum April 13, 1946.

145 Crestfallen and humiliated. RG 59 1945–9 Box 4206 March 27, 1946.

146 "The Swiss delegation." Négotiations de 1945; Guerre Economique, Côte Z424–1, 2, 4, vol. 26, p. 129.
"We are isolated." TB/Schaffner.

147 His principal successor. E 2800 (-) 1990/106 Bd 16 (Handakten Petitpierre).

148 "a decent and." RG 59 1945–9 Box 4206 "Gold" Swiss memorandum April 13, 1946.
"It's imperative to." FO 371/60479 April 11, 1945.
"a part of." FO 371/60479.
"Half a loaf." FO 944/305 April 24, 1946.

149 "a large portion." Memorandum: German Foreign Assets p. 6, RG 59 1945–9 Bx 4206.

150 "a complete rupture." FO 371/60479 May 3, 1946.
were "kicking violently." FO 371/60479 May 4, 1946.

151 "bring out influential." Allemagne, Régime des biens allemands, série P9713, vol. 113, pp. 306–8.

152 "insists [that] rapid." Allemagne, Régime des biens allemands, dec. 1945—mai 1946, série P9715 vol. 113, pp. 334–6.
Stucki, he believed. Allemagne, Régime des biens allemands, juin 1946-mai 1947, série P9716, vol. 114, p. 50.

153 "We relied upon." TB/Rubin.
"specifically excluded Jews." U.S. Dept of Treasury, *History of Foreign Funds Control* (1946), pp. 165, 182.
an "informal agreement." RG 59 1945–9 Box 4236 Rubin/Adams Memorandum of a conversation October 23, 1947.

154 "I cannot," he. E 2001 (E) 1967/113 Bd 374 (III) March 20, 1950.

154 "No distinction was." Ibid.

155 When all this. 50 million kroner from Sweden; 100 million
escudos from Portugal and SF50 million from Switzerland. By
1953, only $17.5 million had been raised—$12.5 million from
Sweden in full and $5 million from Switzerland. The non-mon-
etary gold and jewelery found in the United States zones in
Germany and Austria was valued at $3 million. (RG 59 State
Department, Legal Advisor Records relating to postwar issues
1939–63 Non-monetary gold, Box 12.)
"It was always." TB/Rubin.

156 "A Swiss lie." Négociations de 1945; Guerre Economique, Côte
Z424–1, 2, 4, vol. 26, pp. 122–8.
"shunt off on to." Ibid., pp. 109–32.
"completely taken in." RG 260 OMGUS Property Control and
External Assets 1945–50 Switzerland Box 654, Harrison to Sec.
of State October 8, 1946.

CHAPTER 10: THE HIDDEN MILLIONS

157 "We had to." TB/Ginzberg.

158 "This government feels." Eli Ginzberg, "Report to the
Secretary of State," Ginzberg private papers, p. 69.
Britain's "delaying tactics." Ibid., p. 10.
"my good friend." Ibid., p. 17.

159 "I do everything." Ibid., p. 19.
"most of the." T 236/1478 May 1, 1946.
"The United States delegate." T 236/1479 May 1946.

160 Mackillop's proposal, to. T 236/1478 May 29, 1946.
Unimpressed, Mackillop coldly. T 236/1478 June 5, 1946.
"The money should." T 236/1478 June 17, 1946.

161 Pérrier's letter to. E 2001 (E) 1967/113 Bd 374.

162 "The present cowardice." Négociations de 1945; Guerre
Economique, Côte Z424–1, 2, 4, vol. 26, p. 153.
By 1949, Switzerland. Allemagne, Avoirs de l'état allemand à
l'étranger, Côte 4–21–2, vol. 1022, pp. 174–7.

162 "the atmosphere might." T 236/1478 May 29, 1946.

Another Swiss reported. Jacques Picard, *Switzerland and the Assets of the Missing Victims of the Nazis* (Bank Baer, 1996).

163 But in May. AJC letter, Gottschalk report, June 14, 1946.

Ginzberg's recommendation was. Ginzberg, "Report," pp. 79–81, June 19, 1946.

164 "entirely unprecedented situation." FO 371/60479 July 10, 1946.

thirteen-page proposal. E 2001 (E) 1967/113 Bd 374 May 6, 1946.

"It should not." E 2001 (E) 1967/113 Bd 374 July 29, 1946.

165 "It is vital." E 2001 (E) 1967/113 Bd 374 August 3, 1946.

The idea of. E 2001 (E) 1967/113 Bd 374 August 26, 1946.

"the approximate number." FO 837/1175a December 20, 1949.

166 "He wants 5,000." E 2001 (E) 1967/113 Bd 374 November 11, 1946.

"the money belonged." E 4001 (C) 1 Bd 309 (1800) November 25, 1946.

167 The Allies' interest. FO 371/60481 February 23, 1946; FO 192/199 January 31, 1947; FO 371/67915A April 11, 1947.

Swiss officials, accepting. Allemagne-Suisse, Côte EU 29–8–3, vol. 21, pp. 149–51.

"The Swiss government." RG 319 Records of Army Staff, Ebrty 85A, Army Intelligence File, Box 2882 February 4, 1948.

Other privileged Germans. RG 59 1945–9 Box 4231 July 17, 1947.

In Davos, the. Allemagne, Question Juive, Côte EU 4–8–3, vol. 330, p. 42.

Rather, they spoke. *Die Nation*, July 23, 1947.

Among the many. RG 59 1945–9 Box 4255 800.515/5–1149 May 11, 1949, Robert Kempner, Nuremberg.

168 The accumulation of. FO 371/60479 September 25, 1946.

"It's contrary to." E 7160 (A) b 1968/27 Bd 151 June 22, 1946.

"There's resistance to." E 7160 (A) i 1968/54 Bd 23 (Nr 1–91).

The lawyers mentioned were Dr. Carl Spahn, Ernst Lochmann, Dr. Kurt Brunner and Dr. Alphons Zuppinger.

169 "It's shameful," said. E 7160 (A) i 1968/54 Bd 23 February 11, 1947.

"I'm pleased with." E 7160 (A) i 1968/54 Bd 1 September 13, 1946.

170 "That's impossible," protested. E 7160 (A) i 1968/54 Bd 1 September 24, 1946.

The subject would. E 7160 (A) i 1968/54 Bd 1 October 2, 1946.

The reply to. FO 371/60479 September 25, 1946.

Britain was asked. T 236/1478 October 5, 1946.

171 The British could. FO 192/199 December 3, 1946.

"throw the ball." T 236/1478 October 31, 1946.

Selous, the commercial. FO 192/199 December 3, 1946.

Since the nonmonetary. T 236/1478 October 21, 1946.

This evasion concealed. T 236/1479 September 13, 1947.

Their fate in. Réparations-Restitutions, Côte Y–59–2, vol. 365, pp. 88, 285–9; vol. 366, p. 28.

"It would be." RG 59 1945–9 Box 4228 800.515/4–2547; AJDC, Abba Schwartz May 1, 1947.

172 The Swiss should. RG 59 1945–9 Box 4215A 800.515/10–946 October 9, 1946.

"fed up with." E 2800 (-) 1967/61 Bd 88 (Société de Banques Suisse) November 26, 1946.

To the minister. RG 131 1942–60 Box 51 February 2, 1947 Ostrow to Washington.

173 Letters addressed to. FO 192/201 pt 5 October 28, 1947.

Inside Switzerland—unlike. RG 260 OMGUS Property Control and External Assets 1945–50 Switzerland Box 654.

Schwab and his. FO 192/199 February 3, 1947.

"We know about." RG 59 1945–9 Box 4218 December 23, 1946.

174 "We're not finding." E 7160 (A) 1 1968/54 November 12, 1946 and October 28, 1947.

"the Germans should." E 7160 (A) 1 1968/54 Bd 29 (Korrespondenz AK 1952–4) June 13, 1952.

Compensation Office's valuation. FO 371/93941 August 10, 1951.

174 "We cannot allow." FO 837/1288.

175 "Homberger's prediction about." E 7160 (A) 1 1968/54 November 12, 1946.

"I believe we." E 7160 (A) i 1968/54 vol. 6 June 1, 1947.

176 Stucki was shocked. E 7160 (A) i 1968/54 Bd 23 (Nr 1–91) September 5, 1947.

"This wasn't done." E 7160 (A) i 1968/54 September 9, 1947.

177 The discrepancies exposed. E 7160 (A) i 1968/54 Bd 23 Exposé Nr 79 October 24, 1947.

"The banks acted." E 7160 (A) i 1968/54 vol. 5 October 28, 1947.

Chapter 11: Perfidious Swiss

179 "The Committee is." E 7160 (A) i 1968/54 Bd 23 March 11, 1947.

"a Galacian Jew." E 7160 (A) i 1968/54 vol. 5 December 16, 1947.

180 Posted during the. RG 56 U.S. Treasury, re Swiss banks and Safehaven, Mann memorandum for the files, February 25, 1947.

The contents could. AJDC, AR 45/64 1207 February 27, 1948.

181 "We've reached the." RG 59 1945–9 Box 4225 800.515/3–2847.

"in full recognition." FO 192/200 Pt 3 April 16, 1947.

"We'll be accused." E 7160 (A) i 1968/54 Bd 23 May 25, 1947.

The Jewish refugees. Stucki was also aware that Sweden had not yet paid its promised 50 million kroner for refugees or returned its looted gold—prompting Desmond Morton's condemnation in London of "the inherent dishonesty of the Swedes" (FO 837/1287 May 31, 1948).

182 The Foreign Office's. FO 837/1288 October 25, 1947.

"I have been." FO 837/1288 October 20, 1947. The Allies proposed that the rate of exchange should be the same as between Nazi Germany and Switzerland during the war—SF173 to RM100. On October 8, Switzerland made a counteroffer of SF43 to RM100.

182 "The Swiss," he. FO 837/128 December 9, 1947.

"We could rely." E7160 (A) i 1968/54 Bd 4 Protokoll AK June 24, 1947.

"suggestions for turning." FO 837/1288 October 25, 1947, November 1 and 29, 1947. Meeting on October 14.

183 "We regard the." FO 837/128 November 29, 1947.

To help Germans. E 7160 (A) i 1968/54 Bd 23 May 27, 1947.

"It seems to." E 2001 (E) 1967/113 Bd 374 (111) March 20, 1950.

"It never crossed." RG 59 1945–9 Box 4236 Rubin/Adams memorandum of a conversation October 23, 1947.

184 had decreed that. Military Law 59.

The AJC's efforts. AJC Hevesi to Frankel, September 17, 1948.

185 "constitutes an act." AJC Memorandum, Eugene Hevesi to Slawson, September 3, 1947. Réparations-Restitutions, Côte Y–59–2, vol. 367, pp. 119–25; vol. 366, p. 295. The Russians had given the heirless property to the East German state.

When the French. Allemagne, Réparations, Côte H–15, 13 State Department 2, vol. 1112, pp. 66–7

"a bad mistake." FO 192/201 pt 5 August 28, 1947.

In Bern, Selous. FO 192/200 Pt 3 May 17, 1947; FO 192/206 June 9, 1948.

"It's not our." E 7160 (A) i 1968/54 May 25, 1947.

186 "The provocation by." E 7160 (A) i 1968/54 Bd 4 Protokoll AK June 24, 1947.

187 "become an amusing." E 7160 (A) i 1968/54 August 26, 1947, and see April 22, 1948; FO 192/201 pt 5 September 9, 1947.

"We can defeat." E 7160 (A) i 1968/54 Bd 23 July 8, 1947.

"War criminals" no. Ibid.

188 "it would not." E 2001 (E) 1967/113 Bd 374 January 22, 1947.

To avoid the. E 2001 (E) 1967/113 Bd 374 May 29, 1947.

189 "We are sure." E 2001 (E) 1967/113 Bd 374 August 21, 1947.

"I confirm," wrote. E 2001 (E) 1967/113 Bd 374 October 30, 1947.

190 By then, the. Picard, *Missing Victims*, p. 7.

190 To the bankers. E 2001 (E) 1967/113 Bd 374 December 23, 1947.

"Millions of Swiss." E 4110 (A) 1973/85 Bd December 1, 1947.

Inspired by a. FO 192/201 pt 5 September 15, 1947.

191 Jewish groups attacked. E 7160 (A) i 1968/54 vol. 5 October 28, 1947.

"preferring to let." FO 192/201 pt 5 September 27, 1947.

"The Americans, of." FO 837/1288 October 24, 1947.

"weaken our bargaining." Ibid.

There had been. RG 59 1945–9 Box 4236 Rubin/Adams memorandum of a conversation October 23, 1947.

192 Rubin and his. RG 59 1945–9 Box 4238 800.515/11–2547 November 25, 1947.

"Regrettably, the Compensation." E 7160 (A) 1 1968/54 Bericht über die Tätigkeit der Abteilung, 1946/47.

"were so convincing." TB/King.

193 "a little dangerous." E 7160 (A) i 1968/54 Bd 23 (Nr 1–91).

a "disadvantageous manner." E 7160 (A) i 1968/54 Bd 639.

Jann presented no. RG 56 U.S. Treasury, re Swiss banks and Safehaven, Mann memorandum for the files, June 3, 1947.

Ott's lack of. RG 56 U.S. Treasury, re Swiss banks and Safehaven, Ostrow to Schwab October 1, 1947.

195 Nothing more, the. E 2800 (-) 1967/61 Bd 91 (Affidavits, fausses certifications).

196 "principles of morality." RG 59 1945–9 Box 4238 King dispatch No. 15567 800.515/11–1947.

The "charade," King. TB/King.

"as only an impotent." RG 59 1945–9 Box 4242 King to Washington February 16, 1948 800.515/2–1948; King's Confidential memorandum 800.515/4–1949 Box 4254.

While the French. RG 59 Swiss Negotiations 1943–54 Box 1 Legg to King February 23, 1948.

197 "The Swiss are." FO 837/1288 September 5, 1947.

the "American intention." FO 192/206 April 21, 1948.

"ignorance and crass." FO 837/1290 October 28, 1948.

197 the "slow tempo." FO 192/206 January 20, 1948.

"We mustn't throw." E7160 (A) i 1968/54 vol. 5 February 22, 1948.

In the meantime. FO 192/206 January 20, 1948.

"I'm not displeased." E 7160 (A) i 1968/54 vol. 5 January 13, 1948.

Officially, the State. State Department instruction 3855 May 19, 1947.

198 "may come with." *The Papers of General Clay* (Indiana University Press, 1974), vol. 2, p. 568.

is "wasting time." FO 837/1290 August 10, 1948.

199 smacked of interference. Public Law 671; RG 59 1945–9 Box 4255 e.g. Congressman Cellar to Thorp May 18, 1949; Senator Howard McGarth to Acheson May 10, 1949. TB/Rubin.

Shortly afterward, Rubin. RG 59 1945–9 800.515/3–2448 Box 4243.

Stucki meanwhile returned. E 7160 (A) i 1968/54 vol. 5 May 11, 1948.

Switzerland's claims that. FO 192/198 "Swiss trade policy during the war, Zurich 1946."

Clever accounting had. FO 371/93941 August 10, 1951.

the "untenable position." FO 192/206 May 5, 1948.

200 By then, Britain's. FO 192/206 April 15, 1948.

"As monstrous a." FO 192/206 June 18, 1948.

"fed up with." FO 837/1174 February 2, 1949.

"It would not." FO 837/1293 June 15, 1949.

201 "I've no doubt." E 7160 (A) i 1968/54 vol. 5 May 11, 1948.

"would create insurmountable." RG 59 Negotiations with Switzerland 1948–57 Box 12 September 28, 1949; FO 192/206 letter February 19, 1948 23rd Mtg, item 2.

"We know that." FO 192/206 letter February 19, 1948 23rd Mtg, item 2.

"did not want." E 7160 (A) i 1968/54 Bd 24 Exposé Nr 94.

202 "The Swiss government." RG 59 State Department 1945–9 800.515/6–1349 Bx 4256 June 13, 1949.

202 In private, Ott. E 7160 (A) i 1968/54 vol. 5 April 22, 1948.
"when the Allies'." E 7160 (A) i 1968/54 vol. 6 November 23, 1948.
Members of the. RG 59 Economic Affairs Branch, Negotiations with Switzerland Acheson 1943–57 Box 11 5/11/50. The case of Günther von Haniel.
"I strongly warn." E 7160 (A) i 1968/54 vol. 5 January 13, 1948. Exceptions were naturally tolerated for the Swiss. Dr. Theodor Eisenring, a rich and influential politician regarded as a feudal lord, effortlessly overcame the rules against trading in German assets by ignoring letters, applications by the Compensation Office to the court and even judgments by the courts (E 7160 (A) i 1968/54 Bd 28 (Korrespondenz) November 22, 1949).

203 "We thought that." E 7160 (A) i 1968/54 vol. 5 June 1, 1948.
"in view of." FO 192/211.
With special permission. TB/Bach.

204 "The Swiss government." AJD letter July 7, 1948 Weiss to Eli Rock.
Both the British. AJDC Rubin Memorandum May 10, 1949.
"I leave it." Réparations-Restitutions, Côte Y–59–2, vol. 362, p. 51.

205 To seize more. *Bundesblatt* 1949, I, S. 769ff April 13, 1949. The Swiss proposal was to stipulate that the qualifying date of residence in Germany should be extended to June 1946, when the Washington Accord had been signed—rather than February 1945, when the freeze had been decreed.
"The negotiations are." AJC memorandum June 6, 1949, and see Rubin memorandum to Hevesi May 11, 1949.

CHAPTER 12: THE POLISH CONSPIRACY

207 He still trusted. TB/Isenbergh.
"The amount of." E 2001 (E) 1967/113 Bd 374 January 21, 1948.

208 Other European countries. AJC letter to von Steiger August 3, 1949; AJC letter September 21, 1949.

209 Switzerland, he warned. AJC report July 11, 1949 Jacobson to Schwartz.

210 "This is a serious." AJC Rubin to Eugene July 22, 1949.

On the other. E 2001 (E) 1967/113 Bd 374 (Polnische Ansprüche).

212 "At the appropriate." E 7110/1967/32/Polen 890.0/1294 See Hug and Perrenound, *Assets*, p. 86.

The origin of. E 2001 (E) 1967/113 Bd 775 (Polen) April 25, 1949.

Speich told Troendle. E 2001 (E) 1967/113 Bd 374 (11) March 18, 1950.

213 "as soon as." E 2001 (E) 1967/113 Bd 374 (Polnische Ansprüche) June 15, 1949.

Knowing of the. E 2001 (E) 1967/113 Bd 374 (11) September 15, 1949.

Alexander had also. E 2001 (E) 1967/113 Bd 374 (Polnische Ansprüche) June 14, 1949.

214 "Your spontaneous solution." Ibid.

"Swiss nationals will." E 2001 (E) 1967/113 Bd 374 (11) August 3, 1949.

"confidential exchange of." E 2001 (E) 1967/113 Bd 374 (11) August 4, 1949.

215 "It is incompatible." E 2001 (E) 1967/113 Bd 374 (11) August 26, 1949.

"I am sure." E 4001 (C) 1 Bd 309 (1800) August 5, 1949.

"this American Jewish." E 4001 (C) 1 Bd 309 (1800) August 19, 1949.

"The agreement contradicts." E 2001 (E) 1967/113 Bd 374 (11) September 1, 1949.

"no great importance." E 2001 (E) 1967/113 Bd 374 (11) September 9, 1949.

216 Parliament was unaware. E 2001 (E) 1967/113 Bd 775 (Polen) September 22, 1949.

"The agreement with." E 2001 (E) 1967/113 Bd 374 (11) September 15, 1949.

216 The secret clause. E 2001 (E) 1967/113 Bd 775 (Polen) October 7, 1949.

the "tragic travesty." AJC Rubin to Fisher October 7, 1949.

The American plan. RG 59 1945–9 Box 4256 800.515/6–949.

"attitude on this." AJC Rubin to Hevesi October 17, 1949.

217 "was like comparing." E 7160 (A) i 1968/54 vol. 7 April 12 and June 17, 1949.

Pompously, he refused. IRO September 30, 1949 Hacking to Jimmy. By May 1949, $18.5 million had been paid over to IRO out of the $25 million promised.

Giving any further. E 7160 (A) i 1968/54 vol. 7 January 24, 1950.

The property of. AJC memorandum Hermann Simon September 28, 1949.

218 By then, Petitpierre's. E 2001 (E) 1967/113 Bd 374 (11) September 15, 1949.

219 "Publicity will be." AJC Central Zionist Archives S43–243.

Isenbergh, he predicted. E 2001 (E) 1967/113 Bd 374 (11) October 17, 1949.

220 "on the same." E 2001 (E) 1967/113 Bd 374 (11) November 4, 1949 and December 1949.

After speaking to. E 2800 (-) 1967/61 Bd 88 (Nationalbank) June 30, 1949.

221 "make the Swiss." AJDC Rubin to Hevesi December 6, 1949.

Objections from Bern. *New York Times* December 7, 1949.

Picard, *Missing Victims*, p. 7.

222 was "excessively feeble." FO 837 1174 February 2, 1949.

"The situation is." AJC letter James Rice to Max Isenbergh December 9, 1949.

223 "The British," wrote. AJDC Jacobson memorandum December 14, 1949.

Convinced that his. AJC letter James Rice to Max Isenbergh December 9, 1949.

During the war. Safehaven Report No. 4 April 9, 1945.

224 Like all the. AJC Isenbergh report December 19, 1949.

224 The British were. AJDC letter Rice to Jacobson December 14, 1949.

"I'll try my." TB/Isenbergh.

"not without a." Allemande-Suisse, Avoirs de l'état, Côte 4–21–2, vol. 1022, pp. 62–6.

"If the agreement." FO 837/1175A December 29, 1949; RG 59 1945–9 Box 4259 800.515/12–2149 December 23, 1949.

225 In the margin. E 2001 (E) 1967/113 Bd 374 (11) December 20, 1949.

"bending the rules." E 1301 1/394 pp. 703/4; Hug and Perrenound, *Assets*, p. 89.

"error, a blunder." E 2001 (E) 1970/217 Bd 209 (Herrenlose Vermoegenswerte) February 13, 1957.

the "unfriendly attitude." AJDC AR 45/64 1207 December 27, 1949.

226 "That point about." AJDC Rubin memorandum January 9, 1950.

If, contrary to. FO 837/1175A January 4, 1950.

227 In a press. Federal Political Dept, press release, February 1, 1950.

Suspecting that the. E 2001 (E) 1967/113 Bd 374 (111) March 14, 1950.

228 The lawyer's dignity. E 2001 (E) 1967/113 Bd 374 (111) January 10, 1950.

"In previous years." E 2001 (E) 1967/113 Bd 374 (111) April 25, 1950.

No one in. AJDC AR 45/64 #1207 Translation of Federal Council statement March 22, 1950.

229 To inquiries from. E 2001 (E) 1967/113 Bd 374 (111) February 28, 1950.

230 Both sides understood. Hug and Perrenound, *Assets*, pp. 76–8.

"A whitewash," commented. AJDC AR 45/64 #1207 Robinson to Rock April 11, 1950.

But Acheson's passing. RG 59 Economics Affairs Branch, Negotiations with Switzerland 1943–57, Swiss Accord Box 3 Acheson to Vincent June 10, 1950.

230 "guilty of grave." Ibid.

"more than content." FO 837/1175A February 28, 1950.

"no such assets." FO 837/1175A March 12, 1950.

"to keep him." FO 837/1175A March 6, 1950.

CHAPTER 13: NEW HOPE

231 Dean Acheson promptly. RG 59 Box 1013 254.0041/6–1550 June 15, 1950.

For the Foreign. FO 837/1175A June 25, 1950.

Given British policies. FO 371/93941 August 2, 1951.

That desire for. State Department to British embassy November 13, 1950.

"fan the flames." FO 837/1175A May 12, 1950.

232 "rather barren argument." FO 837/1175A May 17, 1950.

"formerly called Hirsch." E 2001 (E) 1967/113 Bd 374 (11) December 30, 1949.

Appreciating that Switzerland's. E 2001 (E) 1967/113 Bd 374 (111) April 26, 1950.

233 This Israeli was. E 2001 (E) 1967/113 Bd 374 (111) April 27, 1950; E 2001 (E) 1967/113 Bd 374 (111) July 4, 1950.

Since this scheme. E 2001 (E) 1967/113 Bd 374 (111) July 18 and October 24, 1950.

234 an "embarrassing" position. FO 837/1298 February 24, 1951.

After negotiating the. FO 837/1304 September 5, 1951.

"It has for." FO 837/1303 July 1951.

Stucki acknowledged the. E 7160 (A) i 1968/54 Bd 28 (Korrespondenz AK) December 1, 1949.

Given renewed swagger. E 7160 (A) i 1968/54 Bd 124 June 20, 1950.

Retreating, Stucki resorted. E 7160 (A) i 1968/54 Bd 124 March 8, 1951.

235 The Germans, he. AJC letter to McCloy July 31, 1951.

"Now that they." Bower, *Blind Eye to Murder*, p. 424.

235 Included in Bonn's. RG 59 1950–54 Box 1013 Vincent to Washington May 2, 1950.

"It's a question." E 2001 (E) 1967/113 Bd 374 (111) March 20, 1950.

Stucki's withdrawal from. Hug and Perrenound, *Assets*, p. 45.

Bill 603, introduced. HR 1849 and HR 2780, two similar bills.

236 To conceal the. E 2001 (E) 1970/217 Bd 29 (Anfragen Privater, Herrenlose Vermoegenswerte) May 15, 1950.

"The Allies never." E 7160 (A) i 1958/54 Bd 28 (Korrespondenz AK) June 20, 1950.

237 "During the whole." E 2001 (E) 1970/217 Bd 209 April 6, 1954.

"Please write to." E 2001 (E) 1970/217 Bd 209.

The "problems," condemned. RG 59 1950–4 Box 1013 254.0041/7–1150.

238 But suddenly the. RG 59 1950–4 Box 1016 254.1141/3–2151.

"do nothing to." E 2001 (E) 1967/113 Bd 374 (111) November 6, 1950.

The bank's objection. E 4264 1985/57 Bd 250 (Dossier Reginek) M 15532. Eventually the Polish government validated the documents.

Too often, the. E 4110 (A) 1973/85 Bd 3 (d).

239 Since their own. E 2001 (E) 1967/113 Bd 374 (111) March 16, 1951.

"We agree," Zehnder. E 2001 (E) 1967/113 Bd 374 (111) August 2, 1951.

"Don't expect any." E 2001 (E) 1967/113 Bd 374 (111) August 13/14, 1951.

240 "Glaringly exposes the." Ibid.

"Israel needs foreign." E 2001 (E) 1967/113 Bd 374 (111) September 17, 1951.

241 "You advised me." E 4110 (A) 1973/84 Bd 4 October 6, 1952.

242 Shaken by Oetterli's. E 2001 (E) 1967/113 Bd 374 (111) December 1, 1951.

Switzerland, they knew. E 2001 (E) 1967/113 Bd 374 (111) December 7, 1951.

242 An official census. Bulletin No. 28, October 1951.

"special legislation introduced." AJC report November 10, 1952.

243 eighteen-page letter. E 2800 (-) 1967/61 Bd 91 (Affidavits, fausses certifications).

By then, the. E 2800 (-) 1967/61 Bd 88 (Banques Suisse) April 7, 1948.

244 "important external considerations." E 2800 (-) 1967/61 Bd 91 (Affidavits, fausses certifications).

245 Mendelssohn-Bartholdy was. E 2001 (E) 1968/79 Bd 2.

Had Frölicher realized. E 2001 (E) 1968/79 Bd 2 (Finanzielles, Depots von Privatpersonen).

246 Protected by British. See Bower, *Blind Eye to Murder*, p. 1 and passim; and see also FO 1046/274 and FO 1046/210 for Abs's interrogations by the British where he lied about his wartime activities.

"The Swiss," commented. FO 371/99856 June 6, 1952; FO 371/99853 March 10, 1952.

Although his continuing. By May 1949, $17.5 million had been paid over to IRO out of the $25 million promised: $12.5 million, Sweden's full payment, $5 million from Switzerland and nothing from Portugal, which refused to abide by the Washington Accord.

"do something about." E 7160 (A) i 1968/54 November 11, 1951; "grotesque': E 7160 (A) i 1968/54 vol. 9 March 13, 1951. "Switzerland stood up." FO 371/99854 February 26, 1952, *Der Bund* article. Among the many excuses given by Bonn to derail the debts conference, the Germans claimed that if they compensated the 3,300 Germans who had lost assets in Switzerland, they would also be obliged to compensate the nine million dispossessed German refugees from Eastern Europe.

247 "On grounds of." RG 59 State Department, The Legal Advisor—Records Relating to Postwar Settlement Issues 1939–63, Gold Netherlands Box 12.

Corroboration was provided. Ibid.

247 "Switzerland has already." RG 59 Records re Negotiations with Switzerland 1943–57 Box 2 August 17, 1948 C87.

Observing the State. FO 837/1159 January 25, 1947.

248 Yet, despite all. State Department Swiss Accord February 23, 1951; FO 837/1287 August 16, 1948.

"It's time for." E 7160 (A) i 1968/54 vol. 9 March 13, 1951.

"They say the." E 7160 (A) i 1968/54 Bd 28 (Korrespondenz AK) August 1951.

Instead they were. E 7160 (A) i 1968/54 Bd 29 (Korrespondenz AK 1952–4) June 13, 1952.

"on behalf of." E 7160 (A) i 1968/54 November 11, 1951.

grateful to receive. FO 371/99848 December 29, 1951.

249 "It was a." E 7160 (A) i 1968/54 October 7, 1952.

"whose epithet as." Allemagne, Côte 4–21–2, vol. 1027, pp. 12–14. Under the agreement, Germany undertook to pay SF121.5 million to Switzerland and SF121.5 million to the Allies to cover the Allies' claims under the Washington Accord. No German assets in Switzerland were sold. In total, Switzerland recovered SF650 million of its loans to Germany, including the SF121.5 million.

"we opposed them." E 7160 (A) i 1958/54 Bd 95 October 9, 1953; E 7160 (A) i 1958/54 vol. 5.

250 On April 7. FO 371/105797.

"have done very." FO 371/105776.

"As usual the." AJC April 3, 1953.

251 "I am astonished." E2001 (E) 1969/121 Bd 155 (Herrenlosen Vermoegen) January 24, 1952.

After conversations with. AJC memorandum October 2, 1952.

252 With little difficulty. RG 59 Negotiations with Switzerland 1943–57 Box 3.

"a most difficult." RG 59 1950–4 Box 1013 254.0041/12–1250 January 11, 1951.

Rubin's only success. AJDC letter Rubin to Blaustein July 7, 1950.

Germany's bid during. FO 371/99852 February 10, 1952.

252 "Unfortunately," commented a. Allemagne, Question juive, Côte Z–16–4, vol. 329, pp. 170–4.

Reports from the. Ibid., pp. 153–7.

253 "willingness of the." RG 59 1950–1 Economic Affairs Branch Box 1046 April 4, 1951.

"The American delegation." RG 59 254.0041/4–0351 April 10, 1951.

"The Americans, British." E 2001 (E) 1967/113 Bd 374 (111) October 31, 1950.

had "revealed no." State Department Swiss Accord file May 21, 1951.

254 "there exist in." Allemagne, Côte 4–21–2, vol. 1025, p. 137.

"There are no." Hug and Perrenound, *Assets*, p. 12; RG 59 1950–4 Box 1017 254.6241/5–2451 June 13, 1951.

"declared that there." E 2801 1968/84 Bd 94 May 5, 1952. Hug and Perrenound, *Assets*, p. 52.

In a final. AJC, August 2, 1951.

Chapter 14: "Keepers of the Flame"

255 In April 1953. E 2001 (E) 1970/217 Bd 209 April 23, 1953; Hug and Perrenound, *Assets*, p. 37.

256 "This case," Bindschedler. E 4110 (A) 1973/85 Bd 4 April 29, 1953.

"The Israelis' imagination." E 2001 (E) 1969/121 Bd 155 (Herrenlose Vermoegen) March 28, 1952.

"Our prospect of." AJDC letter Jacobson to Leavitt May 19, 1953.

"What is the." AJC memorandum October 2, 1952.

257 Alexander sensed that. E 4110 (A) 1973/85 Bd 1 (Erbenlose Vermoegen in der Schweiz) January 22, 1952.

Noncooperation was the. E 2001 (E) 1969/121 Bd 155 (Herrenlose Vermoegen) June 3 and July 23, 1952.

"There must be." E 2801 1968/84 Bd 93 September 9/10, 1952; Hug and Perrenound, *Assets*, p. 52.

257 After all, the. Hug and Perrenound, *Assets*, p. 45.
Without moral qualms. Allemagne, Questions financiers, Côte EU 4–15–7, vol. 1006, p. 33.

258 "Most Germans," he. Allemagne, Commission Tripartite des Dettes, vol. 1017, p. 223.
"Undoubtedly this will." E 2001 (E) 1970/217 Bd 209 April 23, 1953; Hug and Perrenound, *Assets*, p. 37.

259 In the code. E 4110 (A) 1973/85 Bd 1 (Erblose Vermoegen)
"isolationist and lacked." E 4110 (A) 1973/85 Bd 1 (Erblose Vermoegen) August 31, 1953.

260 "whether it is." E 4110 (A) 1973/85 Bd 1 (JPD, Erbenlose Vermoegen) February 12, 1954.
"some preliminary work." AJC Hevesi to Rubin March 1, 1954.
"An official of." SIG Archives, Zurich, Erblose Vermoegen.

261 "If, despite our." E 4110 (A) 1973/85 Bd 1 (JPD Erbenlose Vermoegen) March 8, 1954.
"Predictable if the." E 2001 (E) 1969/221 Bd 155 (Herrenlose Vermoegen) July 14, 1954.

262 Max Troendle, the. E 2001 (E) 1969/221 Bd 155 (Herrenlose Vermoegen) September 28, 1954.
"Perhaps the banks." E 2001 (E) 1970/217 Bd 209 (Herrenlose Vermoegen) March 28, 1955.
"after the expiry." E 2801 1968/84 Bd 98 (W.45) July 7, 1955.
Hug and Perrenound, *Assets*, p. 39.

263 "We must solve." E 4110 (A) 1973/85 Bd 4 March 28, 1955.

264 "Each delay." Feldmann. E 4110 (A) 1973/85 Bd 1 March 31, 1955.

265 Jews were never. E 4110 (A) 1973/85 Bd 1 June 11, 1955.
"the agreement with." E 2001 (E) 1970/217 Bd 209 (Herrenlose Vermoegenswerte) May 3, 1955.
"We've told [the." E 2001 (E) 1970/217 Bd 209 (Herrenlose Vermoegenswerte) September 15, 1955.
But, since Feldmann. E 4110 (A) 1973/85 Bd 1 September 12, 1955.
What was more. E 4110 (A) 1973/85 Bd 1 November 12, 1955.

265 The bankers departed. E 4110 (A) 1973/85 Bd 1 June 4 and September 24, 1956.

266 "confirm in writing." E 4110 (A) 1973/85 Bd 1 September 26, 1956.

The bank's dishonesty. E 2001 (E) 1970/217 Bd 209 (Herrenlose Vermoegenswerte) June 6, 1956.

Either there was. E 4110 (A) 1973/85 Bd 2 (XII) April 15, 1957.

"It would look." E 6100 (B) 1973/141 Bd 182 (987.2) May 13, 1957; Hug and Perrenound, *Assets*, p. 51.

"has simply capitulated." E 2801 1968/84 Bd 98 (W.45) May 23, 1957; Hug and Perrenound, *Assets*, p. 52.

"hoped that there." E 2001 (E) 1972/33 Bd 280 August 9, 1957; Hug and Perrenound, *Assets*, p. 52.

267 The Bankers Association's. E 4110 (A) 1973/85 Bd 2 (XIII) January 14, 1958.

"Delay telling anything." E 2001 (E) 1970/217 Bd 209 (Herrenlose Vermoegenswerte) November 18 and December 6, 1957.

"Switzerland has always." E 4110 (A) 1973/85 Bd 2 (XIII) January 14, 1958.

"We will not." E 4110 (A) 1973/85 Bd 2 (XIII) December 3, 1957; E 4110 (A) 1973/85 Bd 2 (XIV) October 30, 1958.

268 "The Swiss Confederation." AJC Jewish Agency for Israel December 16, 1958.

"A specialist banker." E 4110 (A) 1973/85 Bd 2 March 26, 1959.

270 Four years earlier. E 4110 (A) 1973/85 Bd 2 February 17, 1959; Hug and Perrenound, *Assets*, p. 56.

It was their fear. Picard, *Die Schweiz*, p. 150.

271 "This all shines." E 4110 (A) 1973/85 Bd 2 (XV) May 22, 1959.

273 To threaten that. April 11, 1959 and March 1959 47th annual report of Bankers Association.

"The Bankers Association's." AJDC Rubin report November 16, 1959.

"We cannot renege." E 2001 (E) 1976/17 Bd 97 November 13, 1959; Hug and Perrenound, *Assets*, p. 58.

273 Reminding the Swiss. 4110 (A) 1973/85 Bd 4 June 1 and July 6, 1960.

274 "Besides the fact." E 2801 1968/84 Bd 98 May 27, 1957; Hug and Perrenound, *Assets*, p. 52.

Days later, Petitpierre's. Jewish Agency for Israel, Bern, July 6, 1960, Federal Policy Bureau to U.S. Embassy Bern; 4110 (A) 1973/85 Bd 4 June 1 and July 6, 1960.

"It would be." E 4110 (A) 1973/85 Bd 2 (XV) October 5, 1960.

275 "The matter must." E 4110 (A) 1973/85 Bd 2 (XV) February 12, 1961.

To help the. Hug and Perrenound, *Assets*, p. 59.

"Israeli exaggerations," the. E 4110 (A) 1973/85 Bd 2 (XIX) August 7, 1961.

"My organization always." E 4110 (A) 1973/85 Bd 2 (XIX) July 7, 1961.

And they loved. E 4110 (A) 1973/85 Bd 2 (XX) August 30, 1961.

276 If the amount. E 4110 (A) 1973/85 Bd 2 (XIX) September 1961.

"Just on the." E 4110 (A) 1973/85 Bd 2 (XIX) October 10, 1961.

"From my own." E 4110 (A) 1973/85 Bd 3 (d) November 21, 1962.

But there was. E 4110 (A) 1973/85 Bd 2 (XIX) August 30, 1961.

277 Oetterli had successfully. E 4110 (A) 1973/85 Bd 3 (d). The law became effective on August 29, 1963.

Chapter 15: Complicating the Riddle

279 "explicitly charged to." Hug and Perrenound, *Assets*, p. 71.

280 "tens of thousands." E4110 (A) 1973/85 Bd 4 (Vollziehungs-verordnung) May 7, 1963.

Panicky Jews evoked. Hug and Perrenound, *Assets*, p. 64.

"Do not waste." E 2001 (E) 1978/84 Bd 144 March 19, 1964; Hug and Perrenound, *Assets*, p. 65.

Unwilling to succumb. E 2001 (E) 1978/84 Bd 144 April 17, 1964; Hug and Perrenound, *Assets*, p. 65.

from "false premises." E 2001 (E) 1976/17 vol 97. (B.42.13); Hug and Perrenound, *Assets*, p. 62.

281 Switzerland's image was. E 2001 (E) 1978/84 Bd 144 April 22, 1964; Hug and Perrenound, *Assets*, p. 65.

"That's all we." E 2001 (E) 1978/84 Bd 144 July 30, 1964; Hug and Perrenound, *Assets*, p. 66.

The lawyer of. E 4111 (A) 1980/13 Bd 159; Hug and Perrenound, *Assets*, p. 68.

282 SBC, which had. Hug and Perrenound, *Assets*, p. 68–9.

Unless Weber pursued. E 4110 (A) 1973/85 Bd 2.

While Switzerland's Jewish. AJDC letter Lack to Leavitt March 13, 1964.

283 No lists of. Hug and Perrenound, *Assets*, pp. 60, 73.

In 1966, Weber. AJDC Jewish Agency for Israel memorandum February 1, 1966; Weber letter November 18, 1964.

Weber's office offered. E 4110 (A) 1973/85 Bd 4 October 16, 1962.

284 The Union Bank. E 4111 (A) 1980/13 Bd 28 (A5028) June 29, 1964; Hug and Perrenound, *Assets*, pp. 44, 70.

285 Always inclined to. Hug and Perrenound, *Assets*, p. 42

286 The money was. E 2001 (E) 1978/84 Bd 144 (B.42.13/4); Hug and Perrenound, *Assets*, pp. 66–8.

287 But Weber didn't. E 4111 (A) 1980/13 vol. 159; Hug and Perrenound, *Assets*, p. 68.

At least a hundred. Hug and Perrenound, *Assets*, p. 111–2.7

288 Häberlin passed their. Ibid., p. 78.

But SF4.8 million. E 4111 (A) 1980/13 Bd 157; Hug and Perrenound, *Assets*, p. 74.

There would be. Hug and Perrenound, *Assets*, p. 76.

Having negotiated. E 4001 (E) 1988/20 Bd 372 (64) March 8, 1972; Hug and Perrenound, *Assets*, p. 76.

289 "great relief and." E 4001 (E) 1988/20 Bd 373 (64) August 11, 1972; Hug and Perrenound, *Assets*, p. 77.

Each file revealed. Hug and Perrenound, *Assets*, p. 80.

That money was. Ibid.

In May 1949. Ibid., p. 86.

291 That money, Weber. Ibid., p. 112.

292 The object, explained. Ibid., p. 114
Its first report. Ibid., p. 117.
"This is thin." Ibid.

Chapter 16: The Deal

309 Headlines reporting that. *Financial Times*, September 20, 1996.
310 "could still be." *Financial Times*, September 12, 1946.
"This is the greatest." *Financial Times*, September 18, 1946.

BIBLIOGRAPHY

Bauer, Yehuda. *Jews for Sale?* (Yale University Press, 1994)

Bower, Tom. *Blind Eye to Murder*, revised edition (Little, Brown, 1996)

———. *The Paperclip Conspiracy* (Paladin, 1988)

Castlemur, Linus von. *Schweizerisch-Alliierte Finanzbeziehungen im Übergang vom Zweiten Welt Kreig* (Cronos, 1992)

Faith, Nicholas. *Safety in Numbers* (Hamish Hamilton, 1982)

Foreign and Commonwealth Office. *Nazi Gold: Information from the British Archives* (September 1996; revised edition, January 1997)

Gilbert, Martin. *The Holocaust* (Collins, 1986)

Haesler, Alfred. *The Lifeboat Is Full* (Funk & Wagnalls, 1969)

Hug, Peter, and Marc Perrenound. *Assets in Switzerland of Victims of Nazism and the Compensation Agreements with East Bloc Countries* (Swiss Foreign Affairs Department, Bern, December 1996; English version, January 1997)

Picard, Jacques. *Die Schweiz und die Juden* (Chronos, 1994)

Rings, Werner. *Raubgold aus Deutschland* (Zurich, 1985)

Sandilands, Roger. *The Life and Political Economy of Lauchlin Currie* (Duke University Press, 1990)

Schneeberger, E. *Wirtschaftskrieg auch in Frieden* (Bern, 1984)

Trepp, Gian. *Bankgeschaefte mit dem Feind* (Rotpunktverlag, 1993)

INDEX